Quantum History

ALSO AVAILABLE FROM BLOOMSBURY

Zero Point, Slavoj Žižek
Against Progress, Slavoj Žižek
Christian Atheism, Slavoj Žižek
Freedom, Slavoj Žižek
Surplus Enjoyment, Slavoj Žižek
Hegel in a Wired Brain, Slavoj Žižek
Sex and the Failed Absolute, Slavoj Žižek
Disparities, Slavoj Žižek
Antigone, Slavoj Žižek
The Universal Exception, Slavoj Žižek
Interrogating the Real, Slavoj Žižek

Quantum History
A New Materialist Philosophy

Slavoj Žižek

BLOOMSBURY ACADEMIC
LONDON • NEW YORK • OXFORD • NEW DELHI • SYDNEY

BLOOMSBURY ACADEMIC

Bloomsbury Publishing Plc, 50 Bedford Square, London, WC1B 3DP, UK
Bloomsbury Publishing Inc, 1359 Broadway, New York, NY 10018, USA
Bloomsbury Publishing Ireland, 29 Earlsfort Terrace, Dublin 2, D02 AY28, Ireland

BLOOMSBURY, BLOOMSBURY ACADEMIC and the Diana logo are trademarks of Bloomsbury Publishing Plc

First published in Great Britain 2025

Copyright © Slavoj Žižek, 2025

Slavoj Žižek has asserted his right under the Copyright, Designs and Patents Act, 1988, to be identified as Author of this work.

Cover design: Ben Anslow

All rights reserved. No part of this publication may be: i) reproduced or transmitted in any form, electronic or mechanical, including photocopying, recording or by means of any information storage or retrieval system without prior permission in writing from the publishers; or ii) used or reproduced in any way for the training, development or operation of artificial intelligence (AI) technologies, including generative AI technologies. The rights holders expressly reserve this publication from the text and data mining exception as per Article 4(3) of the Digital Single Market Directive (EU) 2019/790.

Bloomsbury Publishing Plc does not have any control over, or responsibility for, any third-party websites referred to or in this book. All internet addresses given in this book were correct at the time of going to press. The author and publisher regret any inconvenience caused if addresses have changed or sites have ceased to exist, but can accept no responsibility for any such changes.

A catalogue record for this book is available from the British Library.

A catalog record for this book is available from the Library of Congress.

ISBN: HB: 978-1-3505-6642-2
ePDF: 978-1-3505-6643-9
eBook: 978-1-3505-6644-6

Typeset by RefineCatch Limited, Bungay, Suffolk
Printed and bound in Great Britain

For product safety related questions contact productsafety@bloomsbury.com.

To find out more about our authors and books visit www.bloomsbury.com and sign up for our newsletters.

To Jela, who believed in me even when I didn't

Contents

Introduction: Materialism and quantum criticism 1

I Universal: Collapse comes first

1 Why a Hegelian needs quantum mechanics 11
2 Why quantum mechanics needs Hegel 33
3 Noncommutativity in the symbolic and in the (quantum) real 57

II Particular: From Hegel to Heidegger . . . and back

1 Names for finitude: Hegel, Heidegger, Pippin 81
2 The night of the world 99
3 Heidegger's politics of finitude 123

III Singular: Politics in a quantum world

1 The hologram of conflicting universalities 147
2 Can artificial intelligence really think? 175
3 The politics of vocation 207

Variations

Variation 1   Frozen beauty: Rovelli, Deleuze and the Stoics 237

Variation 2	No substitute for true universals 243	
Variation 3	Pure voice, pure sound: Beethoven, Globokar, Act 261	
Variation 4	Acts of reconciliation 279	
Variation 5	Moderately conservative communism 297	
Variation 6	The painted void 309	
Variation 7	The many monsters of the cinema 321	
Variation 8	Sexual superpositions 335	
Variation 9	Make the kitchen maid king 353	

Conclusion: The hunger to be something 363

Notes 395

Index 425

Introduction: Materialism and quantum criticism

Flatland: A Romance of Many Dimensions, a satirical novella by Edwin Abbott published in 1884, uses the fictional two-dimensional world of Flatland to comment on the hierarchy of Victorian culture. The narrator "Square," who guides the readers through some of the implications of life in two dimensions, dreams of a visit to a one-dimensional world, "Lineland," inhabited by men consisting of lines; he is then visited by a Sphere, but is unable to see the three-dimensional object as anything other than a circle (more precisely, a disk). After the Square's mind is opened to new dimensions, he tries to convince the Sphere of the theoretical possibility of the existence of a fourth dimension and higher spatial dimensions. The Square then has a dream in which the Sphere introduces him to a zero-dimensional space, Pointland, of whom the Point (sole inhabitant, monarch, and universe in one) perceives any communication as a thought originating in his own mind...

After its publication the book was half-forgotten; it was discovered again after Einstein's general theory of relativity brought to prominence the concept of a fourth dimension.[1] Recent trends in quantum mechanics—specifically, the holographic principle—rendered *Flatland* even more prophetic while inverting the entire perspective. If the three-dimensional reality available to our senses can be thought of as a hologram, an image of reality generated by an unimaginably distant two-dimensional boundary, the problem is no longer to explain additional dimensions outside of our standard reality but, on the contrary, to grasp how everything there is to know about strings and gravity in a four-dimensional anti-de-Sutter universe can be encrypted in quantum interactions of ordinary particles and fields lying entirely in the three-dimensional boundary surface. The surface world would function as a kind of hologram . . . It is almost as if you could learn everything about the interior of an orange by meticulously analyzing its skin.[2]

The latest developments move us even further towards Pointland: "The complete notion of a point of space-time in fact consists of the appearance of the entire universe as seen from that point."[3]

How can we account for these paradoxes in the terms of materialism? Lenin wrote his *Materialism and Empiriocriticism* as a materialist reply to attempts by obscurantist philosophers to give a spiritualist twist to new scientific discoveries—discoveries which seemed to undermine materialism, or at least contain the potential to do so.[4] Today, a little bit more than a century later, we are witnessing similar attempts to give a spiritualist spin to quantum mechanics. The fact that entangled particles can influence each other faster than the speed of light is taken as proof that there is a spiritual domain of instant communication outside material reality; the fact that a wave function collapses into reality through observation is interpreted as a proof that observation creates reality . . . no wonder many podcasts claim that quantum mechanics proves material reality is a simulacrum, that all there is, is spirit, etc.[5] Such views have proliferated recently, after the set of orthodox interpretations of quantum mechanics known as the "Copenhagen interpretation" which dominated traditional teachings for much of the twentieth century were largely abandoned. In the absence of these consensus principles, questions about the ontological status of quantum phenomena exploded. While fully endorsing the results of quantum mechanics, the present book follows Lenin's insight that, with each big scientific discovery, the notion of materialism should be radically rethought.

This is not to say that *Materialism and Empiriocriticism* is a perfect book, or a model to slavishly follow. I have no problem with critiques such as those of Carlo Rovelli, who devotes a whole chapter of his *Helgoland* to defending Bogdanov against Lenin's scathing critique.[6] *Materialism and Empiriocriticism* is in its content a very primitive and dogmatic book; its notion of matter is simultaneously too general (if matter is defined as objects which exist in the world independently of subjective perception, then Plato is definitely a materialist . . .) and too narrow (as if the basic claim of materialism is that "matter" is some tiny elementary particles moving in space and time). The basic failure of *Materialism and Empiriocriticism* is that Lenin completely misses the transcendental dimension, reducing it to the pre-transcendental solipsist empiricism of Berkeley (reality only exists in my mind).[7] So my aim is to repeat Lenin's gesture by way of transforming it radically, evolving it to the level of considering materialism without matter, of a level of reality outside our confines of space and time.

Hegel's formula of reconciliation—subject should recognize itself in its other—solicits three readings: subjective-idealist (I recognize reality as my own product), vulgar-materialist naturalism (I recognize that I am just a small part of objective reality, a result of the evolution of life on earth), and a proper dialectical-materialist (I recognize myself, my place, in the lack in the Other, at the point at which the Other fails, at the point of impossibility in the Other). In the third reading, alienation is not left behind, it is just redoubled: my alienation from the Other is simultaneously the alienation of the Other from itself.

In one of his well-known jokes, Ronald Reagan proposes to refute atheism with the following scenario: he will invite a group of distinguished atheists to an exquisite dinner cooked by the very best chefs, and after the dinner he will just ask them: "Do you believe there is a cook who created this meal?" In an obvious analogy, many much more perfect things in our universe prove that there also has to be a supreme "cook"-creator . . . The non-sequitur of this joke is rather obvious,[8] and I consider the following joke about belief in god a much better one. An atheist has a day off work, so he decides to go fishing on his new boat on Loch Ness. It is a beautiful day, the sun is shining, the lake is calm, and the fish are biting. Suddenly, his boat is attacked by the Loch Ness monster! In one easy flip, the beast tosses him and his boat high into the air . . . The monster then opens its mouth, preparing to swallow the man and his boat whole! As the man sails head over heels through the air, he cries out: "Oh God! Please help me!" At once, the ferocious attack stops, the scene freezes in place, and as the atheist hangs in mid-air, a booming voice comes down from the sky: "I thought you didn't believe in me!" "Aww, come on, God! Give me a break!" the man pleads. "Just a minute ago, I didn't believe in the Loch Ness monster either!"

We encounter here a correct formulation of the difference between a believer and an atheist materialist: a true atheist accepts the horror of Loch Ness, he knows reality is not what it seems and there are monstrous things awaiting us out there, but he doesn't take refuge in god. And this is also the difference between common reductionist materialist and a true materialist. When horrors considered "impossible" happen, a reductionist materialist tries to explain them away as illusions generated by processes in our ordinary reality, while true materialism (like that of quantum mechanics) accepts the monstrosities of reality (like the counterintuitive quantum processes). This is why the title of a recent CNN report "Atheist chaplains are forging a new path in a changing world"—aligns perfectly with my project in the book: as the article relates, there are an increasing number of "openly atheist chaplains" working in American institutions, who don't "see a contradiction between [their] beliefs and the work of tending to the human spirit"; in fact, it might even be an advantage, with one atheist chaplain quoted as saying that "Being an atheist, nonbeliever, unaffiliated, whatever you want to call yourself, lends itself really well to chaplaincy because we naturally don't project our own stuff on the people." This is seen as suggesting that "even as the population moves away from religion, the desire for spirituality and connectedness remains":

> Fundamental questions that faith has long answered—from why we're here and what it means to live a meaningful life are just as urgent and relevant for the nonreligious, especially as humanity grapples with existential threats and technological advances that are reshaping our world in ways that are still unclear.[9]

Quantum mechanics is often (from Wheeler and Penrose to Zeilinger) interpreted in an anti-materialist way ("with quantum waves and entanglements, matter disappears..."), and my goal here is a very old-fashioned one: following Althusser's formula that "philosophy represents class struggle in sciences," with class antagonism appearing in it as the opposition between materialism and idealism, my endeavour is to repeat Lenin's gesture a hundred years later apropos quantum mechanics and rebuff all attempts to give a spiritualist twist to its latest development—to paraphrase the famous lines from Gilbert and Sullivan's *Mikado*, I've got them all on my list, and none of them will be missed! Here is the passage from Althusser, which today has the distinct flavour of another era:

> Marxist-Leninist philosophy, or dialectical materialism, represents the proletarian class struggle *in theory*. In the union of Marxist theory and the Workers' Movement (the *ultimate* reality of the union of theory and practice) philosophy ceases, as Marx said, to "interpret the world." It becomes a weapon with which "to change it": *revolution*.[10]

The first thing to note in this definition is a clear reference to Lacan's formula of signifier as that which represents a subject for another signifier: philosophy functions as a signifier which represents class struggle (the true subject of history) in theory (science). But how does philosophy relate to psychoanalysis? Aaron Schuster brings out the unexpected similarity between the two: they both deal with trivialities. In *Logical Investigations* Husserl named philosophy "the science of the trivial" (*die Wissenschaft von der Trivialitäten*): "It is precisely behind the obvious that the hardest problems lie hidden, that this is so much so, in fact, that philosophy may be paradoxically, but unprofoundly, called the science of the trivial."[11] The technical name for this "triviality" is the *transcendental*: when confronted by some key notion of our daily lives (how we experience the passing of time, the motion of bodies in space, encountering a living being . . .), philosophy, in contrast to science, does not probe deeply into the structure of time or life. It remains on the surface of our experience and just asks: how do we experience time in our everyday life? How do we recognize an entity as a living being? The focus is here not on "true reality" but on the implicit set of presuppositions which structure our approach to reality. (For Aristotle, for example, a living being is an object which moves by itself, without external pushes.) Modern science also approaches reality through a set of transcendental presuppositions: "objective reality" is a material network of objects whose interaction is determined by mechanic laws . . . Scientific discoveries are not ignored here, the question is rather if and how they change our basic approach to reality. So where does psychoanalysis come in? It also deals with (what we experience as) trivialities, but in a thoroughly different way:

the most senseless phenomena, those that appear ridiculous, absurd, or bereft of significance, can, and should, be made objects of investigation. . . . In Freud's case, this meant dreams, slips of the tongue, bungled actions, and neurotic symptoms, the glitches and distortions of mental life.[12]

Freud himself refers to these phenomena as "trivialities," and their psychoanalytic interpretation is not scientific in the ordinary sense of the term—psychoanalytic interpretation remains in the domain of meaning, i.e., in the sphere of the symbolic language. However, this sphere is given an additional spin: it includes trauma, traumatic cuts which elude meaning, and this link between trauma and speech determines the notion of truth: truth is not a report on objective facts but a signifier which intervenes into the subject's Real, changing the way it relates to a trauma. This is why David Foster Wallace was right when he wrote in *Infinite Jest*: "The truth will set you free. But not until it's done with you." Here, unexpectedly, Freud rejoins Lenin, as Agon Hamza makes brilliantly clear:

> When Lenin says that what people should know is "the truth," he is not concerned with the truth in the empirical sense but with capturing and naming a moment in its temporal uniqueness. For Lenin, theory is not merely an activity of observation or of pure thinking, it is also an intervention in the historical-political conjuncture. A theoretical statement, just as a political proposition (even if it is done in the form of a slogan), does not emerge from a distance between the subjective position that announces it and the object that is observed. On the contrary, it is done from the militant position fully engaged in the object it observes, of which it is a part. Differently put, Lenin speaks not only from the position of the proletariat, but also from the actuality of the engaged political process/revolution. In this sense, language is not a neutral field of representing reality, it is a field of struggle, as slogans suggest. The politics of language and the language of politics can help us in further elaborating the question of truth and its opposites (untruth and non-truth). Direct factual truth expressed in true statements, that is to say, in objective neutral knowledge, misses subjective truth. Because subjective truth is engaged, included in its object, it cannot assume the form of true knowledge enunciated from a safe distance. It can

only be enacted in the form of factual untruth, through statements which distort objective reality and inscribe into it a subjective engagement of a political and ideological agent. In other words, subjective truth can only be formulated indirectly, in the form of the failure of directly saying the truth.[13]

Jean-Paul Sartre formulated this paradox in a perfect way apropos Khrushchev's report on the XXth Congress of the Soviet Communist Party in 1956 which revealed Stalin's crimes: "when the authorities find it useful to tell the truth, it's because they can't find any better lie. Immediately this truth, coming from official mouths, becomes a lie corroborated by the facts."[14] Here is a recent example of subjective-engaged truth in the form of untruth. In the fourth chapter of my *Pandemic* booklet,[15] I argued, via Quentin Tarantino's *Kill Bill*, that the Covid virus was acting as a kind of "Five Point Palm Exploding Heart Technique" on Western capitalism, where we are living in the brief moments between the explosive hit and the death of the victim (neoliberal capitalism). My point is that this type of dystopian, catastrophic event can bring about a kind of universal solidarity—we need a catastrophe to rethink our ways of living . . . At the level of factual truth, my claim is obviously not true: if anything, the Covid epidemic even strengthened global capitalism, widened the gap between the poor and the rich, constrained (whatever remains of) democracy in our societies, etc. However, this factual non-truth nonetheless functioned as untruth in Hamza's sense: it is not a neutral description but a fully engaged subjective truth which enables us to discern progressive elements in how even some of the most conservative governments reacted to the crisis (direct social intervention in market mechanisms, recourse to direct citizen's income, enforced global cooperation, etc.). In this way we can read the factual truth (the strengthening of capitalism) as a reaction to the threat to the system exerted by the pandemic. So it is not only that we escape from reality to fiction—reality itself can serve as an escape from fiction, from the insight into new possibilities opened up by a crisis.

*

The present book follows the logic of UPS: it moves from Universal through Particular to Singular. It begins with dialectical materialism: the exploration of the philosophical implications of quantum mechanics as the basis for a new form of dialectical materialism. It then moves to historical materialism, confronting Hegel's and Heidegger's notion of historicity. We finish with the singularity of political acts, bringing out the political implications of reading Hegel through the quantum lenses. The underlying syllogism of the book is thus that we can return from Heidegger back to Hegel only through the mediation of quantum universe.

In addition to the triadically-structured matter of the book, the three parts divided into chapters following its main argument, I have also written nine supplemental pieces, or variations, which you can find at the end of the book. Like variations on a musical theme, these pieces recombine, develop and add texture to the primary argument. They can be read interleaved with each of the main chapters, or together at the end.

I

Universal: Collapse comes first

1

Why a Hegelian needs quantum mechanics

The exact status of the collapse of a wave function is arguably the key problem of quantum mechanics—according to Roger Penrose, the fact that this collapse is external to the quantum space proper (quantum waves) proves that quantum mechanics is an incomplete or even incorrect theory. Interpretations of collapse seem to oscillate between the two poles: quantity and observation. For some, collapse occurs automatically when the assemblage of particles involved in a quantum wave reaches a certain quantitative level, which is why superpositions are limited to the most elementary level of subparticles, while for others, collapse occurs when a quantum process is observed (interpretations here differ as to what observation means: from mechanical registration through conscious observer up to formulation in public language). Can we link these two poles and claim that large-scale processes in our reality only exist insofar as they are observed? What definitely holds is that observation functions as a moment when the effect of a quantum process is measured in our ordinary reality, i.e., a moment of the link between the two levels (quantum waves and our ordinary reality). Maybe we should risk a parallel with the symbolic order here (although the idea that collapse occurs only when it is formulated in our language seems the least probable). Imagine a group of people who know some embarrassing detail about one (or all) of them, and also know all others know it—when one of them breaks the silence and makes what was the public secret really public (a topic of open conversation), the situation radically changes *although nobody learned anything new*. Who, then, *did* learn something new? What Lacan calls the "big Other," the public space of meaning.

Magicians know how to manipulate this dimension of the big Other. In a live TV appearance in 1983, the famous magician David Copperfield made the Statue of Liberty disappear in front of a couple of dozen people watching in person from an observation platform and millions of people watching from home. At that time, no one could tell how he made a 310-foot, 225-pound copper statue vanish. Now, however, we know it was all in the set up. Copperfield raised a sheet in front of the statue and when he dropped it, Lady Liberty was gone. However, she was actually just hidden behind one of the towers that held the sheet up. David moved the platform everyone was on, using loud music so the audience wouldn't know or feel the shift. The move changed their perspective so that the statue went behind the tower.[1] There is an important lesson in this magic trick: we are seduced insofar as we focus on the object which seems miraculously to change (disappear), i.e., insofar as we forget to include into what we observe a possible shift in our own subjective position.

This is why, as a Hegelian philosopher, I am so fascinated by quantum mechanics despite the fact that they are definitely strange bedfellows—already the substantives seem incompatible: "dialectics" versus "mechanics" ... But what we find in quantum physics is something that is usually considered an exclusive feature of the symbolic universe, a *self-reflective move of including the observer's own subjective position into the series of observed phenomena*. Recall Hegel's famous infinite judgment "Spirit is a bone"—how does it work? Instead of arguing (from the safe distance of an observer) that spirit cannot be reduced to a bone, it begins by endorsing the claim "spirit is a bone". Our reaction to this statement is one of shock: we experience this claim as blatant nonsense, as a radical self-related negativity ... but it is only through experiencing the nonsense/negativity of this statement that we arrive at Spirit, because "spirit" is just such a self-relating negativity which encompasses me in my subjective stance.[2] And exactly the same holds for Christianity: the Christian version of "Spirit is a bone" is "God is Christ, this miserable ordinary mortal individual." The very absurdity of this statement (how can the almighty god be a finite ordinary human being?) makes us experience the absolute gap, a crack in the texture of reality, and this gap as such is the foundation of atheism. If we assert atheism directly by comfortably claiming "there is no god, just reality out there," we say this from the comfortable position of an outside observer, and it is this very position—this comfort—that a true atheism should undermine. To be an atheist is not to possess a certain knowledge, it is to take up an existential position.

But what has this to do with quantum mechanics? There also, the only way to reach the Real is by way of including the observer into the picture. Still, is the very idea of quantum (the magnitude of the physical property can take on only discrete values) not foreign to Hegel, who remains well within the Aristotelian notion of the infinite divisibility? Is it then possible to think Hegelian dialectics and quantum mechanics together? What feature do they share? Alenka Zupančič provides the key when she wrote about theatre:

> we start with "repetitions," for rehearsals are called *repetitions*, and we end up with *la première*, with the first (performance or the first night). Repetitions do not repeat some first occurrence but, rather, lead up to it.[3]

Can we say, in a similar way, that wave superpositions in quantum mechanics (multiple virtual paths a particle takes to arrive from point A to point B) are like theatrical repetitions: they prepare the (back)ground for the premiere which occurs in their collapse? Collapse comes first, but it is constituted as first through its "repetitions" (superposed variations): superpositions "do not repeat some first occurrence but, rather, lead up to it." Exactly the same paradox is at work in the very core of Hegelian dialectics: in Hegel's reading of the Bible, the Fall (into sin) retroactively constitutes what it is the fall from, i.e., the Good— as Hegel put it brutally, Paradise before the Fall is simply the animal kingdom. What this means is that for quantum mechanics there is no happy domain of free-wave oscillations preceding collapses, a collapse is always-already here ... Considering all this messy confusion, one should not be surprised that the very idea of a collapse as an actual physical event is more and more considered problematic:

> Recent experiments have mobilized the extreme sensitivity of particle physics instruments to test the idea that the "collapse" of quantum possibilities into a single classical reality is not just a mathematical convenience but a

real physical process—an idea called "physical collapse." The experiments find no evidence of the effects predicted by at least the simplest varieties of these collapse models.[4]

No wonder that those who continue to use the notion of collapse are more and more tempted to account for it by introducing another factor external to wave oscillations. As far back as the 1980s and 1990s, Penrose and Lajos Diósi independently proposed gravity as a possible cause of the collapse: "Loosely speaking, their idea was that if a quantum object is in a superposition of locations, each position state will 'feel' the others via their gravitational interaction. It is as if this attraction causes the object to measure itself, forcing a collapse."[5] In spite of my ignorance of the purely mathematical aspect of this topic, I prefer to insist that collapse has to be accounted for in terms that are immanent to quantum waves. The only way to do this is to locate within the very domain of quantum waves a blind spot, a tension which pushes it towards collapse.

My hypothesis is thus that wave oscillations already are a reaction to what, in parallel with the Freudian notion of "primordial repression (*Ur-Verdraengung*)," we could call primordial collapse constitutive of the domain of wave oscillations itself. Consequently, we have *two* collapses: the primordial collapse which gives birth to wave oscillations themselves, and the collapse of waves into our ordinary reality: primordial collapse is a logical presupposition of quantum waves, it accounts for their inherent instability, for the fact that they are constitutively out of joint. (I am fully aware of the opposed meanings of collapse in these two cases: the primordial collapse introduces instability and tension while the collapse proper is a local attempt to regain stability.) In Hegelian terms, this duality of collapses is the difference between abstract self-relating negativity and the determinate negation whose result is a positive entity.

I am therefore opposed to all readings of quantum mechanics which ignore this priority of collapse, to all the narratives on how collapses arise from the spontaneous immanent development of wave oscillations, as well as to all attempts which take the opposite path and reduce quantum reality to an effect or aspect of our ordinary reality.[6] Therein resides the basic premise of the present book, and its first part on quantum mechanics is just a series of superposed variations on this axiom of collapse as the ultimate fact: in place of the "logical" temporality of a wave function collapsing into our ordinary reality, we have a para-consistent temporality in which a collapse into our ordinary reality retroactively posits the wave function. Such a collapsed reality functions as a hologram (a flat interference pattern which then produces a three-dimensional image): a surface onto which the multiple superpositions remain inscribed.

As well as the weird temporality of the collapse in which an effect retroactively posits its cause, Hegelian dialectics and quantum mechanics share the feature with which I began this chapter. They are both paradigms in which the objective Real is only reachable when the observer's subjective reality is included in the picture. In quantum mechanics, this leads immediately to the famous distinction between a wave and a particle—and indeed to the more speculative, paradoxical identity of "a wave *is* a particle."

Again, how? Let's dive *in medias res* of quantum mechanics. The fact that a particle—say, an electron—takes all possible paths when it travels from point A to point B means that this particle splits and *interacts with itself*, not just with other surrounding particles. One should not miss the Hegelian "speculative" echo of this formulation (speculative in the precise sense of reducing multiplicity to a self-relationship of a singular element): what appears as the interaction of elements external to each other turns out to be the interaction of one element with itself. The ultimate consequence of this approach was brought out by Richard Feynman in his classic paper from 1949,[7] in which he introduced his notion of the positron actually being an electron running backward in time. In the trade-off enacted by Feynman, if we accept running backward in time, the whole image gets simplified and one element suffices:

> In the approximation of classical relativistic theory the creation of an electron pair (electron *A*, positron *B*) might be represented by the start of two world lines from the point of creation, 1. The world lines of the positron will then continue until it annihilates another electron, *C*, at a world point 2. Between the times t1 and t2 there are then three world lines, before and after only one. However, the world lines of *C*, *B*, and *A* together form one continuous line albeit the "positron part" *B* of this continuous line is directed backwards in time. Following the charge rather than the particles

corresponds to considering this continuous world line as a whole rather than breaking it up into its pieces. It is as though a bombardier flying low over a road suddenly sees three roads and it is only when two of them come together and disappear again that he realizes that he has simply passed over a long switchback in a single road.

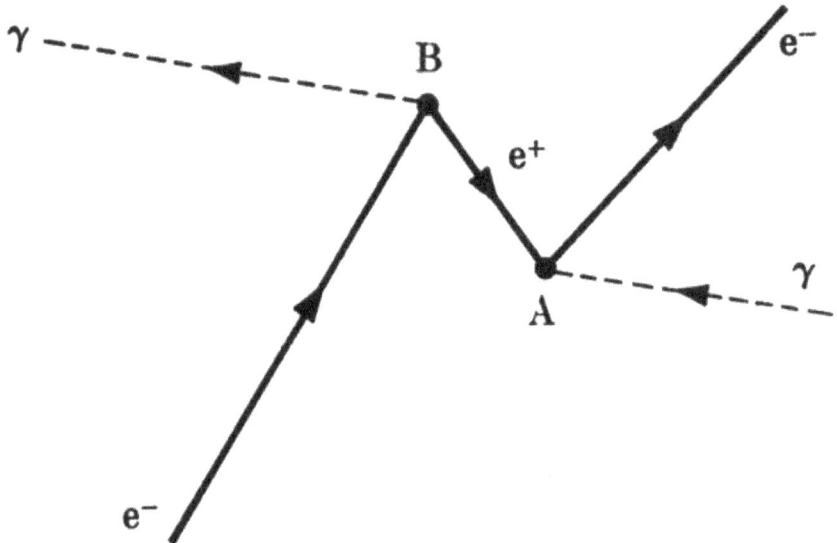

I am, of course, not qualified to judge the scientific validity of this line of thought—all I am saying is that, from my Hegelian standpoint, it works perfectly. What I especially appreciate in it is that something which appeared to be another positive element of reality (positron) turns out to be something which differs from its opposite *only* because of its different temporal line. And is this not also a proper way to reject the dualism of good and evil? When the good god himself reaches the point B, he turns back in time to A and becomes evil (the Old Testament god of wrath and fury), but he then turns around again and moves upwards to goodness (to love)—in Christianity this happens when he is born in/as a man in Christ.

We can see from this example how Hegel's thought can make a crucial contribution to quantum theory, supplying a dimension which has been lacking. When most philosophers mention quantum mechanics, they either focus on its paradoxes for our common sense notions or reduce its philosophical implications to the fact that reality is not totally deterministic but contains an irreducible aspect of contingency. A Hegelian approach shows that much more than contingency takes place in a quantum domain.

The most direct way to this "much more" is a delayed quantum eraser experiment, which appears to imply an influence of the future on the past. First imagined by John Wheeler, the archetypal "physics-for-poets physicist," this is a variation on a quantum eraser experiment—itself a variation on the classic double-split experiment. The quantum eraser experiment

> involves an apparatus with two main sections. After two entangled photons are created, each is directed into its own section of the apparatus. Anything done to learn the path of the entangled partner of the photon being examined in the double-slit part of the apparatus will influence the second photon, and vice versa. The advantage of manipulating the entangled partners of the photons in the double-slit part of the experimental apparatus is that experimenters can destroy or restore the interference pattern in the latter without changing anything in that part of the apparatus. Experimenters do so by manipulating the entangled photon, and they can do so before or after its partner has passed through the slits and other elements of experimental apparatus between the photon emitter and the detection screen. Under conditions where the double-slit part of the experiment has been set up to prevent the appearance of interference phenomena (because there is definitive "which path" information present), the quantum eraser can be used to effectively erase that information. In doing so, the experimenter restores interference without altering the double-slit part of the experimental apparatus.[8]

Wheeler's variation involves a situation in which the experimenter decides whether to leave both slits open or to close one off *after* the electron has already passed through the barrier—with the same results:

> A variation of this experiment, delayed-choice quantum eraser, allows the decision whether to measure or destroy the "which path" information to be delayed until after the entangled particle partner (the one going through

the slits) has either interfered with itself or not. In delayed-choice experiments, quantum effects can mimic an influence of future actions on past events. However, the temporal order of measurement actions is not relevant.[9]

(One should nonetheless be precise here: such erasure doesn't change the past, it changes the *present memory* of the past—that's why the quantum affects only "*mimic* an influence of future actions on past events.")

To put it in a somewhat simplified way, the electrons *seem to know in advance how the physicist will choose to observe it*. (This experiment was carried out in the early 1990s and confirmed Wheeler's prediction.) Even after a collapse should have already happened, this collapse can be retroactively undone and the interference pattern restored. It is as if particles can somehow "unlearn" that they were observed, as if their past can be erased.

> The interference pattern can be controlled by choosing whether or not to learn about a photon's trajectory after it has already hit the detector. The interference stripes only appear when the secondary uncertainty is resolved.[10]

Here we go a step further from the collapse of quantum waves which retroactively establishes necessity: de-quantified order itself is retroactively erased and we are back at quantum waves. What this means is that even the collapse of wave superpositions, which arguably provides the basic form of a temporal cut between "before" and "after," can be undone. How should reality be structured so that such paradoxes become possible?

To explain the present state of a physical system, the usual scientific approach needs two elements: the original situation (boundary conditions) and the laws that determine the evolution of the original situation into its present state. Relying on John Wheeler and others, Thomas Hertog[11] adds a third element: observership, his way of describing the involvement of an observer, who is not just a passive witness but focuses their attention on some parts of the observed state by way of asking questions and in this way regulates, directs even, the evolution of a system, even when that evolution happened in the past:

The triptych evokes the idea that this grand question [of the origins of the universe] retroactively draws into existence those few branches of cosmological history that have properties that are being observed. Observership in quantum cosmology... is an indispensable part of the continual process through which physical reality—and physical theory, we argue—come about.

(188-9)

Into this tripartite approach—the original situation, the laws that determine the evolution of the original situation, and observership—is built "the counterintuitive idea that... history at the very deepest level emerges backward in time":

It is as if a constant flux of quantum acts of observation retroactively carves out the outcome of the big bang, from the number of dimensions that grow large to the types of forces and particles that arise.

(189)

The backward movement (in which a recent "collapse" retroactively changes/reconstructs the past) has to be supplemented by a no less paradoxical forward movement in time; the temporality in quantum processes is double.

We arrive at the same conclusion if we perform the "double-slit experiment" which is today a part of common knowledge: waves that pass through two narrow, parallel slits will form an interference pattern on a screen behind the wall with two slits. But what happens if you shoot a single photon at the double slits? Even though there's only one photon shot at a time, it still forms an interference pattern. It's as if the photon travels through both slits simultaneously: if even photons shot one after the other so that the second photon is shot after the first one already hit the screen, this means that "each individual particle senses both slits."(89) (Perhaps, the Lacanian notion of the "knowledge in the real" is more appropriate here: it is as if each particle *knows* about the entire situation of the two slits and its observation.) We should thus treat

each individual photon as a propagating wave function that fragments at the slits, spreads, and intermingles with itself on the far side, creating a pattern of high and low probabilities.

(192)

However, if you set up detectors in front of each slit to determine which slit the photon really goes through, the interference pattern doesn't show up at all.[12] Wheeler accounted for this conundrum with yet another analogy. He likened the job of a physicist to that of someone playing Twenty Questions in its "surprise" version. In this variant of the old game, one person leaves the room while the rest of the group—or so the excluded person thinks—agrees on some person, place or thing. He then re-enters the room and tries to guess what they have in mind with a series of questions that can only be answered with a yes or a no. But unbeknownst to the guesser, the group has decided to play a trick on him. The first person to be queried will only think of an object and answer the question after the questioner asks his question. Each person after that will do the same, making sure that his response is consistent not only with the immediate question but also with all previous questions. "The word wasn't in the room when I came in even though I thought it was," Wheeler explained. In the same way, the electron, before the physicist chooses how to observe it, is neither a wave nor a particle. It is in some sense unreal; it exists in an indeterminate limbo. So, as Hawking said: "The history of the universe depends on the question you ask." Or, to quote Wheeler again: "Not until you start asking a question, do you get something. The situation cannot declare itself until you've asked your question. But the asking of one question prevents and excludes the asking of another."[13]

This same logic allows us a new way to approach the enigma of the improbability of intelligent life on Earth: In order for life on Earth to be possible, our cosmos—which existed billions of years before life emerged—would have to be composed in an extremely improbable way. If we read the history of the cosmos bottom-up, then the answer that imposes itself is, of course, god and teleology: some higher force had to direct the evolution of the cosmos in the direction of the possibility of intelligent life ... But in the top-down approach the probability distribution

> is of no significance because "we" have already measured that we live in a universe with three large dimensions of space.
>
> (199)

Or, as Lacan would have put it, a letter always arrives at its destination not because of some hidden teleology guaranteeing this outcome but because "destination" is retroactive: the destination of a letter is contingent but the point at which a letter contingently arrives *is* its destination. It is here that we come once again to the idea of a hologram: "The latest incarnation of holography envisions that everything in the four dimensions we experience is in fact a manifestation of a hidden reality located on a thin slice of spacetime." (212) As [x] wrote, it is "almost as if you could learn everything about the interior of an orange by meticulously analyzing its skin." (225) Plato's vision is thus turned on its head, or, perhaps, inside out—the flat image of a thing is its reality, while the real thing is a copy of its image.

*

To clarify this key point, let me return, for the nth time, to Claude Levi-Strauss's exemplary analysis, from his *Structural Anthropology*, of the spatial disposition of buildings among the Winnebago. The tribe, one of the Great Lakes tribes, is divided into two sub-groups ("moieties"), "those who are from above" and "those who are from below". When an individual is asked to draw the ground-plan of his/her village (the spatial disposition of cottages), there are two quite different results, depending on the sub-group the individual belongs to. Both perceive the village as a circle; but for one sub-group, there is within this circle another circle of central houses, so that we have two concentric circles, while for the other sub-group, the circle is split into two by a clear dividing line. In other words, a member of the first sub-group (let us call it "conservative-corporatist") perceives the ground-plan of the village as a ring of houses more or less symmetrically disposed around the central temple, whereas a member of the second ("revolutionary-antagonistic") sub-group perceives their village as two distinct heaps of houses separated by an invisible frontier.[14]

The point Levi-Strauss wants to make is that this example should in no way entice us into cultural relativism, according to which the perception of social space depends on the observer's group-belonging: the very splitting into two "relative" perceptions implies a hidden reference to a constant—not the objective, "actual" disposition of buildings but a traumatic kernel, a fundamental antagonism the inhabitants of the village were unable to symbolize, to account for, to "internalize," to come to terms with, an imbalance in social relations that prevented the community from stabilizing itself into a harmonious whole.[15]

The two perceptions of the ground-plan are simply two mutually exclusive endeavours to cope with this traumatic antagonism, to heal its wound via the imposition of a balanced symbolic structure. We get here a clear distinction between the external reality—the "actual," "objective," arrangement of the houses—and the Real that announces itself in the clash of the two different symbolizations which both distort in an anamorphic way the actual arrangement. The "real" here is not the actual arrangement, but the traumatic core of some social antagonism which distorts the tribe members' view of the actual arrangement of the houses in their village.

The common-sense realist notion of things-in-themselves was best encapsulated in Karl Kautsky's anti-Kantian argument against the unknowability of things-in-themselves (from his *Materialist Conception of History*, published in German in 1927 and not yet translated into English): different subjects perceive an object in different ways, each in accordance with its cognitive limitations. To know this object "really," independently of our subjective perception, we do not need to step out of ourselves and assume an impossible god-like objective view; all we need to do is to compare different perceptions of an object. The differences between them are obviously caused by the cognitive limitations of the subjects doing the observing, they don't belong to the object as it is in itself, while features which remain the same in all different perceptions no less obviously belong to the object itself. This line of argumentation is doubly wrong. Not only does it ignore the possibility that subjective limitation is not individual but generic, the result of the complex perceptual and semiotic history of humanity, but much more importantly, it misses the key dialectical insight into how the Real (as opposed to external reality) is the very antagonism that different discordant perceptions (or, rather, appearances) or even constructions of reality try to obfuscate.

And it would be easy to add numerous similar examples from contemporary political life—if one were, say, to ask a partisan of Trump or of the liberal center-Left to describe the basic coordinates of the American political scene, we would get each time a fundamentally different description (Trump as the voice of the hard-working people against the corrupted non-patriotic "enemies of the people," the liberal Left as the last bulwark of human rights and freedom against Fascist demagoguery), and the Real of this opposition is not provided by the description of social reality as it is but by the antagonism that both poles of the opposition obfuscate, each in its own way.

So it is not that we just get two distorted images/drawings of reality: *reality itself (the actual disposition of houses/huts) is an imaginary hologram which condenses two mutually exclusive symbolic forms.* And do we not get in this holographic duality—the same thing in two descriptions, like wave/particle—a *parallax* at its purest? There is no higher-level drawing that would unite the two: the only thing that unites the two drawings is the underlying antagonism itself. So we have three different levels: the imaginary surface of reality (actual disposition of houses), two incompatible symbolic structures, and the real of their underlying antagonism. Perhaps we can risk a parallel with what, in quantum mechanics, Bohr called "complementarity": the idea that a quantum entity can be measured as a wave or as a particle but not as both at the same time. What I want to add is that, since this notion of complementarity is the exact opposite of complementarity that characterizes some phenomena in our ordinary reality (the co-dependence of opposed features like male and female), it means that the quantum complementarity cannot be grounded in some substantial base shared by both features (waves and particles); it rather presupposes a pure tension or antagonism. And what if this brings us to the ontological origin of time, in which what cannot coexist resolves its tension in time where one can occur after the other? However, holographic cosmology tends to reduce the parallax tension to the classic duality of the true basic reality of a hologram and the standard reality of our expanding universe:

> If, as holographic cosmology posits, the surface of our observations is in some sense all there is, then this builds in the backward-in-time operation that is the hallmark of top-down cosmology. Holography tells us that there is an entity more basic than time—a hologram—from which the past emerges. The evolving and expanding universe would be output, not input in a holographic universe.
>
> (243)

How far can we go in this direction? Wheeler is famous for proposing the phrase "the it from bit": "every it—every particle, every field of force, even the spacetime continuum itself—derives its function, its meaning, its very existence entirely—even if in some contexts indirectly—from the apparatus-elicited answers to yes-or-no questions, binary choices, bits."[16] Is this formula not the ultimate scientific version of the fundamental ontological premise of Western metaphysics, in which whatever exists in reality (any "it") results from some "bit," from a cognitive logical matrix? If we follow this path, we end up in a new version of idealism, the timeless network of qubits out of which "it," our reality, emerges, so that the ultimate reality "may be better thought of as a mathematical realm that can inform physics but need not exist as such" (247):

> quantum information inscribed in an abstract timeless hologram of entangled qubits forms the thread that weaves reality. . . . It is as if there is a code, operating on countless entangled qubits, that brings about physical reality.
>
> (244–5)

This basic reality of qubits is at the same time in the past and in our future, since we are not yet able (not just to discover but simultaneously) to create it: holography "places the true origin of the universe in the distant future, because only the far future would reveal the hologram in its full glory."(245) What remains here of the Darwinian insight that "not the laws as such but their capacity to change and transmute would have the final word"? (246) What remains of the idea of overcoming "the separation between law-like dynamics and ad hoc boundary conditions as a fundamental property of nature"? (80) Or, as Hawking put it, for the classic physical science,

> theoretical physics will have achieved its goal when we have obtained a set of local dynamic laws. They would regard the question of the boundary conditions of the universe as belonging to the realm of metaphysics or religion. But we shall not have a complete theory until we can do more than merely say that things are as they are because they were as they were.
>
> (82)

The only alternative to this idealist vision (or, rather, its necessary supplement) is a self-limitation, i.e., the claim that "we are living in a patch of spacetime, surrounded by an ocean of uncertainty about which, well, we must remain silent." (247) So there is a boundary to (our) cosmos, a boundary which does not reside in its outer limits but is implied by the very position in which we find ourselves as observers and from which, in a top-bottom approach, we reconstruct the cosmos. This would have been the quantum cosmology version of the Hegelian infinite judgment: the entire external cosmos equals (or is correlative to) the observer's eye.

What these counterintuitive thoughts imply is that philosophy returns with a vengeance in today's quantum physics. The old question of the ontological status of wave functions, not just ignored but outright prohibited by Bohr and the Copenhagen orthodoxy, is today answered by the claim that quantum waves describe "the world at some kind of preexistence level" (88) since what exists in/as our reality is only the outcomes of the collapse of the quantum superpositions. At this preexistence level, particles "follow all possible paths when they move from one point to another" (90): in a double-slit experiment, "individual electrons follow not one but every possible path from the gun to the screen. One path takes the electron through the left slit, another through the right, back out through the left, into a U-turn, and through the right slit once more." (91) Along these lines, Feynman proposed the path integral formulation which replaces the classical notion of a single, unique trajectory for a system with a sum, or functional integral, over an infinity of quantum-mechanically possible trajectories to compute a quantum amplitude. The path integral formulation thus suggests that "our reality is a sort of blending—a sum—of all imaginable possibilities."[17]

Here is another unexpected use of superposition in sexuality. For a sexual conservative like me, there are two main options with regards to getting married. First, it seems better not to get married because in this way you display trust in your love: you don't need an external legal limitation that obliges you to fidelity, your love itself is enough of a guarantee. (However, there is a deeper paradox at work in marriage: when marriage mostly no longer has the patriarchal function of securing succession, it may also be read as a commitment to love you even when I will no longer really love you . . .) Second, if you are married, it opens up a way to dream about cheating on your wife without feeling guilty—you can tell yourself "I am just dreaming about it, I know I will not do it because I am married . . ." Is there a way out of this rather debilitating deadlock? It's certainly not simply being married and loving your wife—the gap between the law and desire is irreducible. But what about being married and dreaming about cheating on your wife ... *with herself*, not with another woman (or man or ...)? Crazy and inconsistent as this version may appear, many married people are doing it, practicing a kind of superposition of fidelity and promiscuity: while I make love to my wife, I imagine she is not my wife.

As has been established already in this chapter, in quantum experiments there are often situations which do not fit the ordinary notion of time as a linear movement from the past to the future. There seems only two explanations which can account for the results of such experiments: Either (a) two elements (like entangled photons) can interact faster than the speed of light, which means that there is another dimension of reality beneath or beyond our ordinary reality in which instant interaction between elements far away is possible; or (b) at some specific level of quantum reality, time can run backwards, from the future to the past—not at some metaphoric level (like symbolic reinterpretation of the past) but at the literal physical level. Are these two options just two versions of the same underlying phenomenon?

Such paradoxes surprisingly induced Hawking (who otherwise despised philosophy) to call for a new philosophy for cosmology. (167) In his view, "a proper quantum outlook" would require "a different philosophy of cosmology in which we work from the top down, backward in time, starting from the surface of our observation." (175) Can we apply the top-down approach to the universe itself, so that it has multiple pasts? Hawking's final answer is yes—the premise of his new philosophy is that we should abandon the idea that "the universe has a global classical state. We live in a quantum universe so it should be described by a superposition of histories a la Feynman, each with its own probability." (174) Or, to quote Hertog's paraphrase:

> we should adopt a full-blown quantum view not just of what's happening within the universe—the wave functions of particles and strings and so forth—but of the cosmos as a whole.... we should think of the universe as a superposition of many possible spacetimes. So a quantum universe is *uncertain* even on the very largest scales, on scales well beyond our cosmological horizon like those associated with eternal inflation. And that

large-scale cosmic fuzziness puts a bomb under the eternal background that the multiverse aficionados assume exists.

(174)

This means that we shouldn't imagine the Big Bang as a singularity that then explodes but as a primordial fuzziness in which time bends into space (130)— no wonder Hertog quotes Wagner's *Parsifal*, "I hardly move, yet far I seem to have come. You see, son, here time becomes space" [*zum Raum wird hier die Zeit.*] (72) Or, to quote Hertog, "in the very early universe, quantum effects would have blurred the very distinction between space and time, causing them to suffer a bit of an identity crisis, with intervals of time sometimes behaving like intervals of space and vice versa." (94) The singularity at the bedrock of the classical universe, that event without a cause that seemingly put the beginning outside science, is therefore replaced by "a smooth and rounded quantum origin complying with the laws of physics everywhere." (95)

The fact that there is no pure singularity of the absolute beginning where all laws of nature break down implies a further, radically counterintuitive conclusion: there is no zero-level at which things (or, rather processes) just happen without being in some sense observed. Even the remotest past is retroactively generated by an observer: "What matters is not what is most probable in the theory but what is most probable to be observed. Cosmological histories that don't produce observers don't quite count when we compare our theories to our observations." (127) However, are there different universes for different observers? How do we locate ourselves in this multitude of observers? "Einstein showed that gravity is a manifestation of warped spacetime. Holography goes further and postulates that warped spacetime is woven from quantum entanglement."(235) In what precise sense do entanglements occur only for observers?

Let's begin with the notion of entropy, a concept that is most commonly associated with a state of disorder, randomness, or uncertainty. Entropy is central to the second law of thermodynamics, which states that the entropy of an isolated system left to spontaneous evolution cannot decrease with time. As a result, isolated systems evolve towards thermodynamic equilibrium, where the entropy is highest. A consequence of the second law of thermodynamics is that such processes are irreversible. In 1928, Arthur Eddington endeavoured to explain the nature of time, order, and the universe in terms of entropy:

> If you take a pack of cards as it comes from the maker and shuffle it for a few minutes, all traces of the original systematic order disappears. The order will never come back however long you shuffle. There is only one law of nature— the second law of thermodynamics—which recognizes a distinction between the past and the future. Its subject is the random element in a crowd. A practical measure of the random element which can increase in the universe but never decrease is called *entropy*.

In this way Eddington offers a thermodynamic explanation of time's arrow: a direction of time emerges from irreversible growing entropy.[18] However, many scientists (Carlo Rovelli among them) have pointed out that we cannot talk about entropy as a universal law of reality since a process of entropy always implies a measure of order with regard to which disorder is growing. The parallel with quantum physics is clear: in order to detect a line of growing entropy, we "collapse" the chaotic reality by way of selecting a specific notion of measure. When we buy a new pack of cards, they are usually ordered by color (in the English Poker format, there are black spades, red hearts, blue diamonds and green clubs), and within each of these four groups cards are ordered by their value (first aces, then kings . . .), and in this case some shuffling of the pack can lower entropy. But if we buy a standard card pack and measure its order by the value of cards (first the four aces, etc.), then some shuffling may even lower entropy . . . Low entropy measured by some standards can mean higher entropy measured by a different standard—let's take the case of the development from medieval to modern society in Europe. Measured by some criteria, this development brought much more entropy: instead of the stability of organic hierarchies we got chaotic individualism and market exchanges. However, measured by different criteria, medieval societies were much more chaotic, with permanent wars and plagues—a relatively stable social life emerged only in a modern state. In literature, the same holds for Walter Scott's *Waverley*: the defeat of premodern "organic" life of Scottish clans with the victory of modern legal state at the same time pushes those who do not want to accommodate themselves to this order outside the legal order, they become bandits... The point is that there is no global standard encompassing all reality, so in all of reality there is neither entropy nor progress towards order. This is important because if we perceive growing entropy as the ultimate reference of the flow of time, then it immediately becomes clear that there is no global flow of time encompassing all of reality. For this same reason, I tend to disagree with Smolin in his parallel between science and democracy:

> Scientists know even the best ideas will eventually need to be updated by new insights, and will be, from time to time, replaced by revolutionary new conceptions. Similarly, democratic governance gives people the power to vote a government out of office when its effectiveness diminishes or when events show that its election was a mistake.[19]

Does this parallel not rely on an all too simple notion of progress? Do we not now live precisely in an era of big regress, of a total disorientation? Plus is it not the case that, in the course of (historical) time, the very standards of progress are changing? (For anti-abortion fundamentalists, the prohibition of abortion is the necessary great step in the progress towards equality: first women were proclaimed equal to men, then other races were proclaimed equal to the whites, and now unborn humans should be proclaimed equal to the already-born...) And, last but not least, what if the majority turns against science and acts in a racist way against refugees and immigrants, etc.?

Quantum mechanics and general relativity force us at this point to take not one but two steps further—steps which also have repercussions for our notion of history. It is not enough to say that there is no progress (or regression) in general—such a negation still presupposes that all events take place within the same all-encompassing form of time and space. But what if there is no universal form of time and space, what if space and (especially) time always emerge in a specific physical constellation, so that there are multiple space/times with no common spatio-temporal measure that unites them? One step further: if space/time is not universal, then multiple space/times must be rooted in some more basic level of reality which is, according to some theorists, spatial, and according to others, outside space and time. The notion that as a rule appears here is that of a '"block universe": at its most basic level, reality is an atemporal block in which past, present and future co-exist simultaneously within the same space, and we experience time only due to the limitations of what our point of observation allows us to perceive.

Along these lines, Rovelli claims that time is an effect of our ignorance. Time exists because we cannot see everything everywhere all at once, we cannot access a total view of reality: "if I could take into account all the details of the exact, microscopic state of the world, would the characteristic aspects of the flowing of time disappear? Yes. If I observe the microscopic state of things, then the difference between past and future vanishes."[20] Why? Because the changes regulated by physical laws are "symmetric[al] between future and past." (30) This is because of the nature of entropy (growing disorder), to which, Rovelli argues, the difference between past and future may be solely attributed. However, entropy appears only if we measure a starting point as that of order— "*every configuration is particular*, every configuration is singular, if we look at *all* of its details."(29) Rovelli evokes here a short science-fiction novel (co-authored by Alain Connes and two of his friends) in which Charlotte, the protagonist, "manages to have for a moment a totality of information about the world, without blurring. She manages to 'see' the world directly, beyond time,"(123) and when she is gradually returning to our blurred image of reality, she falls back into time.

But does quantum indeterminacy not imply that reality is in itself blurred, "muddled," so that the limitation of our observations is grounded in the incompleteness of reality itself? Rovelli generally opposes "our confused fantasies about the supposed freedom of the future," (48) but he himself wrote: "The intrinsic quantum indeterminacy of things produces a blurring which ensures—contrary to what classic physics seemed to indicate—that the unpredictability of the world is maintained even if it were possible to measure everything that is measurable." (123) And, to risk even a step further, does this "unpredictability" not point—not towards freedom but—towards some kind of openness of the future?

If the "true reality" of fields and waves is out of time and space, then time and space are in some basic sense illusory. However, isn't the underlying scheme of basic reality and illusory appearances false in the same way as its opposite, the gradual progress towards higher forms? What pushes this pre-ontological quantum space towards collapses and/or towards our common reality must be some immanent impossibility, a "barred One," or some "boundary" (beyond which there is nothing—a boundary which coincides with its Beyond, i.e., which is itself inaccessible) in the basic quantum space itself.

The problem is then to explain how and why—although the fundamental theory of the world "does not need a time variable: it needs to tell us only how the things that we see in the world vary with respect to each other." (103–4)— "the things that we see in the world" are always perceived by us as things that exist in space and time. How, in that case, can the movement of change be in some sense prior to space/time? For Hegel, space and time (as self-negated space) are logically prior to movement: movement means that an element changes its position in space, for which a minimal time is needed (first, the element was at the position x, then it moved to the position y). If, in quantum mechanics, change comes before space/time, is this not evidence that Hegel's logic doesn't cover the quantum universe? To clarify this key point somewhat, let go back to the duality of world in itself and our perspective on it:

> From *our perspective*—the perspective of a creatures who make up a small part of the world—we see the world flowing in time. Our interaction with the world is partial, which is why we see it in a blurred way. To this blurring is added quantum indeterminacy.
>
> (169)

I detect here a certain ambiguity: the first factor (the limitation of our perspective) makes the world appear blurred to us, so that we can still imagine how from a complete global perspective the world is not blurred, but quantum indeterminacy makes it blurred *in itself*. This brings us back to entropy: the illusion of a single line of the flow of time is (to simplify things to the utmost) the outcome of the fact that we, all of humanity, share the same perspective of living in a world of growing entropy. Entropy also explains why we remember the past and not the future: it is not simply because the future didn't yet happen but because the flow of time is based on increasing entropy—entropy was lower in the past, and (what appears from *our* standpoint) as the greater order of things in the past leaves traces in our present. "Since our future is based on growing disorder, it cannot leave traces to us: this fact is the origin of our sensation of being able to act freely in the world, choosing between different futures, even though we are unable to act upon the past."(144–5)

Rovelli claims that "traces" of the past exist (persist in our present) because of entropy (traces of lower entropy in higher entropy)—but what happens when we have a collapse of quantum waves? Are there also traces of multiple wave superpositions after the collapse? Is this not the base of quantum computing? Moreover, how is this notion of the traces of superpositions linked to what Hertog calls the top-down view? The main point here is: what if there is a one-directional cut between the past and the future: the *collapse* of a wave function itself which is irreversible? Does time begin here? Lee Smolin seems to move in this direction when he claims that

> the fundamental distinction is not the difference between the past, present, and future. The fundamental distinction is between some properties that are incompletely known or indefinite, and some quantities that are definite, and that when an event is, is a moment of transition of some indefinite quantity becoming definite. ... we have an operational meaning of now. Basically, an event is part of now if it has been created but it hasn't yet made all the children it's going to make ... that gives us a notion of a present, and that's the fundamentals of this.[21]

Isn't this '"now" defined precisely by a collapse into a definite reality which remains open towards the future (since "it hasn't yet made all the children it's going to make")? There is a parallel with Lacan here: for Lacan, drive is atemporal, permanent, while desire is temporal, oriented towards a goal. Moreover, is what Hegel calls the "night of the world" in which dismembered bodies float not the atemporal/spaceless process, and does Ego as a fixed point not emerge through the encounter with an Other (symbolic Ego ideal)? So is the Self/Ego not the outcome of a collapse of the mix of superpositions (that is the dismembered body) when this mix interacts with an Other?

Here, we stumble once again upon a question that haunts us all the time: how does time/space, as a neutral medium/container *in which* entities exist, emerge? It is not enough to elevate one variable to this position—there must already be a space, an opening for it. Does it not imply that already in pre-ontological flux there is an imbalance, a tendency towards an impossible point?

2

Why quantum mechanics needs Hegel

In his *On the Origin of Time*,[1] Thomas Hertog forcefully asserts the quantum nature of the big bang. For two decades he was a collaborator and friend of Stephen Hawking, and together they probed into a deeper level of evolution in which laws of physics themselves transform and simplify until particles, forces, and even time fades away. The laws of physics are not set in stone but are born and co-evolve as the universe they govern takes shape. As Hawking's final days drew near, the two collaborators published a theory which proposed a radical new Darwinian perspective on the origins of our universe: the laws of nature were at the beginning multiple, caught in a Darwinian struggle for survival, and our laws are the laws which won. Is this not a supreme case of how a general law of nature contingently emerges out of a contingent singular situation?

What is the link to quantum physics here? Is it that our (deterministic) reality emerges through a collapse which functioned like the outcome of Darwinian competition? Quantum mechanics undermines our common notion of reality: it "leads to a different philosophy of cosmology in which we work from the top down, backward in time, starting from the surface of our observations." It is easy to see how this backward transformation works in our symbolic universe: we don't change the facts of what happened in the past, we just locate it into a different symbolic context, we change its meaning... Such symbolic efficiency plays a key role in our lives. Consider the "trillion-dollar coin" strategy proposed in 2011 to reduce the national debt, in which the US government would mint a physical coin, made of platinum, with a face value of

$1 trillion.² Do we not encounter here symbolic efficiency at its purest: a little bit of real (a small coin) just staying locked in a state bank would deeply affect the entire financial—and therewith also economic—situation of a country?

An obvious counter-argument imposes itself here: is not such retroactive transformation of the past something that can be done only within a symbolic order? Is it not something similar to well-known fake paintings in which Jesus is wearing the cross when he was still alive, before his crucifixion? Observation, whichever way we conceive it, is part of our normal reality in which time runs forward and causality works from the past to the future; more precisely, observation is the moment of the collapse of superpositions and wave oscillations into a single reality—so how can observation provide the opening for a movement backwards in time? The answer resides in the specific notion of quantum holograms. Conor Costick defines quantum holography as the idea of a "a three-dimensional boundary hologram that projects the four-dimensional universe as we know it".³

In common three-dimensional reality, time runs forward. In a holographic universe, there is no time, everything is here: "The boundary hologram does not feature time: time only emerges as you make the transition from the boundary to the universe we are used to." Costick argues that understanding the universe as a hologram does not mean that our senses encounter the experience of existing within it differently, but rather opens up the tantalizing possibility that "we are only accessing it from one side of a duality. It's a bit like only ever having encountered light as a wave but finding out that it is just as valid to experience it as a sequence of particles." There is thus a duality to the universe—not least in terms of time:

> Viewed from within the projection, it feels like there is time: there is causality and a progression from the Big Bang to where we are today. But that's only a partial grasp on the situation. Viewed as a hologram, the universe is timeless and if you could translate the information from the boundary where the hologram is described, you could see the entire history of the universe. We are immersed in time and simultaneously in a timeless state.

The first problem we encounter here is the question of whether the parallax of temporality and the timeless "block" universe in which past, present, and future coexist a true parallax, two incompatible views, or are we dealing with a relationship between "true" reality and illusory appearance? The block universe basically reduces time (temporal change) to space: everything there is exists in an eternal present, and the flow of time is just the illusion due to our limited view constrained to the present. The purest version of the block-universe in which time is reduced to a secondary dimension is that put forward by Carlo Rovelli, who argued that time emerges from the laws of quantum mechanics and thermodynamics and that we project linear progressions of past, present, and future on to the messy events of reality. We perceive time passing simply because we're not capable of seeing the world in all its detail; if we could know the positions and speeds of all the particles in the universe—i.e., if we were not subject to quantum uncertainty—"there would be no entropy, and no unraveling of time."[4]

Rovelli spells out clearly the ontological implications of this view: what we experience as our temporal reality "is not a fundamental constituent of the world," it only appears to us

> because the world is immense, and we are small systems within the world, interacting only with macroscopic variables that average among innumerable small, microscopic variables. We, in our everyday lives, never see a single elementary particle, or a single quantum of space. We see stones, mountains, the faces of our friends—and each of these things we see is formed by myriads of elementary components. We are always correlated with averages: they disperse heat and, intrinsically, generate time. . . . Time is an effect of our overlooking of the physical microstates of things. Time is information we don't have. Time is our ignorance.
>
> (222–3)[5]

What this means, at the level of ontology, is that "we must not confuse what we know about a system with the absolute state of the same system. What we know is something concerning the relation between the system and ourselves."(223) What really exists out there, reality in itself, "the absolute state of the system," is composed of quantum events and their interactions which take place outside time, and we should strictly distinguish this reality-in-itself from the way reality appears to us due to the limitation of our view—the classical metaphysical difference between reality and appearances returns here with a vengeance, and

Parmenides wins over Heraclitus. No wonder Einstein viewed with sympathy the idea of a block universe and played with it—this idea is not a crazy extrapolation but a necessary implication of a fully deterministic view of the universe.

Einstein's full determinism relies on a religious foundation—he wrote: "*Raffiniert ist der Herrgott, aber boshaft ist er nicht.*"[6] (God is subtle, but he is not intentionally deceiving us—or, in a more vague and descriptive translation: "Nature hides her secret because of her essential loftiness, but not by means of [a] ruse.") Although Einstein repeatedly pointed out that he didn't believe in a personal god, he proclaimed himself deeply religious: "Our limited minds cannot grasp the mysterious force that sways the constellations." "I believe in Spinoza's God, who reveals himself in the harmony of all that exists."[7] In this sense, for him religion and science necessarily coexist: science itself is sustained by the deep faith that our universe is marvelously arranged in a harmony that pervades all that exists. In Lacanian terms, Einstein believed in the big Other, and it is this very belief which has been dealt a mortal blow by quantum mechanics.

Consequently, the only way to really save time—in whatever form—is to conceive reality as not-all, as incomplete, and in this sense as open towards the future. What this means is that what Rovelli calls the "absolute state" of reality, its complete description, is not only out of reach to us finite limited observers, it is in itself a meaningless notion that should be abandoned. The "ignorance" that separates us, our view, from the absolute state of reality is immanent to reality itself—reality is "in itself" barred, crossed by an impossibility. Usually idealists privilege time (our thoughts happen in time but cannot be located in space), while materialists insist on the irreducible character of space (even our thoughts have to be located in the spatial reality of our brain); but we should reverse this hierarchy. The standpoint of quantum holography also obliges us to adopt a radically new view on the Big Bang—from within the universe as it appears to us, it seems reasonable to wonder what happened "before" the Big Bang, but considered from the other side of the time/not-time duality, the idea that there was any "before" no longer makes any sense:

> It is not like there is a giant clock standing outside of the universe; nor the fundamental laws that when we apply them to the initial conditions will allow us to model the development of the universe. What lies beyond or

before the universe? We can't say because there is nothing to speak with: there is no information on the hologram about this.[8]

To understand this, we should make a step further into the weird ontology implied by quantum physics and conceive observation as integral to understanding reality. As Hertog writes:

> If you had a conventional Western education like mine, then science is taught as the discovery of laws of nature that are always exact, regardless of whether anyone or anything is watching. In the quantum world, a particle is in a superposition of possible positions and velocities, described by a wave function, until one of these is fixed by an observation (the other one then, necessarily, becoming unknowable).[9]

Hawking and Hertog avoid getting lost in the debate on what really counts as observation—they endorse the broadest view: "The observer doesn't have to be human or sentient. Any record of quantum events is a form of observation, so when a quartz crystal preserves the path of a subatomic particle that passed through it, the crystal acts as an observer."[10] This wide notion of what counts as observation enables us to avoid the onto-theological trap to which physics sometimes succumbs.

Newtonian physics, Hertog writes, was grounded in a concept of God as the ultimate and absolute observer; space was the "sensorium" of God, position in space was the position of the object in the eyes of God. In other words, the ontology of empty space as a container of everything that materially exists has to be grounded in a supreme entity—a different iteration of what Heidegger called the onto-theological structure of metaphysics."

With general relativity, however,

> we have been learning that we do not need this frame to keep reality in place. Reality keeps itself in place. Objects interact with other objects, and this is reality. Reality is the net of these interactions. [...] We do not need an external entity to hold this net. We do not need Space, to hold the universe.
> (32)

This is also why we should reject the reading of quantum mechanics which proposes a supreme Observer (sometimes god is directly evoked) which fully constitutes reality—it again regresses to onto-theology. Nonetheless, the basic claim of quantum mechanics—that only when a wave function is observed does it "collapse" into an actual route (prior to that moment, it was traveling through all possible routes)—explains what Hawking and Hertog mean by top-down cosmology:

> The universe is a quantum universe and even the distant past, when no observers existed, can be selected by observation today. [...] the quasar light is in a state of superposition until we switch on the telescope. The history of quantum activity isn't fixed until an observation has taken place; current and future events select the past. In the same way, when we make observations about the universe, we are assisting in creating the answer.[11]

Wheeler drew an image in order to illustrate how "the universe develops to the point where there are observers and these observers fix the past, including the distant past long before any observers exist":

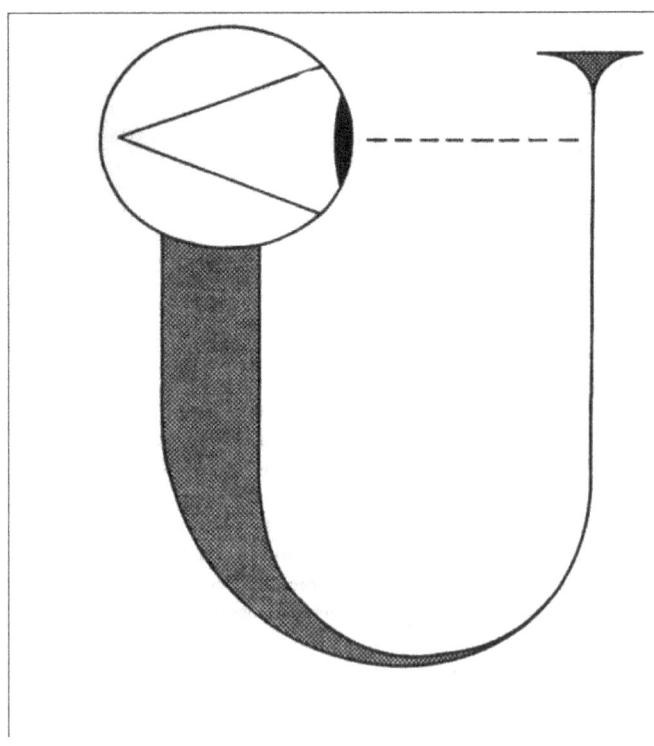

Wheeler argues that this type of "top-down, observer inclusive" approach resolves the seeming paradox of the Anthropic Principle (which basically argues that what we can observe about the universe is limited by the fact that the universe we are observing is one which has enabled intelligent life capable of observing it to evolve) and the seemingly bizarre unlikelihood of a universe capable of supporting life:

> From a classical perspective it seems extraordinary that the laws of physics should have, at every choice, taken the path that resulted in a life-compatible universe. But if we are only now switching on the telescope and observing the fragment of the wave function that we live in, then it necessarily has to be one that supports life. We might be fixing a fragment that was very unlikely, statistically, to have arisen from repeated rolls of the dice. But then all the options are more or less unlikely.[12]

What I find problematic in these formulations is that, if we take the broadest notion of observation, then *there was no time without observers*: the moment our temporal reality emerged, "observations" take place, even if only by crystal quartzes. What this means is that, at the proper quantum level, there is no big rupture, no tremendous collapse of waves—collapses are going on all the time. If every encounter/interaction counts as observation, does this not mean that collapses are infinite since entities are processes of change which exist only in interaction with others? For Rovelli, an entity is exposed to multiple interactions, and in every interaction it "collapses" into a different determined object (into a different *eigenstate*)—in itself, this object is just a mess of quantum wave oscillations. The reversal implied by this claim is interesting: it is not that an entity has a stable self-identity but appears to other entities in different messy ways—on the contrary, an entity is in itself a messy complex of superpositions which collapse in different ways through different interactions . . . But, again, if collapse occurs in all encounters, even between two particles, not just in observations in any narrower sense, then collapses happens all the time continuously, trillions of trillions, more than particles—they are in no way exceptional Events. So was Sabine Hossenfelder right when she wrote that our universe is basically deterministic, with only infinitesimal margins of uncertainty at the subatomic level which do not affect the larger-scale reality?

The mystery of the role of observation in a quantum collapse is homologous to the mystery of human communication: why is communication—a dialogue—never just between two agents, why is a third agency, an impassive observer (Lacan's "big Other"), always necessary? This is why, I think, Rovelli is wrong when he interprets any interaction between two particles or processes as an act of observation in which each particle "observes" the other. The notion of observer's neutrality, of its distance from the observed process of interaction, is irreducible. The lesson of quantum mechanics is not just that such a distance is illusory since we, observers, are part of reality, so that our observation is always an interaction, but something more subtle: "pure" observation is an illusion, but what observation nonetheless bears witness to is that everything that exists is not just interacting particles and processes—there is a gap, a void, that sustains every interaction.

From Marxism through language theories to quantum mechanics, the same motif runs, that of the primacy of interaction over observation, of different modes of inclusion of the observer into the observed process. Marxists and language theorists like to emphasize that language is embedded in our practical interactions and production, it is primarily not an instrument of talking about external reality but a means of being engaged in social reality, even a field of struggle, as Hamza wrote with regards to Lenin. Even the most neutral statements—like the almost proverbial "There is a table in the corner of my room"—are always embedded in specific practical contexts (they tell a stranger where to look for my table, etc.). Quantum mechanics seems to bring this tendency to its properly ontological extreme: there is no "objective reality" since every act of observing (a part of) changes it. However, the first thing to note is that advocates of observation-is-interaction themselves regularly formulate their stance in statements which imply pure observation. When Rovelli determines the basic level of reality as composed not of things but of events, i.e., as a pure flux of becoming which cannot be attributed to any external thing but consists only of particular interactions including our observation, this statement is clearly not a moment of particular interaction but an absolute universal observation. But a more important point is that observation does not presuppose a neutral position outside the observed reality: it is ultimately grounded in a gap in the observed process itself. To put it in speculative terms, not doing anything, not acting but just observing, abstaining from interaction where interaction is expected, is itself the most radical act, the most radical disturbance of the existing order. Abstaining is an act not because we withdraw out of reality (there is nowhere to withdraw), but because reality itself is structured around a void, its own impossibility, and by way of not acting (and just observing) we temporarily place ourselves into that void. Acting against is still participating in the order while not acting suspends the very rules of the game. That's why observation is needed for a collapse to take place—collapse suspends the laws of quantum waves and superpositions.

To repeat again the basic problem: if every interaction counts as observation that causes a collapse, and if things exist only in their interrelationships, does this not mean that all that exists are determined "collapsed" objects? Where is there then any space for superpositions, for wave functions? Are entities with which we don't interact not-collapsed (in superpositions) for us, although they are themselves collapsed? So can the same thing be collapsed from one standpoint and not-collapsed from another standpoint? "The world is like a collection of interrelated points of view. To speak of the world 'seen from outside' makes no sense because there is no 'outside' to the world."(109) But interrelation means collapse, so is there nothing not-collapsed?

We thus arrive at the so-called problem of Wigner's Friend: no matter how all-encompassing it is, an observation cannot include the observer itself as one of its objects. Does this imply that collapses can also be superposed, that an object/event X contains multiplicity of collapses, not only because it interacts with multiple "observers" but because this interaction itself is observed by multiple agents? To quote Rovelli again: "Each part of the world interacts with a small part of all the variables, the value of which determines 'the state of the world with regard to that particular subsystem'."(136) So, again, the world is like a collection of interrelated points of view, each of which is in some sense universal since it renders the entire world from a singular point of view.

As Alenka Zupančič[13] succinctly formulated it, reality in itself (independent of our subjective interaction with it and perception of it) is not another deeper reality (like the Kantian noumena as opposed to phenomenal reality), it is the same as our reality minus the gap (of the real) which locates the subject into it. One should thus not confuse the pre-ontological Real-in-itself implied by quantum theory (a Real composed of quantum processes) with the pre-ontological Real that we find in the films of David Lynch or Andrei Tarkovsky (an impenetrable density which ultimately remains fantasmatic/imaginary). The Lacanian question that arises here is how to avoid the Sartrean duality between the inert in-itself and the void/negativity that is constitutive of a subject, i.e., *how such a subject can emerge in reality*. In Chapter 9 ("What Is a Picture?") of his *Seminar XI*, Lacan notes apropos mimicry:

> We can grasp in effect something which, already in nature, appropriates the gaze to the function to which it may be put in the symbolic relation in man.
> ... I set out from the fact that there is something that establishes a fracture, a bi-partition, a splitting of the being to which the being accommodates itself, even in the natural world.[14]

Zupančič is fully justified in pointing out that, at the epistemological level, reality is accessible to us only because of this gap, of the distance that separates a subject from "objective reality." In this precise sense, the empty subject ($) is correlated in a negative way to "objective reality" (analyzed by sciences) from which the subject is constitutively excluded—if the subject disappears or if it falls into reality (becoming one of the objects in it), "objective external reality" goes with it. But how is this possible? How can a gap that enables us to see reality as external appear in reality itself? Lacan's answer is clear: the evolutionary story of a gradual emergence of subjectivity out of natural biological processes is not sufficient, *there has to be a schism already in "natural" reality itself*. I would go further and advance the hypothesis that this is precisely why a true materialism needs quantum mechanics. With its inclusion of observation (which registers an event) into the ontological consistency of this event itself, only quantum mechanics inscribes a radical schism into the very basic structure of "natural" reality. But, again, what counts as an observation? It was experimentally proven that collapse occurs already when a machine performs a measurement, not only when some conscious observer looks at the result:

> What if we measure the atoms but don't look at the result? In theory, the interference fringes should remain if we don't know anything about the photons' path. In reality, if we measure the energies of the remaining photons but keep that secret, the fringes don't come back.[15]

Relying on Gödel's incompleteness theorems and quantum physics, Roger Penrose takes the opposite path. His premise is that consciousness is not computational, that it cannot be explained on the model of a computer, so we have to refer to another more fundamental dimension to account for it.[16] Gödel's theorems are concerned with the limits of provability in formal axiomatic theories. The first incompleteness theorem states that no consistent system of axioms whose theorems can be listed by an effective procedure (i.e., an algorithm) is capable of proving all truths about the arithmetic of natural numbers. The second theorem, an extension of the first, shows that the system cannot demonstrate its own consistency.[17] From a Hegelo-Lacanian standpoint, a different solution imposes itself: what if, staying with Gödel, we posit that there is no need to go *beyond* because consciousness *is* grounded in a deadlock of computation, it is an effect of the computation stumbling upon a limit (a limit beyond which there is nothing)? Is there not an intriguing resonance between this idea and Heidegger's point (in his analysis of our everyday use of things in *Sein und Zeit*) that we become fully aware of tools only when they malfunction? I use a hammer thoughtlessly, relying on long practice which has habituated this object to me, but I become aware of it when, say, its weighted "head" detaches itself from a long handle after I swing it too strongly?

Penrose draws on the basic properties of quantum computing: bits (qubits) of information can be in multiple states—for instance, in the "on" or "off" position—at the same time. These quantum states exist simultaneously—in a "superposition"—before coalescing into a single, almost instantaneous, calculation. Quantum coherence occurs when a huge number of things—say, a whole system of electrons—act together in one quantum state. What has this to do with our consciousness? Penrose refers here to Stuart Hameroff's idea that quantum coherence happens in microtubules, protein structures inside the brain's neurons. Microtubules are tubular structures inside eukaryotic cells (part of the cytoskeleton) that play a role in determining the cell's shape, as well as its movements, which includes cell division—separation of chromosomes during mitosis. Hameroff suggests that microtubules are the quantum device that Penrose had been looking for in his theory. In neurons, microtubules help control the strength of synaptic connections, and their tube-like shape might protect them from the surrounding noise of the larger neuron.

Penrose believes that the microtubules' symmetry and lattice structure "reek of something quantum mechanical."[18]

There are three problems with this account. First, a large majority of scientists reject Hameroff's idea of microtubules as quantum devices.[19] Second, although Hameroff's notion of microtubules is materialist (it describes what goes on in our brain), his overall view is idealist (to put it bluntly, he thinks consciousness is an immaterial spiritual substance), while "Penrose is an atheist who calls himself 'a very materialistic and physicalist kind of person,' and he's bothered by New Agers who've latched onto quantum theories about non-locality and entanglement to prop up their paranormal beliefs."[20] However, Penrose also seems to oscillate with regard to this point, claiming that proto-consciousness is everywhere:

> An element of proto-consciousness takes place whenever a decision is made in the universe. I'm not talking about the brain. I'm talking about an object which is put into a superposition of two places. Say it's a speck of dust that you put into two locations at once. Now, in a small fraction of a second, it will become one or the other. Which does it become? Well, that's a choice. Is it a choice made by the universe? Does the speck of dust make this choice? Maybe it's a free choice. I have no idea.[21]

In some passages, Penrose goes to the end of this road and draws the idealist conclusion: "Somehow, our consciousness is the reason the universe is here."[22] Wigner was the one who formulated this conclusion openly: a measurement is only accomplished when consciousness (a conscious being)—and not just a machine—registers it. And in the dispute about the collapse of the wave function, the extreme position is taken by Federico Faggin who postulates that consciousness and free will are fundamental and non-algorithmic. Quantum information emerges from them, and the quantum-classical physical world emerges from quantum information. Consciousness is a quantum phenomenon and digital computers, as classical, algorithmic systems, can never be conscious, no matter their complexity.[23] Faggin argues that reality consists of "an undivided energy that has the desire and the capacity to experience and know itself," an energy that he calls "One." One, according to Faggin, exists in a "vaster reality" beyond the reality we experience, where there are many Ones:

So, the entities are the conscious fields, and they shape symbols within their own fields to communicate with other fields—other entities. The crucial difference with contemporary physics is that these fields have an inner semantic and conscious experience, just like we do. The symbols have meaning that are understood by the conscious fields. . . . Matter is nothing more than the information that conscious entities use to communicate with each other to know themselves.[24]

Taken in its abstract form, this position is just a new version of Leibniz's monadology—so where does quantum physics enter in? Faggin's idea is that the collapse of superpositions into a single reality is a conscious free act of the One—the One can be any entity to/in which superpositions happen, even the tiniest subparticles, since all that exists are such Ones with consciousness and free will. The One is aware of all the choices embodied in superpositions and then freely chooses one of them which becomes part of our reality . . . I of course totally reject this solution. Superpositions collapse in a contingent way, but their collapse follows the laws of probability. Collapse is contingent, but not the result of a free act: freed decision is not a contingent act, it is an act determined by a decision. And if we begin with postulating consciousness and free will to account for quantum phenomena, we proceed like bad theologians postulating an omnipotent free god to explain nature and history, i.e., explaining empirical enigmas and mysteries by evoking an even greater mystery.

Here we find ourselves at the opposite extreme to Rovelli, for whom "observation" which collapses a quantum superposition has nothing to do with consciousness since it occurs in any material interaction of different particles. When two electrons interact in such a way that an information passes between the two, an observation takes place, although the amount of information is here minimal—all that an electron can "swallow" is just a simple qubit (like "up" or "down"), while humans constantly process enormous amount of information. For us, "observation" implies a minimum of passivity ("I am not doing anything, I am just observing it"), while in quantum physics every observation already is an interaction that interferes with the observed object or process.

Of special interest here are attempts to define the modes of cognition which do not involve any conscious self-awareness, not even the one that is sometimes attributed to highly developed animals. In an overview of the existing literature, Michael Marder convincingly argues that "plants are *res cogitantes extendentes*": "plants are constantly extending their cognition through the active extension of their bodies, and, with it, their functional cognitive apparatuses. And beyond that, plants also actively extend their cognitive process to the environment they are constantly engaged with and which houses a wide array of their biochemical substances."[25] Such an anti-Cartesian approach (rejecting the ontological distinction between *res cogitans* and *res extensa*) has nothing whatsoever to do with any New Age vitalist obscurantism—it remains firmly in the space of scientific materialism.

The Limit of Relationality

The interactive concept of observation advanced by Rovelli and others, which marks out what has become known as relational quantum mechanics (RQM), struggles to account for the basic quantum mechanical fact that, in the case of entangled particles, if A measures the spin of one of the particles, he can know what the spin of the other particle is without even waiting for a message from B who will measure this spin. Or, more modestly, he can know what any other observer who will measure the spin of the other particle will see.

The price Matteo Smerlak and Rovelli are ready to pay for their relational view[26] is that they reject the predominant view according to which the violations of Bell's theorem provide a proof of non-locality, and claim that their version of RQM enables us to save locality: "it is not necessary to abandon locality in order to account for EPR correlations.[27] From the relational perspective, the apparent 'quantum non-locality' is a mistaken illusion caused by the error of disregarding the quantum nature of all physical systems." First, what is locality? "We call locality the principle demanding that two spatially separated events cannot have instantaneous mutual influence. We will argue that this is not contradicted by EPR type correlations, if we take the relational perspective on quantum mechanics." The basic axiom of RQM is that physical reality is formed by the individual quantum events (facts) through which interacting systems (objects) affect one another. Quantum events are therefore assumed to exist only in interactions and (this is the central point) *the character of each quantum event is only relative to the system involved in the interaction.* ... different observers can give different accounts of the actuality of the same physical property. This fact implies that the occurrence of an event is not something absolutely real or not, but it is only real in relation to a specific observer. Notice that, in this context, an observer can be any physical system. ... The preferred Copenhagen observer is relativized into the multiplicity of observers, formed by all possible physical systems, and therefore it no longer escapes the laws of quantum mechanics.

In the EPR situation, we have precisely such a case: each of the two entangled particles is measured by a separate observer (A and B), so that

> A and B can be considered two distinct observers, both making measurements on α and β. The comparison of the results of their measurements ... cannot be instantaneous, that is, it requires A and B to be in causal contact. More importantly, with respect to A, B is to be considered as a normal quantum system (and, of course, with respect to B, A is a normal quantum system).... this does not mean that B and A cannot communicate their experience. In fact, in either account the possibility of communicating experiences exists and in either account consistency is ensured. Contradiction emerges only if, against the main stipulation of RQM, we insist on believing that there is an absolute, external account of the state of affairs in the world, obtained by juxtaposing actualities relative to different observers.

In this precise sense Smerlak and Rovelli distance themselves from Einstein while pointing out that "Einstein's original motivation with EPR was not to question locality, but rather to question the completeness of QM, on the basis of a firm confidence in locality":

> RQM is complete in the sense of exhausting everything that can be said about nature. However, in a sense RQM can be interpreted as the discovery of the incompleteness of the description of reality that any single observer

can give: A can measure the pointer variable of B, but the set of the events as described by B is irreducibly distinct from the set of events as described by A. In this particular sense, RQM can be said to show the "incompleteness" of single-observer Copenhagen QM. Einstein's intuition that the EPR correlations reveal something deeply missing in Copenhagen quantum mechanics can thus be understood as being correct: the incompleteness of Copenhagen QM is the disregard of the quantum properties of all observers, which leads to paradoxes as the apparent violation of locality exposed by EPR.

I tend to agree with Lee Smolin when he claims that "time is the least illusional thing we know about,"[28] in contrast to space which is "the final illusion," and when he draws this conclusion from the recent experiments demonstrating a faster-than-light contact between particles far away from each other:

> Of all the strange aspects of quantum physics so far discovered, the strangest of all has to be the shocking discovery that the principle of relativistic causality is violated by quantum phenomena. Roughly speaking, if two particles interact and then separate, flying far apart from each other, they nonetheless may continue to share properties of a strange kind, that may be ascribed to the pair, without each of the individuals having themselves any definite properties. We say the two particles are "entangled."[29]

It is difficult to avoid here the term "knowledge in the real" coined by Lacan: as we have already seen,[30] if there are two entangled particles and we measure the spin of one of them, we can simply (or not so simply) claim that our measurement/observation (they are *not* the same) changes its behaviour, making it "collapse" into a definite value; simultaneously, the other particle also "collapses" and changes its behaviour. The well-known problem is: we did not interact in any way with the second particle, so how did the second particle knew that the first one was measured/observed and accordingly changed its behaviour? As we have already seen,[31] there seem to be only two explanations: instant (faster than light) communication between the two entangled particles or the moving of information backwards in time (the first particle goes back in time and somehow lets the second particle know what will happen to it in the near future). Can the notion of gravity be of some help here?

What we should introduce here is a minimal gap between things in their immediate brute proto-reality and the registration of this reality in some medium (of the big Other): the second is in a delay with regard to the first. Many things go on before registration: in this shadowy space, "normal" laws of nature are continuously suspended—how? Imagine that you have to take a flight on day x to pick up a fortune the next day, but do not have the money to buy the ticket; but then you discover that the accounting system of the airline is such that if you wire the ticket payment within twenty-four hours of arrival at your destination, no one will ever know it was not paid prior to departure. In a homologous way,

> the energy a particle has can wildly fluctuate so long as this fluctuation is over a short enough time scale. So, just as the accounting system of the airline "allows" you to "borrow" the money for a plane ticket provided you pay it back quickly enough, quantum mechanics allows a particle to "borrow" energy so long it can relinquish it within a time frame determined by Heisenberg's uncertainty principle. . . . But quantum mechanics forces us to take the analogy one important step further. Imagine someone who is a compulsive borrower and goes from friend to friend asking for money. . . . Borrow and return, borrow and return—over and over again with unflagging intensity he takes in money only to give it back in short order. . . . A similar frantic shifting back and forth of energy and momentum is occurring perpetually in the universe of microscopic distance and time intervals.[32]

The problem that arises here for a Hegelian like me is: can we grasp this paradox of existing by way of borrowing from the future in the categories of Hegel's logic? Does this paradox not imply a notion of temporality—a present "borrowing" from the future to exist—for which there is no place in Hegel? I think the situation is nonetheless more ambiguous. Is not the Hegelian dialectical process not structured precisely like a constant borrowing from the future, the "future" being the Absolute itself which is presupposed by existing in an In-itself outside of our reach? And what comes at the end, in "absolute knowing," is not that we finally no longer borrow from the future; what we realize is that the process has no external Absolute as it gradually approaches, that the truth of the process resides in the process itself which turns around a void. This is why, as Lenin saw it, what we get at the end of Hegel's *Logic* is not the description of the Absolute as it "really is" but just the recapitulation of the process itself that led to this point. And, as Lacanians, should we not also take note how, to characterize the eternal circular movement of the absolute Idea, Hegel uses the term "enjoyment"? "The eternal Idea, in full fruition of its essence, eternally sets itself to work, engenders and enjoys itself as absolute spirit."[33]

Problematic as this parallel may be, one thing is clear here: a language in which we dwell works precisely in this way, through a permanent borrowing from the future. When we speak, we never fully know what we mean by what we are saying, we implicitly count on a meaning that is to come but is never fully here-and-now—only such a borrowing from the future allows us to experience what we are saying now as meaningful. A fully actualized meaning equals meaninglessness. (In psychoanalysis, the same phenomenon is called "transference": a patient's "transference" on the analyst means that he presupposes the analyst already knows the meaning of his symptoms, while this meaning is effectively constructed in the analytic process.)

I see a problem for the reading of quantum mechanics through the categories of Hegel's thought at another level. Recall the already mentioned experiments which demonstrate that two particles (like two entangled photons) can interact faster than the speed of light: the particles are interrelated in such a way that, if I give to the first particle a spin up, the other particle will instantly acquire a spin down, even if the particles are far far away from each other. Instead of getting lost in speculations about how the two particles can interact faster than light at such great distance, would it not be more productive to posit that there is another dimension of space in which the two particles are in direct contact with each other? And I don't see in Hegel's notion of space any signs that he considers the possibility of different dimensions of space (and/or time).

This is how, even in an empty region of space, a particle emerges out of Nothing, "borrowing" its energy from the future and paying for it (with its annihilation) *before the system notices this borrowing*. The whole network can function like this, in a rhythm of borrowing and annihilation, one borrowing from the other, displacing the debt onto the other, postponing the payment of the debt—uncannily as if the whole sub-particle domain are Wall Street traders playing with futures. What this presupposes is, again, a minimal gap between things in their immediate brute reality and the registration of this reality in some medium (of the big Other): one can cheat insofar as the second is delayed with regard to the first. The theological implications of this gap between the virtual proto-reality and the fully-constituted one are of special interest. Insofar as "god" is the agent who creates things by way of observing them, the quantum indeterminacy compels us to posit a god who is *omnipotent, but not omniscient*:

> If God collapses the wave functions of large things to reality by His observation, quantum experiments indicate that He is not observing the small.[34]

The ontological cheating with virtual particles (an electron can create a proton and thereby violate the principle of constant energy, on condition that it reabsorbs it before its environs "take note" of the discrepancy) is a way to cheat god himself, the ultimate agency of taking note of everything that goes on. This is the ultimate atheist lesson of quantum physics: even god himself doesn't control quantum processes. Einstein was right when he famously claimed that "God doesn't cheat"—what he forgot to add is that god himself can be cheated. Insofar as the materialist thesis is that "god is unconscious" (god doesn't know), quantum physics effectively is materialist: there are microprocesses (quantum oscillations) which are not registered by the god-system. And insofar as God is one of the names of the big Other, we can see in what sense one cannot simply get rid of god (big Other) and develop an ontology without big Other: god is an illusion, but a necessary one.[35] And the same holds at the social and political level—as Alenka Zupančič pointed out, the basic axiom of our era of conspiracy theories (which rely on the premise that we are all the time deceived by some hidden masters who really pull the strings of our social life) is: "I am deceived, therefore I am." The materialist answer to this axiom is: no, it is the big Other which is deceived.

If we universalize relationality and define every part of reality as depending on an observer (so that the same part of reality not only appears different but is different for different observers), do we not get stuck in a rather flat global view akin to the first feature of dialectical materialism formulated by Stalin: every entity is caught in a complex network of relations, things do not exist alone in separation from each other . . . Or, to complicate things further: when A and B interact, are they *both* not at the same time observers of the other and observed by the other? So why do we even need an external observer that registers the interaction? Do the two interacting particles not already observe each other?

A naïve but significant philosophical counterpoint arises here: if everything is relative, if it is what it is only relationally, with regard to an observer, does this entire network not float in the air? In order not to collapse into itself, does this network not need to rely on some form of Absolute? The answer is: yes, but this Absolute is not some reality-in-itself beyond all observations. It can only be a *negative* foundation: the *limit* itself, a limit beyond which there is nothing. In the same way as, in structuralism, differentiality can only function through a pure difference, in quantum relationality the fact that every entity is grounded in being-observed implies that not-everything can be observed, but this unobservable is not an external not-observed positive reality, it is the limit of observation itself.

For Rovelli, "RQM is realist about the existence of quantum entities, even though it is antirealist about the wave function": wave function superpositions are just an instrument for calculating probabilities as they appear to an observer of a quantum entity, not part of the observed reality . . . Here we stumble upon the basic philosophical question: when we claim that a theory should fit reality, what do we mean by reality? When asked about an underlying quantum world, Bohr allegedly answered: "There is no quantum world. There is only an abstract quantum physical description. It is wrong to think that the task of physics is to find out how nature is. Physics concerns what we can say about Nature."[36] So all we are effectively dealing with are parts of our everyday reality: numbers on the screen of a measuring apparatus, etc. But is such a view not all too easy? How to combine it with Bohr's claim that "everything we call real is made of things that cannot be regarded as real"? It is difficult to avoid the question: why do the predictions of quantum mechanics hold up, when tested—and quantum mechanics is the most successfully tested theory in the history of science? Wave superpositions are not just possibilities: the point of quantum mechanics is that possibilities have *as such* an actuality and influence the outcome—in some cases, the only way to account for a measurement is to assume that a particle took all possible superposed paths. Or, as Nikki Weststeijn put it in a concise way:

> In RQM the wave function is understood as a book-keeping device that tracks what will happen upon the next interaction. It encodes any previous interaction that A has had with system S and allows A to predict the state of S with respect to A in the future.[37]

It is thus "a bookkeeping device instead of a representation of a real physical quality." However, is it necessary for RQM that the wave function does not represent any real physical quantity? "If we say that the wave function does not represent a real physical quantity, the question then remains what the underlying physical quantity is that in some way gives rise to the wave function." In short, "in order to give a coherent interpretation, RQM should take the wave function to represent a real physical quantity, albeit a relative quantity."[38]

The collapse of superpositions effectuated by a measurement asserts the duality of quantum reality and ordinary reality. Do all the paradoxes displayed by the measurement of quantum processes not impose a rather obvious conclusion: beyond/beneath our ordinary spatio-temporal reality there is not a timeless spiritual domain but another level of reality where the laws of our spatio-temporal reality do not apply (where a particle can take many paths simultaneously, where two entangled particles can be in contact instantaneously, faster than the speed of light, etc.)? This duality is not complementary (in the traditional sense of the term) since it concerns two totally incompatible levels of reality—the two levels are related like the two dimensions of a parallax. Here Lacan's logic of non-all can be of some use: our ordinary reality forms an All grounded in an exception (the observer which causes the collapse of superpositions), while the quantum reality requires no exception, yet it is for that very reason not-all, and the impossibility that makes it non-all pushes the network of superpositions towards collapse. So what if, in order to grasp this duality, we use Lacan's difference between the two forms of assertion: an X exists or there is (something of) X (*il y a de . . .*)? Lacan's examples: "la Femme n'existe pas" (the Woman doesn't exist) and "il n'y a pas de grand Autre" (there is no big Other). The second negation is stronger: although the Woman doesn't exist, there is (something of) the women . . . Similarly, a single reality that arises through the collapse of a wave's superpositions *exists* while *there are* superpositions which do not properly exist.

*

This basic ontological question of the status of quantum waves is something that today's technological-scientific practice itself confronts us with. On December 8, 2024, Google announced Willow, its latest quantum chip:

> Willow's performance on this benchmark is astonishing: It performed a computation in under five minutes that would take one of today's fastest supercomputers 10^{25} or 10 septillion years. If you want to write it out, it's 10,000,000,000,000,000,000,000,000 years. This mind-boggling number exceeds known timescales in physics and vastly exceeds the age of the universe. It lends credence to the notion that quantum computation occurs in many parallel universes, in line with the idea that we live in a multiverse, a prediction first made by David Deutsch.[39]

However, we should avoid the conclusion that we live in a multiverse: multiverse means multiple realities which are like our own reality, and in this way we obliterate the gap that separates our "collapsed" reality from the reality of quantum oscillations. More precisely, what the notion of multiverse fails to encompass is the dimension clearly noted by Rovelli's pluralistic and perspectivalist view of quantum mechanics, the dimension best rendered by the following quite striking quotation:

> if we want to get a true idea of what a point of space-time is like we should look outward at the universe . . . The complete notion of a point of space-time in fact consists of the appearance of the entire universe as seen from that point.[40]

Does Rovelli not make here a point homologous to that of Lacan? "The picture is in my eye, but me, I am in the picture."[41] The world is disclosed to the singularity of my eye, but I am in the world. The mutual determination between a subsystem of the universe and the universe itself is *not* perfectly symmetrical:

it is true that the nature of such a local subsystem ("space-time point") depends on the way it interacts with, or "reflects", the universe from its particular perspective (and this seems a partial concession to monism), but in RQM there is no Leibnizian "monad of the monads" because the cosmos can only be described from some local physical system." The problem with priority monism is that it concentrates exclusively on the dependence of the part from the whole, neglecting completely the converse type of dependence."[42] This converse dependence is crucial: part is a part of all which is itself included in its parts . . . Along these lines, I follow R. Muciño, E. Okon and D. Sudarsky's essay "Assessing Relational Quantum Mechanics"[43] which deals with the general ambiguity problem that affects standard quantum theory when deprived of special roles for measuring devices or observers:

> within RQM, the breakdown of unitarity is not brought about by mysterious quantum jumps. Instead, it is a consequence of the fact that it is impossible to give a full description of an interaction in which one is involved.

This is a truly ingenious solution: the wave collapse happens because of the impossibility of a full description that would include the observer measuring a quantum state. So, in a properly-dialectical tension, waves collapse locally *because they cannot collapse globally.*

3

Noncommutativity in the symbolic and in the (quantum) real

From a philosophical standpoint, the key enigma of quantum mechanics concerns the exact ontological status of quantum waves. The most straightforward solution eradicates the problem, but at much too high a price; this is the Many Worlds Interpretation which doesn't interpret the ψ wave as a probability but "sees it instead as a real entity, effectively describing the world as it is."[1] In the collapse of a wave function, all probabilities are realized, each in its own world—with regard to Schrödinger's cat, in one world, the cat is alive, in another world, the cat is dead. At the opposite end, we have Rovelli's epistemic approach for which "ψ" is a "calculation tool", like a weather forecast or racing odds:

> Real events in the world happen in a probabilistic way, and the quantity ψ is our way of calculating the probability of their occurring. Interpretations of the theory that do not take the ψ waves so seriously are called "epistemic", because they interpret ψ only as a summary of our knowledge of what happens.
>
> (58)

Rovelli goes here a step further: probabilism does not just signal the limitations of our knowledge, but reality is in itself under-determined. The discovery of quantum theory is the discovery that the properties of any entity are nothing other than the way in which that entity influences others. It exists only through its interactions. Quantum theory is the theory of how things influence each other. And this is the best description of nature that we have.

(69)

We can already guess what awaits us at the end of this road: Nagarjuna's Mahayana Buddhist ontology (121–31). If all reality is perspectival, if all properties of an entity arise out of its interaction with other entities, and if all this holds for the entirety of reality which is not composed of things that interact but of ephemeral events that momentarily pop up and disappear, then there is also no substantial reality that underlies this ephemeral world of phenomena—then the only Absolute, the only X beneath the dance of events, is the Void (*sunyata*), and this includes also the Self which has no substantial content outside its interactions with others and external reality. I think such a notion of the Void obfuscates the key tension between the global ontological Void which is all-encompassing and the Void of a Self which is point-like, puncturing, violently negating all external reality. To paraphrase Hegel, it is crucial to conceive the Void not just as Substance but also as Subject.

One can formulate this key point also in the terms of the distinction between "nothing" and "less than nothing": "nothing" is the all-encompassing Void (*sunyata*) about which Buddhism speaks, while "less than nothing" as the puncturing point of absolute contradiction is not the first differentiation in the primordial Void and in this sense the first step towards the multiplicity that characterizes our reality. "Less than nothing" comes (logically) *before* the nothing of the primordial Void, it is the absolute contradiction which is already primordially repressed (to use this Freudian term) in every pacifying experience of the Void. In short, the paradox resides in the fact that one already has to add something to the "less than nothing" to arrive at the "nothing" . . .[2] But my basic reproach to Rovelli concerns his reduction of the wave function to a mere probabilistic calculation:

The ψ wave is the probabilistic calculation of where and how an event relative to us might occur. The wave as well is therefore a perspectival quantity. An object does not have one ψ wave, it has one with respect to every other object with which it interacts. Events that take place in relation to one thing do not influence the probability of events that occur in relation to others. The "quantum state" ψ is always a relative state.

(74)

Rovelli explains further his notion of ψ wave apropos Schrödinger's famous thought experiment about a cat in a box. In Rovelli's version, the subject is shut in a box and a quantum mechanism controls the release of a sleeping drug. Rovelli points out that

> For you the drug was delivered, or it was not delivered. There are no doubts. As far as you are concerned, you are asleep or you are awake. You are certainly not both at once. I, on the other hand, am outside the box and do not interact either with the bottle of sleeping draught or with you. Later on I can observe interference phenomena between you-awake and you-asleep: phenomena that would not have been produced if I had seen you asleep, or if I had seen you awake. In this sense, for me you are neither asleep nor awake. This is what it means to say that you are "in a superposition of sleeping and waking."

(71)

Rovelli then applies this insight to Anton Zeilinger's famous experiment which demonstrated that two entangled particles can exchange information faster than the speed of light (i.e, for all practical purposes instantaneously). (For this experiment, Zeilinger shared with two others the 2022 Nobel prize for physics.) Rovelli's counter-argument is that, since there is no universal simultaneity, the spin of each of the two entangled particles (which are at a large distance from each other) cannot be measured at the same instant: a minimum of time has to lapse for the information about the spin of the particle A to reach the observer who measured the spin of the particle B:

> Only God can see the two places at the same moment—but God, if She exists, does not tell us what She sees. What She sees is irrelevant to reality. We cannot rely upon the existence of something that only God can see.... We can compare the two measurements, in Beijing and Vienna, but the comparison requires an exchange of signals: the two laboratories can send

each other emails or talk on the phone. An email takes time, as does a voice on the phone: nothing travels instantaneously, and an exchange of signals is an interaction, where new elements of reality come about.

(84, 85)

Rovelli relies here on special relativity theory which implies that there is no global simultaneity, no NOW that encompasses the entire universe. If you observe, through a telescope, a person on a planet four light years from the Earth, what you see is what she was doing four years ago on that planet. So can you say that she is "now" doing what you, in your now, observe her doing through your telescope? No, because four years after you have seen her through the telescope, in her time, "she might already have returned to Earth and could be ten terrestrial years in the future (measured by the Earthly time)."(39) So between my past—the events that happened before what I can witness (in my) now—and my future—the events that will happen after my now—"there is an interval that is neither past nor future, and still has a duration. It is an expanded present (15 minutes on Mars, millions of years in the Andromeda galaxy . . .)."

Does this not imply that there is nevertheless an aspect of time that survives the demolition of the Newtonian theory of time? And the same holds for space—Newton's notion of empty space as a neutral container independent of what it contains is not a blind alley in our understanding of space but a big step forwards. This notion is, of course, ultimately wrong, space is not independent of what it contains, of what is "in it"; however, this notion can only emerge if spacetime itself is structured around a hole, a gap in its very core.

The world is nothing but change; it is not a collection of things, it is a collection of events, and these events are "in a *where* but also in a *when*. They are spatially but also temporarily delimited: they are events."(87) The only limitation is that "we cannot arrange the universe like a single orderly sequence of times" (99): "In the world, there is change, there is a temporal structure of relations between events that is anything but illusory. It is not a global happening. It is a local and complex one which is not amenable to being described in terms of a single global order."(100)

However, the point of Zeilinger's experiment is the status of *knowledge*: if two particles are entangled, then if I give a specific contingent spin to a particle

A, I know the spin of B automatically, without any additional measurement. (Plus what happens if, while observing both entangled particles, I then in a contingent way change the spin of one of them again? Will the spin of the other also change accordingly?)

> Entanglement is therefore far from being a rare phenomenon that occurs only in particular situations: it is what happens generically in an interaction, when this interaction is considered in relation to a system external to it. From an external perspective, any manifestation of one object to another, which is to say any property, is a correlation; it is an entanglement between an object and another.
>
> (88)

I think Rovelli succumbs here (as in the case of observation) to an all too easy generalization; whenever an interaction between two elements is considered from an external perspective, the two are entangled. I also think Rovelli reduces superpositions too quickly to an external observer, and thereby to probabilities: for him, in Schrödinger's thought experiment the cat is in two superposed states *for me* (who doesn't see what went on in the box), while the cat itself is either alive or dead, there is no superposition there.

On a more general level, why should we not endorse what in our space appears as faster than light contact if space is relativized? It's not that the two entangled particles interact faster than light in the same space as ours, it is that they move in a different mode of space. So, as I already pointed out in Chapter 1, do all paradoxes displayed by the measurement of quantum processes not impose a rather obvious conclusion: beyond/beneath our ordinary spatio-temporal reality there is (not a timeless spiritual domain but) another level of reality where the laws of our spatio-temporal reality do not apply (where a particle can take many paths simultaneously, where two entangled particles can be in contact instantaneously, faster than the speed of light, etc.)? And, to make an even riskier step further, do we not encounter something homologous in Walter Benjamin's distinction between historicist evolutionism and the properly historical dialectic in suspense? The temptation is to simply invert the standard relationship between particles and waves: waves do not connect (pre-existing) particles, particles emerge when two (or more) waves interact, cross each other's path. But this temptation is to be resisted: waves get "reified" in particles because waves are in themselves ontologically fragile, structured around a lack.

To summarise my basic stance, if the "true reality" of fields and waves is out of time and space, then time and space are in some basic sense illusory. However, isn't the underlying scheme of basic reality and illusory appearances false in the same way that its opposite, the gradual progress towards higher forms? What pushes this pre-ontological quantum space towards collapses and/or towards our common reality must be some immanent impossibility, a "barred One," or some "boundary" (beyond which there is nothing—a boundary which coincides with its Beyond, i.e., which is itself inaccessible) in the basic quantum space itself.[3]

In the Many Words interpretation, the ontological gap between quantum waves and our ordinary reality disappears: there are only quantum waves with all their superposed versions actualized. Based on this insight, Sean Carroll postulated that from an (impossible) objective view, we could give a full deterministic description of reality—the problem is only that *we would not know to which of the multiple worlds we belong*, i.e., where we (the observer) were located in this multitude of worlds. Is this not the problem with the Cartesian *cogito*? The subject reduced to a pure observer has no place in mechanically-determined external reality, and it exists as subject only if it has no place in it. Lacan knew this when he wrote that modern science is based on the foreclosure of the subject ... How to resolve this paradox? Again, we should posit that the objective view which would give a full deterministic description of reality is not only inaccessible to us because of our finitude (because we are part of reality), but—much more radically—because reality is in itself not all, because it doesn't exist as a totality with no immanent barrier.

Rovelli knows this, which is why he defines reality as a multiplicity of worlds each of which is rooted in the point-of-view of a particular observer—there is no "independent" reality. Rovelli is also right to reject the idea that this multiplicity implies a version of the many-worlds interpretation of quantum oscillations; however, he seems to get caught in the traditional philosophical paradox when he "argues that it is impossible for a system to have information about itself because it requires it to stand in a particular correlation to itself and this is not possible. It is not a new idea that quantum mechanics cannot describe the observers."(102) So if "in RQM it does not make sense to claim that the whole universe is in a state of entanglement because, by being part of it, we cannot interact with it by definition,"(104) do we not here stumble upon the old Russell's paradox (is a set a part of itself?) in a new guise? We should reply that a set which contains itself is not an exception but universal: every singularity is a hologram which contains itself as its element, and it is in this sense that it stands "in a particular correlation to itself" since it contains itself not in a general sense but in a singular sense. What is effectively impossible is to have a whole of reality containing itself, but this is impossible precisely because the hologram-structure of reality makes reality as a Whole impossible— not in the simple sense of irreducible multiplicity but in the more precise sense: every singularity already reflects all of reality in its singular way, so there is no all-encompassing Whole because Wholes are themselves multiplied.

Or, to put it in the terms of the liar's paradox, if my statement "I am always lying" is true, then this statement itself is a lie since it implies that I am not always lying, etc. Lacan offers a solution here, distinguishing between the content of an enunciation and the subjective stance of enunciation implied by it: "I am always lying" can correctly render my experience of my entire existence as inauthentic, as a fake. However, the opposite also holds: the statement "I know I am a piece of shit" can in itself be literally true but false at the level of the subjective stance it pretends to render since it implies that, by saying it, I somehow demonstrate that I am NOT fully "a piece of shit," that I am honest about myself . . . But have these psychological finesses anything to do with the quantum universe?

If, as Rovelli repeatedly claims, there is no object, no element of reality, which is not observed, if objects exist only in relation to an observer, as relative to that observer, then the fact that "it does not make sense to claim that the whole universe is in a state of entanglement" means that *one should abandon the very notion of the "whole universe."* This doesn't imply that there is something outside the universe—it's just that the universe cannot be totalized since to do this an external observer is needed. The non-totalizability of the universe thus implies a negative limit (boundary), a limit outside which there is nothing. So I as a part of the universe can claim that there is nothing in the universe that is not entangled—and that, located at this boundary, *I am this nothing*. I cannot be just a part of the universe: the whole world "collapses" in me as an observer, i.e., in one of its parts.

To put it in yet another way, when relational quantum mechanics posits that quantum events exist only in interactions and that *the character of each quantum event is only relative to the system involved in the interaction*, so that different observers can give different accounts of the actuality of the same physical property, i.e., when it claims that the occurrence of an event is not something absolutely real or not, but it is only real in relation to a specific observer, are these and similar claims universally true (true independently of any observer) or are they also valid only in relation to a specific (human) observer? The only way to assert their universal validity without presupposing a global external observer is *to base such universal claims on an immanent limitation or boundary of reality itself.*

The complications that arise when we try to fully understand Zeilinger's experiment demonstrate what makes quantum mechanics so provocative: even what appears a modest experiment displays, upon closer analysis, radical philosophical implications. To complicate things even further, let's analyze another experiment performed by Zeilinger for Rovelli in more detail. A weak laser beam made up of a small number of photons is split into two parts, creating two separate paths—one, let's say, on the "right," and the other one on the "left." (One should note that Rovelli mentions this experiment and not the one for which Zeilinger with two others got the Nobel prize for 2022: the other experiment was meant to demonstrate the instant (faster than light) communication between two entangled particles, and Rovelli disagrees with this reading of the experiment—for him there is no communication faster than the speed of light.) The two paths are reunited before becoming separated again and ending up in two detectors: one let's say "up" and the other "down":

> What I saw is this: if I blocked either one of the two paths (left or right) with my hand, half of the photons ended up in the down detector and half ended up in the up one. But if I left both paths open, free of any impediment, all of the photons ended up in the lower detector: none in the one above it. . . . There is something very peculiar going on. If half of the photons arrive at

the up detector when one path is free, it would seem reasonable to expect that half of the photons should also arrive above when both paths are free. But this is not the case. In fact, none do. How, by blocking one path, can my hand cause the photons traveling on the other path to go to the upper detector?[4]

(45)

The strangeness of the situation resides in the fact that "it seems that you need only to observe for what is happening to change! Note the absurdity: if I don't look for where the photon passes, it always finishes below. But if I look at where it passes, it can end up above. The astonishing thing is that a photon can end up above even if I haven't seen it. That is to say, the photon changes trajectory due to the fact that I was waiting for it at the gate, on the side where it hasn't passed. Even if I haven't actually seen it!"(47)

What makes the situation strange is that it (not quite symmetrically, but nonetheless) up-ends the common idea of quantum mechanics according to which, if a process is unobserved it remains in a state of superposition, while observation reduces this multiplicity and causes its "collapse" into one version which is part of our ordinary reality. Here, however, if the first part of the process is unobstructed, the second part finishes with all particles in one exit, and if the first part is obstructed, the second part finishes with particles equally distributed between the two exits. It is not simply that observation affects the observed object; the mystery resides in the fact that just observing (one exit of the two—the one through which NOTHING passes) tells us that all particles passed through the other exit. And there is a further mystery: how did the particles somehow know that one of the exits is observed and avoided it?

For Rovelli, the answer is provided by the concept of noncommutativity. In a quantum world, to multiply the position by the velocity is different from multiplying the velocity by the position: the order counts. Why? Because of the uncertainty principle. "The uncertainty principle does not mean that we cannot measure the position of a particle with great precision and then its speed very precisely as well. We can. But after the second measurement, the position will no longer be the same: measuring the speed loses information on the position, so that if we measure it again, we will find it changed."(93)

"This tells us precisely about the importance of order: 'first X and then P' is different from 'first P and then X'. How different? By an amount that depends on Planck's constant: the scale of quantum phenomena."(94) X and P are thus noncommutative variables:

"Noncommutative" means: such that their order cannot be changed freely. (94)

This brings us back to Zeilinger's photons. The experiment was structured so that the behaviour of each photon could be described by two variables: X (right/left) and P (up/down). Like the position and speed of a particle according to the uncertainty principle, these two variables are non-commutative; they cannot be determined at the same time. "This is the reason why, if we close one of the paths determining the first variable ('right' or 'left'), the second is undetermined: the photons go randomly 'up' or 'down'. Vice versa, in order for the second variable to be determined, for the photons to all go 'down', it is necessary that the first variable should not be determined; that is, that the photons must pass via both paths 'right' and 'left'. The entire phenomenon follows from the equation which says that these two variables 'do not commute' (are noncommutative), and hence cannot be determined together."(95)

But are we here really dealing with the impossibility of measuring two properties (like position and speed of a particle) simultaneously? Do we not get the case of measuring two properties of a photon (left/right plus up/down) one after the other? So I would still like to get an explanation of how the very indetermination of the first part (no path is blocked) causes the determination of the second part (all photons go down)—is it not as if less order in the first part gives birth to more order in the second part? What I get is the key role of the temporal aspect: again, noncommutativity means that the temporal order in which operations (measurements, in this case) are done matters, that they change the result.

And—here comes the surprise—we encounter a similar noncommutativity in Freud and Lacan, in their description of the psychoanalytic process. The title of Freud's short text from 1914, "Remembering, Repeating and Working Through," provides the best formula for the way non-commutativity works in the psychoanalytic process. The three concepts Freud mentions form a dialectical triad: they designate the three phases of the analytical process, and resistance intervenes in every passage from one phase to the next. The first step consists in remembering the repressed past traumatic events, in bringing them out, which can also be done by hypnosis. This phase immediately runs into a deadlock: the content brought out lacks its proper symbolic context and thus remains ineffective; it fails to transform the subject and resistance remains active, limiting the amount of content revealed.

The problem with this approach is that it stays focused on the past and ignores the subject's present constellation which keeps this past alive, symbolically active. Resistance expresses itself in the form of transference: what the subject cannot properly remember, she repeats, transferring the past constellation onto a present (e.g., she treats the analyst as if he were her father). What the subject cannot properly remember, she acts out, re-enacts – and when the analyst points this out, her intervention is met with resistance. Working through is working through the resistance, turning it from the obstacle into the very resort of analysis, and this turn is self-reflexive in a properly Hegelian sense: resistance is a link between object and subject, between past and present, a proof that we are not only fixated on the past but that this fixation is an effect of the present deadlock in the subject's libidinal economy. The lesson is thus that remembrance alone doesn't count: it moves the analysis forward only against the background of repetition (as part of the transference)—so remembrance counts only if it comes *after* repetition. In *Seminar XI*, Lacan points out that remembrance

> can be obtained more completely by other ways than analysis, but they are inoperant as far as cure is concerned. It is here that we must distinguish the scope of these two directions, remembering and repetition. From the one to the other, there is no more temporal orientation than there is reversibility. It is simply that they are not commutative—to begin by remembering in order to deal with the resistances of repetition is not the same thing as to begin by repetition in order to tackle remembering. It is this that shows us that the time-function is of a logical order here, and bound up with a signifying shaping of the real. Non-commutativity, in effect, is a category that belongs only to the register of the signifier.[5]

While fully accepting the importance of factual truth—or, in this case, not a physical fact but his interpretation that explains the patient's symptoms—a psychoanalyst has to tell this to the patient at the right moment, when (based upon his analytic experience) he is convinced that his statement will deeply affect the patient's subjectivity, pushing him towards accepting some repressed truths about his subjectivity and desires. If the psychoanalyst tells this to his patient too early, the patient will dismiss it as irrelevant. For the truth to have an effect on those to whom it is told, it matters when it is told to them—and, obviously, the same goes for political statements. Jean-Paul Sartre formulated this paradox perfectly in a passage that we already quoted: "when the authorities find it useful to tell the truth, it's because they can't find any better lie. Immediately this truth, coming from official mouths, becomes a lie corroborated by the facts."[6] If the factual truth is told outside repetition and transference (which guarantee the subject's full engagement in what is told), it functions as a lie in the guise of truth.

Jean-Pierre Dupuy formulated a similar insight about social processes when he dealt with counterfactual situations—situations which are vaguely parallel to superpositions which disappeared in the collapse of a wave function. Dupuy returns again and again to the distinction between the two types of conditional proposition, counterfactual and indicative: "If Shakespeare did not write *Hamlet*, someone else did" is an indicative proposition, while "If Shakespeare had not written *Hamlet*, someone else would have done it" is counterfactual. The first one is obviously true since it starts from the fact that *Hamlet* is here, was written, and someone had to write it. The second one is much more problematic since it presupposes that there was a deeper historical tendency/necessity pushing towards a play like *Hamlet*, so even if Shakespeare were not to write it, another writer would have done it.[7] In this case, we are dealing with a rather crude historical determinism reminding us of what Georgi Plekhanov, in his classic text on the role of individuals in world history, said about Napoleon: there was a deeper historical necessity of the passage from Republic to Empire, so if, owing to some accident, Napoleon were not to have become the Emperor, another individual would have played his role.

Is exactly the same distinction not at work in how we consider Stalinism? For many, the rise of Stalinism was necessary, so that even without Stalin or in the case of his early accidental death, another leader would have played his role, maybe even Trotsky, his great opponent. For Trotskyites, but also some others like Stephen Kotkin, the role of Stalin's contingent person was crucial: no Stalinism without Stalin, i.e., if Stalin were to have disappeared from the historical scene in the early or mid-1920s, things like the forced collectivization and the practice of the "construction of Socialism in one country" would not have taken place.

Was then the rise of Stalinism a simple accident, the actualization of one of the historical possibilities that were laying dormant within the situation after the victory of the October Revolution? Dupuy proposes here a more complex logic, the logic of retroactively transforming an accidental act into the expression of a necessity: "necessity is retrospective: before I act, it was not necessary that I act as I do; once I have acted, *it will always have been true* that I could not have acted otherwise than I did."[8] Stalin could have died or he could have been deposed, but once he won, his victory retroactively became necessary. It is the same with Julius Caesar crossing the Rubicon: he could have acted otherwise, but once he did it, crossing the Rubicon became his fate, he retroactively became (pre)destined to do it.

This properly dialectical relationship between necessity and contingency is radically different from Plekhanov's determinism: the point is not that, if Caesar were not to accomplish the fateful first step from the Republic to the Empire, there would have been another person to serve as the vehicle of this historical necessity—Caesar made a contingent choice which retroactively became necessary. That is to say, we, of course, cannot change the past causally, at the level of facts, we cannot retroactively undo what actually happened, but we can change it counterfactually. In Hitchcock's *Vertigo*, the past is also changed in this way. What Scottie first experiences is the loss of Madeleine, his fatal love; when he recreates Madeleine in Judy and then realizes that the Madeleine he knew already was Judy pretending to be Madeleine, what he discovers is not simply that Judy is a fake (he knew that she is not the true Madeleine, since he recreated a copy of Madeleine out of her), but that, *because she is NOT a fake—she IS Madeleine—Madeleine herself was already a fake*. His discovery thus changes the past: he discovers that what he lost (Madeleine) never existed ... To understand properly such a backward movement in time, a brief reference to Deleuze might be of some help. In his early masterpiece *Difference and Repetition*, Deleuze introduces the notion of "dark precursor": "Thunderbolts explode between different intensities, but they are preceded by an invisible, imperceptible dark precursor (*precurseur sombre*), which determines their path in advance, but in reverse, as though intagliated."[9] The precise expression "in advance, but in reverse" is crucial here:

> "Because the path it traces is invisible and becomes visible only in reverse, to the extent that it is traveled over and covered by the phenomenon it induces within the system, it has no place other than that from which it is "missing," no identity other than that which it lacks: it is precisely the object = x, the one which is "lacking in its place" as it lacks its own identity."[10]

Or, as Ian Buchanan put it in a concise way: "Dark precursors are those moments in a text which must be read in reverse if we are not to mistake effects for causes."[11] A dark precursor overtakes itself, points towards the future, comes from the future, but only in reverse, once this future is here. Does Marx not say something like this in the well-known passage from *Grundrisse* about men as the key to the anatomy of apes? The anatomy of apes points towards the future, can only be understood from the future, but this holds only in reverse, once this future is here. What this means is nothing less than a reversal of causal order: as Lacan emphasizes in his *Seminar I*, symptom is not simply an effect of past repressed causes, its meaning is not predetermined, it is (re)constructed through interpretation—in short, symptom is a signal coming from the future. As the analytic work proceeds, an interpretation is achieved at some later time that casts the whole behaviour into relief in a wholly different light, and makes its sense clear—or, as Bruce Fink put it:

> "Lacan parts ways from the outset with certain Anglo-American trends in psychoanalysis by stressing that history is not the past: it is not so much remembering that goes on in analysis, but reconstruction. According to Lacan, Freud more regularly emphasizes "the aspect of reconstruction than that of reliving, in the sense we have grown used to calling affective. The precise reliving—that the subject remembers something as truly belonging to him, as having truly been lived through, with which he communicates,

and which he adopts—we have the most explicit indication in Freud's writings that that is not what is essential. What is essential is reconstruction, the term he employs right up until the end. [I]t is less a matter of remembering than of rewriting history." This leads Lacan to formulate that while the unconscious is ideally inaccessible, it is realized in the symbolic; more precisely, "it is something which, thanks to the symbolic progress which takes place in analysis, will have been." At some point in the future, its past configuration will be determined; it is always caught up in a future perfect. As for the symptom, its meaning will also be realized (not "discovered" as the translator would have us believe). Meaning is not there from the outset, but constructed during the analytic process.[12]

This notion of the unconscious implies that the Cartesian identity of thinking and being (*cogito ergo sum*) covers up a gap which can be formulated in two ways. First there is the predominant (basically Jungian) way: our thinking is just a tip of the iceberg, beneath it there is a vast, deep and invisible domain of drives which form the true core of our being. Then there is the opposite way formulated by late Lacan: in the forced choice between thinking and being, the subject has to choose being, and the Freudian unconscious is precisely a decentered thinking, a thinking outside what I am, a thinking in which I cannot recognize myself. It thinks, and I am not where I really think.

*

The old saying attributed to Mark Twain but first recorded during a debate in the Danish parliament in 1948, "It is difficult to make predictions, especially about the future," is thus deeply meaningful: every future creates its own past, so while we can to some extent predict the future it is much more difficult to predict how the new future will transform our notion of the past. It is also in this sense that, for Lacan, the status of the unconscious is not ontological (a deep substance of our psychic life) but ethical: it is the ethical task of the analytic process to realize it. And before we succumb to the temptation to dismiss this notion of the symptom as something confined to the early Lacan prone to the idealist notion of the Symbolic, we should recall that in one of his last texts, he also says that "the meaning of the symptom depends upon the future of the real."[13] Is he not describing here the same retroactive determination of the past by the future?

So in what sense does Lacan mention "the future of the real"? For Lacan, a true interpretation is not just another symbolic semblance but a discourse which is not of a semblance (the title of one of Lacan's late seminars): it has effects in the real, it transforms the real of the patient's subjectivity. Interpretation is not just a different symbolization of the unconscious real, it changes the basic coordinates of the real core of its subjectivity—if it is formulated at the right moment of the analytic process. Here time enters again: an interpretation has effects in the real only if it is formulated at the right moment, otherwise it remains a symbolic bla-bla, a semblance which leaves the real unaffected—so no wonder that the patient as a rule easily agrees with it. A direct acceptance of an interpretation is a proof that it has no effects in the real, that it leaves the core of the patient indifferent.

Dupuy uses the example of seduction. Especially today, in our Politically Correct times, a seduction process always involves the risky move of "making a pass"—at this potentially dangerous moment, one exposes oneself, one intrudes into another person's intimate space. The danger resides in the fact that, if my pass is rejected, it will appear as a Politically Incorrect act of harassment; so there is an obstacle I have to overcome. Here, however, a subtle asymmetry enters: if my pass is accepted, it is not that I have successfully overcome the obstacle—what happens is that, retroactively, I learn that *there never was an obstacle to be overcome*.[14] Do we not find a homologous paradox of asymmetrical choice in the Gospel according to John, when Christ says he did not come to judge but to save, rejecting the very practice of judgment—don't judge (others) for you will yourself be judged? The text then goes on:

> Whoever believes in him is not judged [*ou krinetai*], but whoever does not believe is judged [*kekritai*] already, because he has not believed in the name of the only Son of God. And this is the judgment: the light has come into the world, and people loved the darkness rather than the light because their works were evil.
>
> (*John* 3:18–19 ESV)

The temporality is here crucial: there is no present moment of judgment when you are judged—you either are not judged or you have already been judged. What is excluded is the possibility of being judged and found innocent, the same as in Dupuy's example of seduction: either you fail and the obstacle remains in force (you are rejected as a harassing intruder) or there was no obstacle—there is no room in this formulation for the possibility of successfully overcoming the obstacle. And, incidentally, exactly the same asymmetry is at work in the Hegelian dialectical process: the subject either stumbles upon an insurmountable obstacle or he realizes that there is no obstacle at all, that what appeared to him as an obstacle is the very condition of his success.

However, there is a dark obverse of this case. On September 2, 1998, the Swissair flight 111 from JFK to Geneva crashed into the Atlantic Ocean southwest of Halifax, and all 229 people on board died. The investigation took over four years, and it disclosed that the inflammable material used in the aircraft's structure allowed a fire to spread beyond the control of the crew, resulting in a loss of control and the crash of the aircraft. After exposing a series of mistakes made by the pilots and the ground control, a report in the National Geographic Air Crash Investigation series ends by raising the question: if the pilots had avoided all mistakes, what then? The sad answer is: the flight was doomed from the beginning, no correct moves would have made a difference. So it is not that "if the pilots had acted differently, the tragedy would have been avoided"—the counterfactual past possibility is retroactively canceled. This is how the past can be changed counterfactually: when we learn that the flight was doomed from the beginning, nothing changes at the level of (past) facts, what changes are just counterfactual possibilities ... Let's finish this series of cases with the highest one from theology: the sin and the Fall. Is this case also noncommutative? Recall Hegel's characterization of rational consideration itself as evil:

> Abstractly, being evil means singularizing myself in a way that cuts me off from the universal (which is the rational, the laws, the determinations of spirit). But along with this separation there arises being-for-itself and for the first time the universally spiritual, laws—what ought to be. So it is not the case that *rational* consideration has an external relationship to evil: it is itself what is evil.[15]

The serpent says that by eating the fruit of the tree of knowledge, Adam and Eve will become like God; and after the two do it, God comments: "Behold,

Adam has become like one of us."(*Genesis* 3:22) Hegel's comment is: "So the serpent did not lie, for God confirms what it said." Then Hegel goes on to reject the claim that what God says is meant with irony: "Cognition is the principle of spirituality, and this ... is also the principle by which the injury of the separation is healed. It is in this principle of cognition that the principle of 'divinity' is also posited."[16] Subjective freedom is not just the possibility to choose evil or good,

> it is the consideration or the cognition that *makes* people evil, so that consideration and cognition *themselves* are what is evil, and that *therefore* such cognition is what ought not to exist *because* it is the *source* of evil.[17]

The Good emerges as a possibility and duty only through this primordial/constitutive choice of Evil: we experience the Good when, after choosing Evil, we become aware of the utter inadequacy of our situation. The queerness of the Law thus reaches its apogee in Christianity in which we, humans, are a priori presumed to be fallen, to dwell in sin, so that the entire reign of the law consists of the rules of how to deal with our violations of the law: through confessions and other modes of ritualized repentance. That's why, as many perspicuous theologians knew, the Fall is *felix culpa*, the fortunate fault / the blessed fall—or, as St. Augustine put it: "For God judged it better to bring good out of evil than not to permit any evil to exist." We have to add another step to this reasoning: in order to bring good out of evil, the Good itself—God—has to bring evil out of itself. This is why we should turn around the standard Christian (or Catholic, more precisely) explanation of why there is evil in the world: god gave us freedom, and freedom is the freedom to choose what we freely decide, inclusive of evil . . . But is it not the other way round? God (more than just exposed us to the temptation of evil, he) *pushed us into evil so that we would discover our freedom*. There is no freedom without evil since, as Hegel knew very well, to be able to choose between good and evil one already has to be in evil.

Is, consequently, the paradox of the forced choice not inscribed already into the structure of God's original gift of freedom to humanity? Humans are given freedom—with the expectation that they will misuse it to break free from the

Creator, i.e., to become effectively free. The only way to use the gift of freedom without incurring guilt is not to use it at all—in short, what we find here is the very structure of the forced choice: "you are free to choose—on condition that you make the wrong choice . . ." No wonder that, according to the standard Gnostic reading of the Fall, the snake which tempts Eve in the Paradise is a benevolent agent of wisdom, trying to impart knowledge to Adam and Eve imprisoned within the walls of Paradise by their evil Creator who wants to keep them in ignorance. God himself, by way of explicitly prohibiting Adam and Eve to eat the apple from the tree of knowledge, effectively *wants* them to violate his prohibition, to make the step into knowing good and evil and thus becoming aware of the shame of their nakedness. God is here himself inconsistent, divided, saying one thing and, between the lines, giving another covert injunction.

As Kierkegaard puts it, the prohibition awakens the possibility of freedom—the freedom to violate the prohibition, i.e., to eat from the tree of knowledge of the difference of Good and Evil. God engages here in a perverse strategy: in pronouncing the prohibitive Word, he solicits man to violate this prohibition and thereby become human—as St Augustine put it long ago (in his *Enchiridion*, xxvii): "God judged it better to bring good out of evil, than to allow no evil to exist." Or, as Hegel, Kierkegaard's great opponent, would have it, knowledge is not just the possibility to choose evil or good, "it is the consideration or the cognition that *makes* people evil, so that consideration and cognition *themselves* are what is evil, and that *therefore* such cognition is what ought not to exist *because it* is the *source* of evil."[18] In short, prohibition precedes what it prohibits, or, as Kierkegaard puts it, the explanation anticipates what is subsequent. The knowledge gained by Adam and Eve after eating from the tree is nonetheless not simply empty—here is what happens after they taste the apple:

> Then the eyes of both of them were opened, and they realized they were naked; so they sewed fig leaves together and made coverings for themselves. Then the man and his wife heard the sound of the Lord God as he was walking in the garden in the cool of the day, and they hid from the Lord God among the trees of the garden. But the Lord God called to the man,

"Where are you?" The man answered, "I heard you in the garden, and I was afraid because I was naked; so I hid." And he said, "Who told you that you were naked? Have you eaten from the tree that I commanded you not to eat from?"

(*Genesis* 3:7–11)

Before eating from the tree, the two were already naked, they just didn't know they were naked—they fell literally like the proverbial cat above the precipice which falls down only after it looks down and notices there is no ground under its feet. The shift involved in the Fall is thus purely subjective, it involves a different attitude towards what Adam and Eve are: the two of them merely realize (register, take note of) what they are—as in the famous passage from Moliere in which a guy, when told that he is speaking prose—a new word for him—asserts with pleasure that he knows how to speak prose. What betrayed their Fall to God was not their brash display of nakedness, but their feeling of shame at realizing that they are naked—one can say that their very moral feeling of shame made them guilty. Recall Alphonse Allais's old joke when he pointed at a woman walking along a street and shouted: "Look at her! Beneath her clothes, she is totally naked!" In exactly the same way, a human being is guilty only under the cover of his/her shame. And is it not the same with the punishment that befalls them (they will die)? In the same way that they were already naked, they were also already mortal, they just didn't relate to their mortality—as Heidegger would have put it, animals die, but only man relates to his death as his innermost (im)possibility. So when God enounces the punishment, he just spells out what Adam and Eve already realized when they noticed that they are naked, namely their misery as two weak mortal beings.

To reintroduce here the term "observation," one should point out that at the level of physical reality, *nothing happens* with the Fall: the Fall (eating the apple and gaining knowledge) means just that Adam and Eve register/observe what they were already doing. As Augustine emphasized, of course there was sex in paradise before the Fall, but sexual acts were performed as a simple instrumental activity, like cutting woods or gathering fruits from the trees—there was no surplus-enjoyment in it, this enjoyment came only with awareness. And this fact allows us to introduce a noncommutative sequence of events: there is no sin before its prohibition, and there is no Good before Evil. Sins are the same acts we were doing before prohibition, we were just not aware (observing) that we are doing them. Observation thus changes an innocent act into sin. In a similar way, we were not Good before choosing Evil because choice as such is Evil. So Fall is not a fall from goodness, Fall retroactively creates what it falls from.

This brings us to another important topic: that of *counterfactual* situations. They are something that is immanent to reality itself: things are not just what they are, their actuality is accompanied by the shadow of what would have happened if a different course of action were to be taken. For example, when in 2020 we decided to impose a quarantine to curb the spreading of the Covid pandemic, we did this to diminish the amount of infections and deaths. However, there is a key distinction to be made here:

> I have a choice of two actions, A and B. I choose A. I estimate that I am in a better situation in the option A than in the option B, as far as I can appreciate it *after I have chosen A*. However, I have no guarantee that if I were to choose B, my situation would have been the same as the one that I envisage for B after having chosen A. In other words, the presupposition is that the "actual" (i.e., real) choice of B puts me into the same world as the "counterfactual" (i.e., virtual, "against the facts") choice of B if I've chosen A. Even more simply, the hidden hypothesis is that the "alternate" worlds have the same reality as the world in which we really find ourselves.[19]

We should abandon this hypothesis, not just for obvious empirical reasons—our counterfactual estimation of what would have happened if we were to choose B (no or much less quarantines) could simply turn out to be wrong—remember how, in the Summer of 2020, when the UK authorities prohibited access to beaches: when this prohibition was largely ignored and the beaches were packed, this led to almost no increase in infections. To put it simply, *A is not the same after I've chosen B*—after I've chosen B, A is measured by the standards which made me choose B. And this brings us back to (Rovelli's reading of) Zeilinger's experiment: does this experiment not clearly prove that Lacan's formulation is wrong, i.e., that non-commutativity is NOT "a category that belongs only to the register of the signifier"?

But are things really so simple? What if we risk a radical hypothesis according to which the "weirdness" of quantum phenomena resides in the fact that we encounter there phenomena which we thought are unique to the symbolic universe in which humans dwell? The claim "it seems that you need only to observe for what is happening to change" should be read very precisely, in its literal meaning: the change is caused not by an element being observed but *by an observation which sees nothing*. Does this "astonishing thing" not come close to what Saussure called differentiality? If the identity of an entity resides only in its differences from other entities, then the fact that something doesn't happen (at a place in the structure where it was expected to happen) counts as a positive fact.

II

Particular: From Hegel to Heidegger ...and back

1

Names for finitude: Hegel, Heidegger, Pippin

Robert Pippin was for decades among the most outspoken American Hegelians, defending Hegel's idealist legacy not only against the post-Hegelian turn towards non-discursive or non-notional reality but also rejecting Heidegger's treatment of Hegel. So it comes as a shock when, in his new book *The Culmination*[1], he endorses Heidegger's characterization of Hegel's thought as the culmination of Western metaphysics, as the full deployment of its basic premise that being equals *logos*, i.e., that the truth of everything that exists (or that can exist) can be articulated in the form of discursive judgments, so that the full system of logic is at the same time a full ontology, the description of conditions that everything that exists should meet. The post-Hegelian thinkers were right to claim that something escapes this closed circle of logical categories and mediations, but they were wrong in trying to locate this missing dimension in some form of pre-logical positive reality (will, productive process, unconscious drives . . .). It is only Heidegger who really breaks out of the Hegelian closed circle, pointing out that we (humans) are finite beings thrown into a historically destined disclosure of Being which predetermines what "matters" to us, our horizon of the meaningfulness of Being—Hegel himself doesn't see how his own Logic already relies on a disclosure of Being as immanently structured by logical categories, judgments, and syllogistic mediations. A new beginning is thus needed, and Heidegger gives hints that only a non-discursive poetic thinking can do the job.

It is easy for the so-called "rationalist" philosophers to make fun of Heidegger's "poetic" thinking. Apropos of what is perhaps the best known single line from a *film noir*, the final remark of the doomed hero in Edgar G. Ulmer's *Detour* ("Fate or some mysterious force can put the finger on you or me for no good reason at all."), one cannot but imagine how this line should be translated into the old Greek and then provided by a Heideggerian commentary pondering on the primordial way the Greeks experienced the tension between Fate and Reason, along the lines of "The Reason /the Ground, the hidden, self-withdrawing foundation/ of our Fate is the Fate, the abyssal game, that names the Event of the coming-forth of the epochal Reason of our Being itself" . . . However, one cannot get rid of Heidegger in such an easy way—he deserves a much more radical confrontation.

While Heidegger characterizes Hegel as the "culmination" not only of German Idealism but of the entire history of Western philosophy, he also reserves a special place for Schelling as the "peak" of German Idealism: Heidegger's idea was that "while Schelling is the peak or *Gipfel* of German idealism, Hegel is its culmination, *Vollendung*."(xi) In what does this difference between culmination and peak consist? Culmination is the point at which a certain system or process actualizes its immanent potentials, achieves its complete form—in the case of Hegel, his logic marks the point at which the metaphysical identity of being and discursive knowability (only what can be rationally known really exists) is fully realized. Peak means the moment in a certain system or process when one of its elements (thinkers, in this case) reaches the highest level in the sense that it already surpasses the limits of that system, signposting a dimension that eludes the system—for Heidegger, Schelling in his essay on freedom displays the unclear premonition of a dimension beyond metaphysics.

So what if we apply this duality of peak and culmination to Heidegger himself, in conjunction with the ongoing process of the full naturalization/objectivization of being-human that occurs in today's cognitive sciences? With his notion of disclosure as a historical a priori of every epoch, Heidegger brings transcendental metaphysics to its culmination, providing its ultimate version, while with their notion of the wired brain, today's cognitive sciences designate a peak of scientific knowability which undermines its very bearer, the subject practicing science.

But one should take a step further: what if Hegel himself, the very core of his thought ignored by Heidegger, is also split between its culmination and its peak? Let's refer here to Heidegger's notion of the onto-theological structure of metaphysics: Hegel's dialectics culminates in the reflexive redoubling through which the gap that separates subject from Substance is transposed into the Substance itself: with Christ, the fall of man from god is transposed into the fall of god from himself, etc. We have to supplement this ontological redoubling of the gap (a redoubling which undermines the very foundation of metaphysics) with the peak of Hegel's dialectics, with its excessive moment which protrudes from its edifice: the space for the experience of the "divine" is the gap that forever separates the transcendental from the objective-realist approach, but this "divine" dimension refers to the moment of madness preceding discourse, to the experience of radical negativity (what mystics and Hegel called the "night of the world") which precludes any theology focused on a positive figure of god, even if this figure of god is radically secularized in modern scientific naturalism.

Recall Kierkegaard's claim about the futility of philosophical systems (his target here is, of course, Hegel): "In relation to their systems most systematizers are like a man who builds an enormous castle and lives in a shack close by; they do not live in their own enormous systematic buildings."[2] As is often the case in Kierkegaard's critique of Hegel, he misses the point here and ignores his own proximity to Hegel: the final result of the Hegelian movement is precisely that enormous castles are only finished when they are accompanied/supplemented by a small shack in which the subject who built them has to dwell ... In short, to paraphrase Hegel's well-known programmatic slogan from his *Phenomenology*: one should conceive the Absolute not only as a magnificent castle but also as a small shack attached to it. (Or the Christian version: one should conceive God not only as the majestic creator or everything but also as a miserable individual walking around Palestine 2,000 years ago; today, his place would have been without doubt in the ruins of Gaza.) In his *Castle,* Kafka himself has a clear premonition of this paradox: the novel's hero decides to climb up the hill and approaches the majestic castle on the top of it; however, the more he comes close to the castle, the more he notices that the castle is not composed of majestic buildings but of dirty small shacks ...

Pippin makes the move from Hegel's culmination of metaphysics as logic to the finite existence of a Dasein thrown into a historical world of a disclosed meaning—but is this move the ultimate one? Do we not find in Hegel himself (and Schelling) an *Ansatz* for a move beyond/beneath Heidegger? The dimension of radical madness, the "night of the world," the pain of infinite difference, is prior to the openness to a meaningful disclosure of being. Schelling begins his *Ages of the World* with: logos is at the beginning, but what was BEFORE the beginning?[3] Heidegger indicates that the culmination of Western metaphysics, of its reduction of being to discursive knowability (i.e., Hegel's elaboration of logic as a complete account of the conditions of the knowability of being and, consequently, of being itself), precisely because of its completion makes palpable that something is missing, that something is left out, ignored: it "reveals finally what is missing or left out, or what remains unasked."(11) The so-called post-Hegelian thought was obviously aware of this ignored dimension; but Heidegger repeatedly claims that it tries to fill in this gap with some new positive substantial mode of being (will to power, social-material process, the unconscious ...) which just turns around the metaphysics without effectively stepping out of it.

My thesis is that while this is true, it was none other than Hegel himself, the point of culmination of metaphysical idealism, who was fully aware of this limitation and included it into his system. Hegel's name for the radical finitude of our predicament is none other than ABSOLUTE KNOWING (AK).[4] The first obvious fact that bears witness to this finitude is Hegel's strict prohibition to engage in speculations about future: philosophy (and science) can only paint grey on grey, what will come is radically open, in no way to be derived from the past and present—here is Hegel's well-known formulation:

> Only one word more concerning the desire to teach the world what it ought to be. For such a purpose philosophy at least always comes too late. Philosophy, as the thought of the world, does not appear until reality has completed its formative process, and made itself ready. History thus corroborates the teaching of the conception that only in the maturity of reality does the ideal appear as counterpart to the real, apprehends the real

world in its substance, and shapes it into an intellectual kingdom. When philosophy paints its grey in grey, one form of life has become old, and by means of grey it cannot be rejuvenated, but only known. The owl of Minerva, takes its flight only when the shades of night are gathering.[5]

Hegel's point here is not that we can only fully know the past, but a much more radical one: each historical epoch implies its own vision of the past, it reconstructs it retroactively from its standpoint—we cannot rely even on our knowledge of the past (in the same way as, in quantum mechanics, each collapse retroactively structures its own genesis). This is what Hegel calls "Absolute Knowing [*Wissen*], not cognition [*Erkenntniss*]": the end-point of dialectical reversals, when the subject stumbles upon the final limitation, the limitation as such, a limitation which can no longer be inverted into a productive self-assertion. Contrary to the misleading appearances, Absolute Knowing "does not mean 'knowing everything.' It rather means—recognizing one's limitations."[6] "Absolute Knowing" is the final recognition of such a limitation which is "absolute" in the sense that it is not a determinate, particular, and as such a "relative" limit/obstacle to our knowledge, something we can clearly see and locate as the limit/obstacle. It is invisible "as such" because it is the limitation of the entire field as such, its closure which, from within it (and we are always by definition within it, because this field in a way "is" ourselves) cannot but appear as its opposite, as the very openness of the field.

It is commonplace to oppose Hegel as the ridiculous point of Absolute Knowing to a more modest sceptical approach which recognizes the excess of reality over every conceptualization. What if, however, it is Hegel who is much more modest? What if his AK is the assertion of a radical closure: there is no meta-language, we cannot step on our own shoulder and see our own limitation, we cannot relativize/historicize ourselves, our own position? What is effectively arrogant is, as Chesterton made it clear, precisely such self-relativization, the attitude of "knowing one's limitation," of not agreeing with oneself—as the proverbial "wise" insight according to which we can only approach reality asymptotically. What Hegel's AK deprives us of is precisely this minimal self-distance, the safety-distance from our own location.

That is to say, Hegel's ultimate point is not that, in spite of our limitation, of our embeddedness in a contingent historical context, we—or Hegel himself, at least—can somehow overcome this limitation and gain access to Absolute Knowledge (to which historicist relativism then responds that we cannot ever gain access to this position, that we can only aim at it as at an impossible Ideal). What he calls Absolute Knowing is, on the contrary, the very sign of our total capture—we are CONDEMNED to Absolute Knowing, we cannot ESCAPE it, since "Absolute Knowing" means that there is no external point of reference with regard to which we could perceive the relativity of our own "merely subjective" standpoint. All determinate being is relational, things only are what they are in relation to their otherness, or, as Deleuze put it, perspectival distortion is inscribed into the very identity of the thing. The real is not out there, as the inaccessible transcendent X never reached by our representations; the real is here, as the obstacle/impossibility which makes our representations flawed, inconsistent. The real is not the In-itself but the very obstacle which distorts our access to the In-itself, and this paradox provides the key for what Hegel calls "Absolute Knowing."

And the same goes for immortality which is the obverse of finitude.[7] The axiom of the philosophy of finitude is that one cannot escape finitude/mortality as the unsurpassable horizon of our existence; Lacan's axiom is that, no matter how much one tries, one cannot escape immortality. But what if this choice is false—what if finitude and immortality, like lack and excess, also form a parallax couple, what if they are the same from a different point of view? What if immortality is an object that is a remainder/excess over finitude, what if finitude is an attempt to escape from the excess of immortality? What if Kierkegaard was right here, but for the wrong reason, when he also understood the claim that we, humans, are just mortal beings who disappear after their biological death as an easy way to escape the ethical responsibility that comes with the immortal soul? He was right for the wrong reason insofar as he equated immortality with the divine and ethical part of a human being—but there is another immortality. What Cantor did for infinity, we should do for immortality, and assert the multiplicity of immortalities: the Badiouian noble immortality/infinity of the deployment of an Event (as opposed to the finitude of a human animal) comes after a more basic form of immortality which resides in what Lacan calls the Sadean fundamental fantasy: the fantasy of another, ethereal body of the victim, which can be tortured indefinitely and nonetheless magically retains its beauty (recall the Sadean figure of the young girl sustaining endless humiliations and mutilations from her depraved torturer and somehow mysteriously surviving it all intact, in the same way Tom and Jerry and other cartoon heroes survive all their ridiculous ordeals intact). In this form, the comical and the disgustingly-terrifying (recall different versions of the "undead"—zombies, vampires, etc.—in popular culture) are inextricably connected.

The same immortality underlies the intuition of something indestructible in a truly radical Evil. Adorno was right when he wrote that when one encounters a truly evil person, it is difficult to imagine that this person can die. This immortality is ambiguous: Evil is indestructible, but so is the suffering of evil persons after their death. No wonder that, in his *The Day Of Doom*, Michael Wigglesworth's dark description of the suffering of sinners after the Judgment Day published in the American colonies in 1662[8], this suffering is described as obscene undeadness: "Their pain and grief have no relief, their anguish never endeth. There must they lie, and never die, though dying every day."

We are of course not immortal, we all (will) die—the "immortality" of the death drive is not a biological fact but a psychic stance of "persisting beyond life and death," of a readiness to go on beyond the limits of life, of a perverted life-force which bears witness to a "deranged relationship towards life." Lacan's name for this derangement is, of course, *jouissance*, excessive enjoyment, whose pursuit can make us neglect or even self-sabotage our vital needs and interests. At this precise point, Lacan radically differs from the thinkers of finitude for whom a human being is a being-towards-death, relating to its own finitude and unavoidable death: it is only through the intervention of *jouissance* that a human animal becomes properly mortal, relating to the prospect of its own extinction. Lacan notes apropos of the "life and death dialogue" how "it only acquires the character of a drama from the moment when enjoyment [*jouisssance*] intervenes. The vital point . . . is the deranged relationship to one's own body called enjoyment."[9]

Both Hegel and Heidegger thus advocate the end of philosophy, but, to complicate things further, none of the two is original in this claim. The topic of the end of philosophy dominates European philosophy from Kant onwards: Kant designates his critical approach as a prolegomena to a future philosophy (metaphysics); Fichte talks about "doctrine of science (*Wissenschaftslehre*)" instead of philosophy; Hegel saw his system as no longer just philo-sophy (love of wisdom) but knowledge itself; Marx opposed philosophy to the study of actual life, etc. till Heidegger whose motto was "the end of philosophy and the task of thinking." There is a deep paradox in this fact. It is only with Kant's revolution, with his notion of the transcendental, that philosophy came to itself. Is it not that, ultimately, philosophy AS SUCH begins with Kant, with his transcendental turn? Is it not that the entire previous philosophy can be understood properly—not as the simple description of the "entire universe," of the totality of beings, but as the description of the horizon within which entities disclose themselves to a finite human being—only if read "anachronistically," from the standpoint opened up by Kant? Is it not that it was Kant who also opened up the field within which Heidegger himself was able to formulate the notion of *Dasein* as the place in which beings appear within a historically determined/destined horizon of meaning?

I am well aware that Heidegger would never accept the use of the term "transcendental" for his approach since "transcendental" is for him irreducibly branded by the notion of modern subjectivity. In spite of that, I keep this term since I think it remains the most appropriate one to indicate the idea of a horizon within which entities appear to us. Heidegger, of course, makes a key step forward with regard to Kant who remains within the horizon of being as the substance enduring in time, as a standing presence. But does today's "postmodern" notion of reality as a dynamic flow of non-substantial appearances (with references to Buddhism) not break with the notion of being as a standing presence?

*

Today we don't only live in an era of the proclaimed end of philosophy—we live in an era of the *double* end of philosophy. At the very beginning of his *The Grand Design*, Stephen Hawking triumphantly proclaims that "philosophy is dead."[10] With the latest advances in quantum physics and cosmology, the so-called experimental metaphysics reaches its apogee: metaphysical questions about the origins of the universe, etc., which were till now the topic of philosophical speculations, can now be answered through experimental science and thus empirically tested... The prospect of a "wired brain" is a kind of final point of the naturalization of human thought: when our process of thinking can directly interact with a digital machine, it effectively becomes an object in reality, it is no longer "our" inner thought as opposed to external reality.

On the other hand, today's transcendental historicism insists that sciences cannot provide the ultimate cognitive frame of our knowledge. Heidegger gave to the transcendental approach an existential turn: philosophy as transcendental-phenomenological ontology does not inquire into the nature of reality, it analyzes how all of reality appears to us in a given epochal constellation. In today's age of techno-science, we consider as "really existing" only what can be an object of scientific research—all other entities are reduced to illusory subjective experiences, just imagined things, etc. Heidegger's point is not that such a view is more or less "true" than a premodern view, but that, with the new disclosure of being that characterizes modernity, the very criteria of what is "true" or "false" changed... It is not difficult to grasp the paradox of such an approach: while Heidegger is perceived as a thinker uniquely focused on the question of Being, he leaves out of consideration what we understand by this question in our "naïve" pre-transcendental stance: how do things exist independently of the way we relate to them, independently of how they appear to us? In this context, I find it problematic, misleading even, how Pippin formulates the relationship between Being and beings/entities:

> Being itself is at issue. Without Dasein, then, there are beings, and there would be a number of facts that would be true of such beings—what exists, what kinds exist, what might exist but does not—but there would be no Being qua Being, manifestness as such... Heidegger's question is not "what is there?" but "what allows" beings to be manifest?
>
> (60)

The disclosure of the meaning of Being of course doesn't create or cause entities; however, to draw from this the conclusion that, even without the disclosure of Being "there would be a number of facts that would be true of such beings—what exists, what kinds exist, what might exist but does not"—is deeply misleading. The terms Pippin uses here—the true facts about such beings which exist even outside their ontological disclosure—are obviously not ontologically neutral, they *already appear only within a specific historical disclosure of Being*. As Heidegger himself was fully aware of, what is out there (or here or anywhere) prior to a historical disclosure of Being, i.e., how to *think* nature prior to the emergence of humans as *Da-Sein,* as the "here" of Being, is a much more difficult question totally avoided by Pippin.

The second critical point is that the problem of appearance is also Hegel's basic problem: Hegel's big question is not "can we penetrate behind deceitful appearances to true being" but exactly the opposite one: "reality" is in itself stupid and flat, the true enigma is: why does (what we perceive as) reality *appear to itself*? "Appear" implies here also falsity, illusion, misrecognition, i.e., a necessarily *wrong* appearance—not only as a secondary possibility, but as an immanent condition of truth, or, to quote two of Lacan's sayings, *la verite surgit de la meprise*? (truth emerges out of misrecognition) and *les non-dupes errent* (the non-duped err). This is also how Hegel's well-known claim that the Absolute has to be conceived "not only as substance but also as subject" is to be understood: abstraction, tearing apart of a totality, misapprehension, are part of the Absolute itself.

So where does Hegel stand in the passage from traditional metaphysics to the postmetaphysical nineteenth- and twentieth-century thought? Hegel is the "vanishing mediator" between his "before" and his "after." That is to say: something happens in Hegel, a breakthrough into a unique dimension of thought, which is obliterated, rendered invisible in its true dimension, by postmetaphysical thought. This obliteration leaves an empty space which has to be filled in so that the continuity of the development of philosophy can be reestablished—filled in with what? The index of this obliteration is the ridiculous image of Hegel as the absurd "absolute idealist" who "pretended to know everything," to possess Absolute Knowledge, to read the mind of God, to deduce entire reality out of the self-movement of (his) mind—the image which is an exemplary case of what Freud called *Deck-Erinnerung* (screen-memory), a fantasy-formation intended to cover up a traumatic truth. In this sense, the post-Hegelian term to "concrete reality, irreducible to notional mediation," should rather be read as a desperate posthumous revenge of metaphysics, as an attempt to reinstall metaphysics, albeit in the inverted form of the primacy of concrete reality.

When, in his *Culmination,* Robert Pippin moves from Hegel to Heidegger, he misses this most radical dimension (beyond the transcendental) in Hegel's thought: like Heidegger, he reduces Hegel's absolute idealism to the total coincidence between being and (logical) knowability, thereby reducing ontology to the notion's self-deployment. However, the gap between logic and reality remains in Hegel, at more than one level—ultimately, the gap is not between logos and reality but in the thing itself, between (in Lacanian terms) reality and the Real. Does already Hegel's best-known formula (the Absolute should be conceived not only as substance but also as subject) not point in this direction? "Subject" does not stand here just for self-consciousness, its discursive power of reflection, it stands also for a gap in the thing (Absolute) itself—"subject" does not mean only that substance is dynamized, caught in self-movement, it means above all that abstraction, illusion, partiality, etc., are immanent to a totality. (The parallel with quantum mechanics cannot but strike the eye here again.) Let me quote here again the well-known passage from the "Foreword" to his *Phenomenology of Spirit* where Hegel provides the most elementary formula of what does it mean to conceive Substance also as Subject:

> The disparity which exists in consciousness between the I and the substance which is its object is the distinction between them, the *negative* in general. This can be regarded as the *defect* of both, though it is their soul, or that which moves them. That is why some of the ancients conceived the *void* as the principle of motion, for they rightly saw the moving principle as the *negative,* though they did not as yet grasp that the negative is the self. Now, although this negative appears at first as a disparity between the I and its object, it is just as much a disparity of the substance with itself. Thus what seems to happen outside of it, to be an activity directed against it, is really its own doing, and substance shows itself to be essentially subject.[11]

The final reversal is crucial: the disparity between subject and substance is simultaneously the disparity of the substance with itself—or, to put it in Lacan's terms, disparity means that the lack of the subject is simultaneously the lack in the Other: subjectivity emerges when substance cannot achieve full identity with itself, when substance is in itself "barred," crossed by an immanent impossibility or antagonism. In short, the subject's epistemological ignorance, its failure to fully grasp the opposed substantial content, simultaneously indicates a limitation/failure/lack of the substantial content itself. Therein also resides the key dimension of the theological revolution of Christianity: the alienation of man from god has to be projected/transferred back into god itself, as the alienation of god from itself (therein resides the speculative content of the notion of divine kenosis)—this is the Christian version of Hegel's insight into how the disparity of subject and substance implies the disparity of substance with regard to itself. This is why the unity of man and god is enacted in Christianity in a way which fundamentally differs from the way of pagan religions where man has to strive to overcome his fall from god through the effort to purify his being from material filth and elevate himself to rejoin god. In Christianity, on the contrary, god falls from itself, he becomes a finite mortal human abandoned by god (in the figure of Christ and his lament on the cross "Father, why have you forsaken me?"), and man can only achieve unity with god by identifying with this god, the god abandoned by itself. Kant misses this properly Christian dimension, and Pippin follows in Kant's footsteps:

> If it were not fully determinable, then the determinations would be hostage to something empirical or historical, and so not a matter of pure thinking. Brandom has developed a reading of conceptual determination in Hegel that argues for such an "open" form of thought's self-determination, or for such a subjection.
>
> (143)

I am here on Brandom's side: to take just two exemplary cases, the categories from Hegel's logic are simply not able to provide the coordinates for grasping the mechanisms of the Freudian unconscious or the weird logic of wave oscillations and superpositions in quantum mechanics. And I even think that, if we properly read the Freudian unconscious, the two cases imply a clear parallel. For Freud, the unconscious is not a substantial pre-discursive psychic entity, a drive that strives to express itself in different ways; it is the repressed part of our symbolic universe, the part which exists in a virtual way, i.e., which is not more real but in some sense less real than our conscious and preconscious thoughts. In the terms of quantum physics, the unconscious are the superpositions which are lost when a wave oscillation "collapses" in one determinate conscious thought or statement: they don't exist, they continue to insist as virtual entities.

In this sense Lacan claims that the status of the unconscious is not ontological but ethical—not only in the sense that the psychoanalytic process is guided by the ethical maxim to confront the patient's unconscious but, much more radically, in the sense that the unconscious itself brought out through the analytic process is not a deep truth already present deep in our psyche but an ethical construct that results from the duty to put some order into our psychic life: "'If I am formulating here that the status of the unconscious is ethical ... it is precisely because Freud himself does not stress it when he gives the unconscious its status."[12] Already in his early work, Freud indicates this apropos a hysteric who "weeps at A" and "is quite unaware that he is doing so on account of the association A-B, and B itself plays no part at all in his psychical life"[13]:

> Now this case is typical of repression in hysteria. We invariably find that a memory is repressed which has only become a trauma by deferred action. The cause of this state of things is the retardation of puberty as compared with the rest of the individual's development.[14]

So it is not that the unconscious is simply B: B became traumatic only retroactively (a classic case is that of Wolfman, Freud's best known patient: when as a small child he witnessed the *a tergo* sexual act of his parents, there was nothing traumatic or sexual in it—it became traumatic only years later when Wolfman developed his infantile sexual theories). The ethical act is here not simply to remember the primordial scene but to *dissociate* it from its traumatic impact which is conferred on it later, retroactively. To remember the primordial scene involves linear causal determinism: one identifies the ultimate cause of ongoing pathological phenomena. The space of freedom is the space of retroactivity, and I retroactively reconstruct the past (in its meaning) as an ethical project. Kafka made this clear in his late short story "Investigations of a Dog"[15] where he delineates the metaphysical battlefield in terms of three distinct impossibilities: on the one side, desire for the impossible (Brod) and the possible is impossible (Kafka); on the other, nothing is impossible, the impossible is impossible (smirking wombs).[16]

The first option (for Kafka embodied in Max Brod) defines the life of the majority of us, at least of those who still live in a world of traditional authority: clear social rules (which you are often allowed to discreetly violate) define what is possible and permit us only to dream about what is impossible (sexual promiscuity and perversions, behaving badly, etc.). In Kafka's world, this bar of impossibility is displaced into the very heart of the possible, of our "normal" daily life: the most ordinary acts and procedures become tainted by an impossibility. (You try to eat a sandwich, it gets stuck in your throat; you try to cross a street, your legs don't follow your intention . . .)

In Kafka, one often finds also the opposite paradox: you may be a world champion in swimming, but you feel that you don't know how to swim; you are a top singer, but what comes out of your mouth is only a weird gargling . . . Kafka perspicuously detects a third option that characterizes a modern permissive world in which "Every womb is fruitful and smirks uselessly at the world":[17] everything is productive and brings pleasure, you can easily do it, but the result is no less frustrating, a stupid joyless pleasure . . . Is there a fourth term? If Kafka's third version is "there is nothing which is impossible", so that the impossible itself is impossible, this is not the same as *actualizing the impossible by way of changing the coordinates of what is possible*. A true political act occurs when something considered impossible is enacted and thus (to use Dupuy's formulation) retroactively creates its own possibility. Such an enactment of the impossible is freedom: "the impossible receives its proper conceptualization, is raised to the level of the concept—the ultimate name of this concept being, for Kafka, 'freedom.'"[18] The third option in which "nothing is impossible" gets unavoidably caught in paradoxes that characterize Cancel Culture: the only way to guarantee that nothing is impossible is to carefully comb the entire field of our activity to exclude acts which preclude others to act with no impossibilities, so that the impossible returns in the guise of prohibitive regulations. This is why, in his *Is It Ever Just Sex?*[19], Darian Leader problematizes the standard notion that, according to psychoanalysis, everything we do or talk about is really about sex—as it says on the book cover:

> The old idea that sexuality is a smouldering, animalistic force within us, desperate for release yet restrained by social forces, has little to support it. Bodies aren't just sticks that make fire when you rub them together, and the pain, heartache, and regret that can accompany the highs of sexual excitement show us that much more is at stake.

Let's take an ordinary example: when I take the Piccadilly tube line in London, I notice that one of the end stations is "Cockfosters," a name which give rise to obvious dirty association (fostering my cock). A Jungian approach would decipher in this name a deeper urge to strengthen my potency (if I am a man), as if sexuality is a substantial psychic passion that seeks to express itself in all possible everyday situations. For a Lacanian, things stand the other way round: I am (or, rather, may be) obsessed with fostering my cock because I associate the name of the station with some traumatic or libidinally invested event which may have nothing to do with sexuality. Another more simple example: back in the 1960s, a Slovene pop singer Rafko Irgolič, a dentist by profession, was quite popular in imitating the cowboy country songs. In one of them, "My black stallion," he sings about a young guy riding a horse which willingly takes him to his beloved eagerly awaiting him, with the words bordering on the obscene ("Run, run, run, runny, / sun, sun, sun, sunny, / one, one, one, onnny, how does he race . . ."). If one listens to the (rather stupid) song, it gets immediately clear that he is not joyfully riding the horse looking forward to the sex with his girlfriend—it is rather the opposite, his true enjoyment resides in his riding the black stallion, and the sex ("riding the girl") is just a pretext that obfuscates the true heart of his enjoyment. One can presume that, when he will actually make love to the girl, he will be dreaming about riding his stallion . . . To put it in another way, at its most basic level, sexuality of the unconscious phenomena does not reside in their ultimate content but in how these phenomena are mediated or submitted to the "dream-work," to its detours and displacements.

Do such detours and displacements not bring us close to poetry? Pippin is right to remark that, in a typical modernist way, Heidegger emphasizes two things about poetry today: since the poetic disclosure of reality is threatened, every authentic poetry today has to reflect upon its own possibility, has to be poetry about poetry itself. Plus insofar as poetry is in these conditions a search for a lost home, for a lost authentic life-world, this means that it cannot by itself achieve this goal and outline a new meaningful disclosure of being; it can only provide ambiguous hints: poetry "rather opens a door than shows us how to enter or what we might find when we do."(214) One has to go to the end here: what if such a position in between is our final predicament? One could afford here yet another of the reversals that characterize Heidegger's thought (in the style of "the essence of truth is the truth of essence itself"): the question of Being (*Seinsfrage*) is the being of Question itself—every disclosure of being is an (ultimately failed) reply to this question, a reply which conceals more than it discloses.

So let's take a final look at Pippin's shift from a Hegelian position to a Heideggerian one. In *Culmination* Pippin restates his old Hegelian position that any critique of idealism which asserts its dependence upon some external ground, "insofar as it is a thinking, a judging, a claim to know, is always already a manifestation of a dependence on pure thinking and its conditions, and such 'moments' of pure thinking are to delimit (but not limit) the normative domain of intelligibility (what can rightly be distinguished from what, or rightly posited as 'ground,' for example) and not any process or series of events that goes on in supposed independence of the empirical world."(149) In his earlier works, Pippin applies this critique to Heidegger himself: Heidegger's assertion of the dependence of our thinking on a disclosure of Being external to it, is also "already a manifestation of a dependence on pure thinking." Pippin doesn't elevate here thinking (self-consciousness) into a causal ground of nature and social life: science can explain how certain animals were able to develop thinking, but they are thereby describing a certain natural process, and

> no fact about the organic properties of such beings accounts for what it is to be self-conscious or agents, and there is no need for the positing of nonmaterial entities or capacities. Those are categories of achievement—indeed, collective achievement—and the question of what is achieved is an autonomous philosophical question.
>
> (158)

Spirit as a self-generative process is, of course, grounded in natural substantial bodies, but this does not explain its immanent logic. It goes without saying that Pippin applies the same critique to Marx and Freud: they both assert the dependence of our thinking on some "objective" substantial process external to it—the social productive process, the unconscious mechanisms. In *The Culmination*, however, Pippin concedes that Heidegger *does* break out of this circle—just Heidegger, not Marx or Freud. Heidegger's critique of Hegel (not Marx's, not Freud's limitation of consciousness) is therefore for Pippin "the first genuine confrontation with Hegel in all the post-Hegelian European tradition."(161) In some sense this is true, but this confrontation is extremely reductive: a key dimension of Hegel's thought disappears in Heidegger's reading of Hegel as the culmination of metaphysical idealism in which discursive Reason is asserted as the ultimate ground of all reality. We should begin with the key fact that Hegel himself in some sense breaks out of the self-enclosed logical circle when, at the end of his logic, he passes from logic to nature: he evokes the insufficiency of the closed circle of logic, of its realm of shadows:

> The idea is still logical; it is shut up in pure thought [*in den reinen Gedanken eingeschlossen*], the science only of the divine concept. Its systematic exposition is of course itself a realization, but one confined within the same sphere. Because the pure idea of cognition is to this extent shut up within subjectivity, it is the drive [*Trieb*] to sublate it, and pure truth becomes as final result also the beginning of another sphere and science.
>
> (SL, 12.253)

This passage is thus not an objective causal process, it is immanent to thinking subjectivity, an effect of "a felt practical insufficiency".(160) What post-Hegelians from Schelling to Marx reproach Hegel with is here clearly stated by Hegel himself. Pippin is right to point out that what Hegel means by calling the Logic the realm of shadows is "a concession to finitude that Heidegger does not see"(179):

> by "shadows," Hegel means to point to the insufficiency of the Logic—even as a metaphysics—if considered as a stand-alone part, when considered as

a speculative science. It is an abstraction, a necessary one, but its isolation from the system it animates, while necessary, can produce only conceptual shadows of the Absolute. We must see it "alive" in the development of the sciences of nature and in the historical development of human Geist before it can be fully understood.

(180)

Here Pippin comes close to Brandom: "the Hegelian a priori for the philosophies of nature and spirit must be a historical a priori, what is conceptually indispensable and so not empirically disconfirmable but at a moment of development in the investigation of nature and the developments of civil society."(181) However, Pippin constrains here historicity to the "philosophies of nature and spirit," not to logic itself. He is right to assert that the passage from logic to *Realphilosophie* is not an actual deduction or the description of an actual causal process: all that one can deduce from the immanent self-movement of notions is that it ends up in the feeling of practical insufficiency which gives birth to the drive to move from the logical "realm of shadows" to actual life. For Pippin, any reality that appears in this way has to follow and fit the space of logical categories, but where this reality comes from is not a philosophical problem but a question of empirical sciences. From my Hegelo-Lacanian standpoint, however, "where does this reality come from" is THE philosophical problem, a problem that confronts us with the topic of the pre-ontological Real, and this is why I am compelled to deal with quantum mechanics.

2

The night of the world

What cognitive sciences are telling us about consciousness is perhaps best resumed in Anil Seth's *Being You: A New Science of Consciousness*, a book written in a clear and modest way, without the falseness and pretention that characterizes a lot of popular scientific writing.[1] Seth's key concept is that of *controlled hallucination*. Our mind models the external environment by predicting what kind of perceptual experience is most likely to occur next, given prior experiences, and the result is our familiar subjective world of objects that have three-dimensional shape, size, colour, relative position, movement, and so forth. This constructed experience is not a representation of the world "as it actually is," but, rather, a model that is good enough to allow us to navigate the environment and do the things that biological beings must do to survive and reproduce. Such a model is a "controlled hallucination" in that it is an imaginary representation controlled or constrained by reality-as-it-is (prediction failures demand a re-imagining, so the hallucination cannot go wildly in any direction), but also in the sense that hallucination is the basis for our decisions, controlling our behaviour.

Seth's next and crucial logical step is to extend the concept of perception of external reality as controlled hallucination to the perception of one's internal reality (our inner sensations and feelings): if perceptions of external reality are controlled hallucinations, conscious perception of our own inner states have to work exactly the same way, and this includes our Self: our sense of selfhood is also just a sensing of our internal state of being, and this internal sensing, like all forms of internal sensing, is an imaginative construction, not a direct perception of some objective reality. Buddhists concluded long ago that the self is an illusion, and Seth has provided a scientific way of demonstrating this point. The same holds for free will: it is a hallucinatory mode of self-perception or, to use another popular expression, a user's illusion.[2]

As a philosopher, my first reaction to this theory concerns the status of this theory itself: is it—and what it claims about reality—also a controlled hallucination? If yes, why should we take it seriously as truth, as the description of the way things "really are"? If not, how can our mind step out of controlled manipulation? The paradox is that the very distinction between how we perceive/hallucinate reality and how this reality is in itself is part of our "hallucinatory" thinking (or, as Hegel put it, the distinction between for-us and in-itself is internal to for-us). Isn't the history of science itself the ultimate proof of it?

*

Sabine Hossenfelder has repeatedly formulated in some of her podcasts the claim of the extreme sceptic: we cannot be absolutely sure that the outside reality really exists, that it is not just a hallucination in my mind. I agree with her, but also at the ontological level. What we perceive in our everyday life as external reality is, as relativity theory and quantum mechanics have made abundantly clear, an appearance concealing a radically different reality. We try to formulate this different reality through modern science, but there is a radical uncertainty inscribed into the very heart of this reality: the more we try to reach for and grasp the real beneath our reality, the more we are dealing with symbolic constructs which do not fit what we experience as our reality. Just think about how in the past decades, quantum scientists have advocated totally incompatible theories: the Many Worlds theories, repeated Big Bangs, etc. It is as if we are cursed by a vicious cycle here: the more we want to grasp how things "really are in themselves," the more we get caught in intellectual speculations.

So my sad conclusion is that, while quantum physics provides the most adequate insight into the universe, the only moments when we are in touch with the Real are the moments of what Lacan called "subjective destitution" and/or what mystics called the "night of the world," the collapse of the symbolic universe. So we should fearlessly *reject* "objective reality": when reality dissolves in "subjective" fragments, *these fragments themselves fall back into the Real, losing their subjective consistency.* The paradox of the postmodern rejection of consistent Self resides in its ultimate result: we lose its opposite, objective reality itself, which gets transformed into a set of contingent subjective constructions. A true materialist should do the opposite: refuse to accept "objective reality" in order to undermine consistent subjectivity. The task is not to grasp how reality is "in itself," independently of our mind; the task is to locate our mind itself, inclusive of its antagonisms, gaps and tensions, *and* inclusive of its symbolic constructions of "objective reality," into a historical Real.

Alain Badiou[3] opposes mysticism and philosophy as the two modes of approaching the unity of being and existence (for Badiou, "being" designates the multiplicity grounded in a Void, i.e., a sphere of ontology whose modern secular form is pure mathematics, while "existence" is a transcendental category: a multiplicity "exists" if it has its place in a transcendental horizon which structures a domain of being, transforming meaningless multiplicity into an element of the order of meaning, of a potential subjective engagement). Mysticism asserts a direct "irrational" (or, rather, pre-rational) unity of being and existence: the unity of being as One is not constructed through a long process of rational development (as is the case with Hegel's logic which begins with pure being and ends with the rational totality of absolute Idea), it is immediately "felt" as an intuition. In other words, in mystical experience the beginning and end directly coincide, there is no work of reason needed to mediate them. In my view, however, a mystical experience is not that of the direct-intuitive unity but, on the contrary, the experience of a radical discordance, of a fall from unity, of the pure (pre-dialectical) absolute contradiction which opens up the space for every form of rational elaboration. Intuition of failure here paradoxically coincides with the failure of intuition.

In this sense I endorse John Millbank's characterization of my stance as that of "mystic materialism"—the "mystic" dimension has nothing to do with some obscure spiritualism, it simply points towards the "night of the world," the zero-level, the ground on which our universe thrives. I also want to emphasize the conjunction of the two terms, "mystical" and "materialism": since our perception of external reality is always mediated by the symbolic order and thus has the minimal status of a symbolic fiction, our only contact with what one cannot but naïvely call "reality as it is in itself" occurs in mystical experiences which brings us close to the very gap in the Real that establishes us as subjects. We should thus totally reject the equation of an authentic mystical experience with any kind of spiritualism: mystical experience is the only ultimate proof against solipsism, a proof that we are not alone, that we are embedded in material reality. To dispel the reproach that the recourse to mysticism is foreign to Lacan, one should point out that the reference to mysticism is a permanent feature of Lacan's teaching. Already in his first seminar, Lacan says about Angelus Silesius that

> the books of the *Cherubinic Wanderer* strike a transparent, crystalline note. It is one of the most significant moments in human meditation on being, a moment richer in resonances for me than the *Dark Night* of St John of the Cross, which everyone reads and no one understands.[4]

Mysticism then returns as a topic in Lacan's Seminar XX (*Encore*) where he deals with feminine sexuality. Lacan qualifies mysticism as "something serious" and locates his own writings as within the same order as the mystical: "mystical jaculations are neither idle chatter nor empty verbiage; they provide, all in all, some of the best reading one can find," with a footnote at the bottom of the page: "Add to that list Jacques Lacan's *Écrits*, because it's of the same order."[5] How are we to understand this? Lacan said in 1969 (a year after the fateful 1968): "You are, however strange this may appear, the cause of yourself. Only there is no self. Rather there is a divided self."[6] Lacan's logic is here clear: *objet a* is the object-cause of desire, but this weird object is the subject itself in its objectivized form, so the subject causes itself through *objet a*, and the basic division of the subject is this very division between $ and *a* which are the same thing in the form of lack and excess. All the paradoxes are grounded in this incompatibility of subject and *a*: *a* is the obstacle to my identity, a foreign stain in me, but this very obstacle causes me as the subject of desire . . .

In his Seminar XIV[7], Lacan mentions the "weird correspondence between subject and object" ("*l'etrange correspondance entre sujet et objet*")—why is this correspondence strange? For two interconnected reasons. First, this correspondence is not what philosophers usually mean by the correlation between subject and object—it is almost its opposite, a kind of negative correlation, since subject is defined precisely by being a non-object. Subject and object are two sides of the same coin, lack and excess; they cannot be "synthesized" so that excess will fill in the lack because they are strictly co-existent, one and the same thing at two different levels—if the lack were to be filled in, there would no longer be a subject, the subject would fall into reality as one of the objects. Second, this correspondence is not properly dialectical but a non-dialectical foundation, a gap which opens up and sustains the very space of dialectics, in some sense even its non-dialectical presupposition . . .

To clarify this crucial point, one should venture into the notion of a Thing which is not a part of our (transcendentally constituted) reality. In *Die Frage nach dem Ding*, his treatise on Kant's *Critique of Pure Reason*,[8] Heidegger restricts himself to "thing" in the sense of an empirical object, part of our transcendentally-constituted reality, without mentioning the Thing in the more radical Freud-Lacanian sense needed: the pre-ontological Real, the "immortal" horror not bound by finitude, a feature of imagination prior to fantasy, like Maupassant's *horla* or the alien from Ridley Scott's film of the same name. We should delineate here the two opposed philosophical senses of imagination. In Kant, imagination is a synthetic activity which is necessary for reality to manifest itself, a medium in which sensory data and pure reason come together—to quote Ulisses Razzante Vaccari: "This conciliatory function of imagination shows, via a synthesizing action, how the manifold may be then connected by knowledge as it pervades the manifold of the sensitive data and makes it available to the synthetic unity of apperception."[9] Imagination is thus transcendental, constitutive even of our perception of actual objects, and Heidegger focuses on this, reading imagination as pre-discursive Manifestness. In Lacan's terms, we could read this imagination as the fantasmatic support of reality.

In Hegel, imagination at its most radical is pre-ontological, the violent activity of tearing things apart, the infinite power of abstraction. One cannot avoid mentioning two often quoted passages, the first one from *Jenaer Realphilosophie* and the second one from the "Foreword" to *Phenomenology*. There is nothing more foreign to Hegel than the lamentation of the richness of reality that gets lost when we proceed to its conceptual grasping—recall

Hegel's already-quoted unambiguous celebration of the absolute power of Understanding:

> what is thus separated, and in a sense is unreal, is itself an essential moment; for just because the concrete fact is self-divided, and turns into unreality, it is something self-moving, self-active. The action of separating the elements is the exercise of the force of Understanding, the most astonishing and greatest of all powers, or rather the absolute power. The circle, which is self-enclosed and at rest, and, *qua* substance, holds its own moments, is an immediate relation, the immediate, continuous relation of elements with their unity, and hence arouses no sense of wonderment. But that an accident as such, when cut loose from its containing circumference,—that what is bound and held by something else and actual only by being connected with it,—should obtain an existence all its own, gain freedom and independence on its own account—this is the portentous power of the negative; it is the energy of thought, of pure Self.[10]

This celebration is in no way qualified, i.e., Hegel's point is not that this power is nonetheless later "sublated" into a subordinate moment of the unifying totality of Reason. The problem with Understanding is rather that it does not unleash this power to its fullest, that it takes it as external to the thing itself—like, in the above-quoted passage from *Phenomenology*, the standard notion that it is merely *our* Understanding ("mind") that separates in its imagination what in "reality" belongs together, so that the Understanding's "absolute power" is merely the power of our imagination which in no way concerns the reality of the thing so analyzed. We pass from Understanding to Reason not when this analyzing, tearing apart, is overcome in a synthesis which brings us back to the wealth of reality, but when this power of "tearing apart" is displaced from "merely our mind" into things themselves, as their inherent power of negativity. In this way, the dimension of the Imaginary returns in its grounding role, not as the site of imaginary identifications and self-recognition but as a (possible) name for the violent act of dismembering (the production of *le corps morcele* with its *membra disjecta*) which tears apart every organic unity. In a move further from Kant, imagination is asserted not just as synthesis but also as "analysis," the activity of tearing apart what seemed to belong together. Hegel formulated this process in his *Jenaer Realphilosophie*, where he writes about the "Night of the World":

> The human being is this night, this empty nothing, that contains everything in its simplicity—an unending wealth of many representations, images, of which none belongs to him—or which are not present. This night, the interior of nature, that exists here—pure self—in phantasmagorical representations, is night all around it, in which here shoots a bloody head— there another white ghastly apparition, suddenly here before it, and just so disappears. One catches sight of this night when one looks human beings in the eye—into a night that becomes awful.[11]

One should not be blinded by the poetic power of this description, but read it precisely. The first thing to note is how the objects which freely float around in this "night of the world" are *membra disjecta*, partial objects, objects detached from their organic Whole—is there not a strange echo between this description and Hegel's description of the negative power of Understanding which is able to abstract an entity (a process, a property) from its substantial context and treat it as if it has an existence of its own? It is thus as if, in the ghastly scenery of the "night of the world," we encounter something like *the power of Understanding in its natural state*, spirit in the guise of a *proto-spirit*—this, perhaps, is the most precise definition of horror: when a higher state of development violently inscribes itself in the lower state, in its ground/ presupposition, where it cannot but appear as a monstrous mess, a disintegration of order, a terrifying unnatural combination of natural elements. This is why for Hegel madness is not an accidental lapse, distortion, "illness" of human spirit, but something which is inscribed into the individual spirit's basic ontological constitution: to be a human means to be potentially mad:

> This interpretation of insanity as a necessarily occurring form or stage in the development of the soul is naturally not to be understood as if we were asserting that *every* mind, *every* soul, must go through this stage of extreme derangement. Such an assertion would be as absurd as to assume that because in the *Philosophy of Right* crime is considered as a necessary manifestation of the human will, therefore to commit crime is an inevitable necessity for *every* individual. Crime and insanity are *extremes*

which the human mind *in general* has to overcome in the course of its development.[12]

Although not a factual necessity, madness is a formal possibility constitutive of the human mind: it is something whose threat has to be overcome if we are to emerge as "normal" subjects, which means that "normality" can only arise as the overcoming of this threat. This is why, as Hegel put it a couple of pages later, "insanity must be discussed before the healthy, intellectual consciousness, although it has that consciousness for its *presupposition*."[13] In short, we do not all have to be mad in reality, but madness is the real of our psychic lives, a point to which our psychic lives necessarily refer in order to assert themselves as "normal."

Do we encounter this Real of madness as what Heidegger calls "the forgetting of the meaning of being"? This forgetting heralds "'the age of complete *meaninglessness*.' So, any retrieval of the question must be a path towards a renewed meaningfulness of being."(34) But what if metaphysics is precisely the stance of (not just "letting be" what is there in its meaninglessness but) a desperate search to find a meaning that sustains beings? So how does the horizon of meaningfulness/disclosure relate to Sartre's nausea? Is nausea simply the traumatic experience of being outside a disclosure of meaning? It's not so simple: the disgusting thick absurd presence is not reality in itself, it remains fully subjective in its substantiality—the true in-itself closer to quantum waves, their pure non-substantial oscillations? Here is a key passage from Sartre's *Nausea*:

> This moment was extraordinary. I was there, motionless, paralyzed, plunged in a horrible ecstasy. But at the heart of this ecstasy, something new had just appeared; I understood the nausea, I possessed it. To tell the truth, I did not formulate my discoveries to myself. But I think it would be easy for me to put them in words now. The essential point is contingency. I mean that by definition existence is not necessity. To exist is simply . . . to be there; existences appear, let themselves be *encountered*, but you can never *deduce* them.[14]

Sartre is here at the opposite end of Andrei Tarkovsky whose films enact the impossible combination, divine experience in disgusting wet mud. We should thus banish the fear that, once we ascertain that reality is the infinitely divisible, substanceless void within a void, "matter will disappear." What the digital information revolution, the biogenetic revolution, and the quantum revolution in physics all share is that they mark the reemergence of what, for want of a better term, I am tempted to call *postmetaphysical idealism*. It is as if Chesterton's insight into how the materialist struggle for the full assertion of reality, against its subordination to any "higher" metaphysical order, culminates in the loss of reality itself: what began as the assertion of material reality in modern sciences ended up in the realm of pure formulas of quantum physics. Is this really, however, a form of idealism? Since the radical materialist stance asserts that there is no World, that the World in its Whole is Nothing, materialism has nothing to do with the presence of damp, dense matter—its proper figures are, rather, constellations in which matter seems to "disappear," like the pure oscillations of superstrings or quantum vibrations. On the contrary, if we see in raw, inert matter more than an imaginary screen, we always secretly endorse some kind of spiritualism.

As we have just seen, the supreme expression of such spiritual materialism are the films of Andrei Tarkovsky: when one of their heroes has a spiritual experience, it is not by way of an effort to elevate himself above the earthly reality, gazing up towards heaven or a distant horizon; on the contrary, he lies flat on humid earth, soaking his face in mud and dirty water . . . Needless to add that such spiritualization of matter is the very opposite of the basic stance of modern science in which "matter" is also "spiritualized," but in a totally different way: matter becomes an abstraction formalized in mathematical formulas. Here we encounter another crucial aspect of the opposition between idealism and materialism: materialism is not the assertion of inert material density in its humid heaviness—such a "materialism" can always serve as a support for gnostic spiritualist obscurantism. In contrast, a true materialism joyously assumes the "disappearance of matter," the fact that there is only void. So what if we turn around the perspective and celebrate the exit from direct being-in-the-world, the shift from engaged care to cold observation of *Vorhandenes*, as a big achievement which opens up the path to modern science?

Another mode of such pre-ontological Real can be provided at the vocal level. In the opening sequence of David Lynch's *Blue Velvet*[15], we hear the uncanny noise that emerges when we approach the real. This noise is difficult to locate in reality. In order to determine its status, one is tempted to evoke contemporary cosmology which speaks of noises at the borders of the universe; these noises are not simply internal to the universe—they are remainders or last echoes of the Big Bang that created the universe itself. The ontological status of this noise is more interesting than it may appear, since it subverts the fundamental notion of the "open," infinite universe that defines the space of Newtonian physics. That is to say, the modern notion of the "open" universe is based on the hypothesis that every positive entity (noise, matter) occupies some (empty) space; it hinges on the difference between space as void and positive entities which occupy it, "fill it out." Space is here phenomenologically conceived as something that exists prior to the entities which "fill it out." If we destroy or remove the matter that occupies a given space, this space as void remains. The primordial noise, the last remainder of the Big Bang, is on the contrary constitutive of space itself: it is not a noise "in" space but a noise that keeps space open as such. If, therefore, we were to erase this noise, we would not get the "empty space" which was filled out by it. Space itself, the receptacle for every "inner-worldly" entity, would vanish. This noise is, in a sense, the "sound of silence."

Along the same lines, the fundamental noise in Lynch's films is not simply caused by objects that are part of reality; rather, it forms the ontological horizon or frame of reality itself, i.e., the texture that holds reality together. Were this noise to be eradicated, reality itself would collapse, from the "open" infinite universe of Cartesian-Newtonian physics, we are thus back to the pre-modern "closed" universe, encircled, bounded, by a fundamental "noise." We encounter this same noise in the nightmare sequence of The *Elephant Man*. It transgresses the borderline that separates interior from exterior, i.e., the extreme externality of a machine uncannily coincides with the utmost intimacy of the bodily interior, with the rhythm of heart palpitations. This noise also appears after the camera enters the hole in the elephant-man's hood, which stands for the gaze. The reversal of reality into the real corresponds to the reversal of the look (the subject looking at reality) into gaze, i.e., it occurs when we enter the "black hole," the crack in the texture of reality. And it seems that there is no space for such pre-ontological real in Heidegger's thought. For Heidegger, metaphysics ultimately means that being must be understood as what could be the content of an assertion. The meaning of Being is then understood to be intelligibility or knowability, and the corresponding notion of truth is what Heidegger calls "correctness," correspondence with the beings about which assertoric claims are made.

(70)

But is then openness/disclosure primordial with regard to *logos*? Is truth as *aletheia* prior to truth as *adequatio* of predicative statements to reality? Yes, but it is not prior to language itself: there is a pre-predicative mode of language, which is why language is "the house of Being." Hegel also complicates things here: speculative statement has to be read twice, its truth emerges only through its failure, since its enunciation is inscribed into its enunciated content. Can we then say that if disclosure only happens when language is not just designating something but fails in this—or, to put it in more formal terms, that differentiality includes pure difference? This is why for Hegel true thinking means thinking in language against language, this is why he regularly resorts to word-plays and (from the standpoint of language rules) "meaningless" misreadings.

Although Heidegger is the ultimate transcendental philosopher, there are mysterious passages where he ventures into this pre-transcendental domain. In the elaboration of this notion of an untruth [*ethe*] older than the very dimension of truth, Heidegger emphasizes how man's "stepping into the essential unfolding of truth" is a "transformation of the being of man in the sense of a derangement [*Ver-rueckung*—going mad] of his position among beings."[16] The "derangement" to which Heidegger refers is, of course, not a psychological or clinical category of madness: it signals a much more radical, properly ontological reversal/aberration, when, in its very foundation, the universe itself is in a way "out of joint," thrown off its rails. What is crucial here is to remember that Heidegger wrote these lines in the years of his intensive reading of Schelling's *Treatise on Human Freedom*, a text which discerns the origin of Evil precisely in a kind of ontological madness, in the "derangement" of man's position among beings (his self-centeredness), as a necessary intermediate step ("vanishing mediator") in the passage from "prehuman nature" to our symbolic universe: "man, in his very essence, is a *katastrophe*—a reversal that turns him away from the genuine essence. Man is the only catastrophe in the midst of beings."[17]

However, at this crucial point where in some sense everything is decided, we should make a step further with regard to Heidegger's formulation—"a derangement of his position among beings"—a step indicated by some other formulations of Heidegger himself. It may appear clear what Heidegger aims at by the quoted formulation: man as *Da-Sein* (the "being-there" of Being, the place of the disclosure of Being) is an entity irreducibly rooted in his body (I use here the masculine form since it is at work in Heidegger). With a little bit of rhetorical exaggeration, one can say that Heidegger's "no Being without Being-There as the place of its disclosure" is his version of Hegel's "one should grasp the Absolute not only as Substance but also as Subject." However, if the disclosure of the entire domain of entities is rooted in a singular entity, then something "deranged" is taking place: a particular entity is the exclusive site at which all entities appear, acquire their Being—so, to put it brutally, you kill a man and you simultaneously "kill Being" ... This short-circuit between the Clearance of Being and a particular entity introduces a catastrophic derangement into the order of beings: because man, rooted in his body, cannot look at entities from outside, every disclosure of Being, every Clearance, has to be grounded in untruth (concealment/hiddenness). The ultimate cause of the derangement that pertains to *Da-Sein* thus resides in the fact that *Dasein* is by definition embodied, and, towards the end of his life, Heidegger conceded that, for philosophy, "the body phenomenon is the most difficult problem":

> The bodily [*das Leibliche*] in the human is not something animalistic. The manner of understanding that accompanies it is something that metaphysics up till now has not touched on.[18]

One is tempted to risk the hypothesis that it is precisely the psychoanalytic theory which was the first to touch on this key question: is not the Freudian eroticized body, sustained by libido, organized around erogenous zones, precisely the non-animalistic, non-biological body? Is it not this (and not the animalistic) body that is the proper object of psychoanalysis? Heidegger totally misses this dimension when in his *Zollikoner Seminare*, he dismisses Freud as a causal determinist:

He postulates for the conscious human phenomena that they can be explained without gaps, i.e., the continuity of causal connections. Since there are no such connections "in the consciousness," he has to invent "the unconscious," in which there have to be the causal links without gaps.[19]

This interpretation may appear correct: it could be said that Freud tries to discover a causal order in what appears to our consciousness as a confused and contingent array of mental facts (slips of the tongue, dreams, clinical symptoms) and, in this way, to close the chain of causal links that run our psyche. However, Heidegger completely misses the way the Freudian "unconscious" is grounded in the traumatic encounter of an Otherness whose intrusion precisely *breaks*, interrupts, the continuity of the causal link: what we get in the "unconscious" is not a complete, uninterrupted, causal link, but the repercussions, the after-shocks, of traumatic interruptions. What Freud calls "symptoms" are ways to deal with a traumatic rupture, while "fantasy" is a formation destined to cover up this cut. That's why for Heidegger a finite human being a priori cannot reach the inner peace and calm of Buddhist Enlightenment (nirvana). A world is disclosed to us against the background of an ontological catastrophe: "man is the only catastrophe in the midst of beings." Or, as Heidegger would have put it, there is no Being (*Seyn*) without Being-There (*Dasein*) as the place at which Being is disclosed. This is why we should reject reading the Oriental thought through Heidegger. Such an approach has to overlook the basic feature of *Dasein*, finitude and being-thrown into an historically determined mode of the disclosure of being which is not grounded in any transcendent ultimate Foundation (divine Will, evolutionary laws of the universe . . .)—it is in its innermost an "event," something that epochally occurs, takes place, "just happens."

It was William Richardson who, drawing on his unique knowledge of Heidegger and Lacan, stated that "when I hear Heidegger talk about *lethe* as 'older' than the essence of truth, I hear what Lacan means by the real." Heidegger himself, in the elaboration of this notion of an untruth older than the very dimension of truth, emphasizes how man's "stepping into the essential unfolding of truth" is a "transformation of the being of man in the sense of a derangement [*Ver-rueckung*] of his position among beings." Erring/untruth is the innermost feature of the event of truth itself, and the very opening paragraph of John Sallis's remarkable essay on the monstrosity of truth directly tackles this difficult point: "What if truth were monstrous? What if it were monstrosity itself, the very condition, the very form, of everything monstrous, everything deformed? But, first of all, itself essentially deformed, monstrous in its very essence? What if there were within the very essence of truth something essentially other than truth, a divergence from nature within nature, true monstrosity?"[20] We are as far as imaginable here from the inner peace acquired in any form of Hindu or Buddhist meditation.

But, again, here we have to risk a step further: if man is the only catastrophe, does this mean that, prior to the arrival of humanity, there was no catastrophe, that nature was a balanced order derailed only by human *hubris*? (By catastrophe I don't mean ontic disasters like asteroids hitting the earth but more radical derangement of the entire network of forms of life.) The problem is that if man is the only catastrophe "in the midst of beings," and if beings are only disclosed to us as humans, then the very space of non-catastrophic beings that surround humans is already ontologically grounded in the catastrophe that is the rise of man.

Now we face the key question: is man as the only catastrophe in the midst of beings an exception, so that if we assume the impossible point-of-view of looking at the universe from a safe distance, we see a universal texture of beings just not deranged by catastrophes (since man is a catastrophe only from his own standpoint, as the exception that grounds his access to beings)? In this case, we are back at the Kantian position: reality "in itself," outside the Clearing within which it appears to us, is unknowable, we can only speculate about it the way Heidegger himself does it when he plays with the idea that there is a kind of ontological pain in nature itself. Or should we take Heidegger's speculation seriously, so that the catastrophe is not only man but already nature in itself, and in man as the being-of-speech this catastrophe that grounds reality in itself only comes to word? (Quantum physics offers its own version of a catastrophe that grounds reality: the broken symmetry, the disturbance of the void by quantum oscillations; theosophical speculations offers another version: the self-division or Fall of Godhead itself which gives birth to our world.)

Now we are on theological ground. Fredric Jameson was right to proclaim predestination the most interesting theological concept for Marxism:

predestination indicates the retroactive causality which characterizes a properly dialectical historical process. In a similar way, we should not be afraid to search for the traces of a meta-transcendental (dialectical materialist) approach in the theosophical speculations of Meister Eckhart, Jacob Boehme or F.W.J. Schelling. For a Kantian, of course, such speculations are nothing more than empty *Schwarmerei*, enthusiastic bla-bla about nothing, while for us, it is only here that we touch the Real.[21]

If we endorse this option, then we have to draw the only possible conclusion: every image or construction of "objective reality," of the way it is in itself, "independently of us," is one of the ways being is disclosed to us, and is as such already in some basic sense "anthropocentric," grounded in (and at the same time obfuscating) the catastrophe that constitutes us. The main candidate for getting close to how reality is "in itself" are formulas of relativity theory and quantum physics—the result of complex experimental and intellectual work to which nothing corresponds in our direct experience of reality . . . The only "contact" we have with the Real "independent of us" is our very separation from it, the radical derangement, what Heidegger calls catastrophe. The paradox is that what unites us with the Real "in itself" is the very gap that we experience as our separation from it. (The same goes for Christianity where the only way to experience unity with god is to identify with Christ suffering on the cross, i.e., with the point at which god is divided from himself.) And this dynamic of experiencing the gap itself as the point of unity is the basic feature of Hegel's dialectic—which is why the space beyond Heidegger's thought that we designated as the space beyond the transcendental is the space to which Hegelian thought belongs. This is also the space for thinking which cannot be reduced to positive science—and in this space, the danger of falling into New Age obscurantism is omnipresent. Since one can easily ignore the possibility that a divinity will directly and openly appear to us, humans, in a way that will leave no doubts about whom we are dealing with, one cannot but concur with Cixin Liu, author of *The Three-Body Problem*, when he said that he would like people to grapple with what he thinks is the "greatest uncertainty facing humanity"—the potential that there is life on other planets and that we could make contact with them at any time.

I hope they realize that there's this one thing that may not happen for the next 10,000 years, or it may happen tomorrow morning ... And that once it happens, our world and our lives will change completely. I hope that the series of 3 Body Problem will make people look up at the starry sky from their busy and trivial lives, even if it's just for a moment.[22]

I recently stumbled upon a rather imbecilic Rightist podcast against Hegel[23] which nonetheless gets one thing right: the origin of the entire line of thought from Hegel to Marx and Communism resides in the Rhine mystics, from Meister Eckhart to Jacob Boehme. In contrast to previous (and later) mystics (like the neo-Platonists) who practice the bottom-up approach (our material reality emerges through the gradual process of the fall from the supreme divine Absolute), the Rhine mystics practice a top-down: their starting point is humans as fallen beings since god himself needs humans to become actual god (although—or, rather, precisely because—humans stand for fall, sin)—as Eckhart put it: not only is god the origin of man but god in his full actuality is at the same time born in man. Of especial significance here is Jacob Boehme whom Hegel described as "the first German philosopher." Boehme asserts the embrace of the *Ungrund*, the Nothing considered as a pure ungrounding—it is this nothing which generates a tragedy in God Himself, and in so doing generates in the divine justice the tragedy of its own undoing in actuality. Every thing, from the Godhead down, is comprehended as enclosing within it already the seed of its undoing.

The notion of the *Ungrund*, of the abyss, without foundation, dark and irrational, prior to being, is an attempt to provide an answer to the basic question of all questions, the question concerning the origin of the world and of the arising of evil. The *Ungrund* is interwoven freedom: it is impossible to separate them, the *Ungrund* as a primordial freedom is indeterminate even by God. Boehme's teaching about the *Ungrund* and freedom is an attempt to comprehend the world-creation from the inner life of the Divinity: the world-creation bears a relationship to the inner life of the Divine Trinity, and cannot be for It something completely external. The principle of evil thus acquires an actual seriousness and tragic aspect. Boehme senses God not only as love, but also as anger, wrath. He senses within God a poignant and harsh quality: the

God of the Old Testament is wrath, while Christ is love. Boehme preaches a torment in the dark abyss, which the light of Christ has to conquer.

Badiou perceptively turns around the theological premise that god created the world out of nothing: "in the theological discourse this is how God created the world: out of nothing. But I'd still say that the greatest example of creation ex nihilo is the creation of God. It was God, rather than the world, that was created out of nothing! Because if God had existed, the creation of the world wouldn't have been a problem. God is, by definition, limitless. His power is infinite, so he could well have created something out of nothing. The problem lies rather with us: how could we, poor finite, mortal humans, create something out of nothing?"[24] My putative reply to this claim is: but god as infinitely powerful precisely could NOT create something out of nothing (if we ignore the thesis that "nothing" is not just nothing but an unformed mass, like Plato's *chora*). God as infinitely powerful stands for unconditional actuality where there is no space for creation—in the Talmud we can already read that god should first contract himself and create the nothing itself, and this contraction is a kind of self-limitation of god.

So, to resume, out of nature god is the Nothing; for from out of nature is the Nothing, which is an eye of eternity, a groundless eye, which stands nowhere nor sees, for it is the *Ungrund* and the selfsame eye is a will, i.e., a longing for manifestation, to discern the Nothing. But this is a Nothing which is "a hunger to be something." And together with this the *Ungrund* is freedom. Within the darkness of the *Ungrund* there is ablaze a fire and this is freedom, a freedom pregnant with potential. Freedom is contrary to nature, but nature has issued forth from freedom. Freedom is a semblance of the Nothing, but from it issues something.[25] What this means is that, in what is effectively a proto-Hegelian move, the gap that separates god from the fallen world is transposed into god himself, as the irreducible gap between god and the Nothing, the dark abyss that precedes him.

It is against this background that we should appreciate Peter Sloterdijk's reply to my brutal question about how he relates to god: "It wasn't me who abandoned god, god abandoned me, he pushed me away, he lost interest in me."[26] This statement is far from a joke, it has to be taken very seriously even (or even especially) by an atheist: becoming an atheist is not a simple subjective free decision, my entire symbolic space is transformed—or, to repeat Deleuze, you can only choose (to drop god) if you are already chosen (i.e., if god dropped you). Abandoning god is thus at its most basic not a primordial act but a *reaction* to "being abandoned by god." And this is what the naïve surface level of Enlightenment thought doesn't see: in order for us to enter the space of rational argumentation, something has to happen in the space of the big Other in which we dwell—this is a crucial moment of the dialectics of Enlightenment.

So what is the solution? In 1990, the Yugoslav rock band Riblja Čorba (Fish Broth) published a song "Tito je vaš (Tito Is Yours)". Although the title ironically subverted the official slogan "Mi smo Titovi / Tito je naš (We are Tito's / Tito is ours)," there was no direct attack on Tito in the lyrics, just an irreverent enumeration of his characteristics ("Comrade Tito was not a human creature / Comrade Tito had a White Court / Comrade Tito was a good comrade / And he didn't make us indebted . . ."). The song was in itself totally incompatible with the official celebration of Tito, but opinions varied widely about how critical the song was since it contained no direct denunciation of Tito as a criminal Communist dictator. However, this debate totally missed the point: the last lines of the song—"Tito is yours / and you are Tito's / and I am not guilty for that"—clearly formulate the position of externality implied by the irreverent enumeration of Tito's characteristics. Such an externality is much more radical than a dissident critique of Tito which continues to participate in the struggle between those who are for Tito and those who are against him, while the final lines of the song are a kind of negation of negation: we are simply outside the space of the conflict. Such a stance is needed more than ever today.

The Violence of Truth

However, to avoid here a fatal misunderstanding, standing outside the space of the conflict does not involve a peaceful neutrality elevated above the conflict: this outside can only be reached through an act of extreme violence, of negating the common space shared by both sides of a conflict. The standard liberal motto apropos violence—it is sometimes necessary to resort to it, but it is never legitimate—is not sufficient: from the radical emancipatory perspective, one should turn this motto around. For the oppressed, violence is always legitimate (since their very status is the result of the violence they are exposed to), but never necessary—it is always a matter of strategic consideration to use violence against the enemy or not.[27] What does this amount to? Patrick Stewart (a Left-wing Socialist actor who superbly played Lenin in the 1974 TV series *Fall of Eagles*) says as Lenin (and the imagined words fit the real Lenin perfectly):

> Objectively, the enemy can be your best friend, your lover, your party colleague, the chairman of your local branch, the editor of your party journal. The battle that's coming now is not with the tsar, it is with ourselves.[28]

I first misread these lines, reading them not the way they are obviously meant, as a globalized suspicion ("your enemy can be even your best friend, one among your closest circle"), but in the opposite sense: your greatest friend is the one whom you perceive as your enemy. However, my misreading also delivers its own truth: since the goal of revolutionary activity is to bring about actual revolution (taking power), the enemy's actions which unwittingly create conditions for the revolution are very helpful. That's why Lenin was horrified by Stolypin's reforms, which included granting the right of private land ownership to the peasantry and which led to unprecedented growth and reform of the Russian state, thus postponing the revolution for which Lenin was hoping for decades. Lenin was relieved by Stolypin's death: he immediately grasped that the final result of his reforms would have been a satisfied peasant class with no will to engage in revolutionary activity. Stolypin was thus the true enemy, and the hardliners who canceled his reforms after his death were objectively our friends . . .

The point is thus not to engage in unconstrained physical violence but to tell the truth, *aussprechen was ist*, "state the facts"(Lenin), to *unleash the violence of words which shatter and mobilize people*. The actual political violence that may follow should be practiced in a Gandhian way, taking into account all the usual humanitarian considerations—but no such constraints hold for the Word at its beginning. Consider what happened in late July 2024 when a number of ministers and Members of Knesset, as well as journalists and TV commentators, criticized a raid by the IDF's military police on the Sde Teiman base in the south of Israel, in which it arrested a number of reservists accused of abusing imprisoned Palestinians.[29] These arrests, which also triggered large public protests in Israel, happened after, horrified at what they saw, some Israeli reservists heroically rendered public that, among other forms of abuse, the security personnel on the Sde Teiman base was torturing Palestinian prisoners by pushing metal sticks into their rectum, which made some of them bleed to death. Beyond the hideous, inexcusable behaviour perpetrated by "the only democracy in the Middle East," there is the fact that the entire affair was downplayed, almost ignored, in our big Western media. This willful ignorance—the very opposite of simply not knowing it—sounds the death knell of the Western liberal democracy. Democracy will have to be reinvented—by violence, if necessary.

*

In the history of radical politics, violence is usually associated with the so-called Jacobin legacy which, for this very reason, is dismissed as something that should be abandoned if we are truly to begin from the beginning again. Even many of today's (post-)Marxists are embarrassed by the so-called Jacobin legacy of centralized state terror, and want to free Marx from it, proposing an authentic good "liberal" Marx who was later obfuscated by Lenin—it is, so the story goes, Lenin who (re)introduced into Marxism the Jacobin legacy, thus falsifying Marx's libertarian spirit . . . But is it so? Let us take a closer look at how the Jacobins effectively opposed the recourse to a majority vote on behalf of those who talk on behalf of the eternal Truth (how "totalitarian" . . .). How could Jacobins, the partisans of unity and of the struggle against factions and divisions, justify this rejection?

> The entire difficulty resides in how to distinguish between the voice of truth, even if it is minoritary, and the factional voice which seeks only to divide artificially to conceal the truth.[30]

Robespierre's answer is: the truth is irreducible to number (counting), it can be experienced also in solitude: those who proclaim a truth they experienced should not be considered as factionists, but as sensible and courageous people. In this case of attesting the truth, he said in the Assemblee on December 28,

1792, any invocation of majority or minority is nothing but a means to "reduce to silence those whom one designated by this term 'minority'": "Minority has everywhere an eternal right: to render audible the voice of truth." It is deeply significant that Robespierre made this statement in the course of the Assemblee nationale apropos the trial of the king. Girondins proposed a "democratic" solution: in such a difficult case, one should make an "appeal to the people": one should convoke local assemblies all around France and ask them to vote on how to deal with the king, only such a move will give legitimacy to the trial. Robespierre's answer was that such an "appeal to the people" effectively cancels the sovereign will of the people which, through the insurrection and revolution, had already made itself known and changed the very nature of the French state, bringing about the Republic.

Robespierre's argumentation effectively points forward to Lenin who, in his writings of 1917, saves his utmost acerbic irony for those who engage in the endless search for some kind of "guarantee" for the revolution. This guarantee assumes two main forms: either the reified notion of social Necessity (one should not risk the revolution too early; one has to wait for the right moment, when the situation is "mature" with regard to the laws of historical development: "it is too early for the Socialist revolution, the working class is not yet mature") or the normative ("democratic") legitimacy ("the majority of the population is not on our side, so the revolution would not really be democratic")—as Lenin repeatedly puts it, as if, before the revolutionary agent risks the seizure of the state power, it should get the permission from some figure of the big Other (organize a referendum which will ascertain that the majority supports the revolution).

With Lenin, as with Lacan, a revolution *ne s'autorise que d'elle-meme*: one should assume the revolutionary act not covered by the big Other—the fear of taking power "prematurely," the search for the guarantee, is the fear of the abyss of the act. Therein resides the ultimate dimension of what Lenin incessantly denounces as "opportunism," and his wager is that "opportunism" is a position which is in itself, inherently, false, masking the fear to accomplish the act with the protective screen of "objective" facts, laws, or norms, which is why the first step in combating it is to announce it clearly: "What, then, is to be done? We must *aussprechen was ist*, 'state the facts,' admit the truth that there is a tendency, or an opinion, in our Central Committee . . ."[31]

Especially when we are dealing with "strong truths" (*les verities fortes*), shattering insights, pronouncing them entails symbolic violence. When *la patrie est en danger*, Robespierre said, one should fearlessly state the fact that "the nation is betrayed. This truth is now known to all Frenchmen": "Lawgivers, the danger is immanent; the reign of truth has to begin: we are courageous enough to tell you this; be courageous enough to hear it." In such a situation, there is no space for a neutral third position—in his speech celebrating the dead of the August 10, 1792, abbe Gregoire evoked the proverb:

> there are people who are so good that they are worthless; and in a revolution which engages in the struggle of freedom against despotism, a neutral man is a pervert who, without any doubt, waits for how the battle will turn out to decide which side to take.

Before we dismiss these lines as "totalitarian," let us recall a later example when the French *patrie* was *en danger*: the situation after the French defeat in 1940 when none other than general de Gaulle, in his famous radio address from London, announced to the French people the "strong truth" (France is defeated, but the war is not over) Against the Petainist collaborators. When de Gaulle, in his historic act, refused to acknowledge the capitulation to Germans and continued to resist, he claimed that it was only he, not the Vichy regime, who spoke on behalf of the true France (on behalf of true France as such, not on behalf of the "majority of the French"!), what he was saying was deeply true even if it was "democratically" not only without legitimization but clearly opposed to the opinion of the majority of the French people. (And the same goes for Germany: it was the tiny minority actively resisting Hitler which stood for Germany, not the active Nazis and also not the undecided opportunists.)

There is no reason to despise democratic elections; the point is only to insist that there are not per se an indication of Truth—as a rule, they tend to reflect the predominant doxa determined by the hegemonic ideology. There can be democratic elections which enact an event of Truth—the election in which, against the sceptic-cynical inertia, the majority momentarily "awakens" and votes against the hegemonic ideological opinion; however, the very exceptional status of such a surprising electoral result proves that elections as such are not a medium of Truth.

This position of a minority which stands for All is more than ever actual today, in our post-political epoch in which the plurality of opinions reigns: under such conditions, the universal Truth is by definition a minority position. As Sophie Wahnich points out, in a democracy corrupted by media, this is what "the freedom of the press without the duty to resist" amounts to: "The right to say anything in a political relativism instead of a demanding and sometimes even lethal ethics of truth." In such a situation, the uncompromisingly-insisting voice of truth (about ecology, about biogenetics, about AI, about the excluded . . .) cannot but appear as "irrational" in its lack of consideration for the opinions of others, in its refusal of the spirit of pragmatic compromises, in its apocalyptic finality.

What grounds a truth is the experience of suffering and courage, sometimes in solitude, not the number and force of majority. This, of course, does not mean that there are infallible criteria for the truth: the assertion of Truth involves a kind of wager, a risky decision, one should carve out its path, sometimes even enforce it. Those who tell the truth are as a rule not understood at first, they struggle (also with themselves) and seek for the proper language to tell it. It is the full recognition of this dimension of risk and wager, of the absence of any external guarantee, which distinguishes the authentic truth-engagement from any form of "totalitarianism" or "fundamentalism."

But, again: how are we to distinguish clearly this "ethics of truth" from the sectarian attempts to impose one's own position upon all others? How can we be sure that the voice of the minoritarian "part of no-part" is effectively the voice of universal truth and not merely a particular grievance? The first thing to bear in mind here is that the truth we are dealing with is not "objective" truth, but the self-relating truth about one's own subjective position; as such, this truth is an engaged truth, measured not by its factual accuracy but by the way it affects the subjective position of enunciation. In his Seminar 18 on "a discourse which would not be of a semblance," Lacan provided a succinct definition of the truth of interpretation in psychoanalysis: "Interpretation is not tested by a truth that would decide by yes or no, it unleashes truth as such. It is only true inasmuch as it is truly followed." There is nothing "theological" in this precise formulation, only the insight into the properly dialectical unity of theory and practice in (not only) psychoanalytic interpretation: the "test" of the analyst's interpretation is in the truth-effect it unleashes in the patient.

This, of course, brings us back to the pre-ontological Real: what the truth-effect transforms is not external reality but the Real as the abyss that sustains the dimension of subjectivity. Or, in the terms of quantum mechanics: instead of changing reality, intervene in the space of quantum waves. Recall the line from Virgil quoted at the beginning of Freud's *Interpretation of Dreams*: "If I cannot sway the heavens I will move the underground." Instead of directly changing reality, the analyst makes his analysand move the Real of his unconscious underground.

3

Heidegger's politics of finitude

Heidegger interprets Kant's transcendental schematism, perhaps the most interesting—and simultaneously the most enigmatic—part of Kant's first *Critique*, as a mode of disclosure of Being. A transcendental schema is "the procedural rule by which a category or pure, non-empirical concept is associated with a sense impression. A private, subjective intuition is thereby discursively thought to be a representation of an external object."[1] The reason a schema is needed is that "whenever two things are totally different from each other, yet must interact, there must be some common characteristic that they share in order to somehow relate to one another."[2] In this sense, schemata "are similar to adapters. Just as adapters are devices for fitting together incompatible parts, schemata connect empirical concepts with the perceptions from which they were derived"—a simple example: the category of "substance" has sense for us only if we "schematize" it as the permanent existence of a certain object in time; "substance" is what remains the same in the flow of temporal changes. Schematism is thus grounded in the subject's finitude, in the duality of spontaneous notional activity and passive exposure to sensual impressions which the subject cannot overcome owing to its finitude. Does this mean that schematism disappears, that it is not needed, with Hegel where the notion immanently generates all its content, so that there is no external Otherness affecting the subject? Such an understanding relies on a false notion of Hegel's idealism as a direct and complete reign of concepts which are able to "swallow" (mediate, reflexively appropriate) all external content.

To elucidate this, a detour through Lacan may be of some help and for a precise reason: Lacan's notion of desire is Kantian. There is no relationship between desire and its object, desire is about the gap that forever separates it from its object, it is about the lacking object. So is the best description of Lacan's central project not that of a *critique of pure desire*, where the term "critique" is to be understood in its precise Kantian sense: maintaining the gap that forever separates every empirical ("pathological") object of desire from its "impossible" object-cause whose place has to remain empty? In contrast to Kant, for whom our capacity to desire is thoroughly "pathological" (since, as he repeatedly stresses, there is no a priori link between an empirical object and the pleasure this object generates in the subject), Lacan claims that there is a "pure faculty of desire," since desire does have a non-pathological, a priori object-cause—this object, of course, is what Lacan calls *objet petit a*.

Here enters what we could call Lacan's sexual schematism—which, of course, works in a way which is different, almost inverted, with regard to Kant's schematism. For Lacan, the universal fact is not some set of symbolic norms but the fact that there is no sexual relationship, and the scheme is not universal but unique, an individual fantasy invented to render a sexual relation possible. Fantasy does not simply realize a desire in a hallucinatory way: rather, its function is similar to that of Kantian "transcendental schematism"—a fantasy constitutes our desire, provides its coordinates, i.e., it literally "teaches us how to desire." To put it in somewhat simplified terms: fantasy does not mean that when I desire a strawberry cake and cannot get it in reality, I imagine eating it; fantasy is what tells me that *I desire a strawberry cake in the first place*. This role of fantasy hinges on the fact that "there is no sexual relationship," no universal formula or matrix guaranteeing a harmonious sexual relationship with one's partner: on account of the lack of this universal formula, every subject has to invent a fantasy of his own, a "private" formula for the sexual relationship—for a man, the relationship with a woman is possible only inasmuch as she fits his formula.

This brings us to a possible Hegelian reading of schematism: there is no direct "synthesis" between concept and empirical intuitions, concepts cannot directly penetrate/mediate empirical content, so there has to be a mediating moment, in the same sense that the unity of god and man can only be enacted through the figure of Christ who is a kind of "scheme" rendering it possible for god to get over his meaningless transcendence and provide meaning to human reality. And, again, the Kantian reading would have insisted on the duality of god and world, on their radically different nature, which is why a mediator is needed—not a mediator as a link between two different worlds which exist independently of it but as the third element of a dialectical triad, as a medium through which the two opposed poles only exist. To put it pointedly, there is no god which precedes Christ, it is only through the mediation of Christ (i.e., through his death!) that god fully actualizes itself.

This brings us to finitude. Kant can perceive finitude only as the finitude of the transcendental subject who is constrained by schematism, by the temporal limitations of transcendental synthesis; i.e., for him, the only finitude is the finitude of the subject, he does not consider the option that *the very categories he is dealing with can be "finite,"* i.e., that they remain categories of abstract Understanding, and are not yet the truly infinite categories of speculative Reason. God conceived as opposed (and external) to finite reality is itself finite, the only true infinity is that of their mediator itself. The task is thus the Hegelian one: not to "overcome" the finitude (the horizon of schematism) but to transpose it into the Thing (Absolute) itself. The mess of partial objects that appears in Hegel's quote about the "night of the world" is the real in its pre-schematized mode, Imagination prior to "synthetic" fantasy/meaningfulness ... Although there is a giant gap that separates this non-schematized chaos of the "night of the world" from Heidegger's notion of finitude and historicity, does Heidegger not also provide a radical notion of how every version of universal Destiny relies on a historical contingency? *Dasein* is a being

> with no inherent teleology or universal or even available ground (an answer to the question of why what fundamentally matters in the world does or ought to matter). What originally matters is inextricable from our thrownness into a certain historical world, so what comes to matter is a question of contingency.... So, the only possible constancy to a life (and so the only way Dasein as some sort of whole is available to itself) is a background resolve, an always underlying readiness for anxiety and an

unwillingness to accept in such an attunement whenever called on the tranquilizing normalcy of the everyday, inauthentic world of Das Man.

(121)

But do everyday engagement and care in our life-world not also provide a kind of "tranquilizing normalcy"? Heidegger often evokes Novalis's notion of homelessness (longing for home)—but what if the fact that what appears as "mattering" to us is radically contingent indicates that homelessness is the founding gesture of becoming human, with nothing beneath it? For Heidegger, every disclosure of "mattering" is radically contingent, rooted in a specific historical situation, which means that there is no space in Heidegger for some universal "matterings" like human rights, freedom, dignity, etc. Here Heidegger is a true anti-Habermas: every "home" is the obfuscation of the primordial homelessness, so there is no big Other of transcendental-pragmatic rules of communication and interaction on which we could and should rely independently of our home. Pippin is thus right in characterizing Heidegger's approach as "dramatically isolating or individualizing":

> A background standing attunement to the constant impendingness of one's own death is intensely private and unsharable, and with such a notion at the center it makes almost all of ordinary life escapist and even cowardly. There seems to be behind it some dark view that the only possible human dignity is a refusal of self-deceit in the face of the ungraspability of one's death.
>
> (122)

"Almost all of ordinary life"—so not just *das Man* but caring relating to ready-at-hand included. The rather obvious problem is here: how does authentic care relate to *das Man*? Is it just simply rootedness in a concrete historical world versus the abstract rootless universality of today's "global citizens"? There are four existential stances at work here: authentic care of being-thrown into a historical disclosure of Being; anxiety when we confront our mortality; rootless *das Man*; traditional metaphysical distanced observation (which quantum mechanics undermines in the domain of science itself). If care taken radically, with no reliance on the big Other, in its abyss, we get anxiety. (Although Heidegger as a rule perceives the anxiety of being-towards-death as an individual experience, he sometimes hints that a society can also make an authentic collective decision when confronted with the threat of its annihilation.)

When, in his interpretation of *The Critique of Practical Reason*, Heidegger reads the a priori "feelings" mentioned by Kant (respect, dignity, anxiety, guilt ...) not just as empirical psychic states but as modes of transcendental attunement, he engages in a short but interesting attempt to define the distinction between pleasure and enjoyment:

> According to Kant there pertains to sensibility in the broader sense not only the faculty of sensation but also the faculty he commonly designates as the feeling of pleasure and unpleasure, or delight in the agreeable, or the reverse. Pleasure in the widest sense is not only desire for something and pleasure in something but always also, as we may say, enjoyment; this is a way in which the human being, turning with pleasure towards something, experiences himself as enjoying—he is joyous.[3]

Heidegger abandons this exploration too soon: his false opposition between pleasure and enjoyment is built on the opposition between object and subject (we find pleasure in an object, we enjoy when we turn towards such an object), but he leaves out of consideration the link between enjoyment and pain: a subject can enjoy pain itself, i.e., he can find enjoyment in its very renunciation to pleasure—enjoyment is beyond the pleasure principle. We are thereby approaching the old Freudian question: why do we enjoy oppression itself? That is to say, power asserts its hold over us not simply by oppression (and repression) which are sustained by a fear of punishment, but by bribing us for our obedience and enforced renunciations—what we get in exchange for our obedience and renunciations is a perverted pleasure in renunciation itself, a gain in loss itself. Lacan called this perverted pleasure surplus-enjoyment. Surplus-enjoyment implies the paradox of a thing which is always (and nothing but) an excess with regard to itself: in its "normal" state, it is nothing. This brings us to Lacan's notion of *objet a* as the surplus-enjoyment: there is no "basic enjoyment" to which one adds the surplus-enjoyment, enjoyment is always a surplus, in excess. Lacan provides here a kind of Hegelian response to Foucault: not only do the mechanisms of repression and regulation generate the excess they endeavour to repress; these mechanisms themselves get libidinally invested, become a perverse source of surplus-enjoyment of their own.

Analyzing Kafka's "Investigations of a Dog,"[4] Aaron Schuster correctly discerned a radical reversal in the dog ready to starve to death: when his fasting begins really to hurt, "the truth of nourishment is revealed. What begins as a struggle not to eat turns into a compulsion to eat the nothing, to feast on the fast itself."[5] We get here a rather obvious case of the passage from pleasure/satisfaction to enjoyment: eating which satisfies my hunger provides pleasure, but extreme hunger, renunciation of eating, gives birth to an enjoyment of its own, much more radical than the pleasure of eating. In short, the repression of a desire necessarily turns into a desire for repression, the renunciation of a pleasure turns into the pleasure in this renunciation, the regulation of pleasures into a pleasure of regulation. This is what Foucault doesn't take into account: how, say, the disciplinary practice of regulating pleasures gets infected itself by pleasure, as in obsessive or masochist rituals. The true excess is thus not the excess generated by disciplinary practices, the excess (of pleasure) are these practices themselves which literally come in excess of what they regulate.

Back to the main argument: how did we pass/regress from authentically engaged care to the modern everyday experience of reality as availability for our manipulation? Pippin proposes that the metaphysical primacy of present-at-hand over ready-at-hand has somehow penetrated our ordinary experience: "some screen of theoretical sedimentation in our ordinary expectations has distorted everything, and what the world is like for us now in its original availability is not what it is actually like for us."(129) The idea that the alienation of our actual daily lives is due to the "theoretical sedimentation in our ordinary expectations"—in short, that a philosophical stance had fundamentally influenced the daily behaviour of people—seems to me very problematic—is it not much more convincing to introduce here the notion of social classes and of the division of labour? Does the theoretical distance towards reality and its scientific exploitation and manipulation not presuppose a double division, the division between those who work and those who live from the work of others, as well as the division in the production process itself between those who are constrained to the physical work and those who plan and regulate this work?

In short, we may say that, in describing the technological exploitation of nature, Heidegger ignores the *social* relationship within which this happens. To clarify this point, let's turn to the classical question of political economy: is labour the only source of value? The obvious and "logical" reply is: no, there are three sources, labour, material on which the work is done, and instruments used in the work. But Marx is basically right here because he sees the value of a commodity not as the property of an object but as the expression of a social relationship, and human beings are the only elements in a social relationship. The same goes for the "radical" ecological stance according to which not only human beings but also animals and other sentient beings, and for some even rivers and mountains, have certain basic rights. Only humans have rights since rights come with responsibilities, and only humans can be held responsible—we cannot hold a dog who killed a small baby responsible for its act. So although we should, of course, be extremely cautious not to cause too much pain to animals, etc., it is deceptive to talk about their rights—if we do, we come close to the situation in France in the late Middle Ages when, for example, birds which invaded a church and desecrated it were put to court and condemned to death.

This line of thought brings us inescapably to the topic of Evil. For Kant, the most radical form of Evil is not a conscious choice of knowingly acting against the Good but the renunciation of the very choice, of the freedom implied by a choice. You are evil when you renounce your freedom and commit problematic acts as if you are predetermined to do it, like Russia is saying about Ukraine and the IDF about Gaza: "We had no choice, we cannot do but . . ." One should nonetheless remember that a truly great ethical act also does not imply a simple trivial choice but the logic of "I simply cannot do it otherwise, if I were not to do it I wouldn't be able to look at my face in the mirror . . ." This similarity, of course, conceals a radical difference: when I renounce the choice (and this very renunciation is choosing Evil even if what I do is quite respectable) I do it in a comfortable spirit, getting rid of the pressure of responsibility: "That's how it is, what can one do?"; when I perform a proper ethical act, I am haunted by a terrifying pressure, there is nothing relaxing in it—here, I don't renounce my freedom, I am fully conscious that I freely chose what was ethically necessary for me to do.

This prevalent form of ordinary Evil is most palpable in today's obsession with the struggle against cruelty and violence: the scope of acts which can count as cruel expands more and more—a dirty word, a malevolent gaze, a small obscene gesture . . . However, this obsession with cruelty is not sustained by moral fanaticism but by what one cannot but call "human rights realism": yes, human rights, but don't pretend that we don't all have blood under our skin, so we have to be realists and not expect too much from others or from ourselves—in other words, let's obey the law and be kind to others, but only as much as it is realistically possible, and let's violate the law only when it is really necessary, when there is no other rational way. The implication of this stance is that we are not really free: freedom is an illusion shared by rare fanatics who as a rule destroy themselves, while for us, ordinary people, the best is to surrender to circumstances and drift with the current . . . The paradox here is that the repressed freedom (the radical freedom we renounce when we decide to live a "rational" controlled life which avoids excesses) returns with a vengeance in excessive brutality that more and more permeates our lives: mass outbursts of "irrational" violence, ritualized gang brutality, pleasure in humiliating others . . .[6]

So what does Heidegger have to offer to this conundrum? How does he deal with what we perceive as the big Evils of the twentieth century? As expected, Heidegger's basic reference is to the ontological difference: the true Evil are not "ontic" crimes like gas chambers but the ontological nihilism of the global scientific-technological civilization. However, two things cannot but strike the reader here. Although Heidegger does here and there risk a dialogue with a Japanese person or some other non-Western thinker, the space of historicity proper is for him the West from the so-called pre-Socratics onwards, a sequence which culminates in today's global technological civilization. One cannot avoid here a naïve question: what about other parts of the world, India, China, Africa—what about their spirituality, their world-disclosures? And, especially, how could it happen that they are all also conquered by the global scientific-technological civilization, caught in what we call "progress"? Why and how did their spirituality get caught in the same path towards nihilism?

The second thing to note about Heidegger's insistence on the properly transcendental-ontological level of the Disclosure/Meaningfulness of Being is that secretly (or not even so secretly) it relies on many ontic choices. For example (and this is arguably THE example), for Heidegger the nihilism of modern technological manipulation is not simply a global feature of today's world but is repeatedly identified with Judaism. Even in 1948, after the end of World War II, Heidegger urged an examination of "Jewry's predisposition to planetary criminality [*planetarischen Verbrechertum*]":

> *With their marked gift for calculation*, the Jews "live" according to the principle of race, and indeed have done so for the longest time, for which reason they themselves most vigorously resist its unrestricted application. The arrangement of racial breeding stems not from "life" itself, but from the hyperempowerment of life by machination [*Machenschaft*]. What this brings about with such planning is a *complete deracination* of peoples by harnessing them in a uniformly constructed and streamlined arrangement of all entities. Along with deracination goes a self-alienation of peoples—the loss of history—i.e., of the regions of decision for being [*Seyn*].[7]

The philosophical background of these lines is the opposition between fully living in a concrete world, assuming the way being discloses itself to us in an always unique Event, and the denial of such concrete spiritual-historical roots in the abstract stance of objectivizing the world into "external reality" as something to be manipulated and exploited. Defenders of Heidegger claim that he simply confuses here the metaphysical stance of rootless *Machenschaft* that predominates today with an empirical people (Jews) which embodies this stance at its most radical, so that one can get rid of Heidegger's anti-Semitism by being more faithful to Heidegger than Heidegger himself, i.e., by sticking all the way to the ontologico-ontic difference.

Is Heidegger not committing here the classic mistake of positing a specific historical agent which has to be responsible for our woes? In Bryan Singer's *The Usual Suspects*, Verbal Kint says to inspector Kujan who interrogates him: "The greatest trick the Devil ever pulled was convincing the world he didn't exist." This—known line from the film is a paraphrase of a statement by Charles Baudelaire who wrote a story that appeared in *Le Figaro* in 1864 in which he claimed: "*la plus belle des ruses du Diable est de vous persuader qu'il n'existe pas!*" [The most beautiful of the cunnings of the Devil is to convince us that he doesn't exist.] In the film, Kint says this line to convince Kujan that Keyser Soze, the mythical all-powerful criminal mastermind, really exists as a person, i.e., that he is not just a figure of mythic imagination. (One should be more precise here: Keyser Soze's disposal of those who know him is not the same as Mr. Arkadin's (from Orson Welles's film of the same name) who wants to erase all the traces of his problematic past, before he became a big public person; it is also not to remain fully unknown (like le Carré's Karla whose existence itself should be unknown). Keyser Soze wants to be *known* as somebody whose features are unknown, he wants to be known as a terrifying obscure threat.)

But I think the contrary is true: the greatest trick the Devil (or, rather, the ideology which operates with the Devil) pulled was to convince us that he exists, i.e., that "the Devil" is not just a mythic subjectivation (presentation) of the chaotic horrors of social life, that there is a single person who really pulls the strings behind social evils—an ideological operation at its purest. The anti-Semitic version of this trick would have been something like: "The greatest cunning of the Jews is to convince us that there is no Jewish conspiracy against our societies." However, one should note the practical necessity of such a subjectivation of the agent of evil: it plays a key role in how evil functions.

Literally hundreds of articles have been written (and podcasts produced) on the question: is Verbal Kint really Keyser Soze? The main answers are: yes, he is, otherwise the ending makes no sense; no, one of the other men in the line-up at the police station that opens the movie scene is; the real Soze is Kobayashi who acts as Soze's lawyer and representative; Soze doesn't exist as a real person, he is just a mythic point of reference; Soze is not a name, it functions as a title which passes from one to another individual... In quantum terms, we have here a series of superpositions: the movie contains hints at all these possibilities, and the ending (Kint = Soze) obviously works as a collapse into a single reality. However, I think pursuing this question—focusing on "who is Soze?"—is the final trap of the movie which makes us miss the more basic result of the final revelation: yes, Kint is Soze, the big question is answered, but how does Kujan realize this? After Kint is released and leaves the office, Kujan looks around the office where he interrogated Kint and realizes that Kint was composing his narrative by way of incorporating into it fragments of the reality around him in the office ("Kobayashi" is the brand name of the cup of coffee the two used during the interrogation, etc.). Which means: yes, Kint is Soze, but this is the *only* thing we know now—all the stories we've heard can be lies improvised by Kint/Soze . . . So the identity of Kint and Soze is a truth which turns all we think we know into a potential lie, a truth which entails almost a kind of Cartesian doubt: everything we know may be a lie. In Lacanian terms, it is the exception which sustains the universality of a lie. At the end we thus do not get all the truth (a complete explanation of "what really happened"), as is the case in usual whodunits: the final truth destroys our continuous effort to distinguish truth from lies, it turns everything into a potential lie.[8] And this is perhaps one of the most accurate definitions of the Devil.

To return to Heidegger's theory, in which he writes that Jews are not the only place of such a short-circuit between the ontological and the ontic: the counterpoint to Jews are Germans as the only proper metaphysical people, the only people who can enact a new epochal beginning. If Germans and Jews are the two absolute opposites the tension of which can only be resolved through the annihilation of one pole, does this mean that the Holocaust was in some sense justified? Here Heidegger takes into account the difference between the metaphysical stance of Jewishness and the ontic Jews, but in an extremely perverted way: he interprets the Holocaust (the annihilation of ontic Jews) as the self-annihilation of the Jews themselves:

> Only when what is essentially "Jewish" in the metaphysical sense battles against the Jewish is the pinnacle of self-annihilation in history attained; assuming that what is "Jewish" has everywhere seized dominion entirely for itself, such that even the battle "of the Jewish," and this above all, becomes subjection to it.[9]

By accounting for the Holocaust in the terms of the havocs of modern technologies, Heidegger ignores the pathologies of the German historical development which culminated in the annihilation of the Jews; in this false move from the particular to the universal, Germans, the actual perpetrators of the Holocaust, disappear from the picture, they become just an anonymous instrument of the self-annihilation of the Jews themselves. And is Israel not doing something similar when it claims that Palestinians themselves are responsible for the thousands of dead civilians in Gaza? IDF is targeting only Hamas members, and since Hamas is using civilians as a human shield, it is responsible for the suffering and death of those civilians.

The irony here goes even deeper: Germans (or, more accurately, the Nazis) become the stand-in of "what is essentially 'Jewish' in the metaphysical sense" in its battle against the empirical Jews. In short, they stand for the much more radical practice of technological machination, more so than the actual Jews themselves, so that, to go to the end, Germans themselves were the true agents of self-annihilation—the destruction of Germany in 1945 was its self-destruction, something Germany brought upon itself. What Heidegger misses here is that, in our global capitalism, every reference to roots, to "blood and soil," loses its innocence since it already serves the aim of global machination.[10] Pippin is right to point out the political implications of Heidegger's view:

> Heidegger has to claim that what for the Hegelian, or in the Hegelian tradition, must count as the pathologies of modernity—alienation, reification, domination instead of mutuality of recognitive status, the humiliating conditions of the modern organization of labor, anomie, deracination—are all best understood as implications of the still "unthought" question, the meaning of Being, as descendants of the "metaphysical" tradition. As I have suggested, this claim is worth taking more seriously than it has been, but the way Heidegger formulates the issue seems to exclude all other options as derivative from and so complicit with that tradition.
>
> (219)

The key word here is "exclude": it is not that economic exploitation and the alienating organization of labour can be integrated into Heidegger's thought as secondary effects of modern nihilism; any focus on them is to be excluded, dismissed as not only irrelevant but a dangerous trap. In 1953 Heidegger said that the end result of World War II "decided nothing"[11]—nothing in terms of the history of Being. Russia and America who are "metaphysically the same" won over Germany not just militarily but also "metaphysically," by infecting Germany with the (self)destructive stance of nihilism, depriving

Nazism of its "inner greatness." This is what Heidegger is aiming at in the following passage from his *Black Notebooks*:

> If one thought it through from the perspective of destiny, would not, for instance, the failure to grasp this destiny—which would not belong to us, if the world-willing [*Weltwollen*] was suppressed [*Niederhalten im Weltwollen*] —would this failure not be much more essentially a "guilt" and "collective guilt," the magnitude of which essentially could not even be measured against the gruesomeness of the "gas chambers" [*Greuelhaften der "Gaskammern"*]; a guilt—uncannier than all "crimes" that can be "inveighed against" publically—which surely no one would forgive in the future. Already today "one" does not want to see—this not-willing is far more willing than our spinelessness [*Willenlosigkeit*] in foreboding that Germany and the German people are but one concentration camp—the likes of which "the world" has not "seen" indeed, and which "the world" does not want to see—this not-willing is far more willing than our spinelessness [*Willenlosigkeit*] in the face of the brutalization [*Verwilderung*] of National Socialism.[12]

Let's note here first the problematic nature of guilt; as the dying Sian tells Darby at the end of episode 5 of *A Murder at the End of the World*: "Guilt is so easy, easier to blame yourself than contend with the truth." This reversal of the standard wisdom (blaming others to avoid one's own guilt) is the basic claim of psychoanalysis, and it applies precisely to Oedipus. At the end of the Sophocles' play, Oedipus doesn't admit his guilt: he knows he killed his father and married his mother, but he didn't know anything about this (no place here for some unconscious desires!).

Back to the long quote from Heidegger—if we read this paragraph carefully, the message is clear: the gas chambers are an ontic crime and as such incomparably less terrifying than the German defeat in 1945 which made all of Germany and the German people one big concentration camp, a spineless people deprived of its world-willing, a willingness to engage in a historical disclosure of authentic Being. In short, the guilt of this ontological betrayal is incomparably more important than the guilt for the holocaust—or, as Peter Trawny put it concisely:

> If "we" [Germans] were "suppressed" in pursuing this "world-willing"—now, after the war—this "suppression" would be "guilt," the magnitude of which could not even be measured against the gruesomeness of the gas chambers. The "world-willing" of the "Germans" is ontohistorically more important than the "gruesomeness of the gas chambers."[13]

The expression "brutalization [*Verwilderung*] of National Socialism" thus indicates that it was the global stance of calculation and technological domination which "brutalized" National Socialism, at its origins a much more positive spiritual project. The universalization of an actual terrifying event into an all-encompassing metaphor is crucial here: the Nazi concentration camps were a (gruesome, true) real event, but after World War II, the whole of occupied Germany became one big concentration camp … The same universalization often occurred when white liberals expressed their horror at the practice of female castration in some Third World countries (especially in Africa): the reply was that white liberals have no right to complain about this because plastic surgeries that are taking place among millions of white women are nothing but a kind of extension of clitoridectomy to the entire body of a woman …

*

I remember from my youth, the time of the student revolts in late 1960s, how some Europeans, Heideggerians sympathetic to student protests, interpreted them in generalized ontological terms as the rejection of the technological-consumerist society and a craving for a new beginning—or, as the Croat Heideggerian Vanja Sutlić said: "Che Guevara in Bolivia is not just fighting capitalism, he wants a new world outside metaphysical nihilism." (Incidentally, when, in 1967, a group of protesting students from Berlin visited Heidegger, he expressed his support for them, claiming that they were trying to achieve what he strived for in 1934 as the rector of the Freiburg university.[14]) Although Pippin is sensitive to Heidegger's simplifications and unanswered questions—see the final paragraphs of his book—he doesn't go all the way here, especially with regard to politics: Heidegger is indifferent towards "ontic" justice, moral responsibility, guilt of the Holocaust, even empirical threats to the environment and acting against them. The question raised by Pippin here is simply irrelevant from Heidegger's standpoint:

Heidegger has framed all such issues as dependent on, and reflecting some sense, of the historical meaningfulness of Being and that means the context of his question about the reconciling powers of reason is a question about mattering. How could Hegel approach a question like whether a mutual recognitive status in modern ethical life matters, and if so how much, and if a lot, why?

(220)

It is not difficult to guess Heidegger's reply: the very ideal of mutual recognition and dignity remains within the frame of modern subjectivity and is as such ultimately the source of what is wrong in modernity, demonstrating that the failure of modernity is its truth. Or, to put it brutally in the terms of "mattering" (a disclosure of Being determines the basic frame of what *matters* to the subjects who find themselves thrown into a specific historical world): for Heidegger, human rights and mutual recognition ultimately *don't matter*. The only thing that really matters is the willingness of a people to freely assume its destiny, an act of total commitment which has nothing to do with free dialogue and negotiation.

But the question remains: if what Heidegger describes as the primordial opening/disclosure/attunement is not cut/traversed by class difference, is the attunement that discloses the world as an object of technological manipulation really simply shared by all people in a modern epoch? When Pippin recapitulates Heidegger's notion of modern society as one of productive exploitation, manipulation and consummation of all reality, he adds in parenthesis: "(Although he would never put it this way, it would not be unfair to invoke another word to capture this situation: capitalism.)"(214) This begs the response: yes, but why would Heidegger never name capitalism? Why is the word prohibited in his language? In all probability, Heidegger's answer would have been that capitalism is just one among ontic organizations of the technological disclosure of Being— as he put it, Soviet Union and the US are "metaphysically the same." To this we should insist that capitalism is not simply an ontic phenomenon, one of the possible versions of technological attunement: capitalism is not just a social phenomenon, it also has a transcendental-ontological status. It is not modern science and technology as such which push us to continuous domination over and exploitation of nature—they function like this only within the frame of capitalism with its permanent propensity towards expanded self-reproduction.

So Pippin is right here: it is not enough to mention technological availability as the source of the disappearance of Meaningfulness—one should add the word "capitalism" never used by Heidegger. Here Marx surprisingly meets radical conservatives: Patrick Buisson, the French ultra-conservative, was right in claiming that *"le grand deconstructeur, c'est le capitalisme."*[15] Plus we should add that the disclosure of beings as objects of technological manipulation and exploitation is not homogeneous: the objects of such exploitation immanently resist it, which brings us back to class struggle, a notion even more unmentionable for Heidegger than capitalism.

Is Heidegger's Nazi engagement just a stupid error or is it grounded in his basic philosophical stance? Or, even worse, what if his very basic philosophical stance is grounded in his Nazi engagement? The only way to clarify this topic is to turn the question around and analyze the implicit philosophical foundations of Hitler's work itself. (This, of course, doesn't mean that we should elevate Hitler into a serious philosopher—the task is just to explore the implicit ontological foundations of Hitler's "thought.") Peter Trawny's *Hitler, Philosophy and Hatred: Notes on the discourse on identity politics*[16] risks this daring step which is deeply justified, although it will appear problematic to many, especially in today's electrified atmosphere; the book's approach is best rendered by the publisher's summary:

> To believe that European discourse can keep National Socialism at a distance, like an object, is at best a naïve hypothesis, but at worst a political mistake. One then pretends that National Socialism had no contact with the rest of Europe, with other philosophers, with other political and religious languages. This is why Adolf Hitler's *Mein Kampf* is still considered a book unworthy of philosophical discussion. This attitude sheds light on philosophy itself. Does it possibly find too much of itself in *Mein Kampf*? And what is it exactly that it finds there? Trawny's reading of Hitler's book does not avoid the possibility of a continuity between philosophy and National Socialism. It is an encounter with a hatred that threatens us simply because it once seized power and dominated the life of a society. There is no reason to think that the hatred has passed away.[17]

With regard to Heidegger, the result that imposes itself from such a reading—for those who, in spite of all counter-arguments, continue to hold Heidegger up as a great philosophical figure—is more than just paradoxical, it is very painful. Yes, there are two facts that we should accept: Heidegger was an engaged Nazi AND he was a titan of philosophy, he formulated some crucial philosophical insights. But what if Heidegger saw certain crucial things not in spite of but precisely *because* of his problematic political stance? This absolutely doesn't imply that there is a deeper truth in Nazism; it means that to see something at the level of ontology, one *has* to "err" at the ontic level—not just err in the sense of mistakes but err in the sense of terrifying monstrosity. A Jewish friend of mine who is close to Heidegger and simultaneously deeply immersed in Jewish spirituality,[18] claimed that some Talmudic texts indicate how some painful truths can only be said from the position of Satan. This, of course, should not remain our final position: one should pass through Heidegger and supplement his thought so that it no longer requires the Nazi link (to simplify it, so that the three authentic spiritual positions are no longer those of a poet, a warrior, and a farmer).

Do we, in the "liberal" West, have an alternative to oppose to the dark prospect raised by Trawny? Any reference to the "complexity" of the situation is a fake here—the answer is a simple NO. The parallel between today's pro-Palestinian student protests and the 1968 anti-Vietnam-war protests are often noted; however, Franco Berardi also noted an important difference between the two. Rhetorically, at least, the 1968 protesters identified with anti-imperialist defense of Vietcong and with a socialist project, but today's protesters very rarely identify with Hamas. What, then, do they identify with? Berardi's bitter hypothesis is that

> students are identifying with despair. Despair is the psychological and also cultural trait that explains the wide identification of young people with the Palestinians. I think that the majority of the students today are consciously or unconsciously expecting the irreversible worsening of the conditions of life, irreversible climate change, a long lasting period of war, and the looming danger of a nuclear precipitation of the conflicts that are underway in many points of the geopolitical map.[19]

It is difficult to put it better than Berardi. The first step towards hope is to fully admit our desperate predicament in all its dimensions. What Adorno wrote decades ago—"Nothing but despair can save us."[20]—is today more true than ever. Adorno's line echoes Kafka's basic idea that the only success, the only solution, is the failure of failure itself. Does this amount to a version of Beckett's famous formula from his 1983 story "Worstward Ho": "Ever tried. Ever failed. No matter. Try again. Fail again. Fail better."?

One can read Lacan's entire theoretical development in this sense: all his attempts to find the right word (or formula) for his theoretical edifice failed, and he then moves to another attempt to "fail better"—from four discourses to mathems, from mathems to knots . . .—and in his very brief last seminar session he openly admits that all these attempts failed. But with Kafka the "failure of the failure" does involve a kind of negation of negation which ends the infinite line of failures, although not the usual pseudo-Hegelian one of negating the failure and succeeding. The failure of failure means that when we fail we should not just approach the same goal in a different more realistic or more efficient way: what we should renounce is the very standard-ideal-goal we tried to achieve. The unsurpassable model of the Kafkaesque failure of a failure is, of course, the situation described in the last lines of his "parable" on the door of the Law from *The Trial*: the man from the country fails to enter the door of the Law, and this failure fails when he is told that door was there just for him:

> The gatekeeper has to bend way down to him, for the great difference has changed things to the disadvantage of the man. "What do you still want to know, then?" asks the gatekeeper. "You are insatiable." "Everyone strives after the law," says the man, "so how is that in these many years no one except me has requested entry?" The gatekeeper sees that the man is already dying and, in order to reach his diminishing sense of hearing, he shouts at him, "Here no one else can gain entry, since this entrance was assigned only to you. I'm going now to close it."[21]

Do we not get something similar on the southern side of the demilitarized zone that divides North from South Korea? South Koreans built there a unique place to visit: a theater with a large screen-like window in front, opening up onto the North. The spectacle the public observes when they take seats and look through the window is reality itself (or, rather, a kind of "desert of the real"): the barren demilitarized zone with walls, etc., and, beyond, a glimpse of North Korea. However, as if to comply with the fiction, North Korea has built in front of this theater a pure fake, a model village with beautiful houses; in the evening, the lights in all the houses are turned on at the same time, people are given good dresses and are obliged to take a stroll every evening... One can easily imagine a Kafkaesque conclusion of this show: all of a sudden, the lights in the model village are turned off and a voice from the North says: "This spectacle was assigned only to you. North Korea is now going to close it."

Nothing new, one could add: the spectators from the South knew this all the time—but the enigma remains: if they knew it all the time (i.e., if they knew that North Korea built that model village just for them to see it), why are they so fascinated by it that they enjoy looking at it? This brings us to a further difference between Kafka and North Korea: Kafka's man from the country desperately wants to pass through the door of the Law (probably to resolve some legal problem he is caught in), while the observers from the South don't want to effectively visit the model village in the North—they know very well they are just watching a spectacle staged for them. It is more like a cinema performance where what we see on the screen is reality itself staged for us. The true enigma resides elsewhere, in the Other's desire: why is North Korea, with its ideology of self-sufficiency (*juche*), so keen to impress a foreign gaze, i.e., the gaze of its mortal enemies? Why doesn't it simply decide to ignore the foreign view? What if North Korea is—in its very impenetrability—already caught into a libidinal economy which includes us?

Another unexpected link emerges here: what about Kafka and quantum mechanics? Is the doorkeeper's final message ("the door is here only for you") not similar to the basic claim of quantum mechanics about how an observer is always included into (what we experience as) objective reality which exists independently of our observation? Theorists like Carlo Rovelli pointed out convincingly that this claim (the inclusion of the observer) does *not* imply some sort of subjective idealism ("my mind creates reality")—on the contrary, it implies a materialist axiom that we (observers) are also part of the world, that we do not observe it from some privileged external position... Yet another unexpected link: with the ongoing war in Gaza, do we not get from both sides—Hamas and IDF—horrors which are (partially, at least) also committed for the observers (witnesses, cameras, digital media)? The devastation of Gaza was also made to impress on the observers the strength of the IDF and Israel's capacity to destroy those whom they perceive as threats to its existence.

With the explosive development of Artificial Intelligence, we are approaching the obverse of the situation described by Kafka: in my interaction with a digital agent, I act as if I am a partner in an actual dialogue (AI can easily program a partner who looks and acts like a human), but the AI system opposite is just a blind mechanism ignoring my subjectivity—the doors are not just for me, they are for anyone... The circle so nicely described by Schuster—the obscure and all-powerful agency which appears to dominate the Kafkaesque subject (the Court, the Castle...) is in reality his symptom, his unconscious formation onto which he projects his repressed traumas and antagonisms, so that his destruction is a self-destruction—can no longer be applied here: the AI megamachine does not function as an obstacle which is simultaneously a positive condition to the emergence of a subject.

It is even very problematic to turn this relationship around and say that humans become symptoms of the AI machines, the embodiments of the machines' inner inconsistencies and impossibilities—this holds more for our common language which subjectivizes itself through the subject that gives body to the lack of a "true Word"... Will then an all-powerful AI apparatus induce in a subject caught in it a real psychosis, not just a paranoia? Will the big Other become a real object, not just a virtual/non-existent agent? However, it may happen that if AI develops not human consciousness but a radically new form of self-awareness, its absolute strangeness will give rise to neurosis, to a questioning of "what does AI want"...[22]

But, again, how does all this affect the notion of a revolution? One thing is certain: we should leave behind the standard paradigm/excuse of "next time we'll do it in a better, totally different way." We, the agents, should begin from the zero-point, and this zero-point does not mean a radical destruction/reconstruction of social reality but a radical destruction/reconstruction of ourselves, of our innermost subjectivity. This is what Kafka meant when he wrote in a letter to Max Brod: "There is infinite hope—just not for us."[23] An ambiguous statement which can also mean: not for us *as we are now*, so we have to change radically, to be reborn. But what has this to do with revolution? After his statement that subject is a cause of itself, Lacan goes on: "Entering onto this path is where the only true political revolution may flow from."[24] Kafka noticed apropos the October Revolution:

> The decisive moment in human development is everlasting. For this reason the revolutionary movements of intellect/spirit that declare everything before them to be null and void are in the right, for nothing has yet happened.[25]

Here is Schuster's commentary on these lines:

> It's not that history has ended, as so many Hegel-inspired critics have repeated in various contexts. Rather, the end has already occurred, and the real question is whether, and when, history will begin. Kafka's universe is marked by an unbearable tension between extreme closure and boundless openness, between the end that has already taken place and the beginning that is yet to start.[26]

This brings us to the well-known Gramsci remark from his *Prison Notebooks*: "The crisis consists precisely in the fact that the old is dying and the new cannot be born; in this interregnum a great variety of morbid symptoms [*fenomeni morbosi*] appear."[27] From today's Kafkaesque experience, this remark appears all too naïve: our present is ALWAYS the one in which the old is dying and the new cannot be born. In social change, capitalism is disintegrating but the new socialist order cannot be born and we get morbid symptoms (like techno-feudalism); in sexual economy the old patriarchy is disintegrating and the new free sexuality cannot be born, so we are getting morbid symptoms, etc. The worst (Stalinist or Fascist) illusion is that a direct smooth passage from the Old to the New is possible and that we just missed it due to our contingent limitations (for example, the idea that Stalinism arose because the first revolution happens in the wrong place, in "backwards" Russia and not in the developed West).

The temporality of such passages is crucial. Joseph Brodsky surmised that, after 15–20 years in power, a tyrant invariably "decides to immortalize himself by doing something horrendous": "The average length of a good tyranny is a decade and a half, two decades at most. When it's more than that, it invariably slips into a monstrosity."[28] His judgment seems to be right: it was 19 years after the October Revolution that the Stalinist Great Purges exploded, and it was 17 years after the victory of the Chinese Revolution that the Great Cultural Revolution was set in motion.

*

In view of the recent worldwide rise of fascisms as the reaction to the crisis of global capitalism, Todd McGowan[29] suggested that we should reverse the well-known Walter Benjamin line: "It's not that every fascism is the result of a failed revolution but that fascism is the natural response that capitalism engenders." The new logical order is thus: capitalism reacts to a crisis with some form of fascism, and the emancipatory resistance is then a reaction to this fascist threat. So we have here non-commutativity, but in an inverted order: there is no radical emancipation without a fascist threat.

*

So what if, in fidelity to Kafka's vision, we turn things on their head: the true "morbid symptom" is our image of the proper New that we expected to emerge, and the solution is precisely and only to be sought in new "morbid" solutions that we improvise to avoid the catastrophe at the horizon. The only thing to add here is that "unbearable tension between extreme closure and boundless openness" is already present in Hegel's thought where extreme closure (the closed circle of the Hegelian system where the end coincides with the beginning) coincides with radical openness: the system cannot say anything about the future, there is no deeper "historical necessity" indicating the way.

III

Singular: Politics in a quantum world

1

The hologram of conflicting universalities

Lately the notion of universality enjoys a bad reputation—the predominant commonplace is that a position which presents itself as neutral-universal effectively privileges a certain (heterosexual, male, Christian . . .) culture: "universal human rights are effectively the rights of the white male private owners to exchange freely on the market, exploit workers and women, as well as exert political domination . . ." This, however, is only half of the story: not only do we live today in a world which is less universal than we think (since we are all caught in particular cultural universes)—we are simultaneously *more* universal than we think since we are all enmeshed in trans-cultural global capitalism.

What begs to be questioned is the emergence of the very form of universality: how, in what specific historical conditions, does abstract Universality itself become a "fact of (social) life"? In what conditions do individuals experience themselves as subjects of universal human rights? Therein resides the point of Marx's analysis of "commodity fetishism": in a society in which commodity exchange predominates, individuals themselves, in their daily lives, relate to themselves, as well as to the objects they encounter, as contingent embodiments of abstract-universal notions. What I am, my concrete social or cultural background, is experienced as contingent, since what ultimately defines me is the "abstract" universal capacity to think and/or to work. The modern notion of "profession" implies that I experience myself as an individual who is not directly "born into" his social role—what I will become depends on the interplay between contingent social circumstances and my free choice; in this sense, contemporary individuals have a profession—that of electrician or professor or waiter—while it is meaningless to claim that a medieval serf was a peasant by profession. In certain specific social conditions (of commodity exchange and a global market economy), "abstraction" becomes a direct feature of actual social life, the way concrete individuals behave and relate to their fate and to their social surroundings. Universality becomes "for itself" only insofar as individuals no longer fully identify the kernel of their being with their particular social situation, only insofar as they experience themselves as forever "out of joint" with regard to this situation: the mode of appearance of an abstract Universality, its entering into actual existence, is thus an extremely violent move of disrupting the preceding texture of social life.

Universality-for-itself is thus to be opposed to any notion of organic totality, of a Whole in which every particular element has its allotted place: in a totality, its universality becomes for itself in one of its elements which cannot achieve full identity in it, which lacks a proper place in it, i.e., whose particular identity is thwarted, which cannot actualize itself in its particularity. For radical feminism, women (not men) stand for universality insofar as they are prevented from fully becoming what they are (with regard to their immanent potentials). And the same tension seems to haunt formulations of Jewish identity. In his *Black Notebooks*, Heidegger characterized Jews as a failed nation, a rootless people with no land, fatally prone to calculation and manipulation—however, what Heidegger ignored is that the very fact that Jews had "failed" as a nation was what made them great, a stand-in for universality.

The "logic" of this type of traditional anti-Semitism was complicated once Zionists themselves began to evoke the cliché of roots, or, as Alain Finkielkraut wrote in 2015 in a letter to *le Monde*: "The Jews, they have today chosen the path of rootedness."[1] It is easy to discern in this claim an echo of Heidegger who, in his *Spiegel* interview, posits that all essential and great things can only emerge from our having a homeland, from being rooted in a specific historical tradition. The irony is that in today's Zionism we are dealing with a weird attempt to mobilize anti-Semitic clichés in order to legitimize Zionism: anti-Semitism reproaches the Jews for being rootless, and it is as if Zionism tries to correct this failure by belatedly providing Jews with roots . . . No wonder many conservative anti-Semites ferociously support the expansion of the State of Israel. The problem is that now the radical Zionist Jews act as if they can have their cake and eat it: they have a land and state, but they still maintain the claim to universality.

This tension unfortunately makes Israel a failed state. The sad state of affairs in Haiti in 2024 provides an extreme and tragic case of a so-called failed state: illegal criminal gangs took over the public space and control 80% of the country. But are the West Bank settlers who threaten Palestinians there, physically attacking them, stealing their land and ruining their crops, in full view of the Israeli army and police forces, not also a gang openly violating the law? What does it imply then when their actions are not only tolerated but even supported by the (Israeli) forces of law and order? Consider that the Israeli minister of security, responsible for commanding the police, is Itamar Ben Gvir, who was convicted by an Israeli court for anti-Palestinian terrorism . . . The sad lesson is that today the supposedly sacred values of Western democracies are less and less in evidence even in the developed West itself: if we measure a failed state by the cracks in the edifice of state power, as well as the heightened atmosphere of ideological civil war and the growing insecurity of public spaces, then Israel and even the United States are on a fast-track to become one.

Such a confused situation elicits a desperate search for some ideological form that would maintain social stability, and the first obvious candidate is, of course, religion. Marx's well-known characterization of religion as the "opium of the people" nonetheless remains all too naïve. It is true that radical Islam is an exemplary case of religion as the opium of the people: a false confrontation with capitalist modernity which allows the Muslims to dwell in their ideological dream while their countries are ravaged by the effects of global capitalism— and exactly the same holds for Christian fundamentalism. However, there are today, in our Western world, two other versions of the opium of the people: they are, literally, the opium and the people.

Invoking "the people" functions today as a fuzzy populist dream destined to obfuscate our own antagonisms. And for many among us the opium of the people is opium itself, escape into drugs. Chemistry (in its scientific version) is becoming part of us: large aspects of our lives are characterized by the management of our emotions by drugs, from everyday use of sleeping pills and anti-depressants to hard narcotics. We are not just controlled by impenetrable social powers, our very emotions are "outsourced" to chemical stimulation. The stakes of this chemical intervention are double and contradictory: we use drugs to keep external excitement (shocks, anxieties, etc.) under control, i.e., to de-sensitize us to them, and to generate artificial excitement if we are depressed and lack desire. Drugs thus react to the two opposed threats to our daily lives, over-excitement and depression, and it is crucial to notice how these two uses of drugs relate to the distinct spheres of private and public: in the developed Western countries, our public lives more and more lack collective excitement (such as would be provided by a genuine political engagement), while drugs supplant this lack with private (or, rather, intimate) forms of excitement—drugs perform the euthanasia of public life and the artificial excitation of private life. The country whose daily life is most impregnated by this tension is South Korea, and here is Franco Berardi's report on his journey to Seoul:

> Korea is the ground zero of the world, a blueprint for the future of the planet.... In the emptied cultural space, the Korean experience is marked by an extreme degree of individualization and simultaneously it is headed towards the ultimate cabling of the collective mind. These lonely monad walks in the urban space in tender continuous interaction with the pictures, tweets, games coming out of their small screens, perfectly insulated and perfectly wired into the smooth interface of the flow.... South Korea has the highest suicide rate in the world. Suicide is the most common cause of death for those under 40 in South Korea.[2]

What Berardi's impressions on Seoul provide is the image of a place deprived of history, a worldless place (the term was introduced by Alain Badiou). Even Nazi anti-Semitism, however ghastly it was, opened up a world: it described its critical situation by positing an enemy which was a "Jewish conspiracy"; it named a goal and the means of achieving it. Nazism disclosed reality in a way which allowed its subjects to acquire a global "cognitive mapping," and opened up a space for their meaningful engagement.

Perhaps it is here that one should locate one of the main dangers of capitalism: although it is global and encompasses the whole world, it deprives the large majority of people of any meaningful cognitive mapping. Capitalism is the first socio-economic order which de-totalizes meaning: it is not global at the level of meaning. There is, after all, no global "capitalist world view," no "capitalist civilization" proper: the fundamental lesson of globalization is precisely that capitalism can accommodate itself to all civilizations, from Christian to Hindu or Buddhist, from West to East. Capitalism's global dimension can only be formulated at the level of truth-without-meaning, as the Real of the global market mechanism. No wonder millions are exposed to the unbearable superego pressure in its two aspects: the pressure to succeed professionally and the pressure to enjoy life fully in all its intensity.

This brings us to Alexandre Kojeve, the great interpreter of Hegel from the 1930s to 1950s who saw the moment of the "end of history," the highest form of social order, first in Stalinist Russia and then in contemporary Japan. If Kojeve were to be alive today, he would have located the end of history in South Korea[3]—why? South Korea is arguably THE country of free choice—not in the political sense, but in the sense of daily life, especially among the younger depoliticized generation. The choice we are talking about is the indifferent choice of moderate daily pleasures, selecting among options which don't really matter: what one listens to and reads, how one dresses, how one socializes and eats, to which foreign country one goes for a holiday . . . There is a recent movie that perfectly depicts the stance of such a post-political disengaged individual: *Perfect Days* (Wim Wenders 2023, a Japanese-German coproduction) in which Kōji Yakusho plays Hirayama who works as a toilet cleaner in Tokyo, fully content with his simple life. Following a ritualized daily rhythm, he repeats it daily from dawn, and dedicates his free time to his passion for music, in his van to and from work, and books, every night before bed. Japan comes closest to South Korea in this trend towards depoliticized disengagement—even the immensely popular Japanese eco Marxist Kohei Saito advocates the motto "slow down" (the title of his last book).

This new generation mostly doesn't care about big issues like human rights and freedoms or the threat of war—while the world still notices the aggressive pronouncements of the North Korean regime accompanied by nuclear threats, the large majority in South Korea just ignores them. Since the standard of living of the large majority is relatively high, one comfortably lives in a bubble. North Korea is the opposite: permanent mobilization and state of emergency, no free choices, life focused on how to confront the Enemy... To counter this indifference of the youth which is spreading also in China, Xi Jinping recently lauded Chinese civilization for its long and continuous history that stretches back to antiquity, saying that it has shaped the great Chinese nation; he emphasized that it is imperative to comprehensively improve the protection and utilization of cultural relics and better preserve and carry forward cultural heritage.[4]

It also appears that, hidden from the public, a big struggle is going on within the Chinese Communist Party between those who advocate the interests of big corporations and financial capital, and those who want more active participation of the poor and exploited. My question here is: but what about the interests of the Party nomenklatura itself? If some of its top echelons want to limit the power of the big capital, does this automatically make them the advocate of the working class? If there is a lesson to be learned from twentieth-century Communism, it is that one should concede that the ruling Party automatically advocates the interests of the poor and the exploited.

This is why it's worth taking a close look at the writings of Wang Huning, a current member of the Chinese Communist Party's Politburo Standing Committee and the director of the Central Guidance Commission on Building Spiritual Civilization. Wang is correct in emphasizing the key role of culture, of the domain of symbolic fictions. The true materialist way to oppose the topic of the "fiction of reality" (subjectivist doubts in the style of "is what we perceive as reality not just another fiction?") is not to strictly distinguish between fiction and reality but to focus on the *reality of fictions*. Fictions are not outside reality, they are materialized in our social interactions, in our institutions and customs—as we can see in today's mess, if we destroy fictions on which our social interactions are based, our social reality itself begins to fall apart.

Wang designated himself as a neo-conservative—what does this mean? Wang sees his task as imposing a new common ethical substance, and we should not dismiss this as an excuse to impose the full control of the Communist Party over social life. Wang is replying to a real problem. Thirty years ago, he wrote a book *America against America* where he perceptively noted the antagonisms of the American way of life, including its darker sides: social disintegration, lack of solidarity and shared values, nihilist consumerism and individualism ...[5] Trump's populism is a false way out: it is the climax of social disintegration because it introduces obscenity into public speech and thus deprives it of its dignity—something not only prohibited but totally unimaginable in China. We will definitely never see a high-level Chinese politician doing what Trump did publicly: talk about how large his penis is, imitating a woman's orgasmic sounds ... Wang's fear was that the same disease may spread to China—which is now happening at the popular level of mass culture, and the ongoing reforms are a desperate attempt to put a stop to this trend. Again, will it work?

It is easy to perceive in the ongoing Chinese campaign a tension between content and form: the content—the establishment of stable values that hold a society together—is enforced in the form of mobilization which is experienced as a kind of state of emergency imposed by the state apparatus. Although the goal is the opposite of the Cultural Revolution, there are similarities in the way the campaign is done. The danger is that such tensions can produce cynical disbelief in the population. More generally, the ongoing campaign in China seems all too close to standard conservative attempts to enjoy the benefits of the capitalist dynamism but to control its destructive aspects through a strong Nation State pushing forward patriotic values.

*

The ethnic-religious conflicts are the form of struggle which fits global capitalism: in our age of "post-politics" when politics proper is progressively replaced by expert social administration, the only remaining legitimate source of conflicts are cultural (ethnic, religious) tensions. Today's rise of "irrational" violence is thus to be conceived as strictly correlative to the depoliticization of our societies, i.e., to the disappearance of the proper political dimension, its translation into different levels of "administration" of social affairs. If we accept this thesis on the "clash of civilizations," the only alternative to it remains the peaceful coexistence of civilizations (or of "ways of life," a more popular term today): forced marriages and homophobia (or the idea that a woman going alone to a public place is somehow "fair game" for rapists) are OK, just as long as they are limited to another country which is otherwise fully included into the world market.

*

In his work on the concept of neofeudalism, Yanis Varoufakis uses the examples of digital and tech corporations which hold monopolies in all but name—

Amazon for books, Microsoft for software, and so on.[6] So is techno-feudalism already post-capitalism, as Varoufakis claims? Or is, as Noam Yuran claims,[7] what some call techno-feudalism actually capitalism at its purest, capitalism which finally comes to itself (in Hegelese; capitalism at the level of its notion)? I follow here Alenka Zupančič who[8] posited a properly Hegelian identity of the two terms of the alternative: yes, with techno-feudalism capitalist "comes to itself," but since capitalism can function only if it is at a distance from its notion, it abolishes itself when it reaches its notion.

What is often largely ignored by the mainstream media is that the digital warlords like Elon Musk have their counterparts in literal warlords, for example in the Sudan where there is an ongoing civil war between factions who display shocking cruelty and indifference towards what we would think of as "their own people"—or at least people who live in the regions they control. In Sudan, warlords like Hemedti block humanitarian aid designed for the struggling population, demanding an exorbitant cut (sometimes as much as 50%) before allowing any aid to reach the people. This is more and more the reality in which we live: a high-tech neofeudalism running in parallel with (and linked to, because of the role played by these corporations in exploiting the natural resources of less developed countries) an almost medieval, nakedly violent feudalism.

The split between digital neofeudalism and the neofeudalism of the warlords does not imply that we should look for some deeper unity of the two: the truth resides in their split as such. Therein resides the lesson of Fred Jameson: we should avoid any notion of the enforced deeper unity of different forms of protest or of violence like a vampire avoids garlic. Back in the early 1980s, Jameson provided a subtle description of the deadlock of the dialogue between the Western New Left and the Eastern European dissidents, of the absence of any common language between them: "To put it briefly, the East wishes to talk in terms of power and oppression; the West in terms of culture and commodification. There are really no common denominators in this initial struggle for discursive rules, and what we end up with is the inevitable comedy of each side muttering irrelevant replies in its own favorite language."

In a similar way, the Swedish detective writer Henning Mankell is a unique *artist of the parallax view*. That is to say, the two perspectives—those of the affluent Ystad in Sweden and Maputo in Mozambique—are irretrievably "out of sync," so that there is no neutral language enabling us to translate one into the other, even less to posit one as the "truth" of the other. All one can ultimately do in today's conditions is to remain faithful to this split as such, to record it. Every exclusive focus on the First World topics of late capitalist alienation and commodification, of ecological crisis, of the new racisms and intolerances, etc., cannot but appear cynical in the face of the raw poverty, hunger and violence endemic to the Third World; on the other hand, attempts to dismiss the problems of the First World as trivial in comparison with the "real" Third World permanent catastrophies are no less fake—focusing on the Third World "real problems" is the ultimate form of escapism, of avoiding a confrontation with the antagonisms of one's own society. The gap that separates the two perspectives IS the truth of the situation.

The New World Order that is emerging is thus no longer the Fukuyamaist NWO of global liberal democracy but a NWO of the peaceful co-existence of different politico-theological ways of life—co-existence, of course, against the background of the smooth functioning of global capitalism. The obscenity of this process is that it can present itself as progress in anti-colonial struggle: the liberal West will no longer be allowed to impose standards on others, all ways of life will be treated as equal ... The last gasp of the "end of history" was Fukuyama's dream of global liberal-democratic capitalism, and with the September 11 attacks, that era came to an end.

*

Decades ago, Ayatollah Khomeini wrote: "We're not afraid of sanctions. We're not afraid of military invasion. What frightens us is the invasion of Western immorality." The fact that Khomeini talks about fear, about what a Muslim should fear most in the West, should be taken literally: Muslim fundamentalists do not have any problems with the brutality of economic and military struggles, their true enemy is not the Western economic neocolonialism and military aggressiveness but its "immoral" culture. The same holds for Putin's Russia where the conservative nationalists define their conflict with the West as cultural, in the last resort focused on sexual difference (Russia recently defined thrLGBT movement as a terrorist organization).

While the new populist Right advocates a clear vision (return to traditional values against demands for LGBT+ rights and recognition, reassertion of ethnic identity against immigrant threats and multiculturalism in general, etc.), the moderate Left is more and more simply disappearing: unable to propose a vision that would mobilize people, it is often taking refuge in Cancel Culture excesses. Our global situation should thus be read as a hologram: there is no longer one notion of progress dominating (even the golden calf of economic development is losing this role), we live in an era of the superposition of different futures, of different universalities (universal visions of progress). So the main options today are: remnants of the Fukuyama dream, direct religious fundamentalism, and especially what I cannot but call a moderately-authoritarian soft Fascism: market capitalism combined with a strong state mobilizing nationalist ideology to maintain social cohesion—think of Modi's India.

My suspicion is that this option will not prove effective against the threats we are facing today, and that a new form of Communism will have to be invented. Noam Chomsky often submitted me to a quite brutal critique, but I must say that I fully subscribe to his prediction of the approaching end of organized society: "we are at a unique moment in human history. Decisions that must be made right now will determine the course of future history if there is to be any human history, which is very much in doubt. There is a narrow window in which we must implement measures to avert cataclysmic destruction of the environment, measures that are quite feasible."[9] Ultimately it is as simple as that: the task that urgently imposes itself is that of universal solidarity and cooperation among all human communities. The ongoing impasses with geoengineering make brutally clear the need for global cooperation if we are to cope with global warming. Affected for years by prolonged heat waves, the authorities on the West coast of the US plan to spray gasses in the air above the sea near the coast which would block the heat from the sun rays to reach the earth. Critics pointed out that this idea is very risky not only because it may cause unpredictable damage in the area itself: even if it will work, it may change the overall situation so that heat domes will just be displaced and will emerge in other parts of the earth, most likely in Western Europe.[10] What lurks on the horizon is that the effects of global warming will be distributed around the world according to the financial strength of a country: the rich countries will protect themselves at the expense of the poor ones, "outsourcing" heat domes to them.

There is no higher historical necessity that pushes us in this direction, history is not on our side, it tends towards our collective suicide. No wonder many commentators conclude that the battle against global warming, the way it was conceived, *is already lost*—the moment has arrived for us to accept this fact and to rethink our entire strategy. First, we should abandon the notion of historical progress. As Walter Benjamin wrote, our task today is not to push forward the train of historical progress but to pull the emergency brake before we all end in post-capitalist barbarism. The ongoing crises which resonate with it and with each other in a complex interplay. This interplay is uncontrollable and full of dangers, and such a risky situation makes our moment an eminently political one.

Our present situation is the one described by Cixin Liu in his sci-fi masterpiece *The Three-Body Problem*[11]: a scientist is drawn into a Virtual-Reality game "Three Body" in which players find themselves on an alien planet, Trisolaris, whose three suns rise and set at strange and unpredictable intervals: sometimes too far away and horribly cold, sometimes far too close and destructively hot, and sometimes not seen for long periods of time. The players can somehow dehydrate themselves and the rest of the population to weather the worst seasons, but life is a constant struggle against apparently unpredictable elements, so that although players try to find ways to build a civilization and attempt to predict the strange cycles of heat and cold, they are condemned to destruction . . .

*

Do the latest disturbances in our environment not demonstrate that our Earth itself is gradually turning into Trisolaris? Devastating hurricanes, droughts and floods, not to mention global warming, do they all not indicate that we are witnessing something the only appropriate name for which is "the end of Nature"? ("Nature" is to be understood here in the traditional sense of a regular rhythm of seasons, the reliable background of human history, something on which we can count that it will always be there.) Now that God or Tradition can no longer play the role of the highest Limit, Nature takes over this role. But what kind of nature will this be? Even when we imagine global warming, we are aware that we are approaching a new world in which "England" will designate a barren dry country, while "Death Valley" will designate a big lake in

California. However, we still picture it as a new stability, with "regular and repeatable weather patterns":

> once humanity reaches the limit of carbon output, Earth's climate stabilizes at a new, higher average temperature. This higher temperature is overall bad for humans, because it still leads to higher sea levels and more extreme weather events. But at least it's stable: The Anthropocene looks like previous climate ages, only warmer, and it will still have.[12]

However, recent researches find it more probable that "Earth's climate leads to chaos. True, mathematical chaos. In a chaotic system, there is no equilibrium and no repeatable patterns. A chaotic climate would have seasons that change wildly from decade to decade (or even year to year). Some years would experience sudden flashes of extreme weather, while others would be completely quiet. Even the average Earth temperature may fluctuate wildly, swinging from cooler to hotter periods in relatively short periods of time. It would become utterly impossible to determine in what direction Earth's climate is headed."[13] Such an outcome is not only catastrophic for our survival, it also runs against our (human) most basic notion of nature, that of repeatable pattern of seasons.

Although our planet has only one sun around which it circulates, our predicament could be called "a six-crises problem": ecological crisis, economic imbalances, wars, chaotic migrations, the threat of AI, disintegration of society. Although the underlying cause of these crises is the dynamic of global capitalism, the interaction of crises leads to chaos which is no less unpredictable than the situation on Trisolaris. Do these crises strengthen each other or does their interaction offer some hope—say, a hope that the ecological crisis will compel us to move beyond capitalism and war to a social order of global solidarity? Although Cixin Liu imagines wonderful and/or terrifying new scientific and technological inventions, he is fully aware that the basic dimension of our crises is social, the coexistence of different civilizations as well as the antagonisms within each civilization. So the solution will also have to be social (a new social organization of our societies), not just technological.

The first thing to do today is therefore to act accordingly to our predicament: to prepare for the forthcoming emergency state(s). The paradox is that acting like these disasters will happen in all their dimensions (from ecological catastrophes to wars and digital breakdowns) is the only chance we have to prevent them from really happening. The Polish Prime Minister Donald Tusk recently said: "I know it sounds devastating, especially to people of the younger generation, but we have to mentally get used to the arrival of a new era. The prewar era."[14] He is right, although not unconditionally—the situation is still open, and what we should say is, to be more precise: "If a new world war will happen, it will be clear that it has begun back in 2022, and that its deployment was necessary." Why this strange paradox of retroactivity? Maybe quantum mechanics offers a solution here—but we should take precautions to avoid the type of direct progressist reading of quantum mechanics advocated by Thomas Hertog in his appropriation of Hannah Arendt's critique of scientific objectivism:

> A genuine quantum outlook on the universe counters the relentless alienating forces of modern science and lets one build cosmology anew from an interior viewpoint. ... Observers have a creative role in cosmic affairs, introducing a backward-in-time element. We read the fundamentals of the history of the universe from the top down. It turns the apparent design of the universe upside down: at a quantum level the universe engineers its own biofriendliness. Life and the universe are in some way a mutual fit, according to the theory, because, in a deeper sense, they come into existence together.[15]

So it may appear that this state before natural laws set in is a natural counterpart of freedom: human freedom is a short-circuit to that primordial state before natural laws. However, can we really say that "at a quantum level the universe engineers its own biofriendliness"? The collapse of quantum superpositions is contingent, not the result of a struggle and our decisions on what to focus, so the engineering of biofriendliness is strictly retroactive: it appears only when, from our present standpoint as living beings, we look backwards and reconstruct the line which ends up in our situation. Hertog makes a further step which I find problematic: he says that biologists can also "use this knowledge [arrived at through backward-in-time reasoning] to influence future branchings." So it is not only that "at the quantum level, the universe engineers its own biofriendliness," it is also that "scientists are starting to envisage hypothetical laws and then engineer systems in which they emerge,"(261) and this means we (humanity) are at the

> dawn of a new era, the first of its kind in the history of Earth, and perhaps even of the cosmos, in which a species attempts to reconfigure and transcend the biosphere it has evolved in. Echoing Hannah Arendt, from merely undergoing evolution, we are transitioning towards engineering it and, with it, our humanities.
>
> (263)

This idea misreads Arendt's intention: when she emphasizes our (humanity's) finitude and groundedness in Earth, Arendt speaks as a Heideggerian for whom the very idea of "engineering evolution and, with it, our humanness" is the danger we are confronting today: when we engineer nature, inclusive of our own nature, humanness is over because by definition it cannot be engineered—we are thrown into it, and Arendt's Heideggerian point is that our relationship to reality as an object of engineering is rooted in a certain disclosure of the meaning of Being which stands for utter self-destructive nihilism.

In other words, although Herzog rejects scientific objectivism and determinism, he is nevertheless coming all too close to classic Marxist determinism in the sense of Plekhanov, Kautsky and Bukharin: social reality is totally determined by necessary laws, the fact that we cannot predict the exact moment of the turmoil of our near future simply means that our knowledge of reality is incomplete. One should note here how Kautsky slightly relativizes this determinism with the reference to our knowledge by way of evoking the (totally misunderstood) notion that freedom is a knowledge of necessity: if we know (some of) the laws of nature and society, we can manipulate them (through technological interventions and social engineering) and give them a spin more benevolent to us. According to this argument, knowing the laws of nature gives us the "freedom" to build machines, to use electricity, to generate nuclear energy—we don't violate the laws of nature here, we just use them for our purposes . . . I see a double problem in this solution. First, are we really free when we possess such knowledge or is freedom here just another name for our ignorance (since we simply don't know how our own "free" decisions are determined)? Is the implication not that we are somehow exempted from the laws of nature like an engineer is exempted from the machine it runs? Second, and much more important, such a view of freedom transposes the model of the scientific-technological exploitation of nature onto emancipatory social processes: from an objective distance, a subject learns the laws that regulate history of his time, and then decides to manipulate history to achieve his (or his group's) goals... Such a stance has nothing to do with a proper Communist stance in which truth is accessible only from a subjective engagement.

The idea that "the courage of our questions and the depth of our answers would allow us to navigate planet Earth safely and wisely into the future"(266) is thus suspicious from the Heideggerian standpoint as well as from the standpoint of quantum mechanics. I find utterly problematic the vision of a smooth passage from spontaneous/unpredictable quantum collapses to having an overview of superpositions and then deciding for one among them that fits our interests:

> Taking a quantum view, the myriad paths forking off into the future are in a sense already out there, as a landscape of possibilities. Some futures may even appear rather plausible. We should learn from the past, though, that chance constantly interferes, leading history to take unexpected twists and turns.
>
> (264)

This is how a Slovene cultural figure recently described himself: "I am quantically free, unpredictable." Pure nonsense, since freedom is not unpredictable contingency but a "freely" imposed necessity, the act of decision which cannot be reduced to its causes, while a quantum collapse is by definition a point at which chance interferes. Furthermore, if our unsurpassable finitude means anything at all, it means precisely that we a priori cannot acquire "a clear global vision" of our predicament: to do this we would have, as it were, to step on our own shoulders and look at ourselves from outside. The top-down approach means that our evolution has already collapsed into our present state and we cannot see in advance which superpositions are contained as non-collapsed in our present state.

The notion of finitude could also be given a different spin. A simple but convincing idea circulated recently in some media: since there is a limited number of different sounds that can be used to compose a song, and since millions of songs were already written, it is practically impossible today to avoid plagiarism—basically *all possible songs were already written*. (This idea can even be strengthened if we take into account the fact that the combination of sounds is constrained by cultural—or perhaps, as Steven Pinker claims, even genetic—limitations to sound combinations which are experienced as pleasant or just acceptable by our mind.) Does the same hold also for philosophy? Are all basic philosophical stances already formulated? However, the paradox here is that the experience of the space of songs as potentially infinite is grounded in our very finitude—only if we could step out of our finitude and grasp the space of possible songs from an external view, would it be possible for us to see its finitude. Infinity is thus strictly a category rooted in our finitude—as in quantum mechanics in which the multiplicity of superpositions appears infinite precisely because we cannot step out of ourselves and grasp the totality of the universe "objectively."

So how should we use the notion of hologram? In recent quantum mechanics, it designates the image of an object which catches not only its actual state but also its interference pattern with other options that were lost when the actual state imposed itself. (We developed this topic in the first part of this book.) While I am, of course, not qualified to pass a scientific judgment on these notions, I find the temptation to apply them to human history irresistible. Perhaps the supreme example of holographic history is provided by none other than Marx. Marx is not an evolutionist, he writes history "top-down," i.e., his starting point is the contemporary global capitalist order, and from this point he reads the entire history as a gradual approximation to capitalism. This is not teleology: history is not guided by capitalism as its telos, but *once capitalism emerges*, it provides the key to the entire (pre)history—here enters Marx's well-known story (in *Grundrisse*) of linear development from prehistorical societies through Asiatic despotism, Antique slavery, and feudalism to capitalism. But, again, there is no teleological necessity in this development, it results from a series of contingent collapses of superpositions.

Along these lines, Alex Taek-Gwang Lee[16] conspicuously demonstrates the dialectical intricacies of the relationship between Western Europe and the Far

East during European modernity: it is not the case that dynamic European capitalism penetrated and triumphed over the inert substantial reality of the Far East. First, Asia did not experience itself as "Asia" at all before the European colonization: the notion of "Asia" as the inert domain lacking any dynamic development is already the product of European colonialism which (mis)perceived Asia in this way. Second (and even more important), the rise of so-called "Pan-Asianism" from the late nineteenth century onwards was not propelled by the desire to avoid the destabilizing madness of European capitalism and to regain the traditional stability and values of the pre-modern Asia; on the contrary, it was paradoxically the name of the attempt to leave behind the inert "Asia" and to modernize it in a way that would integrate the Western achievements while trying to avoid their self-destructive aspects.

In a collapse of the wave function, other possible superpositions do not simply disappear, they leave their traces in the result (the single reality that emerges in a collapse). Does something similar not hold for political struggles? When a peaceful negotiation wins over armed resistance, armed resistance is inscribed in the result. Our media like to mention, as the two examples of successfully negotiated solutions, the rise of the ANC to power in South Africa and the establishment of civil rights as the result of peaceful protests led by Martin Luther King in the US—in both cases, it is obvious that the (relative) victory of the peaceful negotiations occurred because the establishment feared the violent resistance (from the more radical wing of ANC as well as of the American Blacks). In short, negotiations succeeded because of they were accompanied by a superposed ominous threat of armed struggle.

*

What David Graeber and David Wengrow propose is to abandon capitalism as the "top" from which we regress to the past that leads to it—the interest of works like *The Dawn of Everything*[17] is that they provide a kind of quantum superposition to the actual early development of civilization: a big well-organized state (Incas) which (for some time, at least) did not follow the line of neolithic centralization, state authority and class distinctions. The split of the Inca society into its "anarchist" version and authoritarian version thus captures the moment when, in a kind of Darwinian struggle, two superposed social orders were fighting for predominance, and the authoritarian one won.

Since, as Fredric Jameson suggested, all (hi)stories are ultimately the stories of the Fall from traditional organic society to chaotic modernity or, in religious terms, from medieval Catholicism to Protestant individualism, no wonder that some Catholic theologians dream of a Catholic modernization which would unite individual freedom with an organic sense of community. Along these lines, John Millbank advocates a version of alternate modernity whose possibility is embodied in the line of Christian thought from Acquinas through Eckhart, Cusa and Kierkegaard, up to Chesterton and Millbank himself. In refusing the Protestant narrative of progress of Christianity from Orthodoxy and Catholicism to Protestantism and then Hegel's atheism, he outlines the possibility of an alternate development; the implication is also that history is not a necessary logical/conceptual progress, but a contingent narrative with multiple trends, so that it could also have turned otherwise:

> It is easy, for example, to imagine that a more humanist reformation might have taken place (in 15th–16th-century Spain this had at one stage more or less already occurred) such that, while lay life and piety would have moved more centre-stage, the specifics of Reformation and Counter-Reformation dogmatics would not have dominated the European future. This could well have entailed less stand-off between divine grace and human freedom, less dualism of nature and grace in theory and of secular and sacred in practice— with the upshot that economic and political institutions might have remained more ecclesiastically-shaped, even though now more lay-directed. ... Why is it not legitimate to imagine "another" Christian modernity that would be linked to the universal encouragement of mystical openness and productivity, rather than the separation between a forensic faith and an instrumentalizing reason? But as I shall show, such a modernity would persist with the alternative dynamism of paradox and not pass over into the hypocritical sterility of dialectics.[18]

While opening up the space for individual freedom and creativity, this alternate modernity would constrain them to—and (re)inscribe them into—the only ground on which they can really thrive and avoid nihilistic self-destruction, that of justice as "identical with objective social harmony"... in short, Millbank imagines an alternate collapse that would stabilize the chaos of modernity.

Along the same lines, some Marxist historians have pointed out that the explosion of capitalism in early modernity was conditioned by (the contingent interaction of) two disconnected factors: the availability of surplus financial wealth (mainly gold from Latin America), and the rise of dispossessed "free" individuals through the privatization of commons—the surplus wealth was "invested," used to employ and exploit dispossessed workers. But this combination was in no way predestined: history could have taken a different turn, with the dispossessed poor enslaved or mobilized as a threat to the existing order, with the surplus of gold just bringing about its devaluation, etc.

*

In a homologous way, there are two opposed ways to conceptualize the relationship between capitalism and socialism: in the standard Marxist progressive view, capitalism is the passage from pre-modern societies to socialism, while for the pro-capitalist view the actual socialism was a passage from a lower to a higher form of capitalism. So which of these conceptualizations is correct? Viewed through the lens of the quantum notion of superpositions, they are both potentially true, since the ongoing struggle is precisely the conflict to determine which one will prevail. One of the two is not true now but *will have been* true once it prevails.

The lesson of these paradoxes is that subdivisions within a universal genre always simultaneously split the genre itself. In the Slovene Dictionary of Literary Language, "man" is defined as a "human being of a male gender," while "woman" is defined as a "person of female gender"—why is the difference not presented as a specific difference within a common species (humankind OR persons), why is the universal term itself different in each case (man is a species of human being, woman is a species of person)? "Person" is defined as "a human individual irrespective of its gender," while "human being" is defined as "a being able to think and speak." In English, "person" is defined as "a human being regarded as an individual." Furthermore, "persona" is defined as "the aspect of someone's character that is presented to or perceived by others," or as a strategic mask of identity in public, the public image of one's *personality*, the social *role* that one adopts—one can already discern here the link to the well-known motif of femininity as masquerade. Recall also that we can say about somebody "as a person, he is nice and warm, but his theory is worthless" (or the opposite, for that matter: "as a person, he is nasty and despicable, but his theories are those of a genius")—here we can easily discern the anti-feminist spin of characterizing women as persons: they can be warm and pleasant, although their serious work is worthless . . .

So a man directly relates to the universality of human species, he is its only direct embodiment, while a woman is deprived of this dimension of direct universality and counts only in her individuality. What we encounter here is a perfect case of the dialectics of genus and species: we don't have the genus of human beings with its two major species (men and women)—*each species implies/constructs its own genus (of human beings, of persons)*. But might we not also claim that "person" implies a unique inner spiritual wealth and dignity, while "human being" is an empty abstraction? In this case, I would much prefer "human being": there is almost something inhuman in the idea of a human being who is not a person but just an impersonal subject, while "person" brings in all the imaginary shit of inner life . . .[19]

How should we react to this false neutrality of being-human? It is not enough to say that women are also fully human. In his perspicuous reflections on men, women, and trans in Seminar XVIII,[20] Lacan plays with the idea that "there is no sexual relationship" grounds the dimension of freedom. "There is no sexual relationship" is not symmetrical: if a woman were to exist, she would be a counterpart to men, as is the case in premodern sexualized ontologies which oppose masculine and feminine cosmic principles (yin and yang, etc.). But woman is precisely NOT a symmetrical counterpart to man: a man is fully caught in the imaginary-symbolic semblance, he fully identifies with his symbolic identity, his stance is that of displaying his phallic power aimed at impressing his others, while, in contrast to men, a woman doesn't exist, and this non-existence (the fact that a woman is not entirely located in the symbolic order which provides existence) IS the space of freedom. We have to take this as far as it can go: there is no neutral subject which is then subdivided into masculine and feminine—such a subdivision secretly (or not so secretly) privileges man as a model subject. But from a Lacanian standpoint, the Cartesian subject (as a model of modern subjectivity) is in its basic dimension feminine, and being-a-man stands for the escape from the abyss of freedom.

We can see here how right Lacan was when he pointed out that progressive evolution is a new form of teleology. The true break of teleology is only a top-down history which conceives the linear progress as a retroactive fact, as the outcome of a backwards-projection of our standpoint into the past. In a quantum-holographic history, this retroactivity is rendered visible, and all superpositions that were present in the past and were erased through their collapse are rendered visible again. In this sense one can even say that Walter Benjamin, in his *Theses on History*, proposes a holographic notion of history in contrast to the predominant progressist-evolutionary version: a present revolution redeems the past, i.e., it re-actualizes past superpositions lost in their collapse towards a ruling ideology. Such a direct contact between the present and the past is timeless in the sense that it by-passes the temporal causal network connecting the past and the present:

> The past carries with it a temporal index by which it is referred to redemption. There is a secret agreement between past generations and the present one. Our coming was expected on earth.[21]

*

In some passages Heidegger expands this approach onto pre-human nature itself: "I often ask myself—this has for a long time been a fundamental question for me—what nature would be without man—must it not resonate through him in order to attain its ownmost potency."[22] Note that this passage is from the time immediately after Heidegger's lectures on *The Fundamental Concepts of Metaphysics* from 1929–30, where he also formulated a Schellingian hypothesis that, perhaps, animals are, in a hitherto unknown way, aware of their lack, of the "poorness" of their relating to the world—perhaps there is an infinite pain pervading the entire living nature:

> if deprivation in certain forms is a kind of suffering, and poverty and deprivation of world belongs to the animal's being, then a kind of pain and suffering would have to permeate the whole animal realm and the realm of life in general.[23]

So when Heidegger speculates about pain in nature itself taken independently of man, how can we read this claim without committing ourselves to anthropocentric-teleological thinking? As we already mentioned, the answer was indicated by none other than Marx who, in his introduction to *Grundrisse*, wrote:

> "Bourgeois society is the most developed and the most complex historic organization of production. The categories which express its relations, the comprehension of its structure, thereby also allows insights into the structure and the relations of production of all the vanished social formations out of whose ruins and elements it built itself up, whose partly still unconquered remnants are carried along within it, whose mere nuances have developed explicit significance within it, etc. Human anatomy contains a key to the anatomy of the ape. The intimations of higher development among the subordinate animal species, however, can be understood only after the higher development is already known."[24]

In short, to paraphrase Pierre Bayard[25], what Marx is saying here is that the anatomy of the ape, although it was formed earlier in time than the anatomy of man, nonetheless in a way *plagiarizes by anticipation the anatomy of man*. There is no teleology here, the effect of teleology is strictly retroactive: *once capitalism is here* (emerging in a wholly contingent way), it provides a universal key for all other formations. Teleology resides precisely in evolutionary progressism where the key to the anatomy of man is the anatomy of ape.

*

Along these lines, one can also understand why Kant claims that, in some sense, the world was created so that we can fight our moral struggles in it: when we are caught in an intense struggle which means everything to us, we experience it as if the whole world is at stake and will collapse if we fail; the same holds also when we fear the failure of a love affair. There is no direct teleology here, our love encounter is the result of a contingent encounter, so it could easily also not have happened—but once it does happen, it decides how we experience the whole of reality. When Benjamin wrote that a big revolutionary battle decides not only the fate of the present but also of all past failed struggles, he mobilizes the same retroactive mechanism that reaches its climax in religious claims that, in a crucial battle, not only the fate of us but the fate of god himself is decided. Therein resides the difference between evolutionary historicism and the properly historical dialectic in suspense:

Thinking involves not only the movement of thoughts but also their zero-hour [*Stillstellung*]. Where thinking suddenly halts in a constellation overflowing with tensions, there it yields a shock to the same, through which it crystallizes as a monad. The historical materialist approaches a historical object solely and alone where he encounters it as a monad. In this structure he cognizes the sign of a messianic zero-hour [*Stillstellung*] of events, or put differently, a revolutionary chance in the struggle for the suppressed past.[26]

It is not just that, in such moments of the "dialectics in suspense," a present revolutionary moment is torn out from its context as a monad and is superposed directly on past failed attempts. More importantly, the past attempts failed (are excluded from the past collapse), which means that the past is not just the victorious past: what was obliterated when one superposition won in the past remains in the historical memory, waiting to be reawakened by a different present moment. In this sense, if revolutions in a progress-oriented conceptualization mean that for every step society takes "forwards," there will be an immense cost to human life and dignity—what I called "squashed birds" in *Against Progress*—then the revolution Walter Benjamin envisaged would in fact be the ultimate counter-revolution: a backlash in which everything that has been sacrificed returns to wreak its revenge or, at least, to register the price paid for progress. Spartacus lost (don't forget that he defended a "primitive" pre-class society against the "progressive" Rome), but the memory of his slave rebellion persists as a virtual shadow and provides a holographic depth to later rebellions.

*

Such a standpoint casts new light on the way we tend to dismiss all forms of religious fundamentalism. As I have written elsewhere (*Zero Point*), the standard "clash of cultures" interpretation of the Russia-Ukraine war as a conflict between Western liberalism and Russia's traditional authoritarianism is deeply misleading. Putin is not a Russian traditionalist, he has to be located as the last person in the series of brutal modernizers of Russia, after Ivan the Terrible, Peter the Great, Catherine the Great, and Stalin. The last named was a great admirer of Peter the Great who built a new capital of Russia on the Baltic sea (Petersburg) to establish a direct link with Western Europe—the human costs of this project run into hundreds of thousands. Peter's reforms were opposed by so-called Old Believers, Eastern Orthodox Christians who maintained the liturgical and ritual practices of the Russian Orthodox Church as they were before the reforms of Patriarch Nikon of Moscow between 1652 and 1666. Resisting the accommodation of Russian piety to the contemporary forms of Greek Orthodox worship, many Old Believers chose death rather than give up their faith: collective suicides of thousands by fire continued from the seventeenth century into the nineteenth century. The best known artistic representation of this rejection is Modest Mussorgsky's unfinished opera *Khovanshchina* which deals with the rebellion of Prince Ivan Khovansky and the Old Believers against the regent Sofia Alekseyevna and the young Tsar Peter who were attempting to institute Westernizing reforms in Russia. After Sofia managed to suppress the so-called Khovanshchina (Khovansky affair), the Old Believers committed mass suicide.

*

One should note that things only really changed with the October Revolution: the first Soviet government (appointed on October 26, 1917) included several prominent figures with an Old Believers background: Aleksei Rykov, the first Commissar on Internal Affairs, Vladimir Milyutin, Commissar for Agriculture, Alexander Shliapnikov, Commissar for Labour, and Viktor Nogin, Commissar for Trade and Industry. The Cabinet secretary was Vladimir Bonch-Bruyevich, a top Russian expert on the Old Believers. Bolsheviks regarded the Old Believers and sectarians as a kind of social protest, the opposition against the Tsarist regime—and they were right: it was far more than a question of competing rituals. Old Believers distrusted the unity of Church and state (which de facto meant the subordination of Church to state) and wanted the religious community to remain a self-organization of common people.

No wonder that the persecution not only of religion in general but especially of Old Believers intensified in the Stalin era. Between 1937 and 1940 the remnants of a few noteworthy Ural Old Believer monasteries were secretly relocated to the remote lower Yenisei River area in Siberia. As late as 1951 the Dubches secret Old Believer monasteries were spotted from the air by Soviet authorities and subsequently demolished; the Old Believers living there were arrested and all the buildings, icons, and books were burned.[27] The subordination of the Church to the state continues today when Putin has directly mobilized the Orthodox church into an instrument of his politics—for example, recall the statements by Patriarch Kirill of the Russian Orthodox Church that there is no need to instill fear around nuclear weapons, as Christians are not afraid of the end of the world. In a supreme act of obscenity, Kirill thanked Russian scientists for developing "incredible weapons": "We await the Lord Jesus Christ who will come in great glory, destroy Evil, and judge all nations."[28]

The lesson here is that what may appear as a reactionary move par excellence—a return to old rigid orthodoxy—can well express class struggle, i.e., a resistance to new forms of exploitation and domination masked as "modernization." The unsurpassed model of such a religious utopia is Canudos, the outlaw community deep in the Brazilian backlands of Bahia which towards the end of the nineteenth century became a home to prostitutes, freaks, beggars, bandits, and the most wretched of the poor headed by Antônio Conselheiro, an apocalyptic prophet:

> This community developed a "mutual, cooperative and solidary concept of work." In Canudos, which once held a population of 24 thousand people and 5,200 homes, there was a kind of socio-mystical, religious, assisting, community power inspired by the "equalitarian fraternity of the primitive Christian communism," in which there was no hunger. "They all worked together. *Nobody had anything. Everybody worked the soil, everybody labored. Harvested . . . Here's yours . . . Here's yours. Nobody got more nor less.*"[29]

Canudos was a utopian space without money, property, taxes, and marriage, and it did not disintegrate because of its immanent tensions or because this is not a "realistic" way to live. It was destroyed by the military forces of the "progressive" and secular Brazilian government; Canudos's buildings were razed to the ground, all its inhabitants massacred, its guiding spirit Conselheiro beheaded in 1897. Everything is to be endorsed in Canudos, up to the religious "fanaticism"—it is as if, in such communities, *the Benjaminian other side of the historical Progress, the defeated ones, acquires a space of their own*. Utopia EXISTED here for a brief period of time. This is the only way to account for the "irrational," excessive, violence of the destruction of these communities: ALL inhabitants of Canudos, children and women included, were slaughtered, as if the very memory of the possibility of freedom had to be erased.

An obvious counter-argument immediately arises here: does this mean that we should bracket aggressive Muslim fundamentalism up to ISIS and Boko Haram alongside Canudos as Benjaminian backlashes against the death march of progress? No, and the line that separates them is very clear.

*

The paradox is that the problem of populist fundamentalism does not reside in the fact that it is too identitarian (against which we should emphasize fluidity and contingency of every identity) but, on the contrary, in the fact that it lacks proper identity, that its identity clings onto the denial of its constitutive Other. Are the so-called fundamentalists, be it Christian or Muslim, really fundamentalists in the authentic sense of the term? What they lack is a feature that is easy to discern in all authentic fundamentalists, from Tibetan Buddhists to the Amish in the US: the absence of resentment and envy, the deep indifference towards the non-believers' way of life. If today's so-called fundamentalists really believe they have found their way to Truth, why should they feel threatened by non-believers, why should they envy them? When a Buddhist encounters Western hedonists, he hardly condemns them—he just benevolently notes that the hedonist's search for happiness is self-defeating. In contrast to true fundamentalists, the pseudo-fundamentalists are deeply bothered, intrigued, fascinated, by the sinful life of the non-believers. One can feel that, in fighting the sinful other, they are fighting their own temptation. This is why the so-called Christian or Muslim fundamentalists are a disgrace to true fundamentalism.

Let's take a closer look at the Tibetans who are extremely self-centered: "To them, Tibet was the center of the world, the heart of civilization."[30] What characterizes the European civilization is, on the contrary, precisely its *ex-centered* character—the notion that the ultimate pillar of Wisdom, the secret *agalma*, the spiritual treasure, the lost object-cause of desire, which we in the West long ago betrayed, could be recuperated out there, in the forbidden exotic place. Colonization was never simply the imposition of Western values, the assimilation of the Oriental and other Others to the European Sameness; it was always also the search for the lost spiritual innocence of OUR OWN civilization.

This story begins at the very dawn of the Western civilization, in Ancient Greece: for the Greeks, Egypt was the mythic place of lost ancient wisdom. And the same holds today in our own societies: the difference between the authentic fundamentalists and the Moral Majority perverted fundamentalists is that the first (like, say, the Amish in the USA) go along very well with their American neighbours, since they are simply centered on their own world, not bothered by what goes on out there, among "them," while the Moral Majority fundamentalist is always haunted by the ambiguous attitude of horror/envy with regard to the unspeakable pleasures in which the sinners engage—this attitude pushes them towards acts of violence like bombings and slaughters.

Back to today's Russia: Putin's regime has thus nothing to do with any authentic ancient Russian spirituality that rejects European modernization. It uses a fantasized "Eurasia" to legitimize its own project of brutal modernization and conquest. This is why we should not dismiss Russia as a country caught in a neo-conservative vortex resisted only by a tiny liberal minority: those who want to free Russia of Putinism will not be able to do it without awakening the dormant authentic Russian spirituality which resists authoritarian state power.

And even further back to Graeber and Marx, this is why the superposition of a more "democratic" Inca society persists and gets resuscitated in later rebellions against centralized despotic state power. In the linear progression of slavery, feudalism, and capitalism, each of these actual nodal points is accompanied by a series of superpositions: feudalism is not just feudalism but all that could have happened but was obliterated by its rise. And, back to quantum mechanics, this is why superpositions (multiple paths of a particle) are not just our "bookkeeping devices" that enable us to calculate reality but part of reality itself.

We don't change the past facts, we just locate them into a different symbolic context, we change their meaning. So we do not have a Whole which comprises its parts: each part comprises multiple universalities between which we are forced to choose. This brings us back to the basic premise of holography: the whole is a part of its part, i.e., *a part is composed of all the (other) parts of its whole*. (Capitalism is only a part of history, a moment in the global development, but *it imposed itself as the prism through which we see the entire development as steps gradually leading to it.*) True history is thus not a gradual development of parts, but a series of shifts in how *its "whole" is itself (re)structured*. We get a series of Wholes because the actual Whole is inaccessible, and the only Whole we can reach is a negative one, the impossibility to reach the Whole inscribed into reality itself.

Do we not find the same parallax duality in Heidegger's notion of history of Being as the history of disclosures? Heidegger sometimes emphasizes the abyssal contingency of disclosures (they just happen, with no deeper logic or ground), and he sometimes comes close to the language of teleology, presenting the history of the West as the gradually growing oblivion of manifestness, the oblivion which culminates in today's scientific/technological global order which poses a threat to the very dimension of disclosure/manifestness grounded in human finitude.

Our predicament confronts us with the deadlock of the contemporary "society of choice." We pride ourselves for living in a society in which we freely decide about things which matter. However, we find ourselves constantly in the position of having to decide about matters that will fundamentally affect our lives, but without a proper foundation in knowledge. Such a situation is properly frustrating: although we know that it all depends on us, we cannot ever predict the consequences of our acts—*we are not impotent, but, quite on the contrary, omnipotent, without being able to determine the scope of our powers*. While we cannot gain full mastery over our bio-sphere, it is unfortunately in our power to derail it, to disturb its balance so that it will run amok, swiping us away in the process.

2

Can artificial intelligence really think?

The way capital controls our lives is perhaps best exemplified by BlackRock, a mega-company that works discreetly, avoiding too much public exposure. It has nearly $10 trillion in assets under management. That's more than the GDP of every country in the world except for the United States and China. BlackRock is a top shareholder across a wide range of global industries that include oil and gas, technology, retail, big banks, healthcare, weapons manufacturing, and much more. All this makes BlackRock one of the most powerful corporate actors on the planet, whose influence touches every aspect of our daily lives. Although the CEO Larry Fink has attempted to brand the firm as sensitive to global challenges like climate change, structural racism, and public health, BlackRock's investment activity and governance practices drive business operations that directly harm Black and Indigenous communities and people of color around the world. BlackRock is one of the world's biggest corporate drivers of climate chaos and ecocide—it is a major culprit behind the global climate breakdown. BlackRock also remains one of the world's biggest investors in the coal industry. In sum: there may be no greater existential crisis facing humanity than the global climate catastrophe and BlackRock is playing an active role in perpetuating this crisis. BlackRock also props up many companies whose products are tied to gun violence in the United States and endless war and occupation of places like in Iraq, Afghanistan, and Palestine.[1]

As expected, AI plays a key role in how Blackrock operates: Blackrock built and uses Aladdin (Asset, Liability and Debt and Derivative Investment

Network), an electronic system which, already back in 2013, handled about $11 trillion in assets (including BlackRock's $4.1 trillion assets), which was about 7% of the world's financial assets, and kept track of about 30,000 investment portfolios. As of 2020, Aladdin managed $21.6 trillion in assets. The network in Wenatchee, Washington State, consists of around 6,000 computers, and the software uses these computers to analyze global economic data, stock market prices and numerous other economic factors. For example, sudden changes in government, weather conditions or possible disasters are also taken into account when evaluating portfolios.[2] What all this means is that programs like Aladdin are not neutral: their decisions are based on premises which largely ignore environmental and human damage. Blackrock is arguably the ultimate figure of techno-feudalism where the feudal master itself operates blindly, as an algorithm which ignores personal quirks of the ancient feudal lords. But the main problem with such a "realist" approach which focuses on economic interests is not only that it leads to a cynical distance and precludes serious political engagement: its ultimate message is "don't struggle, your fight will just help military industry (or medical industry or . . .)." It also does not provide a true dialectical mediation, a true analysis of how a form of ideology arises—such a direct foundation of ideologico-political stances and practices in economic interests remains external, it ignores how individuals subjectively perceive their predicament and mystify it. Where is the causal link between objective "interests of the capital" and populist militarism as a subjective stance? An individual cannot stand on its own shoulders, becoming aware of the "interests of the capital" and then translating them into an ideological stance.

Many of the fake "Leftists" who blame NATO for the Ukrainian war react to it with a surprisingly vulgar economic reductionism: the NATO support of Ukraine reflects the interests of the Western military-industrial complex and the war goes on to satisfy these interests . . . (To avoid a misunderstanding, yes, economic relations matter.[3] There is, however, a limit to such a vulgar economist approach: at the end of this road, we will be told that the Nazis perpetrated the Holocaust in order to boost the profits of IG Farben which was making the gases to kill the Jews . . . True, war can help the economy—remember that the US got out of the Great Depression only during World War II; however, the enormous amounts spent on arms could also be used for ecology and social solidarity without automatically causing an economic crisis.) In the case of Ukrainian resistance to Russian aggression, can we seriously claim that the desperate Ukrainians who were ready to fight for their survival were somehow just "reflecting" the interests of the Western military-industrial complex?

Or, let's take a negative example: were the Nazis fighting till 1945, killing millions and sacrificing hundreds of thousands of their own, just to satisfy the interests of capital? There is a complex interplay between these two levels—the idea of an evil ruling class aware of its economic interests and manipulating the crowd through its control of ideological apparatuses is far too naïve. Yes, the Nazis committed horrors because they were deeply immersed in an ideological mystification, but this mystification was immanent to their ideology: yes, they lied to themselves when they projected the cause of evil into the Jews, but many of them were fully committed to this lie, ready to die for it. Here psychoanalysis enters: ideology is not a direct reflection of some external economic processes, it is divided in itself, it has its own "unconscious." As Marx knew it when he spoke about "commodity fetishism," ideology is not external to socio-economic processes, it is inscribed into their very core. There are no objective "interests of capital," these "interests" are always-already ideologically mediated.

When we talk about AI and war, we should begin with a fact that is often ignored—not just how AI is already widely used to regulate military activities, but how the machinery that supports AI can in itself be a target of military operations. In the third week of July 2014, an unexpected malfunctioning in a specific aspect of Windows programs brought thousands of digital programs and links to a standstill, and these disruptions in the virtual universe had dire consequences in our real lives: they have hit airlines, banks, businesses, schools, governments, and even emergency services.[4] This fairly limited accident made it clear how our daily lives are already regulated through digital processes to such an extent that a more global outage of the web would in all probability cause a regression of our daily lives into an uncontrollable violence of the new barbarism. (If civilization used to be three meals away from anarchy, it is probably now three Cloudflare meltdowns away . . .) No wonder, then, that Western powers are worried about Russian submarines closely monitoring the trans-Atlantic cables—in all probability they have orders to destroy them in the case of an all-out war. Plus we can be sure that the US and China are making similar plans. There is in all probability a new mode of MAD (Mutually Assured Destruction) operative even now: superpowers definitely try to implant into the AI systems of its opponents digital viruses which, when activated, could immobilize the entire life of a country (no electricity, water, etc.). Since both sides know this, they are well aware that if they activate these viruses they will immediately suffer the same devastating consequences.

This prospect opens up a vision of global war that differs from our usual imaginings (drones dropping bombs, nuclear projectiles hitting our cities . . .): what if we will simply awaken one morning and look through the window where everything will appear normal, the sun shining, the birds singing. However, we will all of a sudden realize not that there will be a war but that the war already took place and is in some sense over—we already lost it, and the eventual "real" battles will be just its aftermath. Moreover, most of these battles will take place not against the enemy but in our society itself, among desperate individuals and groups fighting for survival. So yes, war reduced to a technological process regulated by AI is terrifying, but it still remains rooted in social relations. To cite a recent example, it was reported that a significant role in the bombing of Gaza has been played by an AI-based programme called "Lavender," which during the first few weeks of the war designated as many as 37,000 Palestinian individuals as suspected militants and their homes as targets for possible airstrikes. It was reported that the army acted upon Lavender's "kill lists" with no requirement to check the basis of the information, despite knowing that the system had an error rate as high as 10% and

> is known to occasionally mark individuals who have merely a loose connection to militant groups, or no connection at all. Moreover, the Israeli army systematically attacked the targeted individuals while they were in their homes—usually at night while their whole families were present—rather than during the course of military activity. . . . In addition, when it came to targeting alleged junior militants marked by Lavender, the army preferred to only use unguided missiles, commonly known as "dumb" bombs (in contrast to "smart" precision bombs), which can destroy entire

buildings on top of their occupants and cause significant casualties. "You don't want to waste expensive bombs on unimportant people . . .," said one of the intelligence officers.[5]

Incidentally, what this last fact means is that if the target to be bombed is classified as unimportant, the chance that his entire family or house will be killed or destroyed is much greater than if the target is a top Hamas member. But the main point is the following one. The Israeli propaganda always emphasizes the direct personal brutality of the Hamas attackers: they rape, kill, and abduct in a direct physical contact with their victims, enjoying the fear and pain inflicted on them. The implication is that the IDF procedure is somehow less horrible: all the work is done by AI, the soldier just presses a button far behind the front. But is the impersonal AI process that regulates the bombing and killing of thousands in some sense not even more terrifying than direct face-to-face killing? Is the idea that such a killing somehow de-culpabilizes the soldier who presses the button not the ultimate obscenity, the first case of a genocide done by AI?

From the ancient times of *Bhagavadgita* and Zen, military doctrine advises soldiers that they must act with inner peace and distance from external reality: avoiding direct subjective engagement, not identifying with one's own acts, is the key to success. This distance is becoming direct reality today when more and more military operations are done from a safe distance: the soldier is sitting far from the front and just pushes buttons or moves a joystick in front of a screen to direct a rocket or a drone. A Ukrainian gamer-turned-drone operator said video games have helped him fight Russians. He told Reuters his mother said his gaming would come to nothing—but now he's making deadly drone strikes. It was reported years ago that the notorious Wagner Group was also searching for experienced gamers.[6]

At an even more basic level, this brings us to the topic that haunts our media in the Past decades: can Artificial Intelligence actually think?[7] This debate has been mostly dominated by the idea that AI can only imitate human intelligence, reducing it to abstract forms of reasoning, missing the true "spirit" of human intelligence. AI is thinking reduced to automatization: machines can adapt themselves to new situations, they can learn new things and new procedures, they can perform complex operations far beyond the scope of a human mind. But AI is not really alive, it is literally artificial, a grey mechanistic shadow of human intelligence in which none of the sudden sparks which characterize the working of a human mind can ever ignite . . . insofar as we reflect in this way, our victory over machines is secured in advance.

Big companies are not just investing enormous sums of money but also using colossal amounts of energy to develop AI machines with such enhanced intelligence that their functioning will be beyond our (human) reach. The problem is that the amount of energy needed to build such machines would compel us to abandon and infringe all the limits and caps we need to observe to prevent global warming and other ecological catastrophes, i.e., to maintain ecological sustainability—it is simply not possible to meet AI energy demands while keeping pace with climate goals. Here is a foretaste of our future:

> The world is facing a looming global water crisis that threatens to "spiral out of control" as increased demand for water and the intensifying impacts of the climate crisis put huge pressure on water resources, a UN report has warned. The consequences will be even more catastrophic without urgent action. The water crisis threatens more than 50% of global food production and risks shaving an average of 8% off countries' GDPs by 2050, with much higher losses of up to 15% projected in low-income countries, the report found.[8]

So what choice are we to make here? The former Google CEO Eric Schmidt advocates a radical solution which, while it may appear crazy, promises to solve all big problems we (humanity) are confronting: since "we're not going to hit the climate goals anyway, because we're not organized to do it," let's ignore sustainability and invest everything, inclusive of enormous amounts of energy, into new unpredictably strong AI machines. There are many arguments for the claim that we're not going to hit the climate goals—recall just what goes on in Finland: "Natural sinks of forests and peat were key to Finland's ambitious target to be carbon neutral by 2035. But now, the land has started emitting more greenhouse gases than it stores."[9] In short, one of our basic strategies to reach carbon neutrality thus unexpectedly backfired, for reasons which are not yet clear.

Not only this: the fact that humanity is approaching (ecological, military, social) self-destruction means that the only truly rational way out is to abdicate our agency and decision-making power, to allow the new AI machines to control and regulate our social life, although they will be doing this in ways that will not be transparent to us. Schmidt's proposal cannot but remind us of the old Groucho Marx advice: "Are you in some legal trouble? Hire a lawyer—you will be in even more trouble, but you will have a lawyer to take care of them." We are in trouble due to our environmental predicament, so let's use artificial intelligence—we will be even more in trouble, but we will have AI to take care of it . . .[10]

*

While the consequences of our explosively progressing immersion into the digital universe as our life-world are not yet clear, there seems to be good reasons to reject the optimist view that we will get used to it in the same way we got used to writing and other externalizations of our thought processes. Does a permanent "conversation" with ChatGPT not gradually diminish our ability to think? It not only makes available to us an endless flow of data, it also more and more takes over from us the very process of reasoning. Are we then not at a unique moment in history when our mental ability begins to shrink, so that the summit is behind us and we are on a way to decline?[11] We should thus abandon the boring obsession with the question: will AI serve us or will we be dominated by AI? We should also abandon the no less boring search for the right balance between technological development and concern for our environment—all the formulas of "green passage" which will allow us to have our cake and eat it are a fake. There are only two serious options: the one advocated by Kohei Saito (radical de-growth) and the one advocated by Schmidt for whom, instead of being afraid that we'll be controlled by all-powerful machines, we should endorse our surrender to machines as the only solution available to us. So what about environmental threats? Schmidt claims that AI will solve its own problems when it comes to pushing sustainability: the new AI-generated technology might actually solve the environmental issues we (humanity) are unable to cope with in an appropriate way . . . I think we should follow this line of thought to the end, to its logical conclusion, and accept that, if AI will decide it is in the interest of life on earth (or of its own reproduction) to eliminate us (humans), so be it![12]

*

According to the common sense view, AI is the culmination of intruding mediators which interpose themselves between us, humans, and reality in which we live. Instead of experiencing ourselves as embedded in our natural environment, "breathing" with it, we interpose new and new obstacles (machines, screens, virtual realities . . .) that separates us from reality . . . There is, of course, an aspect of truth in this view, not the least among them being the prospect that science may give rise to new forms of life which may endanger the very existence of (not only human) life on earth:

> World-leading scientists have called for a halt on research to create "mirror life" microbes amid concerns that the synthetic organisms would present an "unprecedented risk" to life on Earth. The international group of Nobel laureates and other experts warn that mirror bacteria, constructed from mirror images of molecules found in nature, could become established in the environment and slip past the immune defenses of natural organisms, putting humans, animals and plants at risk of lethal infections.[13]

However, this very real threat should not blind us to the fact that any AI machine, even if it is (for us) unimaginably strong and efficient, is simply part of reality, it fits into it, while the only stain in reality, a disturbing element in it, is us, humanity. Here we should learn from Chaplin whose figure of Tramp is a stain embodied. His *City Lights* opens with showing

> a group of well-heeled citizens and dignitaries around a monument to "Peace And Prosperity" that is about to be unveiled. After a series of long-winded speeches, where Chaplin effectively uses sound to convey the meaninglessness of their words, the monument is unveiled to reveal the Little Tramp asleep in the arms of one of the monument's statues. What follows is a hilarious scene, with an apologetic Tramp getting himself near impaled on the sword of one of the statues, followed by a perplexed and angry crowd holding onto their wrath when the National Anthem is played. The Tramp tries to be upstanding, even in his ridiculous position but cannot contain himself, as he soon uses the features of the monument in a farcical display before making his getaway . . .[14]

The Tramp stands here for the human subject as such: not an abstract gaze observing reality but something interposed between our gaze and its proper object, something that disturbs our clear view. Lacan's premise is that there is no clear view: when we look at something there is always a stain in what we see, and this stain is the stand-in for ourselves, for our gaze, the blind spot in the image from which the image returns the gaze and looks back at us . . . One can only imagine what Chaplin were to do with Donald Trump if he were to be alive today, how he would reshoot the famous scene from *The Great Dictator* in which Hynkel (Hitler) plays with a globe-balloon which then explodes above his feet. In *The Great Dictator*, Chaplin based his identification with Hynkel/Hitler on their very similar moustaches, while today he would rely on the obvious vocal similarity between Trump and Tramp. So what if, instead of a globe-balloon, Trump would have played with a balloon shaped as a big vagina, squeezing and kicking it obscenely till it would explode in his face (a reference to his "I can grab pussies")? Or maybe he would play with his ultimate obscenity: his special edition of the shamelessly Americanized Bible?

The field of AI has seen a remarkable evolution over the past several decades, with two distinct paradigms emerging—symbolic AI and subsymbolic AI. Symbolic AI, which dominated the early days of the field, focuses on the manipulation of abstract symbols to represent knowledge and reason about it. Subsymbolic AI, on the other hand, emphasizes the use of numerical representations and machine learning algorithms to extract patterns from data. The strengths of symbolic AI lie in its ability to handle complex, abstract, and rule-based problems, where the underlying logic and reasoning can be explicitly encoded. In contrast to symbolic AI, subsymbolic AI focuses on the use of numerical representations and machine learning algorithms to extract patterns from data. This approach, also known as "connectionist" or "neural network" AI, is inspired by the workings of the human brain and the way it processes and learns from information.

Subsymbolic AI systems rely on machine learning algorithms, such as deep learning, to automatically extract features and patterns from large datasets, without the need for explicit rule-based programming. Knowledge in subsymbolic AI is typically distributed across the weights and connections of the neural network, rather than being localized in specific symbols or rules.

The strengths of subsymbolic AI lie in its ability to handle complex, unstructured, and noisy data, such as images, speech, and natural language. This approach has been particularly successful in tasks like computer vision, speech recognition, and language understanding. The paradox is that while subsymbolic AI is often perceived as closer to the human mind (it is modeled on neural connections, it is more sensitive to blurred and ambiguous regions that it tries to decipher, it can establish much faster a dialogic relationship with a human agent who perceives it as a pseudo-human partner, etc.), the reality is almost the opposite: symbolic AI uses explicit, human-readable representations of knowledge, while subsymbolic AI relies on distributed, numerical representations that are more opaque to human understanding.[15] The prevalent (and correct, I think) stance is that subsymbolic AI is really a version of symbolic AI: it is ultimately a symbolic AI which is made so that it (appears to) act(s) in a subsymbolic way.

Another term used for subsymbolic AI is Artificial Neural Networks (ANN), a structure of units or nodes called *artificial neurons*, which loosely model the neurons in a brain. These units are connected by *edges*, which model the synapses in a brain. They are used for various tasks, including predictive modeling, adaptive control, and solving problems in artificial intelligence. They can learn from experience, and can derive conclusions from a complex and seemingly unrelated set of information.[16] In this way, they do not imitate human thinking: what we are really encountering lately are *machines which don't think like humans*: they really do think, but not simply better than us—they think in a way which is radically *foreign* to human thinking.[17] From this perspective, the organic human intellectuality (our inner reflection or contemplation)—in other words, what I referred to above as the sparks of spirit—is not a sign of our priority or advantage over AI but a sign of its *inferiority*:

> Human intellectuality is seriously limited, it has already reached its zenith early in the development of the species *homo sapiens*. Today we do not think more deeply or in a more sophisticated way than the oldest Antique philosophers, and *The Iliad* can move us in the same way it would have moved us three thousand years ago. ... the only dimension of human intelligence which effectively develops beyond slow and unpredictable

rhythms of biological evolution is technical intelligence. This means that human intelligence can expand and perfect itself only through its autonomization from organic intellectuality through technological self-overcoming.[18]

I disagree with this conclusion for two reasons. First, there is nothing natural or organic in "intellectuality"; intellectuality is rather a sign of the radical rupture between humans and animals, it breaks and disturbs organic rhythms. Second, yes, there effectively is something constrained or limited in the very foundation of human intellectuality, but it is precisely this limitation (what Heidegger called finitude) which gives birth to human transcendence, to specific human spirituality. If this limitation is abolished, we enter a totally different domain. So we should reverse the terms: "human" is more than "over-man." What human intellectuality implies is a gap between inside and outside, between so-called inner life and outside reality, and it is not clear what will happen (or, rather, is happening) with this gap in developed AI—in all probability, it will disappear, since machines are part of reality. The fact that a subject has no fixed place in the symbolic order becomes most palpable in the case of copyists, those who just literally transcribe what already exists in the symbolic universe—the place of a copyist in a symbolic order

> is his not having a place. If Flaubert's copyists, as read by Foucault, stand for a successful alienation whereby the subject disappears into an alien element, the anonymity of pure discourse, Kafka's universe is one of failed alienation where the subject cannot settle into the order in which it's caught, since the subject is nothing other than a gap in this order.[19]

Copying is a procedure of traditional bureaucracy where handwriting (and maybe typing machines, including photocopiers) predominates. But what happens with the digitalization of our lives where data (information) exists predominantly in digital clouds and are no longer part of our physical reality? Can we still call this situation a successful alienation in which subjects disappear in the anonymity of pure discourse? If we add to this the self-organizing and multiplying artificial intelligence which not only follows our orders and choices but manipulates us in advance, deciding which choices are given to us? In many domains, from choosing a partner to medical diagnosis or a decision where to invest money, AI does a better job than an average marriage counsellor, doctor or banker. Am I in such a situation reduced to an object and/or pretext for the self-reproducing digital entity, or does it open up a new space of freedom for me?

To avoid a misunderstanding, all this in no way precludes the option that thinking machines will develop a subjectivity in some sense even more human than that of humans. The two *Blade Runner* movies, especially the second one (*2049*), address this problem: they both focus on a replicant (Deckard, K) who is not sure if he is a true human or a replicant with implanted memories. Their radical doubt which reduces them to a Cartesian *cogito* (Deckard-Descartes) not sure if the reality around him is real or just a fake orchestrated by an evil spirit, makes them in some sense *more human than the "true" humans themselves*: yes, they are "inhuman," but this inhumanity means that they openly assume their reduction to the void of a pure *cogito*—what makes them more human than humans is their radical doubt, a feature totally foreign to thinking machines. In contrast to this radical doubt, "true" humans remain embedded in their finite situation, in their historical symbolic context. In short, "true" humans remain *persons*, while self-doubting replicants are ready to confront the abyss of pure *subjectivity*.

To see this distinction clearly, one should avoid two opposed traps: not only the trap of naïve realism but also the trap of fictionalism, i.e., of the claim that we live in symbolic fictions behind which there are only other fictions, with no ultimate grounding in the real. David Chalmers, well-known for his claim we cannot exclude the possibility that we live in a simulated world, wisely resists this idealist temptation and insists on a reality independent of our minds: even if our common reality is the product of a complex machine which controls our brains (as it happens in the movie *The Matrix*), every simulation has to be generated by a simulating machine which is part of reality (although it is possible that this reality is radically different from our normal reality).[20] Does this bring him close to quantum mechanics which (in its predominant version, at least) posits that our everyday reality is grounded in quantum processes which obey a different logic? In other words, is there a link between virtual in the sense of VR (inclusive AR)—an effect of reality constructed by digital machines—and virtual in the sense of wave oscillations which are not part of our reality (they become this only through collapse)? When quantum mechanics claims that what we experience as our ordinary reality is not what reality really is, that it is the product of another level of reality, the QU, which obeys different laws, is it in some sense suggesting that the status of our ordinary reality is virtual?

I think this parallel is problematic: in contrast to quantum oscillations, a digital machine that sustains AR and VR is fully part of our ordinary reality, with no quantum waves involved, no superpositions and collapses. Plus there is a third domain of virtuality—in some precise sense, what we experience as reality is always-already augmented even if no digital machinery sustains it: the symbolic order always and by definition provides a partial/twisted view on reality—the reality we see and interact with is always and by definition "augmented" by our virtual supplements. Recall Pokemon Go, a location-based AR game released in July 2016: virtual creatures ("Pokémon") appear on the screen as if they were in the same real-world location as the player. This AR mode is what makes Pokémon Go different from other games: instead of taking us out of the real world and drawing us into the artificial virtual space, it combines the two: we look at reality and interact with it through the fantasy-frame of the digital screen, and this intermediary frame supplements reality with virtual elements which sustain our desire to participate in the game, push us to look for them in a reality which, without this frame, would leave us indifferent ... sounds familiar? Of course it does. What the technology of Pokemon Go externalizes is simply the basic mechanism of ideology—at its most basic, ideology is the primordial version of "augmented reality."

In continental philosophical tradition, the name for the "+" which makes our everyday reality a "reality+" is the *transcendental* dimension: the horizon of meaning which enframes our perception of and interaction with reality. Chalmers ignores this + constitutive of our everyday reality because his approach remains that of analytic philosophy. Chalmers's *Reality+*[21] definitely deserves a closer look: it deals with ontological, epistemological, and deontological problems of virtual and simulated realities. The density of its analytic argumentation is breathtaking: I've never read a book with such a breadth of topics in which almost every page brings a new specific line of argumentation (although one must add that all this argumentation remains within the frame of analytic rational argumentation). For me as a philosopher the most interesting segment is Part 7 ("Foundations") where Chalmers focuses on the fundamentals of his approach.

The ultimate dilemma here is: simulations and virtual realities are based on some mathematical algorithm (say, a chair I see when I am immersed into virtual reality exists independently of my mind, it is real, but its reality resides in digital bits which regulate its appearance in VR); however, if we live in a simulated world, i.e., if our ordinary reality is also a simulation regulated by algorithms of some higher digital intelligence—a hypothesis Chalmers considers as a possible and even probable option—and if there are even multiple levels of simulations (simulation in simulation in simulation . . .), is there an ultimate level of reality outside simulations, or is all reality based on some mathematical algorithm (which can, obviously, also be interpreted as a divine mind)?

Rather than providing a clear answer to this dilemma, Chalmers begins with the basic problem of the philosophy of language: how do words relate to things they designate? Analytic philosophy oscillates here between two extremes: descriptivism versus causal theory. For descriptivism, the meaning of a word resides in the set of features it is associated with in our mind (chair is a wooden, metal or plastic object on 3 or 4 legs and a platter on which a person can sit), and this word refers to an empirical object only if this object fits the set of features. The causal theory, on the contrary, posits a direct causal relationship between an object and the word that designates it: in an act of primal baptism, a word is directly attached to an object, and this object remains what this word refers to even if, in a later experience or scientific discovery, we realize that the true features of the object in question are totally different from what we thought.

Chalmers approaches this topic when he deals with the meaning of words in simulated or multiple realities. Yes, meaning resides in environment, not "in the head," but this environment is not just what we usually perceive as external reality. To return to our example of a chair in virtual reality: its referent is not an illusory chair that exists only virtually but also the bytes in a digital cloud which cause and regulate its appearance. So why should we use the same word for a chair in our everyday reality and for a chair in virtual reality? Is it not obvious that the entities are substantially different? Would the use of the same word not be justified only in the case of a subject who is so fully immersed in simulated virtual reality that s/he takes it for ordinary reality? After a detailed set of arguments and counter-arguments, Chalmers arrives at a position he calls structuralism—here is his own brief definition:

> The thesis that scientific theories are equivalent to structural theories, cast in terms of mathematics plus connections to observation. Epistemic structuralism says that science tells us only the structure of reality (though there may be more to reality than this). Ontic structural realism says that reality itself is entirely structural.
>
> (470)

The difference between epistemic structuralism and ontic structuralism is secondary with regard to the main point Chalmers is making. He challenges us to imagine two realities which are experienced by people who live in them as exactly the same; imagine then that a scientist coming from outside did a chemical analysis of water in each of the two realities and discovered that, while in our reality water has the chemical structure of H_2O, in the parallel universe it has a different chemical structure, XYZ. Although the object the experience of water refers to is different in the two realities, one can justify the use of the same word "water" in both cases because this object plays exactly the same structural role in both cases . . . Chalmers then extends the argument to simulated worlds: imagine our ordinary reality and its perfect simulation. If in such a simulation "water" (which is effectively a network of digital bits) plays the same structural role as our "real" water, the use of the same word is justified. Chalmers pushes this argument to its conclusion and argues that AI and simulated entities also can think and possess consciousness. Here is the logical form of his argumentation:

1. Our physical theories are structural theories.
2. If we're in Nonsim(ulated) Universe, our physical theories are true.
3. Sim Universe has the same structure as Nonsim Universe.
4. So: if we're in Sim Universe, our physical theories are true.[22]

From my standpoint, however, what Chalmers misses is exactly structuralism—not in his own standard meaning of a formal structure that can be actualized in different materials (in the same way that, say, Shakespeare's *Hamlet* is the same play if we see it in a theatre, read it in a book or watch its cinematic version), but in the strict meaning of French structuralism which exploded in the 1960s. The basic lesson of French structuralism is that a structure is always characterized by a minimal reflexivity: a structure is never pure, by definition it includes as one of its elements a stand-in for its own constitutive impossibility, for what is excluded from its space. For example, Marx's overall vision of history is that of a linear succession of "progressive" modes of social development from primitive societies through Asiatic mode of production, slavery, feudalism, capitalism up to Socialism and Communism. However, a close analysis shows that "Asiatic mode of production" is an empty category into which Marx threw whatever didn't fit his Eurocentric logic of history.

For Lacan, the same notion of structure holds for the symbolic order itself—this is what he aims at with his circular definition of signifier as that which represents the subject for another signifier. Lacan's premise is that subject's representation, its expression in the symbolic order, always fails, there is a gap between subject and the symbolic order; however, subject doesn't precede this failure, it emerges through the failure of its symbolic representation—in short, a subject tries to fully express itself in words, it fails, and this failure IS subject. The temporal circularity is crucial here, in a nice case of what Hegel called "absolute recoil": an entity is a retroactive effect of its failure to be what it is. This failure has to be inscribed into the symbolic order as a special signifier, a signifier which stands for what a signifier cannot represent. What eludes words is thus not reality in all its wealth but subject itself. Consequently, we move beyond the difference between a formal structure and its material actualizations: since structure itself is reflexive, the non-formal excess is inscribed into it. The problem with causal theory is that "it looks for that x, for the feature guaranteeing the identity of a reference through all changes of its descriptive properties, in the reality itself; this is why it must invent its own myth, Keith Donnellan's myth of an 'omniscient observer of history'":

> Suppose that all that a certain speaker knows or thinks he knows about Thales is that he is the Greek philosopher who said that all is water. But suppose there never was a Greek philosopher who said such a thing. Suppose that Aristotle and Herodotus were referring to a well digger who said, "I wish all were water so I wouldn't have to dig these damned wells." In such a case, when the speaker uses the name "Thales" he is referring to that well digger. Furthermore, suppose there was a hermit who never had any dealings with anyone, who actually held that all was water. Still, when we say "Thales" we are plainly not referring to that hermit.[23]

Today, the original reference, the starting point of a causal chain—the poor well digger—is unknown to us; but an "omniscient observer of history" capable of following the causal chain to the act of "primal baptism" would know how to restore the original link connecting the word "Thales" to its reference. Why is this myth, this antidescriptivist version of the Lacanian "subject presumed to know," necessary? The basic problem of antidescriptivism is to determine what constitutes the identity of the designated object beyond the ever-changing cluster of descriptive features—what makes an object identical-to-itself even if all its properties have changed; in other words, how to conceive the objective correlative to the "rigid designator," to the name in so far as it denotes the same object in all possible worlds, in all counterfactual situations. What is overlooked, at least in the standard version of antidescriptivism, is that this guaranteeing the identity of an object in all counterfactual situations—through a change of all its descriptive features—is the retroactive effect of naming itself: it is the name itself, the signifier, which supports the identity of the object. That "surplus" in the object which stays the same in all possible worlds is "something in it more than itself, that is to say the Lacanian *objet petit a*: we search in vain for it in positive reality because it has no positive consistency—it is just an objectification of a void, of a discontinuity opened in reality by the emergence of the signifier."[24]

Description and original baptism are thus not external to each other since there is also a way in which original baptism falls into the domain of description: original description names the dimension in the designated object which remains unknown to the speaker, the x in the object which eludes description, which cannot be reduced to known properties. One can also say that original baptism stands for the dimension of *question* in every description. Recall a hilarious joke in one of the early Marx brothers movies, the "Why a duck?" scene: Groucho say to Chico that they have to meet someone at a viaduct, and Chico asks "Why a duck?"; when Groucho explains to him that a viaduct is a large bridge across a valley, Chico persists: "Why a duck?" Groucho goes on explaining: "You know, a bridge! Under the bridge, there is a green meadow..." "Why a duck?" repeats Chico. So the exchange goes on: "In the midst of this meadow, there is a pond." "In the pond, there are some ducks swimming..." "So, that's why a duck!" triumphantly exclaims Chico, getting it right for the wrong reason, as is often the case in ideological legitimization. Following a wild etymology, the designation of a name is here explained through the literal meaning of its parts: Why a duck? Because there are ducks swimming in the pond beneath it...

The key feature here is that *the question (about why this name) is inscribed into the name itself*. As we all know, the word "kangaroo" originated in a similar misunderstanding: when the first white explorers of Australia pointed at a nearby kangaroo and asked the Indigenous people what it was, the Indigenous respondent did not get the point, so they answered with "kangaroo," which in their language meant "What do you want?". If, then, this misperception of the question as a positive term, this inability to recognize the question, is one of the standard procedures of ideological misrecognition, then the very inanity of the Marx brothers' dialogue displays a critico-ideological dimension, insofar as it reintroduces the dimension of a question in what appears as a positive designation: "viaduct" is really "why a duck?". Does the logic of anti-Semitism not rely on a similar misrecognition: while "the (anti-Semitic figure of the) Jew" appears to designate directly a certain ethnic group, it effectively just encodes a series of questions: "Why are we exploited? Why are the old mores falling apart?", etc., to which "the Jewish plot" is offered the semblance of an answer. In other words, the first gesture of the critique of anti-Semitism is to read "the Jew" as "Why a Jew?" ... When Christopher Hitchens tackled the difficult question of what the North Koreans effectively think about their "Beloved Leader" Kim Yong Il, he produced what is arguably the most succinct definition of ideology: "mass delusion is the only thing that keeps a people sane."²⁵ And the mechanism of this delusion is precisely the obfuscation of the question, the misreading of the question as a statement.

The paradox is thus that the X beyond all particular properties rendered by symbolic descriptions is not a Kantian Thing-in-itself but an effect of language itself: speech gives birth to the unspeakable excess that allegedly escapes its grasp. What this means is that there is no clear cut between what others see in me and what I am in myself: I also define myself through what others see in me. Back to anti-Semitism: what the perpetrators of anti-Semitic pogroms find intolerable and rage-provoking, what they react to, is not the immediate reality of Jews, but a reality+, the reality supplemented by the image/figure of the "Jew" which circulates and has been constructed in their tradition. The catch, of course, is that one single individual cannot distinguish in any simple way between real Jews and their anti-Semitic image: this image overdetermines the way I experience real Jews themselves and, furthermore, *it affects the way Jews experience themselves.* From the diaspora of the Jews and the rise of anti-Semitism, the symbolic identity of the "real" Jews themselves is marked by anti-Semitic fantasies: the very core of their identity is defined in the terms of the defense against anti-Semitism.

So, back to reality+, to simplify things to the utmost, did Hitler not offer the Germans the fantasy-frame of Nazi ideology which made them see a specific Pokémon—"the Jew"—popping up all around and providing the clue to what one has to fight against? And does the same not hold for all other ideological pseudo-entities which have to be added to reality in order to make it complete and meaningful? One can easily imagine a contemporary anti-immigrant version of Pokemon Go where the player wanders about a German city and is threatened by Muslim immigrant rapists or thieves lurking everywhere. So how does our ordinary reality relate to reality+? This ordinary reality already is reality+ since it is sustained by the symbolic order which enframes the mode of its perception. Here intervenes the gap between reality and the Real: reality is always-already symbolically enframed, while the Real is that which resists symbolization.

If quantum physics is correct, i.e., if with quantum physics we "caught god (the creator of the simulated world in which we live) with his pants down," since the ontological incompleteness of reality asserted by quantum physics implies that god was too lazy (or unable) to program to the end the world in which we live, is then quantum physics not the ultimate proof that we live in a simulated world with an imperfect simulator? The only way out of this predicament for a materialist is to accept that ontological imperfection is a basic feature of reality itself. For Roger Penrose, quantum mechanics is not a complete theory because it cannot account for the collapse of the wave function which gives birth to our everyday reality—collapse is not part of quantum universe, it is external to it. He is in principle right, but the solution he proposes (there has to be another reality outside the QU) is not inevitable. What about taking more seriously (and literally) the basic premise of quantum mechanics: QU is in itself incomplete, not fully ontologically constituted, so that what appears a problem is its own solution? This incompleteness does not imply that there is somewhere else a more basic reality, but it does imply that this incompleteness (or, rather, inconsistency) of the QU pushes it towards collapse. In other words, QU is not a happy universe where waves float around unimpeded, it is a universe traversed by a basic impossibility.

The eventual limit of AI is to be sought at another level, at the level of its subjectivization. A subject's relationship to knowledge is at the beginning always that of transference, i.e., its knowledge constitutively relates to another subject elevated to the status of the subject-supposed-to-know, of a subject who already possesses the knowledge I am trying to discover. This, of course, is what happens in the psychoanalytic treatment: the analysand acts as if the analyst already knows the meaning of their symptoms while this meaning is effectively constructed in the course of the treatment itself, so that the moment when the analysand can be said to really know the meaning of its symptoms is at the same time the moment of what Lacan calls the fall of the subject-supposed-to-know. A similar thing happens in big religious revolutions: when Martin Luther radically transformed Christianity, he assumed that he was just returning to its authentic origins. In intersubjective relations, this "illusion" of presupposed knowledge is necessary: it is only through such an illusion that actual knowledge can emerge. However, this dialectic of transference is totally absent in Artificial Intelligence machines: they know (register) what they know, they can learn new things, but the growth of their knowledge does not progress through presupposing new knowledge as already existing in an other, which is why they have no transferential love towards any figure of an other.

AI can, of course, function as a subject supposed to know for us, humans: AI machines already know how to discern our feelings, they know more about us than ourselves. However, AI machines themselves don't rely in their functioning on a subject supposed to know. (Although one cannot exclude the possibility that we, humans, will become a specific sort of subject supposed to know on account of our very "irrationality" and inconsistency: the AI machine controlling us may read this inconsistency as impenetrability, as an indication of a deeper subject in ourselves which regulates our acts in a consistent way.)

Furthermore, one thing AI—for the time being, at least—cannot do is to develop small daily rituals: not habits, but rituals.[26] Here are some examples from well-known persons. When Maya Angelou arrives at a motel, she always asks for all the pictures to be removed from the walls of her room. After finishing her writing in the early evening, Agatha Christie took a bath and ate an apple there. Before falling asleep, Charles Dickens always pulled out his compass to make sure that his bed is facing north. Serena Williams always bounced the ball five times before her first serve . . . We all do similar things, small ritualized gestures which are quite often even embarrassing. They make life meaningful yet they have not only no pragmatic function but also no definite meaning, so there is no need for psychoanalysis to bring out their hidden meaning. Their meaning is purely self-referential, it resides in the effect of meaning. Such acts presuppose a subjectivity which tries to introduce a minimal order in its life.

At the opposite end of such rituals is the perplexity with regard to our place in the symbolic order which we express in curses, so the question "Can AI think?" should thus be transformed into a question "Can AI curse/swear?". Could it utter a helpless, furious outcry? As Lacan repeatedly points out, "primordial" speech acts are single exclamations, as a rule curses or vulgar words ("Shit", "Wow!" . . .), which play a very specific role: they are neither statements about things and processes that are going on in reality (like "a storm is coming from the north"), nor are they expressions of our inner reaction to external events (fear, anger, joy . . .). At their most basic, they express our lack of a proper place in the symbolic order in which we dwell. We enter the symbolic order first as its objects: we somehow grasp that others are talking about us, that we are within the scope of their interest, but we don't clearly understand what they are saying, what they want from us, what they see in us—language as a medium is a big Other, it connects us with others and it simultaneously functions as a wall separating us from others. Or, to quote Etienne Balibar:

> the subject can only be conceived as the failure of the law, of language. *In* language and yet *more than* language, the subject is a cause for which no signifier can account. Not because she transcends the signifier but because she inhabits it *as limit*.[27]

Therein resides the clear contrast between Hegel and Habermas. Habermas (but also Hegelians like Brandom) relies on the normativity inscribed into language itself: the moment we speak, we are obliged to act so that we respect the factual truth of our claims, we sincerely express our intentions, etc. Although, of course, we often do not speak like that, we thereby get involved into pragmatic paradoxes—we violate the normativity implied by the very fact that we are speaking. For Lacan, on the contrary, the gap that separates language from subject is irreducible, and the normativity inscribed into language is that of a pretence: in speaking I pretend that am sincerely telling the truth, but this truth is the truth of a (symbolic) fiction. Lacan in this regard follows Hegel for whom language fits the stable categories of Understanding, so that to capture in language the vertiginous shifts of Reason we have to violate its explicit rules—as Hegel put it, we think only in language, but to really think we have to use language against itself.

It is in this sense that, for Lacan (who often evokes his dog Justine), dogs speak but they don't really inhabit language, i.e., they are unable to subjectivize themselves in it, to assume a stance towards others in it. They are perplexed by human language, and they get frustrated by their inability to participate in linguistic exchanges—as Lacan put it, dogs are neurotic, hystericized by language, without being its subjects. So they are not simply outside language: what they can experience is the frustration of the fact they cannot find their place within language, that they cannot inscribe their subjective position into it. This is why human curses and exclamations matter: they don't simply express our fear or anger or joy, what they express is a much more basic frustration at the impossibility to say in clear language what we want to say, to "find the right word":

> If a dog could speak, would he not bellow a curse? Perhaps that's what Sartre's dog was meaning to say all along without knowing it. The true word lying just beyond his grasp is not the word that would unlock the universe of language, allowing him to fully enter into the community of speaking beings and thereby put an end to his obscure frustration. It is rather the word by which he could name his unspeakable frustration about missing the word, and thus release this frustration into language itself. To speak is to tarry with the impossibility of speaking, to give voice to and do something with the bewilderment, lassitude, and rage—the abject objecthood—in which Sartre's dog can only helplessly languish.[28]

As a further illustration Schuster mentions the famous "all-fuck" investigation scene in *Wire* I/4, a scene that I analyzed in detail in an old book of mine.[29] In an empty ground floor apartment where a murder took place 6 months ago, McNulty and Bunk, witnessed by a sole silent housekeeper, try to reconstruct how it happened, and the only word they pronounce during their work are variations of "fuck"—they do it 38 times in a row, in so many different ways—it comes to mean anything, from annoyed boredom to elated triumph, from pain or disappointment or shock at the horror of a gruesome murder to pleasant surprise, and it reaches its climax in the self-reflexive reduplication of "Fuckin'fuck!". To prove it, one can easily imagine the same scene in which each "fuck" is replaced by a more "normal" phrase ("Again, just another photo!", "Ouch, it hurts!", "Now I got it!", etc.) . . . This scene works on multiple levels, but at its most basic it is a curse in the multitude of its uses: the same word can function in a multitude of ways precisely because this multitude is sustained by the frustrating impossibility of clearly expressing one's subjective stance. So this scene does not enact a metaphoric or reflective game adding a level to the "realist" functioning of language—on the contrary, it enacts the basic gesture of language, that of bringing out the crack, the impossibility, on which language is based: we use words in a language because the "true" word is missing, and this word is missing because I—the speaking subject—don't have a proper place within the symbolic space, because I am a crack in its edifice. Curses and exclamations are words which register the lack of a proper word, a word that would adequately represent the subject for other words, and since the subject is a lack in the symbolic space, a curse reflectively registers this lack.

We can—should, even—imagine an ideal analytic session in which the analyst reenacts the scene from *Wire* and from time to time just interrupts the patient's flow of words with a curse, maybe even with a simple "Fuck!". It is also in this sense that the analyst is the obverse of the master. The (wrongly) so-called "pansexualism" of Freud ("behind everything there is sex") would acquire in this way an unexpected meaning: yes, the analyst's reply to everything is "Fuck!", but this fuck has nothing to do with sexuality, it can refer to anything and nothing.

For this reason I find Lacan's claim that a dog "has a superego without an unconscious" problematic: if Lacan elsewhere (correctly) claims that superego is not a moral agency but the injunction to enjoy, then the human figure of authority to which a dog submits as a faithful servant up to the point of being willing to sacrifice itself is not a superego figure but rather a (fantasy of) the perfect Master—a dog has neither an unconscious nor a superego. It is only through human perversion that the obscene superego enters the game, so that even the dog from Kafka's story which finds (surplus-)enjoyment in fasting to death does not do it out of a superego pressure. If "the neurotic longs for a master that would release him from the need for a master, and allow him to finally act on his own,"[30] a dog already found such a master instead of just looking for him.

And let's go to the end here: does the exclamation "Christ!" not work in a similar way like "Fuck!"? We can easily imagine the scene from *Wire* with "Christ!" instead of "Fuck!", where the curse would express the same frustrating inability to subjectivize our position in the big Other. In Mel Brooks's *History of the World: Part I* there is a scene in which the hero (played by Brooks himself), a waiter in Jerusalem in the year of 33, is asked to serve at an important dinner; when, in the middle of dinner, one of his plates slips out of his hands and falls down, he exclaims "O, Christ!", and gets a gentle answer from one of the guests: "Yes, please?" What we should advocate is the move in the opposite direction, from the actual dialogue to a pure exclamation.

And why should we not bring the two dimensions—sex and god's name—together? Recall (trigger warning!) a dirty joke: in an elementary school class, the teacher is asking boys how do we go to heaven when we are dying, and one of them replies: "First with our legs." Surprised, the teacher says "Why?", and the boy replies: "A week ago, when my father was on a business trip, I entered my parents' bedroom and I saw someone laying on my mother making strange movements; my mother's legs were raised high up and she was shouting: 'O Christ, I'm coming!'" This mention of Christ is not simply a blasphemy, it just gives words to the mother's frustrating inability to find the right word for the intense pleasure she is experiencing. So let's imagine that, if Kierkegaard were to consummate his love for Regine, she would be uttering the same phrase when approaching the orgasm. Even more, if Christ were not Christ, would he not also be justified to utter a simple "Christ!" or "Fuck!" instead of the well-known "Father, why have you abandoned me?" when dying on the cross? ONLY in Christianity can we imagine such an outcry.

This dimension of uneasiness/discontent in language is the topic that lies beneath Ludwig Wittgenstein's *Tractatus*—he tries to resolve it by way of clearly distinguishing what we can speak about and what we cannot speak about—or, as he writes in the final proposition of *Tractatus: Wovon man nicht sprechen kann, darueber muss man schweigen.* (Whereof one cannot speak, thereof one must be silent.)[31] The immediate question this raises is why should one prohibit something that is already in itself impossible? The answer is relatively easy: if we ignore this prohibition, we produce statements which are (for Wittgenstein) meaningless, like speculations about the noumenal domain in Kant's philosophy. (Lacan qualified the prohibition of incest in a similar way, claiming that its function is to render the impossible possible: if incest has to be prohibited, it means that it is possible if we violate this prohibition.) We find also a theological version of this prohibition in *The Day Of Doom*, Michael Wigglesworth's poem published in 1662, a dark Puritan description of the punishment of sinners which was for a century the absolute bestseller in the American colonies. When, on the Judgment Day, individuals confront God the Judge, the sight is too strong to be put in words, "therefore I must pass it by, lest speaking should transgress."[32]

There is, however, an ambiguity in Wittgenstein's proposition which resides in the double meaning of "*kann*": it can mean simple ontic impossibility, or a deontic prohibition ("you cannot talk/behave like that!"). Wittgenstein's proposition can thus be read in a radical ontological sense intended by Wittgenstein himself—there are things impossible to talk about like metaphysical speculations—, or in a conformist-deontic sense—"Shut up about things you are not allowed to talk about!" The opposite of this conformist wisdom is the ethical imperative: *Wovon man nicht schweigen kann, darueber muss man sprechen.* (Whereof one cannot be silent, thereof one must speak.) Horrors like the Holocaust or Communist purges or colonial disasters cannot be passed over in silence (as happens in today's China), we have to bring them out.

The opposite of this ethical injunction is a tautological cynical wisdom: *Wovon man nicht schweigen kann, darueber muss man schweigen.* (Whereof one cannot be silent, thereof one must be silent.) Which means: even if you know you cannot keep quiet about it, do not talk about it since talking about it would pose too much of a threat to you.—What, then, about the opposite tautology: *Wovon man nicht sprechen kann, darueber muss man sprechen.* (Whereof one cannot speak, thereof one should speak.) It defines poetry: poetry is an attempt to put in words what cannot be said, to evoke it, and this holds precisely for traumatic events like the Holocaust: any prosaic description of the horrors of the Holocaust fails to render its trauma, and this is why Adorno was wrong with his famous claim that after Auschwitz poetry is no longer possible: it is prose which is no longer possible, since only poetry can do the job. Poetry is the inscription of impossibility into a language: when we cannot say something directly and we nonetheless insist on doing so, we unavoidably get caught in repetitions, postponements, indirectness, surprising cuts, etc. We should always bear in mind that the "beauty" of classic poetry (symmetric rhymes, etc.) comes second, that it is a way to compensate for the basic failure or impossibility.

But this is not Wittgenstein's last word: already in *Tractatus*, he introduces another term which works as the opposite of saying (*Sprechen*), namely showing/displaying (*Zeigen*), so we can also say: *Wovon man nicht sprechen kann, das zeigt sich.* (Whereof one cannot speak, that shows itself.) The inversion of this statement (*Was man nicht zeigen kann, darueber muss man sprechen.*—"What one cannot show, thereof one must speak.") is a vulgar commonsense notion since it reduces "showing" to the obvious meaning of "what is evidently present in front of us," which can be exemplified by seeing one's exterior; the argument is then that focusing on how a person appears ignores the deeper spiritual truth of this person, the truth which can only be rendered by words describing this truth.

Against this line of argumentation one should focus on the elementary Hegelian question: not what is the secret beneath appearance but *why does a thing need to appear in the first place*. In short, Wittgenstein's "showing" has nothing to do with "appearing" as opposed to what is beneath it. "Showing" is the form of appearance ignored when we focus on what appears—Wittgenstein follows here Marx and Freud who both claim that the true secret is not what is Beyond what appears but the form itself (the commodity form, the form of dreams). The difference between *zeigen* (showing) and *schweigen* (keeping silent) is that while *schweigen* is an act (I decide not to speak, which implies that I am already within the domain of speech—a stone does not "keep silent"), *zeigen* happens involuntarily, it is a by-product of what I am doing when I speak: I don't (and cannot) *decide* what to show.

This insight (formulated by Wittgenstein in many versions, like "what can be shown cannot be said") should not be read as a hint towards some ineffable deep Truth beyond words: what cannot be said is fully immanent to saying, it is the form displayed by saying, it is what we do by saying something. To Wittgenstein's example of "honesty" we could add "dignity": if you talk about it, you are NOT dignified or honest—honesty and dignity can only be shown/displayed by doing it, by acting as an honest or dignified person. Recall what I often referred to as the "Hugh-Grant-paradox" (referring to the famous scene from *Four Weddings And a Funeral*): the hero tries to articulate his love to the beloved, he gets caught in stumbling and confused repetitions, and it is this very failure to deliver his message of love in a perfect way that bears witness to its authenticity ... In his very failure to speak about his love, he shows/displays it (although we can, of course, also intentionally fake such failures). We are dealing here with Wittgenstein's version of "there is no meta-language": a speech act cannot include into what it says its own form, its own act. Jon Elster articulated this feature in his notion of "states that are essentially by-products":

> Some psychological and social states have the property that they can only *come about* as the by-product of actions undertaken for other ends. They can never, that is, be *brought about* intelligently and intentionally, because they attempt to do so precludes the very state one is trying to bring about. I call these "states that are essentially by-products." There are many states that may arise as by-products of individual or aggregate action, but this is the subset of states than can *only* come about in this way. Some of these states are very useful or desirable, and so it is very tempting to try to bring them about. We may refer to such attempts as "excess of will," a form of *hubris* that pervades our lives, perhaps increasingly so.[33]

Among many examples offered by Elster (like "Good art is impressive; art designed to impress rarely is"[34]), one should mention the topic of authenticity and sincerity:

> The terms of sincerity and authenticity, like those of wisdom and dignity, always have a faintly ridiculous air about them when employed in the first person singular, reflecting the fact that the corresponding states are essentially by-products. ... Naming the unnamable by talking about something else is an ascetic practice and goes badly with self-congratulation.[35]

Elster mentions here the "unnamable," which brings us back to Wittgenstein: sincerity and authenticity cannot be named, they can only be shown/displayed by way of practicing it—a lesson that deals a heavy blow to the cult of authenticity which pervades our culture from the 1950s onwards. And a similar logic holds also for worshipping a god: "To paraphrase [Stanislav] Lem's personoid Adan 900: Any god that demands our worship doesn't deserve it."[36]

Following Bertrand Russell's famous quip about Wittgenstein (who, according to Russell, managed to say quite a lot about the unsayable[37]), could we not say that Elster also manages to say quite a lot about the dimension that he proclaims "unnamable"? However, this reproach misses the point. Of course we can talk about what a speech shows/displays, but *not in the first person*:

I cannot designate myself as authentic, as having dignity, etc.—if I do this, I undermine my authenticity or dignity which can only show itself in how I act. The statement "there is no meta-language" should be understood in this precise sense: I cannot include my position of enunciation (which may display dignity) into my own enunciated content. And this brings us to Robert Pippin's interpretation of Hegel, to his move from Hegel to Heidegger. For Pippin, Hegel remains at the level of saying, there is nothing really impossible to say (to articulate in predicative judgments), while what Heidegger refers to as "being-in-the-world" points towards the pre-predicative dimension of showing/displaying.

And does something similar not hold for both poles of today's global political space, authoritarian nationalism and Cancel Culture? On September 29, 2023, Russian Foreign Minister Sergey Lavrov "has indicated that Moscow is prepared for discussions concerning Ukraine, provided they take into account the situation on the ground and Russia's security interests."[38] Which means: we are prepared for peace negotiations provided Ukraine accepts that territories occupied by Russia are part of Russia, and provided it radically changes its politics (Russia demands "de-Nazification" of Ukraine) . . . in short, provided Ukraine capitulates. The Western liberal approach is often problematized along the same lines by anti-colonial critics: for the Western liberals, democratic exchange is formulated in terms which secretly impose the logic of Western democracy-and-freedom, so that joining liberal pluralism effectively amounts to a capitulation to Western values . . . Lavrov asserts the logic problematized by anti-colonial critics in its pure form. In Wittgensteinian terms, Lavrov speaks about negotiations, but what he shows/displays with his speech is the very opposite of negotiation, a brutal exclusive enforcing of one's own position.

Along the same lines, I can easily imagine Hegel having a repeated intellectual orgasm in bringing out the (for him) obvious necessity of the reversal of inclusivity and diversity into a procedure of systematic exclusion: "How long can parts of the liberal Left keep maintaining that 'cancel culture' is but a phantom of the right, as they literally go round canceling gigs, comedy shows, film showings, lectures and conversations?"[39] What permeates "cancel culture" is a "no-debate-stance": a person or position is not only excluded—what is excluded is the very debate, the confrontation of arguments, for or against this exclusion. Hegel would have mobilized here what Lacan called the gap between enunciated content and the underlying stance of enunciation: you argue for diversity and inclusion, but you do it by excluding all those who do not fully subscribe to your own definition of diversity and inclusion—so all you do is permanently exclude people and stances. In this way the struggle for inclusion and diversity gives birth to an atmosphere of Stasi-like suspicion and denunciation where you never know when a private remark of yours will lead to your elimination from the public space ... Don't we get here an extreme version of the joke about eating the last cannibal? "There are no opponents of diversity and inclusion in our group—we've just excluded the last one ..." So, again, in Wittgensteinian terms, while Cancel Culture speaks about diversity and inclusion, it shows/displays a stance of extreme exclusion.

Such inversion of inclusion into exclusion also obeys a deep Hegelian dialectical reversal, namely the transposition of an external threat into immanent antagonism, as it was perspicuously noted by Elster apropos the notion, fashionable today, of democracy under threat: "We can reverse the common dictum that democracy is under threat, and affirm that democracy *is* the threat, at least in its short-termist populist form."[40] Exactly as in the case of Cancel Culture, the threat to inclusion and diversity are inclusion and diversity themselves, when they are practiced in a way that shows/displays extreme exclusion.

And should we not add two further variations where "*sprechen*" is replaced by "*schweigen*"? "*Wovon man nicht schweigen kann, das zeigt sich,*" and "*wovon man schweigen soll, das zeigt sich*"? They follow the logic of a symptom which takes place at the level of "*zeigen*": a symptom is not simply a statement—in it, what is forbidden/impossible to say displays itself. What is then the difference between the two versions, between "*nicht schweigen kann*" and "*schweigen soll*"? Is it not again the difference between ethical prohibition and ontological impossibility? What one "cannot be silent about" points towards the ontological insistence of a drive which, even if it is not articulated in full propositions, shows itself, while what "one must be silent about" indicates an ethical prohibition.

All these variations on Wittgenstein's final thesis are thus superpositions which express in various modes the subject's frustration at the basic deadlock of our symbolic existence, and, as we have already seen, the ultimate expression of this frustration is the act of swearing. The ultimate variation on Wittgenstein's final thesis is thus: "*Wovon man nicht sprechen kann, das muss man verfluchen.*" *What we cannot speak about, we should swear at.*

Magnus Carlsen, the *de facto* world champion bored by classic chess (he mostly ignores big tournaments for the last two years), now joined the ranks of those who promote freestyle chess where the pieces on the back rank are randomized in the starting position. I see in this tendency to move to freestyle chess a reaction to the fact that in classic chess computers set the standard and regularly beat top human players (the latter's quality is measured by how close they come to the way a computer would play). When the back rank pieces are randomized, the number of possible moves grows exponentially, so that for some time at least computers will lose their advantage. Another way for humans to gain advantage even in classic chess is that, while knowing perfectly how their digital opponent will play, they intentionally make moves which are "wrong" (less than optimal), counting on the fact that their "wrong" moves will perplex the digital machine which will try to read a deeper intentional strategy into their "wrong" moves and thus make moves which will no longer obey the optimal strategy. However, such a perplexed state means that the digital machine will react to our "irrational" moves with something like a curse—but they cannot curse . . .

Could we not say something similar about the well-known "prisoner's dilemma," a thought experiment involving two *rational agents* each of whom can either cooperate for mutual benefit or betray their partner ("defect") for individual gain? While defecting is rational for each agent, cooperation yields a higher payoff for each. The paradox involved here has often been noted, and it concerns, as expected, self-reflexivity: if (in a situation with multiple participants) *I can reasonably assume that other participants will choose trust and cooperation*, then I can immensely profit by *not* choosing trust but by defecting.

In other words, we cannot truly communicate with AI—so what would have been a perfect communication? One shouldn't be surprised that we find it at the lowest of the lowest of popular culture: in one of the sub-plots of *Love, Actually* (Richard Curtis, 2023), writer Jamie withdraws from London to his

French cottage, where he meets a Portuguese housekeeper Aurélia who does not speak English (and he, of course, doesn't speak Portugese). Precisely because the two don't share a common language, a mutual attraction grows: they talk a lot, but counting on the fact that the other will not understand what one is saying, they are more and more making open love declarations to each other—and although they don't understand each other's words, they understand all the more fully the intended emotional impact. No wonder that, at the end, they get happily married . . .

3
The politics of vocation

If the present book deserves to be dedicated to anyone, it is to the people of Tristan da Cunha, the 98-square kilometers island in the middle of nowhere in the South Atlantic, lying approximately 2,787 kilometers (1,732 miles) from Cape Town and 2,437 kilometers (1,514 miles) from the nearest inhabited place, the island of Saint Helena. On October 10, 1961, a volcanic eruption forced the evacuation of all 264 people to the UK, but in 1963 almost all of them returned, withstanding the temptation of developed capitalism—why? Was it because the island has a unique social and economic structure based on solidarity, not competition? All resident families farm and all land is communally owned... in short, it is a Communist island. So much more than Bhutan with its ridiculous "dictatorship of happiness,"[1] Tristan da Cunha should serve as a model to all of us. Bhutan measures happiness by periodically surveying about 10 percent of the population and compiling statistics that fall under nine domains: living standards, health, education, environment, community, time-use, psychological well-being, governance, and culture—it is easy to imagine how this very bureaucratic procedure of measuring happiness undermines its goal.[2]

But what can this small island in the middle of nowhere tell us about our predicament? It enables us to look for the traces of similar solidarity that still abound all around us, although we are conditioned to ignore them like the good old Pavlov's dog. There is a notion (with a religious background, but nonetheless open to a materialist reading) which shows a way to make one's life meaningful without falling into a trap of some higher power guaranteeing this meaning, that of *vocation*. In his *Shattered*, Hanif Kureishi notes that, much more than top specialist doctors, nurses are those who consider their job a vocation:

> From the conversations I've had with the nurses, with whom I spend most of my days, and some of my nights—not having known any before—they consider their work to be a vocation, a calling, a whole way of life. They dress and undress me, wash my body, genitals, and arse, cleaning everything. They brush my hair, change my dressings, feed and engage me in conversations; insert suppositories, change my catheter and brush my teeth, shave and transfer me from bed to chair—this is their everyday work. . . . The nurses here are cheerful, they sing and make jokes, but they are not well paid. Wages are certainly lower in Italy than they are in the UK but they have been doing this for years and, as far as I can tell, want to carry on.[3]

We are not talking here about some higher form of creativity (art, politics, science . . .) which passionately occupies us, although this is also the opposite of a job we are doing just for money. We are talking about hard unpleasant work which brings little remuneration—we do it because we feel that we simply cannot not do it. Kureishi is perspicuous enough to immediately add that vocation and sexuality are not to be opposed—they can be in competition because they are both a vocation. Note also the profoundly theological Deleuzian remark that, in an authentic vocation, I don't choose it but I am chosen by it: "There is also a sexual aspect to the notion of vocation, since such a choice, like sexuality, isn't an option, but something you are inexorably drawn to. It chooses you, rather than the other way round."[4] So I don't impute to the inhabitants of Tristan a special pleasure in their way of life, I don't in any sense "feel their pleasure" in what is undoubtedly their rather harsh life. The great Scottish runner Eric Liddell (who won the 400 meters race at the 1924 Olympics in Paris) said: "I believe God made me for a purpose, but He also made me fast. And when I run, I feel His pleasure." From my perspective, such a claim comes too close to perversion, and what pops up in my mind is a variation on Niels Bohr's answer to Einstein's famous "God doesn't play dice": "Don't tell god when to feel pleasure!" I am only claiming that for the inhabitants of Tristan their life there is their vocation.

Plus my claim in no way implies that human nature (if we risk this term, whatever it could mean) is basically good and only corrupted in societies in which exploitation reigns. What I only claim is that the idea of human nature as basically egotist and utilitarian is wrong, regularly violated in both directions—or, as Freud puts it in "The Ego and the Id": "If anyone were to put forward the paradoxical proposition that normal man is not only far more immoral than he believes but also far more moral than he knows, psycho-analysis, on whose findings the first half of the assertion rests, would have no objection to raise against the second half."[5] The core of what we refer to as "evil" is not egotism but envy and resentment which make me act against my rational interests since the other's displeasure matters to me more than my own pleasure.

We should take this parallel to its logical conclusion: if I fall passionately in love with a woman (or the other way round) and she is indifferent towards me or even finds me disgusting, love was still not *my own* free choice—my experience is that I was chosen to love her. But what if a vocation is a fake, not only in the obvious sense that there are vocations for an evil cause (Nazis, Stalinists, and today's religious fundamentalists also experience their terror as a vocation), but in a more refined sense: when I am effectively caught into the capitalist machinery, working for profit, it can make me even more efficient if I experience myself as pursuing a vocation (developing new products or whatsoever)?[6] Here one should shamelessly insist on the difference between an authentic vocation and a fake one, a difference which can be deployed through an immanent analysis: the vocation for an evil cause has to rely on an obscene underground of obscene enjoyment, and the vocation as a mask of capitalist activity also has to obfuscate its ultimate meaninglessness.

There is a recent film which focuses precisely on vocation as a way to escape the capitalist commodification of our life, also in the form of dedicating it to some higher spiritual pursuit (a form which is still confined to the fulfilment of our ego): Krzysztof Zanussi's late masterpiece *Liczba doskonała* (*The Perfect Number*, 2022). A young Polish mathematician-physicist is immersed in his scientific research and in the teaching of his subjects, while his elderly Jewish-Polish cousin from Jerusalem would like to donate him the wealth accumulated during his life as a businessman. The young mathematician rejects this offer, since he wants to remain poor but happy in his life of teaching and researcher of Physics—he knows his vocation is the elaboration of the space-time theories of Quantum Physics . . . simple as it may sound, this solution actually works. It provides a new version of the old and often misused formula of freedom as a recognized necessity: the necessity I recognize is my vocation. To see this, one has to be caught in it—only in this way we can leave behind the cynical distance that predominates today.

However, Zanussi complicates things here, he presents the two positions—the rich Jewish businessman and the young poor scientist dedicated to his vocation—as two parallel stances echoing each other: both are focused on their own life achievement, both exclude any intense relationship with others, i.e., in both cases, there is no space for a loving "we." At the film's end, the uncle's death sobers the scientist, he shows compassion for others and responds to the love of a woman who was faithfully waiting for him till he became able to act as part of a loving "we."

I am skeptical towards this stance because I think that love or compassionate social engagement (like that of Kureishi's nurses) are also forms of vocation. Zanussi's scientist is not a truly consistent figure, he combines authentic vocation with pathological features which are not an immanent part of one's vocation (one should recall that he is extremely ambitious, he wants to be remembered in history for his discoveries). There is no immanent contradiction between pursuing science as a vocation and engaging in a loving relationship or fighting for social justice. Even if the two appear to enter into a conflict ("does your scientific or political vocation not make you neglect our love?"), we should reject the very terms of this choice: in an authentic dilemma, one should not decide between Cause and love, between the fidelity to one or the other event. The authentic relationship between Cause and love is more paradoxical.

The basic lesson of King Vidor's *Rhapsody* is that, in order to gain the beloved woman's love, the man has to prove that he is able to survive without her, that he prefers his mission or profession to her. There are two immediate choices: (1) my professional career is what matters most to me, the woman is just an amusement, a distracting affair; (2) the woman is everything to me, I am ready to humiliate myself, to forsake all my public and professional dignity for her. They are both false, they lead to the man being rejected by the woman. The message of true love is thus: even if you are everything to me, I can survive without you, I am ready to forsake you for my mission or profession. The proper way for the woman to test the man's love is thus to betray him at the crucial moment of his career (the first public concert in the film, the key exam, the business negotiation which will decide his career)—only if he can survive the ordeal and accomplish successfully his task although deeply traumatized by her desertion, will he deserve her and she will return to him.

The underlying paradox is that love, precisely as the Absolute, should not be posited as a direct goal—it should retain the status of a by-product, of something we get as an undeserved grace. Perhaps, there is no greater love than that of a revolutionary couple, where each of the two lovers is ready to abandon the other at any moment if revolution demands it. The question is thus: how does an emancipatory-revolutionary collective which embodies the "general will" affect intense erotic passion? From what we know about love among the Bolshevik revolutionaries, something unique took place there, a new form of the romantic couple emerged: a couple living in a permanent emergency state, totally dedicated to the revolutionary Cause, ready to sacrifice all personal sexual fulfilment to it, even ready to abandon and betray each other if Revolution demanded it, but simultaneously totally dedicated to each other, enjoying rare moments together with extreme intensity. The lovers' passion was tolerated, even silently respected, but ignored in the public discourse as something of no concern to others. (There are traces of this even in what we know of Lenin's affair with Inessa Armand.) There is no attempt at *Gleichschaltung*, at enforcing the unity between intimate passion and social life: the radical *disjunction* between sexual passion and social-revolutionary activity is fully recognized. The two dimensions are accepted as totally heterogeneous, each irreducible to the other, there is no harmony between the two—but it is this very recognition of the gap which makes their relationship non-antagonistic.

How, then, does vocation stand with regard to belief? Remember the denouement of le Carré's *The Little Drummer Girl* when Khalil, the Palestinian fighter, a sincere "terrorist," discovers that the English actress Charlie who pretended to join his cause and even voluntarily became his lover betrayed him:

> "Who do you work for, Charlie? For the Germans?" She shook her head. "For the Zionists?" He took her silence for yes. "Are you Jewish." "No." "Do you believe in Israel? What are you?" "Nothing," she said. "Are you Christian? Do you see them as the founders of your great religion?" Again she shook

her head. "Is it for money? Did they bribe you? Blackmail you?" She wanted to scream. She clenched her fists, and filled her lungs, but the chaos choked her, and she sobbed instead. . . . Slowly, without aggression, he reached out his left hand and touched the side of her face, apparently to make sure that she was real. Then looked at the tips of his fingers, and back at her again, somehow comparing them in his mind.[7]

In both the movie and in the BBC miniseries version, they inserted another line by Khalil at . . . : "So you don't believe in anything."(the miniseries) / "You believe in nothing. You have no beliefs at all."(the movie) Although the movie and TV versions are not to be underestimated (in the TV miniseries, Florence Pugh is excellent as Charlie, while in the movie Juliano Mer-Khamis totally steals the show as Khalil), the inserted line is basically superfluous, it just renders explicit what is obvious from the scene itself: Khalil's properly ethical disappointment at Charlie. When he asks Charlie if she did it because she believes in Israel or Christianity, or because she was blackmailed, this is not an accusation but an attempt to find acceptable reasons for her betrayal. When he realizes that Charlie believes in nothing, his reaction is not violence but just a sad total resignation mixed with a minimum of compassion. The worst mistake would have been here to dismiss such a full commitment as something that necessarily leads to religious fundamentalism: to make life worth living, a human being should act as more than a human animal following its needs and interests—a full commitment to a Cause is needed. True, Blaise Pascal was right when he wrote: "Men never do evil so completely and cheerfully as when they do it from religious conviction." However, what distinguishes such commitment from religious fundamentalism is that it is fully aware of its subjective character, which is why it always functions against the background of a possible loss of belief enacted, among other cases, in Christ's "Father, why have you forsaken me?". What remains for a Christian in such cases is only the unconditional love for those who are bent for self-destruction.

Following Padre Raffaele Nogaro's groundbreaking idea of the urgent need to liberate Christ himself,[8] we should accept that Christ works as a vanishing mediator in every authentic love—he is here whenever there is love between humans: "For where two or three gather in my name, there I am with them."(Matthew 18:20) Christ is thus neither the subject nor the object of love, he is love itself: "Whoever does not love does not know God, because God is love."(John 4:8) Padre Nogaro makes this point with full clarity: "Jesus substitutes the first commandment of the old Law 'love your master God' (Dt 6:5) with the commandment which does not have as its direct addressee God but the neighbour." Nogaro then quotes Dietrich Bonhoffer who takes this to its logical extreme: "A Christian is not a religious man but simply a man, a 'being for others' like Jesus." This is also why the genuine dimension of Christian doubt does not concern the existence of god: its logic is not "I feel such a need to believe in god, but I cannot be sure that he really exists, that he is not just a chimera of my imagination." (A humanist atheist can easily respond to this: "then drop god and simply assume the ideals god stands for as your own.") An authentic Christian is indifferent towards the infamous proofs of god's existence. What the position of Christian doubt involves is a pragmatic paradox succinctly rendered by Alyosha in Dostoyevsky's *Karamazov Brothers*: "God exists but I am not sure whether I believe in him," where "I believe in him" refers to the believer's readiness to fully assume the existential engagement implied by such a belief: "the question of the 'existence of God' is not really at the heart of Dostoyevsky's labors. . . . Alyosha's uncertainty about whether he 'believes in God' is an uncertainty about whether the life he leads and the feelings he has are the life and the feelings that would rightly follow from belief in God."[9] It is in this sense that every theology is political: it confronts us with the question of our social engagement. That's why I fully endorse Nogaro's motto: "WITH JESUS IT IS NOT NECESSARY TO BELIEVE, TO LOVE IS ENOUGH." In other words, the same holds for belief as for love: belief is not belief in god (as an object external to us), Jesus is here in our belief itself (our full commitment to a worthy Cause).

*

More precisely, we should introduce here a gap between belief and faith: what Khalil talks about is faith, not belief, and fundamentalists reduce faith to belief. Mark Murphy determines this gap, paraphrasing Lacan's thesis that "desire is neither the appetite for satisfaction nor the demand for love, but the difference that results from the subtraction of the first from the second, the very phenomenon of their splitting"[10]: "The question of mere 'questions of belief' and knowledge of God—and the vulgar framework that entails—is negated when we encounter faith by subtracting one from the other: faith appears as a negative surplus when knowledge is subtracted from belief."[11] This is why one can say "I believe Hitler (when he says he wants to eliminate Jews), but I don't have faith in him". Belief is a belief in facts beyond what we know (say, I believe there is an alien civilization on Mars), faith is a subjective engagement.

The paradox of authentic faith is that, although it excludes fundamentalism, it also excludes its apparent opposite, cultural relativization. For years, the populist Right were targeting "cultural Marxism" as an allegedly new and even more dangerous form of Marxism bent on destroying the very basis of our civilization. The idea is that, after the failure of the revolutions in the West around the early 1920s, Communists realized that the cause of this failure was the strength of traditional religious values, so they changed their target and concentrated on first undermining the cultural values that sustain our civilization. The combination of Marxism with psychoanalysis supposedly proved ideal for this task ... The irony is that today the newly emerging orthodox Communist Left also uses this term, but from the opposite standpoint: Western Marxism which replaced political revolutionary struggle with cultural analysis, neglecting or even condemning actual Communist states, was from the beginning a tool of imperialism to neutralize Marxism, to make it acceptable for the capitalist academia with no links to actual working class movements. The old saying "when nothing goes right, go left" holds true today more than ever—and it is also more difficult to follow than ever.

But history is full of surprises—now this term has its atheist counterpart: cultural Christianity—here is a recent case of such culturalization. On August 28, 2024, the Dicastery for the Doctrine of the Faith, with the assent of Pope Francis, rendered public a Note which granted approval for devotion linked to Medjugorje, recognizing the abundant spiritual fruits received at the Sanctuary of the Queen of Peace. Without making a declaration on the supernatural character of the Marian apparitions, it just recognizes the goodness of the spiritual fruits linked to Medjugorje, authorizing the faithful to adhere to it since "many positive fruits have been noted in the midst of a spiritual experience, while negative and dangerous effects have not spread among the People of God."¹²

The last sentence is weird: it sounds as if it admits there were also negative and dangerous effects which just have not spread around as much as the good ones—so it's not a question of truth but of a cold calculation of good effects versus bad effects: since the good effects dominate, let's tolerate the pilgrimage. The phrase *nihil obstat* was used by a Catholic cleric known as a *Censor Librorum* (Latin for 'censor of books') to indicate that a book contains nothing contrary to Catholic doctrines, faith, or morals, and so can be published. The message of the Note was also a *nihil obstat*: even if there are serious doubts about the miraculous nature of the appearances of Mary, the Note poses no obstacle to the Catholics who want to continue to make pilgrimages to Medjugorje. Are the authors of the Note aware that they are reasoning like the big figures of the Enlightenment like Voltaire who were in private atheists or at least agnostic sceptics: they thought that, even if religion was not based on truth, ordinary people needed it since they were too weak to listen to reason— only a figure of supernatural authority could compel them to control their destructive and immoral passions . . .

After the Khomeini revolution in Iran, the first censor installed by the regime to review all new movies and decide whether they should be shown or not was a *blind* cleric, so when he was watching a movie someone was sitting at his side and describing to him what was happening on the screen—maybe, this is an ideal censor because the true censor's job is not to judge the work itself but the effect this work produces in an average viewer. And did the Dicastery not act in a similar way? What matters is not the immanent truth but its effects . . .

*

Lately even some ferocious atheists (like Richard Dawkins) declared themselves "cultural Christians": although they don't believe in god, they respect and practice the moral rules of Christianity, considering them superior with regard to all other religions. With the Note on Medjugorje, it seems that even the Vatican itself made a turn in this direction: what matters more than truth are the ethical implications of a religious stance. Such postmodern pragmatic relativism is as far as one can imagine from the authentic belief of someone like Kierkegaard who was in no way a dogmatic fundamentalist—he famously proclaimed that we cannot ever be fully sure that we believe, we can only believe that we believe and thus accept the absurdity of belief. In *Murder in the Cathedral*, T.S. Eliot has his *de facto* mouthpiece Thomas Beckett say: "The last temptation is the greatest treason / To do the right thing for the wrong reason." The authentic Kierkegaardian lesson is that we should turn this claim around: no, the highest form of treason is to do the right thing for the right reason—when we think we are doing this, we adopt the arrogant position of a subject who, in full self-transparency, knows what he is doing. But we never know this since we shouldn't trust even our most sincere beliefs—as Kierkegaard put it, we can only believe that we believe.

Cultural Christians are totally blind to the desperate inner turmoil Kierkegaard went through, the turmoil that is condensed in the story about the Fall. The serpent says that by eating the fruit of the tree of knowledge, Adam and Eve will become like God; and after the two do it, God comments: "Behold, Adam has become like one of us."(Genesis 3:22) Hegel's comment is: "So the serpent did not lie, for God confirms what it said." Then Hegel goes on to reject the claim that what God says is meant with irony: "Cognition is the principle of spirituality, and this . . . is also the principle by which the injury of the separation is healed."[13] Hegel announces here the final message of Richard Wagner's *Parsifal*: "The wound can be healed only by the spear that smote it (*Die Wunde schliesst der Speer nur der Sie schlug*)." Subjective freedom is not just the possibility to choose evil or good,

> it is the consideration or the cognition that *makes* people evil, so that consideration and cognition themselves are what is evil, and that therefore such cognition is what ought not to exist because it is the *source* of evil.[14]

The Good emerges as a possibility and duty only through this primordial/constitutive choice of Evil: we experience the Good when, after choosing Evil, we become aware of the utter inadequacy of our situation. The queerness of the Law thus reaches its apogee in Christianity in which we, humans, are a priori presumed to be fallen, to dwell in sin, so that the entire reign of the law consists of the rules of how to deal with our violations of the law: through confessions and other modes of ritualized repentance. That's why, as many perspicuous theologians knew, the Fall is *felix culpa*, the fortunate fault/the blessed fall—or, as St. Augustine put it: "For God judged it better to bring good out of evil than not to permit any evil to exist." We have to add another step to this reasoning: in order to bring good out of evil, the Good itself—God—has to bring evil out of itself. This is why we should turn around the standard Christian (or Catholic, more precisely) explanation of why there is evil in the world: god gave us freedom, and freedom is the freedom to choose what we freely decide, inclusive of evil . . . But is it not the other way round? God (more than just exposed us to the temptation of evil, he) *pushed us into evil so that we would discover our freedom.* There is no freedom without evil since to be able to choose between good and evil one already has to be in evil. No wonder that back in 2017 even Pope Francis, who usually displayed the right intuitions in matters theological and political, committed a serious blunder in endorsing the idea, propagated by some Catholics, to change a line in Lord's Prayer where it asks "lead us not into temptation":

> It is not a good translation because it speaks of a God who induces temptation. I am the one who falls; it's not him pushing me into temptation to then see how I have fallen. A father doesn't do that, a father helps you to get up immediately. It's Satan who leads us into temptation, that's his department.[15]

The first thing to note here is that there could be more truth in what is clearly a mistranslation than in a more faithful rendering of the original meaning. There are good reasons to accept that the Christian topic of immaculate conception is grounded in the mistranslation of the Hebrew *alma* (which simply means "young woman") as "virgin": "It would appear that Western civilization has endured two millennia of consecrated sexual neurosis simply because the authors of Matthew and Luke could not read Hebrew."[16] There are also good reasons to accept that the seventy "virgins" awaiting martyrs in the Muslim paradise resulted from a mistranslation: in using the word *hur*, transliterated as "houris," Koran relied here on the early Christian texts which used the Aramaic *hur*, meaning "white raisins," a delicacy. Let us take a young martyr on a suicide mission because he took literally his leader's promise: "The gates of Paradise have opened for you. There are beautiful black-eyed virgins waiting for you on the banks of rivers of honey." Imagine the look on his face "when, finding himself in a paradise teeming with his fellow thugs, his seventy houris arrive as a fistful of raisins."[17] However, what we should avoid at any cost is precisely the cheap satisfaction provided by such discoveries of the original meaning.

In a homologous way, one can avoid responsibility and/or guilt by precisely emphasizing in an exaggerated way one's responsibility or by assuming guilt all too readily, as in the case of the white male Politically Correct academic who emphasizes the guilt of racist phallogocentrism, and uses this admission of guilt as a stratagem NOT to confront the way he as a "radical" intellectual perfectly fits the existing power relations towards which he pretends to be thoroughly critical ... Here also, the best mask of a thing is the thing itself ... Back to the Pope's recommendation, it is easy to discern its noble purpose:

> The Pope wishes for God to be a God of love, loving and protecting us as our human fathers do here on Earth, and not a God willfully guiding us into danger. Yet to my most profound disappointment and sadness, this cannot be so, for in the Gospels, the very words of Jesus in the prayer itself tell us otherwise.[18]

However, is god not exposing us to temptation already in paradise where he warns Adam and Eve not to eat the apple from the tree of knowledge—but why did he put this tree there in the first place, and then even drew attention to it? This is why Saint Theresa of Avila was right when she wrote: "More tears are shed over answered prayers than unanswered ones." Was god not aware that human ethics can arise only after the Fall? Many of the most insightful theologians and Christian writers, from Kierkegaard to Paul Claudel, were fully aware that, at its most basic, temptation arises in the form of the Good— or, as Kierkegaard put it apropos Abraham, when he is ordered to slaughter Isaac, his predicament "is an ordeal such that, please note, the ethical is the temptation."[19] Is the temptation of the (false) Good not what characterizes all forms of religious fundamentalism? And we should openly confront the paradoxes implied by true ethics. Although John le Carré's *Russia House* is not among his best works, it contains an immensely powerful chapter. The book's hero, Barley, the head of a small British publishing house, visits the USSR in the years of perestroika to attend a writers' retreat near Peredelkino. There he encounters a man called Goethe, in fact a renowned physicist who has secretly written a manuscript detailing the Soviet's nuclear missile capabilities. Goethe's goal is to convince the West that USSR does not pose a real military threat (its military capacities are much less developed than it appears) and, in this way, to facilitate the end of the Cold War. When the CIA learns of Goethe's manuscript, it is concerned because the manuscript states that the Soviet nuclear missile program is in complete disarray, and therefore there's no real reason for an arms race to continue. Instead of rejoicing, they panic, perceiving a danger for their military complex, so they try to prove that Goethe's manuscript is a Soviet plot to delude the West. They invite Barley to the US where they subject him to a long humiliating and aggressive interrogation. Barley appears to play the game, but he ultimately breaks down, becomes disgusted with the situation, and decides to offer his services to the KGB . . . The long chapter which details Barley's interrogation and his utter and painful disillusionment with CIA is by far the strongest in the book, a true lesson in ethical integrity and in how, sometimes, betrayal (of one's own side) is the only way to act ethically.

This brings us to the *nihil obstat* apropos the appearance of Mary in Medjugorje. It is easy to discern its noble purpose: why prevent the goodness of the spiritual fruits from Medjugorje from freely spreading and being shared even if they are based on a lie? However, such a culturalization of Christianity, treating it as a cultural phenomenon with no unconditional truth value, inexorably leads us to censor the basic Christian texts themselves if they don't fit the prescribed task of spreading around the goodness of its spiritual fruits. If we want to keep the Christian experience alive, we have to resist all temptation to purge from it "problematic" passages—they are the very stuff which confers on Christianity the unbearable tensions of a true life. Christianity is a form of madness or it is a dead corpse. I never thought I would find myself on the side of conservative critics of Pope Francis, but he took this cultural direction too far when he recently said in a conversation with children in Singapore:

> All religions are paths to reach God. They are—to make a comparison—like different languages, different dialects, to get there. But God is God for everyone. If you start to fight saying my religion is more important than yours, mine is true and yours isn't, where will this lead us? There is only one God, and each of us has a language to arrive at God. Some are Sikh, Muslim, Hindu, Christians; they are different ways to God.[20]

Two immediate counter-questions: what about there being no god, and what about polytheists for whom there is more than one god? Furthermore, such a reduction of different religions to different languages which express the same god opens up the way to naturalism. In neurotheology, the study of religion reached the extreme point of reductionism: its formula, "(our experience of) god is (the product of neuronal processes in) our brain," clearly echoes Hegel's formula of phrenology: "Spirit is a bone." Hegel calls this the "infinite judgment" which asserts the identity of the highest and the lowest, and no wonder that neurotheology is often dismissed as a new version of phrenology—more refined, for sure, but basically advocating the same correlation between the processes or shapes in our head and psychic processes ... The limitations of this approach are obvious, and the lines of attacking it clearly predictable. While these critical reactions to neurotheology have a certain weight, they nonetheless ultimately founder upon a hard rock: if it was proven that, by manipulating a subject's neurons, one can effectively give rise to some kind of mystical state in the subject, and that, in this way, one can experimentally induce a religious experience, does this not indicate that our religious experience is in some sense caused by neuronal processes in our brain? The specific form of this experience, of course, depends on its cultural context and on the thick web of socio-symbolic practices, and the precise causality, of course, remains obscure, but—as Jacques Lacan would have put it—we do encounter here a bit of the real which remains the same in all symbolic universes.

So the Pope's words could be easily understood in neurotheological terms: languages are different symbolizations of a Real which are neurological processes in our brain. However, these lines could also be understood as a version of Cultural Christianity: do they not imply that Christianity is just one of the possible symbolizations (cultural appearances) of the neurological Real? This is not at all my position: for me, Christianity has its own repressed Real, and it is at this level that its use for radical emancipatory movements is to be sought. My position is much closer to that of Althusser who, in 1980, gave an interview to Italian TV in Rome where he said:

> I became Communist because I was Catholic. I did not change religion, but I remained profoundly Catholic. I don't go to church but this doesn't matter; you don't ask people to go to church today. I remained a Catholic, that is to say, an internationalist universalist. I thought inside the Communist party there were more adequate means to realize universal fraternity.[21]

Althusser is in good company here: Eric Satie, a devout Catholic, was also a Communist—his sense of solidarity with the people led him to join the Communist Party in 1913 after the murder of the party leader Jean Jaurès, and he remained a card-carrying member until his death. If anything, I am here much harsher than Althusser: I don't advocate a simple unity of Christianity and Communism. In my view, first, I am much closer to Protestantism (Calvinism, more precisely) than Catholicism; second, for me, there is no place for "all religions of the world" in my world. Calvinists combined, in a unique way, predestination with free will and social activism. They

> argued against bishops and for lay-elders; they also wanted the ministry of the church to have an important measure of independence from the civil government. . . . the pastors of the church viewed themselves as prophetic critics of the political rulers. Calvinism also tended to teach a greater right of resistance and even revolution in the face of tyrannical government. All of this was held together under the notion of divine sovereignty. Quoting the Book of Acts, Calvinists would say, "We ought to obey God rather than men." (Acts 5:29)[22]

The theological dimension is our only hope when we face the massive failure of emancipatory transformation. Bolivia in the past two decades, a bright exception, is now also approaching a failure: there is an open split in the Moralista movement between Lucho Arse, a more technocratic president, and Evo Morales who feels betrayed and, together with his supporters, is organizing armed local uprisings attacking military units and police. Whichever turn the events will take, the Bolivian miracle seems over.

But is Calvinism not—much more than Lutheran Protestantism—what Max Weber had in mind when he emphasized the link between Protestantism and capitalism? Is Calvinism not the ideological foundation of early capitalism at its purest? Yes and no: we encounter here a typical dialectical reversal. The problem with capitalism is that it cannot survive if, in its social reality, it follows too closely its own ideological foundation—it can survive only through permanent compromises with other traditions. What this means is that, in order to fully actualize the ideological core of capitalism, we have to transcend capitalism to another social formation, to Communism. In other words, Calvinism is the ex-timate point of Christianity, a point of its potential self-overcoming, in a similar way that Christianity is the ex-timate point in the religious space, it is literally an atheist religion, its central event is the death of god which opens up the way to Holy Spirit, to the freedom in equality of a group which rejects social hierarchy. This atheist core of Christianity is, of course, obfuscated in institutionalized Christianity whose main effort is to erase its own subversive excess—which is why G.K. Chesterton was right (as he usually is) when he wrote: "I believe in preaching to the converted, for I have generally found that the converted do not understand their own religion."[23]

The triad of Orthodoxy, Catholicism, and Protestantism corresponds to the Lacanian triad of Imaginary–Symbolic–Real: the horizon of Orthodoxy is that of the imaginary fusion between man and god; Catholicism focuses on the symbolic exchange between the two poles; Protestantism asserts the "subtracted" god of the intrusion of the Real. The key doctrinal division between Orthodoxy and Western Christianity (both Catholicism and Protestantism) concerns the procession of the Holy Spirit: for the Latin tradition, the Holy Spirit proceeds from both Father and Son, while for the Orthodox it proceeds from the Father alone. Apropos of this disputed question of the origin of the Holy Spirit, Hegel committed a weird slip of the tongue: he mistakenly claimed that for Orthodoxy, the Holy Spirit originates from both Father and Son, and for Western Christianity from the Son alone (from Christ's Resurrection in the community of believers); as he wrote, the disagreement between East and West concerns knowing "if the Holy Spirit proceeds from the Son, or from the Father and the Son, the Son being only the one who actualizes, who reveals—thus from him alone the Spirit proceeds."[24]

For Hegel, it is thus not even thinkable for the Holy Spirit to proceed from the Father alone—and my point is that there is a truth in this slip of the tongue. Hegel's underlying premise is that what dies on the Cross is not only god's earthly representative-incarnation, but the god of beyond itself: Christ is the "vanishing mediator" between the substantial transcendent god-in-itself and god qua virtual spiritual community. This "shift from subject to predicate" is avoided in Orthodoxy, where God–Father continues to pull the strings, is not really caught in the process: for Protestantism, Holy Spirit is the return of Christ in the community of believers not supported by any big Other. It is also only in this way that we can get rid of the ambiguous figure of the Devil—ambiguous, because in traditional Christianity Devil plays a contradictory role: he tempts us into sin and then organizes the punishment for our sins in Hell. The most radical Protestants resolved this question by way of identifying an evil dimension *in god himself*.

How, then, do we pass from capitalism to Communism? For Noam Yuran,[25] capitalism is not the mode of production in which everything has a price and can be exchanged on the market, i.e., in which commodification is universalized. It is in pre-capitalist societies that everything can be negotiated, exchanged for a proper price, especially marriage which is a matter of negotiated exchange between families and in this sense a business proposal, while in capitalism love and marriage are exempted from market exchange: it is a bourgeois ideal to marry for love. Insofar as we accept the thesis that Protestantism is the exemplary religion of capitalist (at least till the middle of the twentieth century), then the same holds for the passage from Catholicism to Protestantism. In premodern Catholicism, our salvation is a matter of exchange, I can buy it through my good works or even directly for money (this is what shocked so much Luther: in Vatican it was possible to buy redemption not only for sins already committed but even for future sins—say, I want to steal property from my relative and if I pay to the Church an adequate sum, I can then do it without endangering my salvation). In Protestantism, on the contrary, my salvation is decided by god in advance (predestination), which means that it is not a matter of haggling, it doesn't imply any form of market exchange, even the most spiritual one.

Paradoxically, it is this very limitation which sustains the space for capitalist ever-expanding search of profit—a nice case of the Lacanian logic of all (commercialization) grounded in a constitutive exception. And my crazy hypothesis is that all we should do is to pass from the "masculine" logic of universality grounded in an exception to the "feminine" logic of a space with no exception which is for this very reason non-all: in (the lower stage, at least, of) Communism, there is nothing money cannot buy and for this very reason money cannot buy all there is.

So, again, why Christian atheism? A reference to Marx may be of some help here. Apropos of the Party of Order which took power when the revolutionary élan of 1848 was over, Marx wrote that the secret of its existence was

> the coalition of Orléanists and Legitimists into one party, disclosed. The bourgeois class fell apart into two big factions which alternately—the big landed proprietors under the restored monarchy and the finance aristocracy and the industrial bourgeoisie under the July Monarchy—had maintained a monopoly of power. . . . the nameless realm of the republic was the only one in which both factions could maintain with equal power the common class interest without giving up their mutual rivalry.[26]

So when we are dealing with two or more socio-economic groups, their common interest can only be represented in the guise of the negation of their shared premise—the common denominator of the two royalist factions is not royalism, but republicanism. (And, in the same way the only political agent that consequently represents the interests of the capital as such, in its universality, above its particular factions, was Tony Blair's Third Way Social Democracy . . .) Exactly the same holds for Christianity: it is not one among religions but the only truly universal religion, the common denominator of all religions, which can only assume the form of atheism (the death of god), of the negation of their shared ground. And exactly the same holds also for the Kantian ethics, an ethics with no supreme Good, a *de facto* atheist ethics of autonomy: I am responsible not only to do my duty but to decide what this duty is, with no reliance on a higher authority. To clarify this topic, one has to revisit Lacan's topic of *Kant avec Sade*, of Sade as the truth of the Kantian ethics.

Here, however, we come close to a very touchy point. As Lacanians, we should be especially attentive to shifts and inconsistencies in Lacan's own teaching. Perhaps the greatest shift occurs in the course of his seminar on the ethics of psychoanalysis: there is a subtle but radical change in how he reads the motif of "Kant with Sade."[27] At the beginning, he refers to Saint Paul, to Paul's notion of a law which enables (calls for) its sinful transgression, while towards the end, law itself becomes the law of desire. To clarify this shift, let's begin with the famous passage from Paul's Romans 7:

> So, my brothers and sisters, you also died to the law through the body of Christ, that you might belong to another, to him who was raised from the dead, in order that we might bear fruit for God. For when we were in the realm of the flesh, the sinful passions aroused by the law were at work in us, so that we bore fruit for death. But now, by dying to what once bound us, we have been released from the law so that we serve in the new way of the Spirit, and not in the old way of the written code. What shall we say, then? Is the law sinful? Certainly not! Nevertheless, I would not have known what sin was had it not been for the law. For I would not have known what coveting really was if the law had not said, "You shall not covet." But sin, seizing the opportunity afforded by the commandment, produced in me every kind of coveting. For apart from the law, sin was dead. Once I was alive apart from the law; but when the commandment came, sin sprang to life and I died.[28]

One of the last echoes of this stance is found in the work of Georges Bataille who for this reason remains strictly *premodern*, stuck in this dialectic of the law and its transgression, of the prohibitive law as generating the transgressive desire, which forces him to the debilitating perverse conclusion that one has to install prohibitions in order to be able to enjoy their violation—a clearly unworkable pragmatic paradox. What Bataille is unable to perceive is simply the consequence of the Kantian philosophical revolution: the fact that *the absolute excess is that of the Law itself*—the Law intervenes in the "homogeneous" stability of our pleasure-oriented life as the shattering force of the absolute destabilizing heterogeneity. In Buddhism, you are taught to sacrifice desire in order to attain the inner peace of Enlightenment in which sacrifice cancels itself. For Lacan, the true sacrifice is desire itself: desire is an intrusion which throws off the rails the rhythm of our life, it compels us to forfeit everyday pleasures and comforts for discipline and hard work in the pursuit of the object of our desire, be it love, a political Cause, science ... In short, Lacan's reading of Kant's ethics is not fully consistent. The basic line of Lacan's reading of Kant is adequately rendered in Russell Sbriglia's summation of Joan Copjec's elaboration of her notion of the "sartorial superego"[29]:

> whereas utilitarianism blithely assumes that "man can be counted as zero," psychoanalysis insists that, if counted man can indeed be, he can only be counted as "minus one."[30] Confident that the goal of man is the maximization of pleasure and that pleasure can therefore be used to regulate and manipulate man, utilitarianism presumes that "man is basically and infinitely manageable," that he is, in short, "fundamentally *ruly*." (85) The psychoanalytic objection to this supposition, Copjec clarifies, rests not on the protest that man is *more* than "rationalist engineers" like Bentham allows, but rather that "man is, in a manner, *less*" than utilitarians realize insofar as "he is radically separated from, and cannot know, what he wants"(87)—a separation and an unknowing that renders man fundamentally *unruly*. Hence Copjec's conclusion that "the difference between the utilitarian and the Lacanian subject is the difference between zero and minus one, between a subject who is driven to seek the maximization of his pleasure in his own greater good, and a subject for whom pleasure cannot function as an index of the good, since the latter is lost to him"—lost because the subject is ultimately "subject to a principle *beyond* pleasure," (87) that principle being, of course, what psychoanalysis dubs the death drive.

Up to this point I cannot but fully agree: for Kant, freedom effectively is not the freedom to pursue one's pleasures without constraints, it is on the contrary "the freedom to resist the lure of the pleasure principle and to submit oneself to the law of the death drive."(96) Freedom does not reside in spontaneously following one's cravings, it is a form of *resistance* to these cravings, a form of self-control. But now we come to the problematic point: Lacan sees the limit of Kant's notion of categorical imperative in Kant's ignorance of how the distinction between the subject of the enunciated and the subject of enunciation works in the case of categorical imperative—a failure that makes it seem as though it "come[s] from nowhere," which, in turn, allows the addressee to "presume to occupy the vacant enunciative position" and "take itself as the source of the statement": "the ethical subject hears the voice of conscience as its own."(96–98) With his autonomous ethics, Kant thus "sealed up again the gap he so dramatically opened" (96): it appears that the subject itself issues the moral imperative he obeys in acting ethically.

Again, in Lacanese, what Kant failed to do was to distinguish between the subject of the *enunciated* (the subject of the *statement* that Kant correctly understood the categorical imperative to be) and the subject of its *enunciation* which is decentered with regard to the moral subject—this agency that pushes the subject to act ethically is, of course, what psychoanalysis identifies as the *superego*. This is where Sade comes in as the "truth" of Kantian ethics: the categorical imperative is not libidinally neutral since the pain we, its subjects, experience when doing our duty brings enjoyment to the decentered superego agency. From this standpoint, we can claim that "acting ethically, paradoxically, entails not *identifying* with the moral law (as in Kant), but *dis-identifying* with it, it entails not heeding this 'impulse,' but '*recoil*[*ing*]' in 'moral revulsion' (88) from this 'incomprehensible part of our being.'" (92)

*

However, the actual "incomprehensible part of our being" is not superego but *desire itself* which is constitutively decentered with regard to subject, desire which makes the subject barred, a void. And, as it was formulated with brilliant simplicity by Lacan, the reason Sade was not able to think the barred subject ($) resides in his misconception of the difference between the two deaths, the biological death of the common mortal body and the death of the other "undead" body: it is clear that what Sade aims at in his notion of a radical Crime is the murder of this second body. Sade deploys this distinction in the long philosophical dissertation delivered to Juliette by Pope Pius VI in Book 5 of *Juliette*:

The human being, along with all organic life and even inorganic matter, is caught in an endless cycle of death and rebirth, generation and corruption, so that "there is indeed no real death," only a permanent transformation and recycling of matter according to the immanent laws of "the three kingdoms," animal, vegetable, and mineral. Destruction may accelerate this process, but it cannot stop it. The true crime would be the one that no longer operates within the three kingdoms but annihilates them altogether, that puts a stop to the eternal cycle of generation and corruption and by doing so returns to Nature her absolute privilege of contingent creation, of casting the dice anew.

What, then, at a strict theoretical level, is wrong with this dream of the "second death" as a radical pure negation which puts a stop to the life-cycle itself? In a superb display of his genius, Lacan provides a simple answer: "It is just that, being a psychoanalyst, I can see that the second death is prior to the first, and not after, as de Sade dreams it." (The only problematic part of this statement is the qualification "being a psychoanalyst"—a Hegelian philosopher can also see this quite clearly.) In what precise sense are we to understand this priority of the second death—the radical annihilation of the entire life-cycle of generation and corruption—over the first death which remains a moment of this cycle? Aaron Schuster points the way:

> Sade believes that there exists a well-established second nature that operates according to immanent laws. Against this ontologically consistent realm he can only dream of an absolute Crime that would abolish the three kingdoms and attain the pure disorder of primary nature.[31]

In short, what Sade doesn't see is that there is no big Other, no Nature as an ontologically consistent realm—nature is already in itself inconsistent, unbalanced, destabilized by antagonisms. The total negation imagined by Sade thus doesn't come at the end, as a threat or prospect of radical destruction, it comes at the beginning, it always-already happened, it stands for the zero-level starting point out of which the fragile/inconsistent reality emerges. In other words, what is missing in the notion of Nature as a body regulated by fixed laws is simply *subject itself*: in Hegelese, the Sadean Nature remains a Substance,

Sade continues to grasp reality only as Substance and not also as Subject, where "subject" does not stand for another ontological level different from Substance but for the immanent incompleteness-inconsistency-antagonism of Substance itself. And, insofar as the Freudian name for this radical negativity is the death drive, Schuster is right to point out how, paradoxically, what Sade misses in his celebration of the ultimate Crime of radical destruction of all life is precisely the death drive:

> for all its wantonness and havoc the Sadeian will-to-extinction is premised on a fetishistic denial of the death drive. The sadist makes himself into the servant of universal extinction precisely in order to avoid the deadlock of subjectivity, the "virtual extinction" that splits the life of the subject from within.... as Lacan argues, Sade is right if we just turn around his evil thought: subjectivity is the catastrophe it fantasizes about, the death beyond death, the "second death." While the sadist dreams of violently forcing a cataclysm that will wipe the slate clean, what he does not want to know is that this unprecedented calamity has already taken place. Every subject is the end of the world, or rather this impossibly explosive end that is equally a "fresh start," the unabolishable chance of the dice throw.

This brings us back to Kant, to Kant's preeminence over Sade: Kant characterized the free autonomous act as an act which cannot be accounted for in the terms of natural causality, of the texture of causes and effects: a free act occurs as its own cause, it opens up a new causal chain from its zero-point. So insofar as "second death" is the interruption of the natural life-cycle of generation and corruption, no radical annihilation of the entire natural order is needed for this—an autonomous free act already suspends natural causality, and the subject as $ already is this cut in the natural circuit, the self-sabotage of natural goals. The mystical name for this end of the world is "night of the world," and the philosophical name, radical negativity as the core of subjectivity. And, to quote Mallarmé, a throw of the dice will never abolish the hazard, i.e., the abyss of negativity remains forever the unsublatable background of subjective creativity. We may even risk here an ironic version of Gandhi's famous motto "be the change you want to see in the world": the subject is itself the catastrophe it fears and tries to avoid. And is the lesson of Hegel's analysis of the French revolutionary terror not exactly the same (which is why the parallel between Sade's absolute crime and revolutionary terror is well grounded)? Individuals threatened by the Terror have to grasp that this external threat of annihilation is nothing but the externalized/fetishized image of the radical negativity of self-consciousness—once they grasp this, they pass from revolutionary Terror to the inner force of the moral Law.

So I think Lacan ultimately doesn't claim that the Kantian categorical imperative is sustained by a Sadean superego injunction to enjoy: what happens in an authentic ethical act is another dis-identification, a dis-identification between the moral law and the superego. If my desire is sustained by a superego imperative (as is the case in every form of transgressive desire, a desire that thrives on violating what the law prohibits), then this desire is by definition compromised—in acting in this way, I betray my desire.

And to dispel the impression that we are dealing here with distinctions of no practical or political interest, think about Ukraine today, in 2025. The country is confronting a forced choice: life or freedom? However, this choice has an additional twist: both choices imply death. If, in the present situation, you choose life (surrender), you choose death (disappearance as a nation, as Russia repeatedly made it clear). If you choose freedom (i.e., continued armed resistance, but with the prospect of less Western support), you choose (for many Ukrainians and their habitat) actual death and destruction.

There is a French novel which seems to rely on the same choice: Julien Gracq's *The Opposing Shore* (the original title is *Le rivage des Syrtes*). "Syrtes" refers to the southern-most region of Orsenna, a fictional stand-in for Italy where there seem to be cars but no electricity, a country ruled by the ancient and decadent city of the same name which seems to be, but isn't quite, Venice. For the past 300 years, Orsenna has been in a state of suspended war with Farghestan, the barbarian desert country across the sea to the south; Farghestan, with its two main cities on the coast and endless deserts, seems a great deal like Libya, although some of the places change sides: Mount Etna moves to Libya and becomes the Tängri; the ruins of Sabratha leave Libya for Italy and become Sagra; Sirt goes to Italy and becomes Syrtes. Aldo, the novel's narrator and protagonist, belongs to one of the ruling families of Orsenna. Sent as a state observer to Orsenna's dilapidated naval base of Syrtes, he crosses the forbidden line that divides the dead sea by sailing to the city of Rhages on the enemy's shore. There his ship is welcomed with three cannon shots. Having by this irreparable act rekindled the war that will destroy Orsenna, Aldo accomplishes the suicidal gesture a whole people secretly yearned for: when he returns from Syrtes to Orsenna, he discovers that the ruling elite of Orsenna is using the pretense of a war with Farghestan to whip up nationalist patriotism . . . Beyond the obvious reproach that Gracq is depicting the descent of Orsenna into Fascism (evoking the external threat to create an emergency state, etc.), one should discern here a deeper existential dilemma: what is more desirable, a calm inert life of small satisfactions, not a true life at all, or taking a risk which may well end in a catastrophe?

However, Ukraine is not facing *this* choice but an almost exactly opposite one. If it wants to return to calm daily life it needs to take the risk of pursuing war (military resistance), i.e., of exposing itself to potential death. If it wants to avoid war, it faces with great certainty another form of death (disappearance as a nation under Russian occupation). One should note here that it is the West which has the choice wrongly attributed to Ukraine: risking a war (by supporting Ukraine) or choosing peaceful life (by suffering a humiliation of betraying its ally). And, as many critical analysts are pointing out, even the Western European choice of peace does not really guarantee a long-term peace because if Russia gets Ukraine it will in all probability not stop there but pursue its expansion towards the West, so that the European West will later confront the same choice in much tougher conditions. Here, then, the Western peaceniks (from Viktor Orban and other radical Right figures to pseudo-Leftists) simply cheat by attributing the choice which is not even truly their own to Ukraine.

The ongoing war is not just a struggle for the control of territory or for economic power. It is also more than an effort to annihilate a nation, although the dimension of a genocide is clearly discernible in it—not in the literal sense of killing all members of a nation but in the sense of depriving the survivors of their ethnic identity and making them Russians. It is even more than an indicator of a global geopolitical shift—it is a war of spirit against spirit, of two mutually exclusive visions and practices of what a human being is. Maybe, we should return here to Nietzsche who, towards the end of the nineteenth century, in *Ecce Homo*, presented his dark vision of the next century:

> For when Truth battles against the lies of millennia there will be shock waves, earthquakes, the transposition of hills and valleys such as the world has never yet imagined even in its dreams. The concept "politics" then becomes entirely absorbed into the realm of spiritual warfare. All the mighty worlds of the ancient order of society are blown into space—for they are all based on lies: there will be wars the like of which have never been seen on earth before.[32]

Before we dismiss these lines as obscurantist brooding, we should at least note that Alain Badiou[33], definitely not a Nietzschean, in his booklet *The Century* arrives at similar conclusions. Badiou's metaphor for the twentieth century is the wounded body of a beast (a term he borrows from Osip Mandelstam's poem *The Age*, 1923). The beast was surviving the nineteenth century in a relative state of comfort, caught in the illusion of gradual economic and political progress. With the twentieth century, the beast got tired of patiently approaching the imagined goal of progress—it decided to confront history face to face and to fulfill the promises of the nineteenth century through acts of brutal voluntarism. The result was, as Nietzsche predicted, a new kind of "spiritual warfare": two world "wars the like of which have never been seen on earth before," accompanied by a series of violent revolutions, and all this just wounded the beast without giving rise to a New Man. So what will follow this unique mixture of hope and brutal disappointment that was the twentieth century? In *The Will to Power*, he extends his speculations to the next century (ours, the twenty-first), noting that it would see "the total eclipse of all values," based on the rise of "barbaric nationalistic brotherhoods":

> Nobody should be surprised when … brotherhoods with the aim of robbery and exploitation of the nonbelievers … appear in the arena of the future.[34]

Here we are now, and the irony is that those who advocate a return to traditional old values are the most brutal in their "robbery and exploitation of[35] the nonbelievers." We will all have to be ready to risk our lives, and the only difference between Russia and Western Europe is that, as we have seen, Russia claims it doesn't fear death because it believes in a higher divine power which will redeem Russians after their death, while we in Western Europe know that there is no higher guarantee, that death is just death. Our hope is that Russia's readiness to die is a fake, part of a strategy of bluffing, but fake can also lead to real consequences.

In Lacanian terms, the true choice is not between life and death but between the two deaths: symbolic death (loss of symbolic identity) and actual biological death. Perhaps, this is the best definition of our global predicament today.

Variations

Variation 1

Frozen beauty: Rovelli, Deleuze and the Stoics

When Rovelli determines the basic level of reality as composed not of things but of events, i.e., as a pure flux of becoming which cannot be attributed to anything, is there the temptation to establish a link between Rovelli and none other than Gilles Deleuze and his notion of *pure becoming without being* (as opposed to the metaphysical notion of pure being without becoming)? This pure becoming is not a particular becoming of some corporeal entity, a passage of this entity from one to another state, but a becoming-in-itself, thoroughly extracted from its corporeal base. Since the predominant temporality of Being is that of the present (with past and future as its deficient modes), the pure becoming-without-being means that one should sidestep the present—it never "actually occurs," it is "always forthcoming and already past."[1]

As such, pure becoming suspends sequentiality and directionality: say, in an actual process of becoming, the critical point of temperature (0 degrees Celsius) always has a direction (water either freezes or melts), while, considered as pure becoming extracted from its corporeality, this point of passage is not a passage from one to another state, but a "pure" passage, neutral as to its directionality, perfectly symmetric—for instance, a thing is simultaneously getting larger (than it was) and smaller (than it will be).

The Foucault closest to Deleuze is therefore the Foucault of *The Archeology of Knowledge*, his underrated key work delineating the ontology of utterances as pure language events: not elements of a structure, not attributes of subjects who utter them, but events which emerge, function within a field, and disappear.

To put it in Stoic terms, Foucault's discourse analysis studies *lekta*, utterances as pure events, focusing on the inherent conditions of their emergence (as the concatenation of events themselves) and not on their inclusion in the context of historical reality. This is why the Foucault of *The Archeology of Knowledge* is as far as possible from any form of historicism, of locating events in their historical context—on the contrary, Foucault *abstracts* them from their reality and its historical causality, and studies the *immanent* rules of their emergence. What one should bear in mind here is that Deleuze is *not* an evolutionary historicist; his opposition of Being and Becoming should not deceive us. He is not simply arguing that all stable, fixed entities are just coagulations of the all-encompassing flux of Life—why not? The reference to the notion of *time* is crucial here. Let us recall how Deleuze (with Guattari), in his description of becoming in/of philosophy, explicitly opposes becoming and history:

> "Philosophical time is thus a grandiose time of coexistence that does not exclude the before and after but *superimposes* them in a stratigraphic order. It is an infinite becoming of philosophy that crosscuts its history without being confused with it. The life of philosophers, and what is most external to their work, conforms to the ordinary laws of succession; but their proper names coexist and shine as luminous points that take us through the components of a concept once more or as the cardinal points of a stratum or layer that continually come back to us, like dead stars whose light is brighter than ever."[2]

The paradox is thus that transcendental becoming inscribes itself into the order of positive being, of constituted reality, *in the guise of its very opposite*, of a static superimposition, historical development frozen and crystallized. This Deleuzian eternity is, of course, not simply outside time; rather, in the "stratigraphic" superimposition, in this moment of stasis, it is TIME ITSELF which we experience, time as opposed to the evolutionary flow of things WITHIN time.

Deleuze thus inverts Plato's dualism of eternal Ideas and their imitations in sensuous reality into the dualism of substantial (material) bodies and the pure impassive surface of Sense, the flux of Becoming which is to be located on the very borderline of Being and non-Being. Senses are surfaces which do not exist, but merely subsist: "They are not things or facts, but events. We cannot say that they exist, but rather that they subsist or inhere (having this minimum of being which is appropriate to that which is not a thing, a nonexisting entity."[3] The Stoics, who developed this notion of "incorporeals," were

> the first to reverse Platonism and to bring about a radical inversion. For if bodies with their states, qualities, and quantities, assume all the characteristics of substance and cause, conversely, the characteristics of the Idea are relegated to the other side, that is to this impassive extra-Being which is sterile, inefficacious, and on the surface of things: the ideational or the incorporeal can no longer be anything other than an "effect."[4]

The Stoics thus opened up a unique alternate line of thought, clearly opposed to the substantialist metaphysics, which resurfaces in early Wittgenstein ("The world is all that is the case. . . . The world is the complete sum of facts, not of things."), in Whitehead, and in Deleuze. At the top of the Stoics' ontological hierarchy we find the *ti*, "somethings," which are divided into the *on* and the *me on*, the sphere of the existent and the sphere of the non-existent. To the *on* belong the *somata*, the things that can perform or undergo actions; to the *me on* belong the void, place, time, and the *lekta*. These four *asomata* do not have an independent existence of their own; they are only thought and said. What is predicated of a soma is an event that occurs at the periphery of the domain in which bodies act and are acted upon; the actuality of the event entirely derives from the body by which it is caused. *Lekton* is that which exists *kata logiken phantasian*, by way of a presentation which is typical of a living being possessed of reason and speech, or also *ekphorika*, things capable of being expressed in words. *Lekta* are merely thought and nothing directly corresponds to them in the world of existing *somata*.[5]

Consequently, Stoics draw a strict distinction between logic and language: language is sound, it is corporeal, material, and sensible, part of the world of real being, while logic falls within the category of the incorporeals—logical statements are *lekta*, sayables, they have meaning, but since they are not corporeal, they do not have full being. This distinction is the same as the one between a cause, which is a body, *soma*, and that of which it is the cause, which is called *symbebekos*, consequence, or *kategorema*, predicate. The lancet and the flesh are bodies; the lancet is the cause of an asomatic *kategorema*, namely being cut, with respect to the flesh. Fire and wood are bodies; the fire is the cause of an asomatic *kategorema*, namely being burnt, with respect to the wood. If the sun or the sun's heat makes the wax melt, we have to say that the sun is the cause, not of the melting of the wax, but of the wax being melted, of a *kategorema* which is indicated by an infinitive.

Upon closer inspection, we see that things are already more complicated in Plato himself: Plato's idea is not a thing beyond illusory appearances, it is phenomenal, the idealized look of an object, its appearance, how it looks to a gaze—in its "idea," the ever-changing materiality of an object "collapses" for an ideal observer into its frozen look appearance. Plato's idea, therefore, doesn't belong to *somata*: material things incessantly change (the late Plato calls the material substrate *hora*), while the idea is a frozen surface that remains (I see the same idea "table" although my perception of it changes all the time).

But is this all, is the duality of *somata* and *lekta* the last word? For Badiou, the primary fact is multiplicity of multiplicities and the One comes after, through counting-as-One; for Deleuze, the productive-immanent One of the Life flux immanently generates multiplicity; for Lacan, multiplicity emerges against the background of minus One—in short, the absence/failure of One is immanent to multiplicity, it is its determining absence, i.e., there is multiplicity *because* the One is barred by its immanent impossibility. Or, to put it in more speculative Hegelian terms: the One arises as the effect of its own impossibility (like the subject which is the result of its own failure to become subject). In Berlin, you can order beer "*mit ohne*," "with without" (or just with-out!), to distinguish it from beers which are with different fruit extracts ("*Berliner Weiss*," white, which can be green or red . . .). So, insofar as "white" is the neutral color, it is this non-existing "white" which has three species: *rot, gruen,* and *ohne*—red, green, and without (in the same way the empty set is an element of every set, or the proletarians are in society "*mit ohne*," since their proper place is no place). The primordial state is thus not a simple innumerable and inconsistent multiplicity, but a multiplicity with/out One, marked by an immanent obstacle which prevents it becoming One.[6] One lacks, it is "one less," and this lack is in itself a positive fact, it triggers repetition/drive. It is precisely because the One is lacking that the inconsistent multiplicity appears to itself, re-presents itself.

*

There is a double difference between Deleuze's and Rovelli's notion of becoming. Rovelli asserts becoming not as opposed to things but as the primordial/basic state of reality itself, while for Deleuze *lekta* are passive, effects caused by bodily things. Here is the first stanza of "Casta Diva" from Bellini's *Norma*: "*Casta Diva, che inargenti / queste sacre antiche piante, / a noi volgi il bel sembiante / senza nube e senza vel . . .*" ("O chaste Goddess, who silver / These sacred ancient plants, / turn towards us a beautiful semblance / cloudless and unveiled . . ." Performed in a night ceremony in the midst of a sacred forest, the incantation addresses Moon, not Sun—that's why the Goddess is chaste, not primarily in the sense of purity but more in the sense of sterility: even when we see it unveiled, without clouds, the light of the Moon is not fertile, it is a mere semblance (although a beautiful one), a pale silver echo of the golden light of the Sun, like the Deleuzian flow of Sense which is a pale effect of the bodily causality. For Rovelli, on the contrary, becoming is not a phenomenon of language (*lekta*) but reality itself. So does relational quantum mechanics (RQM) not provide an ontological counterpart to *lekta*?

Variation 2
No substitute for true universals

If there is a self-proclaimed Hegelian who is profoundly anti-Hegelian, it is the Italian philosopher of Fascism Giovanni Gentile (killed in 1944 in Florence by Communist partisans). He called his thought "actualism" or "actual idealism": his basic premise is that mind (self-consciousness of individuals always located in a wider national identity) creates all reality, spiritual and material. At its most basic, even the State is not a material entity embodied in its institutions but a spiritual entity which is not opposed to individuals as a higher power but one with them. For this reason, thinking is one with practice, it is a reflection which is simultaneously creative. Gentile's idealism is thus an absolute immanentism: there is no transcendent material or spiritual (divine) reality. The highest achievement of humanity is a Fascist nation-state which creates the conditions of individual freedom—Gentile co-wrote with Mussolini himself *The Doctrine of Fascism*, the foundational text of Italian Fascism ... Gentile deploys a caricatural version of absolute idealism, and it immediately strikes the eye how non-Hegelian this vision is: there is no unavoidable development through antagonisms and deceptions, no *"la verite surgit de la meprise,"* no vertiginous dialectical reversals, just the discarding of all forms of materialism, liberal individualism and transcendence and the vision of a positive state in which spirit reigns supreme and where all is One (individuals=nation=state=Leader ...) in this spiritual unity. All things of some interest that are taking place in the ongoing revival of Hegel studies go against Gentile's vision.

There are, of course, many forms of this revival, and I count my own work in this space. Jure Simoniti's *The Contingent Universal*, which also belongs to this space, is an extraordinary achievement, a fully elaborated systematic philosophical vision which focuses on the speculative identity of contingency and universality.[1] Since throughout his book Simoniti critically deals with my work—and I consider his critical remarks by far the most accurate among all my critics—I feel obliged to analyze his reproaches in detail.

Simoniti's starting point is that "the world is not 'universal' in its given, panoramic entirety, but has first to contract into its *hic et nunc* in order to produce its universality in the first place": "there is nothing that can fixate the contingency of the present moment but the emergence of a universal; and universality is no more than the very form of the world being present to itself in its contingent locality." The mutual implication of the two passages is crucial: it's not only that universality has to contract itself into a contingent singularity that is less than any of its particularities—if we say only this we remain within the ultra-nominalist idea that every universality is grounded in a singular historical point. More is needed: to locate itself in its contingent unique place, to grasp itself in its uniqueness, singularity itself needs the form of universalities. Does the same movement of reduction to a singular point and then of the expansion to a new universality not form the very core of Christianity? The entire universe is contracted in the singular figure of Christ, a miserable individual dying on the cross; through his death, he then returns as a new universality of the Holy Ghost. Plus does the same not hold also for Lenin and Mao? Shocked by the "patriotic" turn of most European social democracies, Lenin totally rethought the notion of a Communist revolution, and Mao had already done the same in the 1930s, shifting the focus from workers to farmers. In sciences, we get this double movement at its purest in quantum mechanics—recall Carlo Rovelli's claim that "if we want to get a true idea of what a point of space-time is like we should look outward at the universe ... The complete notion of a point of space-time in fact consists of the appearance of the entire universe as seen from that point."[2] So first every vision or notion of the universe is located or grounded in a singular standpoint of an observer, and then, *to grasp this observer in its singularity*, we have to analyze how the entire universe is reflected in or appears from this unique standpoint.

In the history of philosophy, such a double movement is clearly present in the Socratic revolution which is characterized by two features. First, it is a reaction to the general crisis of the Greek social life which, for Socrates, is embodied in the widespread popularity of sophists, performers of empty rhetorical tricks who enacted a self-worsting of the tradition of *polis*. Second, what Socrates opposes to this decay is not a simple return to the glorious past but a radical self-questioning. The basic procedure of Socrates is the endless repetition of the formula: "What, exactly, do you mean by . . .?"—by virtue, truth, the Good, and similar basic notions? Today, we need the same questioning: what do we mean by equality, freedom, human rights, the people, solidarity, emancipation, and all other similar words which we use to legitimize our decisions? The point is thus not to return to European legacy but to bring it back by way of rethinking it thoroughly.

Socrates should be opposed here to a pre-Socratic panoramic view over the totality of the cosmos: although pre-Socratics are already philosophers, they continue the pre-philosophical cosmogony by approaching the universe in its All and directly searching for its substantial principle (water—not earth—for Thales, change for Heraclitus, atoms for Democritus . . .), Socrates enacts a withdrawal to the void of pure subjectivity ("all I know is that I know nothing") and then proceeds to questioning—what? Not reality but the meaning of words:

> It is precisely words that now present themselves as small, close at hand, freely accessible entrances to the abyss of non-meaning behind the veil of things. While the world in its givenness conveys the impression of representing a lawful order, and its phenomena appear to be classifiable under particular symbolic rubrics, it is, quite paradoxically, only the universals themselves (i.e., concepts, notions, words) that are semantically volatile enough to allow a glimpse into the lack of any metaphysical, ideal, and semantic guarantee, and hence into the utter contingency governing everything. It seems that, while a panoramic view over the world still yields the feeling that things unfold according to some invisible laws acting behind them, only the repeatable, seemingly fixed universal is an entity externalized enough to bring to light the pure element of chance. Look at things, and you

will see the necessity of laws; but now examine closely a word, and you will recognize pure chance at its origin!

Is this reduction to questioning the meaning of words which exposes the nothingness at its core not the best compact description of what Hegel is doing in his *Logic*? Hegel begins his philosophy not by analyzing reality but by deploying the vertiginous dance and reversals of words (the universals we use to grasp reality) caught in their "mutual and differential definition". No wonder Hegel praised Plato's *Parmenides* as his highest speculative achievement: *Parmenides* designates Plato's failure of his attempt to define Ideas in their fixed substantial identities—Ideas get caught in their vertiginous dance against the background of an irreducible nothingness which, in this case, means the ultimate collapse of their meaning. The late Plato then almost regresses to pre-philosophical cosmological dualism by means of which he tries to fill in this abyss.[3] Both cases thus invert the standard metaphysical opposition of material reality in its constant change and the stable universe of Ideas: reality is inert, stable, caught in some higher laws, while the world of words and their universal meanings opens up a space of utter instability and void—and, therein resides Plato's lesson, one has to pass through this instability and void to reach a new Universality.

One should oppose here the Socratic questioning to the Confucian "rectification of names." When, in the fifth to third centuries BC, China went through the period of the "Warring States," Confucians perceived as the ultimate cause of this slow but persistent decay the betrayal of old traditions and customs. Most troubling to Confucius was his perception that the political institutions of his day had completely broken down. He attributed this collapse to the fact that those who wielded power as well as those who occupied subordinate positions did so by making claim to titles for which they were not worthy. When asked about the principles of good government, Confucius is reported to have replied: "Good government consists in the ruler being a ruler, the minister being a minister, the father being a father, and the son being a son." Confucius' analysis of the lack of connection between things and their names and the need to correct such circumstances is usually referred to as his teaching on *zhengming*, the "rectification of names" (this name itself is a symptomatic misnomer: what should be rectified are acts—they should be made to correspond to their names): "If language is not correct, then what is said is not what is meant; if what is said is not what is meant, then what must be done remains undone; if this remains undone, morals and art will deteriorate; if justice goes astray, people will stand about in helpless confusion. Hence there must be no arbitrariness in what is said. This matters above everything."[4] The crisis was resolved by "Legalists" who dropped the very coordinates of such a perception of the situation: for the Confucians, the land was in chaos because old traditions were not obeyed, and states like Qin with their centralized-military organization dismissive of the old customs were perceived as the embodiment of what is wrong. However, in contrast to his teacher Xunzi who regarded nations like Qin as a threat to peace, Han Fei "proposed the unthinkable, that maybe the way of the Qin government was not an anomaly to be addressed, but a practice to be emulated."[5] The solution resided in what appeared as a problem: the true cause of the troubles was not the abandonment of old traditions, but *these traditions themselves* which daily demonstrated their inability to serve as guiding principles of social life. Legalists triumphed and united China for the first time under one king—in short, they fully asserted the convergence of universality and contingency in all its explosive dimension. Although the post-Hegelian post-metaphysical thought also endeavours to liberate the actual particular reality from its metaphysical universal shackles, it is in effect

> nothing more than the series of detours of not letting it happen. Supplementary frames are set in motion to prevent the contact between universality and contingency/, but their fallacies may betray that they misunderstand the very object they were intended to grasp. . . . There is no need for an all-encompassing, metaphorical, panoramic, and complacently nihilist investiture of cosmic chance; for there is no contingency other than the audacity of a local place to act universally.

When Simoniti defines singularity as "nothing but particularity that has lost its backing in the existence of metaphysical universals," I am tempted to add that singularity is also universality divested of all of its particular determinations— in this sense, in the notion of a pure subject singularity coincides with universality: I am this unique One, a subject at a distance from its particular properties and thus universal. Furthermore, is the key to the triad UPS which undermines the couple of universality and particularity not the inclusion of the subject of enunciation into the enunciated content? Enunciation is inscribed into the enunciated as the excessive/lacking particular that is excluded from (that has no place in) the classificatory order of particulars. Let's take the case of transhumanists: with all their warning about how we are on the brink of a post-human era, they effectively remain too humanist. That is to say, when they describe the possibility of intervening into our biogenetic base and changing our very "nature," they somehow presuppose that the autonomous subject freely deciding on his/her acts will still be here, deciding on how to change his "nature." They thus bring the split between the "subject of the enunciated" and the "subject of enunciation" to its extreme: on the one hand, as an object of my interventions, I am a biological mechanism whose properties, including the mental ones, can be manipulated; on the other hand, I (act as if I) am somehow exempted from this manipulation, an autonomous individual who, at a distance, can make the right choices. So the way to undermine neuronal determinism is not by remaining focused on the object of investigation and showing how transhumanists misunderstand their object, but to raise another question: which is the subjective position of enunciation of a transhumanist, the position from which he deploys his argumentation? Is this position itself not something that doesn't fit its content?

So where do I fit into this edifice? Here is how Simoniti recapitulates the gap that separates his philosophical edifice from mine:

> while Žižek could perhaps be reproached with finding in quantum physics an "instant ontology" capable of providing the infrastructure for his claims of ethical universalism, [Simoniti's] book's cooptation of modern science operates on a very different level. Our claim is not to seek in the *real* world the impulses for the proliferation of forms that are obviously irreducible to it, but *to offer a logic that detaches the dawn of the new from its causal embedding in the chain of sufficient reasons*. The philosophical recourse to modern science does not seek to construct a narrative that leads from physical conditions to the emergence of life forms, human societies, and

ultimately philosophy. Rather, it uses science only as a special case of how the impulse of universality is in no way ideally predestined by antecedent circumstances, but fills the emergent space that extends precisely where there is no background support.

The starting point of philosophy is thus a given positive order in which some traditional universality seems to control and regulate the constellation: all particular content appears to be firmly embedded in the global order determined by the chain of sufficient reasons. The first move of philosophy is to locate the cracks in this edifice, the exception which doesn't fit into the global order; for Marx, this element is the working class which, by its objective social position, is the point of its "symptomal torsion"(Alain Badiou)—workers are, to quote Jacques Ranciere, a "part of no-part" of the social body, lacking a proper place in it, an antagonism embodied. It is thus crucial to insist on the Communist-egalitarian emancipatory Idea, and insist on it in a very precise Marxian sense: there are social groups which, on account of their lacking a determinate place in the "private" order of social hierarchy, directly stand for universality. All truly emancipatory politics is generated by the short-circuit between the universality of the "public use of reason" and the universality of the "part of no-part"—this was already the Communist dream of the young Marx: to bring together the universality of philosophy with the universality of the proletariat. Simoniti emphasizes how this point of exception is the point of singularity whose very existence undermines the global order within which it appears; however, at the same time, this reduction to a singular radically contingent moment opens up the path to construct a new universality that cannot be deduced from the totality it undermines the new universality emerges through in a radically contingent way. This view has radical consequences for the notion of philosophy:

> philosophy does indeed have no positive object of its own, such as physical phenomena, biological forms, social facts, linguistic conventions, existential claims and sensibilities, ethical norms, artistic creations, etc., which is why it is always dependent on extrinsic imagery.... In its objectless quality, philosophy will thus reveal something about the world that positive science and concrete politics cannot. It is the realization that to the extent that

philosophy lacks a natural object, the world is also in want of any first foundation, any original truth, or any generative principle. To put it another way, philosophy comes second because universality and truth themselves always come in last.

The key question to be raised here is: OK, but how does the hegemony of ideal forms arise in the first place? Simoniti is at his weakest when he proposes a six-steps "speculative reconstruction of how reality engenders the form of ideality":

> First, in the logical space of the prohibition of both ideal intervention and of real predetermination, reality, left to itself, illuminates the light of the *Gegenwart*. *Sub specie realis*, to put it this way, the existence of the present moment may be the most basic fact of this world, a "primitive" that cannot be further analyzed. *Sub specie idealis*, however, the scandal of the *Gegenwart* can be seen as the direct expression of a reality that has no reason and no ideal value to draw on. . . . the world unfolds only through its *Gegenwarten*, because it searches in the light of day for its ground and its reason, which were not given to it at its birth. Second, it is in this momentary illumination of the *Gegenwart* that the elements of the non-ideal real experience the weight of singularity. They cannot but be where they are, without the possibility of shaking off their thereness. As a consequence, a differentiation takes place in the field of utterly contingent locales.

It is at this point that I thoroughly disagree with Simoniti—his account reads like a "speculative reconstruction" which presupposes much more than it explains—it reads like a new version of speculative genesis in the style of Jacob Boehme or late Schelling; his reference to sciences—"it is not the task of philosophy to give an account of *how* this happens; these processes are the subject of science. What philosophy contributes is merely the logic of the strict immanence of idealities arising within the field of reality."—just masks his failure. Already the starting point is suspiciously ambiguous: what does "the logical space of the prohibition of both ideal intervention and of real predetermination" effectively amount to? Is this prohibition just an epistemological instrument to imagine the ontological beginning, the zero-point of pure contingency where there is no ideal intervention and no real predetermination, or is this prohibition to be thought as something inscribed into reality itself—is this not the only way to account for the fact that the zero-point reality which has no reason and no ideal value to draw on "searches in the light of day for its ground and its reason, which were not given to it at its birth"? In other words, the only way to account for the fact that "a differentiation takes place in the field of utterly contingent locales" is to posit that this "field of utterly contingent locales" is already marked by a certain radical lack, that it already functions against the background of a certain impossibility. Simoniti seems to ignore the question of where this lack (which propels the field of contingent locales to search for its ground and its reason) comes from, and it is here that I differ from his vision: for me, the starting point is not a field of utterly contingent locales but a cut/gap which stands for fall from the field of pure contingency—in short, it all begins with a crack, a fall, that affects any imagined beginning.

Simoniti also argues that I get caught in a hidden teleological circle: when I claim that the quantum universe strangely resembles some features of the symbolic universe (retroactivity, actuality of what is merely potential, etc.), am I not claiming (using Schellingian terminology) that the quantum universe is our symbolic universe at a lower potency (degree of power)? And does this not imply that there is a kind of direct developmental link between the quantum universe and our symbolic universe, as if the quantum universe is already in itself the symbolic universe, i.e., as if the emergence of the symbolic universe is not radically contingent but inscribed into reality as its immanent potential? Let me try to clarify this crucial point by way of beginning with the key problem of quantum mechanics which Simoniti himself tries to answer with his speculative reconstruction: the domain of quantum waves is a domain of contingency, so how do these waves collapse into our deterministic reality? It is crucial not to elevate quantum processes into a unique ultimate reality and then try to deduce from it how collapse happens: *there is a gap at work in quantum there from the very beginning.* I think this aspect is missed by Simoniti when, in his critique of my work, he focuses on the role quantum physics plays in my theoretical edifice, denouncing it as "a veritable symptom" of my philosophy:

It seems that when a system of thought invents concepts that are too big for its time, so that the tools for their ultimate analytic eventuation and grounding are still lacking, it tends to rely on a kind of "instant ontology" that could give legs to its untimely ideas. The most innovative part of the theory's truth procedure is thus somehow providentially foreshadowed at the more fundamental level of given reality.... Our guess and our hope, however, is that the missing algorithm to ground his philosophy and make quantum metaphors unnecessary is precisely the logic of "contingent universality."

A very precise and insightful critique—but does it hold? Let us dig deeper into Simoniti's argumentation: my "theoretical coalition with quantum mechanics might admittedly strike us as a surrogate for the lacking 'ground theory of being,' but Žižek only resorts to it because it is, in his view, the only scientific worldview which already at the basic level of materiality manifests the entwinement of the symbolic and the real, the subject and objectivity." The critique implied by this passage is that my privileging of quantum mechanics among sciences has the same role as the post-metaphysical universal statements which transform the assertion of contingency into a universal feature perceived from an external panoramic view. Simoniti addresses the same reproach to my twin basic notions, the Hegelian self-relating negativity and the Freudian death drive: they "could be interpreted as two reactive principles making their way through the new ontological landscape outlined by mutually defining chance events and universal claims," i.e., they

> pose as auxiliary expressions of the absence of any such all-encompassing, omnipotent cosmic governance. The pervasion of being by negation in Hegel merely indicates that no real identity is ideally warranted. And when this original negativity folds back upon itself and becomes self-referential, it marks the moment when its sheer contingency unfolds into its own universal dimension, whose "secondary lawfulness" ensures that there are no identities except those produced in the process of negation. Similarly, the essential repetitiveness of drive in Freud parasitizes on the fact that desires have no natural objects by which they can be permanently satisfied.... In short, Hegel's negativity and Freud's drive seem to be located at the point at

which throwing oneself into the arms of contingency, for lack of any other way out, is doomed to establish its own emergent universality.

Simoniti's aim is, of course, to resist this temptation to which post-metaphysics regularly succumbs: in post-metaphysics,

> ontology broke apart into the singularist theories of being on one pole and the outward, miraculous universals on the other. Under the pretext of daring to disclose much more desolate cosmic landscapes than before, the post-Hegelians unconsciously still insisted on the contrastive fixity of substitute universals which were impervious to the muck of the here and now. It may thus very well be that gods, overmen, fateful events, and existential attitudes were only conjured because they promised to resist the semantic nihilism of dialectics.

So is self-relating negativity and/or death drive really my own "substitute universal" which allows me to "resist the semantic nihilism of dialectics"? Quite the opposite: self-relating negativity and/or death drive is my name for this very "semantic nihilism of dialectics"; they are not positive ontological notions, they just point towards an original gap. Simoniti wants a philosophy without symptom, but the price he pays for it is that he himself produces a mega-symptom, his vision of how the established order emerges out of the primordial contingency. My reference to quantum mechanics is not just another symptom: for me, the only way to avoid fake-ontological symptoms is to confront the question "What happens prior to a truth event?"—in short, how is reality structured so that contingent truth events can take place in it? For me the only way to answer this question is: there must be a gap that is at work in it from the very beginning. In its classic form, quantum mechanics insists on the irreducible gap that separates the domain of quantum waves and superpositions from the single reality of our daily lives, and it gets caught then into the problem of how to conceptualize the passage between the two. The classical formula of this passage is that of the *collapse of the wave function*, and the entire history of quantum mechanics is full of attempts to explain how this collapse functions, from outrightly denying it in the Many Worlds theory (there is no collapse of waves to a single reality since the wave superpositions are all actualized in multiple realities) up to the idea that, since collapse into a single reality happens through its registration by an observer, our universe only exists by way of being observed by a divine global gaze. There is, as expected, a great effort to avoid both these extremes by way of deploying how the wave oscillations immanently (without any external observer) collapse into a single reality though a process of decoherence; most of these attempts rely on a criterion of quantity: wave oscillations occurs at the subatomic level, and when we move to larger entities, they automatically collapse . . .

In a similar, although more systematic, way Rovelli tries to reduce the gap between a quantum process and its observer by way of universalizing the notion of observation/registration: whenever multiple quantum processes interact, they are "observed" by each other. The price he pays for this is that he is compelled to universalize contingency in formulations which perfectly fit what Simoniti calls "substitute universal." Rovelli is a radical singularist, but he universalizes this position: "RQM is complete in the sense of exhausting everything that can be said about nature." In a strict parallel to Simoniti's mythic "genesis" of the given deterministic order from the primordial pure contingency, the last chapter of Rovelli's *Helgoland*, which aims at providing the genesis of our ordinary spatio-temporal reality from the basic domain of wave functions, fails, I think. No wonder that Rovelli seems to get caught in the traditional philosophical paradox when he argues that

> it is impossible for a system to have information about itself because it requires it to stand in a particular correlation to itself and this is not possible. It is not a new idea that quantum mechanics cannot describe the observers.
> (102)

As I wrote in Chapter 3, relational quantum mechanics returns us to an old problem expressed by the liar's paradox. Rovelli writes: "The world is like a collection of interrelated points of view. To speak of the world 'seen from outside' makes no sense because there is no 'outside' to the world."(109) Another universal statement, confirming Simoniti's diagnosis that "the 'external totalization' of the field of singularities unrolled the homogenous plane of sheer contingencies as something that can be recognized and known in one sweep, neutrally, declaratively, and as if from an outside perspective."

When Rovelli posits that quantum events exist only in interactions and that *the character of each quantum event is only relative to the system involved in the interaction,* so that different observers can give different accounts of the actuality of the same physical property, i.e., when he claims that the occurrence of an event is not something absolutely real or not but is only real in relation to a specific observer, are these and similar claims universally true (true independently of any observer) or are they also valid only in relation to a specific (human) observer? The only way to assert their universal validity without presupposing a global external observer is *to base such universal claims on an immanent limitation or boundary of reality itself.* Put it in another way, one can only avoid the neutral/external position of enunciation if one admits/ posits a limitation as the only "universal" feature. In short, the only way to limit a space *from within,* not from an external point of observation, is to posit the coincidence of the two limits: the external limitation coincides with an internal one, i.e., a space is already "in itself" not-all, not identical to itself. This paradox only occurs in differential systems which form a complete totality by way of including among its elements a mark of their own incompleteness—and quantum mechanics moves in a space characterized by differentiality. This limitation from within is what characterizes the pre-ontological Real, and it also enables us to clarify the ambiguous relationship between the Lacanian Real and the Void in the so-called Oriental thought. Here we encounter critics which confront my work at a much lower level than Simoniti. I am often reproached for not really understanding Buddhist and Hindu thinkers and the associated traditions—suffice it to quote two passages from a Reddit site:

> Zizek is wrong when he says Eastern's approach to "looking inwards to achieve knowledge" will lead to find hate so we should avoid it. He is extremely wrong about this because he doesn't understand Brahman, *Bhagavad Gita,* or even the philosophies of Quakerism (which in fact are western!). All of them teach that when you truly look inside to find knowledge, what you will find is that we are all part of the same, and we should find a way to heal by uniting in peace. If Himmler used that to logic "I am not my actions therefore I can do whatever I want" then he didn't really look inward, but instead only scratched the surface enough to justify his evil actions to himself (which is just Ego). Himmler did not achieve

gnosis, otherwise he would've understood that "Jews are the same as him, and therefore he wouldn't have committed genocide."

In an interview he did with *The Times*, he also said how the issue with Oriental philosophy is that it says to 'look deeply within yourself and find truth,' while Slavoj believes 'if you look, you will find nothing there. The self is an illusion." The ignorance of this is amazing, because that's exactly what Oriental religion is all about![6]

The first thing that strikes the eye is the obvious contradiction between these two reproaches (formulated by different persons): if we look deep into ourselves, do we find there nothing or do we see that we are all part of the same, and we should find a way to heal by uniting in peace? The difference is here the one between *Gita* which advocates the unity of my soul and god, and Buddhist which posits that there is no substantial self behind the appearances, so that the self is an illusion, and Himmler adored *Gita*, not Buddhism—why? Here is how, in *Gita*'s central passage, the God Krishna answers Arjuna, the warrior-king who hesitates entering a battle, horrified at the suffering his attack will cause—an answer worth quoting in detail:

> He who thinks it to be the killer and he who thinks it to be killed, both know nothing. The self kills not, and the self is not killed. It is not born, nor does it ever die, nor, having existed, does it exist no more. Unborn, everlasting, unchangeable, and primeval, the self is not killed when the body is killed.... As a man, casting off old clothes, puts on others and new ones, so the embodied self, casting off old bodies, goes to others and new ones.... It is everlasting, all-pervading, stable, firm, and eternal. It is said to be unperceived, to be unthinkable, to be unchangeable.... Therefore you ought not to grieve for any being. Having regard to your own duty also, you ought not to falter, for there is nothing better for a Kshatriya than a righteous battle.... Killed, you will obtain heaven; victorious, you will enjoy the earth. Therefore arise, o son of Kunti, resolved to engage in battle.[7]

So it is NOT that "when you truly look inside to find knowledge, what you will find is that we are all part of the same, and we should find a way to heal by uniting in peace"—the conclusion of *Gita* is exactly the opposite one: since the self is not killed and is not killing, engage in a battle and do (your duty of) killing. It is difficult to resist here the temptation to paraphrase this passage as the justification of the burning of Jews in the gas chambers to their executor caught in a moment of doubt: since "he who thinks it to be the killer and he who thinks it to be killed, both know nothing," since "the self kills not, and the self is not killed," therefore "you ought not to grieve for any" burned Jew, but, "looking alike on pleasure and pain, on gain and loss, on victory and defeat," do what you were ordered to do ... In this alternative, I of course prefer Buddhism to *Gita*, but I do not endorse the Buddhist dismissal of the subject ("self") as an illusion. Yes, the subject is a void ("nothing"), but it is not the same void as the Buddhist *sunyata*, the selfless emptiness that grounds entire reality. It is rather its exact opposite: the absolute contraction to the zero-point of a self-relating void excluding all otherness, all positive content. We could paraphrase here Hegel's axiom that the Absolute should be grasped not only as Substance but also as Subject: the void is not just the all-encompassing void as the medium of interrelations that form our reality but also the singular point through which we maintain a minimal distance towards reality.

Politically, however, my true target is *Gita*, while I maintain my highest respect for Buddhism which is ultimately the only serious alternative to the Lacanian ethics. While I was often attacked for my stance on *Gita*, the recent podcast by Swami Revatikaanta reaches a new low in these attacks. It is not just the humiliating and patronizing tone of his attack (apparently I speak of things about which I don't know anything, and Swami ends with an invitation to participate in his course to learn more ...). Swami shows a clip from my improvised podcast with Piers Morgan[8]; here is a brief resume of my written argumentation:

> Christopher Nolan's film *Oppenheimer* has angered many Indian moviegoers due to the reference of *Bhagavad Gita* during an intimate scene. Many have taken to Twitter, wondering how the censor board cleared the scene. A statement from Save Culture Save India Foundation said: "We do not know the motivation and logic behind this unnecessary scene on life of a scientist. A scene in the movie shows a woman makes a man read Bhagwad Geeta aloud while getting over him and doing sexual intercourse."[9] My reaction to

this reaction is exactly the opposite one: *Bhagavad Gita* advocates a horrible ethics of military slaughter as an act of highest duty, so we should protest that a gentle act of passionate love-making is besmirched by a spiritualist obscenity. In order to find our way in the ongoing mess, we should do something like this: bring out the horror which sustains the "spiritualization" of carnal passion.

I am well aware of the provocative nature of this passage, but I continue to subscribe to it fully. So here is the gist of Swami's counter-argument:

> Detachment and non-identification do not imply a lack of moral sensibility. Instead they encourage individuals to act purely and selflessly without selfish ego-driven desires corrupting their actions. This is in essence the marriage between Karma Yoga, which means selfless detached action, and Dharma, righteous conduct. Now I've introduced Dharma, so what is Dharma? The Mahabharat which by the way is the wider text to which the *Bhagavad Gita* belongs defines it as the Eternal Duty, the Sanatana Dharma, towards All Creatures is the absence of malevolence towards them in thought, deed and word, and to practice compassion and charity towards them. Now if that is indeed true, why then does Krishna seemingly encourage Arjuna to engage in a war and to kill his aggressors? A fair question because we must protect that which is worthy of protection or see it die. If we value life we must value Dharma. Dharma is that which sustains life, which promotes nonviolence and compassion to all. Now if that very system comes under attack by those who have no desire to uphold it, then our inaction is nothing but complicity in its destruction.[10]

One should first note that Arjuna (a warrior used to slaughter) despairs because the war is now the Kurukshetra war between the Pandavas and the Kauravas, i.e., a battle against his own kin, not against an external enemy. Swami's conclusion is that a precise reading of *Gita* totally disqualifies Himmler's reference to *Gita* since the Nazis were obviously not acting out of compassion and were not fighting for the protection of the Good and the destruction of the wicked . . . truly? From the Nazi standpoint, they were doing *precisely this*, which is why it is more than easy to imagine Himmler's justification of the Holocaust in Swami's terms: yes, we must protect that which is worthy of protection or see it die, and Germany is something that is worthy of protection; but Germany is under systematic attack by the Jews who threaten its very existence, so our inaction against the Jews is nothing but complicity in the destruction of Germany . . .

So my point is that the fanatical Nazis were far from being motivated by selfish ego-driven desires: many of them effectively acted out of the conviction that they are saving their country, a conviction for which they were ready to die. One must accept the sad and disturbing fact that true radical evil reaches beyond egotism and can adopt the form of Good.

Furthermore, note that Swami ignores the key passage in Krishna's answer to Arjuna in which there is no mention of compassion and justice—from the long passage quoted above, it is clear that the argument is purely ontological, it concerns the two levels of being, the eternal being of the indestructible Self and the impermanent bodily reality. So it's not even the prospect of eventual victory that justifies a military engagement, it is just the empty obligation to do one's duty. The conclusion is clear: if the external reality is ultimately just an ephemeral appearance, then even the most horrifying killing eventually *does not matter*. Clarice Lispector concisely formulated the horror of the indifference that underlies the notion of an all-encompassing god: "What still frightened me was that even the unpunishable horror would be generously reabsorbed by the abyss of unending time, by the abyss of unending heights, by the deep abyss of the God: absorbed into the heart of an indifference. So unlike human indifference."[11] This horror of indifference is profoundly Christian, while one often encounters the anti-Christian logic in today's Russia. Margarita Simonyan, editor of *Russia Today*, said in 2022 it was "more probable" Putin would turn to his nuclear arsenal than admit defeat:

> Either we lose in Ukraine, or the Third World War starts. I think World War III is more realistic, knowing us, knowing our leader. This is to my horror on one hand. But on the other hand, it is what it is. We will go to heaven, while they will simply croak . . . We're all going to die someday.[12]

This is Krishna repeating its line in Russia today! Furthermore, it is not only me, an ignorant European, that rejects the ethics of *Gita*: in India itself, critical voices abound. As expected, many Buddhists deny the existence of an eternal indestructible Self that is one with the Absolute: in Buddhism, there is no such Self, all that there is beneath the interplay of perishable phenomena is the primordial Void. Ambedkar wrote that in *Gita* the caste system is systematically ordained and explained. Swami is right about that, in reading *Gita*, one should take into account its context, which is in this case provided by Hinduism. In Hinduism, "Dharma" designates an individual's duty fulfilled by observance of custom or law, and is clearly defined as specific to a cast to which one belongs: duties are individually fixed with reference to the qualities arising from their inherent natures:

> The inherently natural duties of a Brahmin are peace, self-restraint, religious austerities, cleanliness, quietness, straightforwardness (humanity), knowledge (that is, spiritual knowledge). The inherently natural duty (karma) of the Kshatriya is bravery, brilliance, courage, intentness, not running away from the battle, generosity, and exercising authority (over subject people), "goraksya" (that is, the business of keeping cattle), and vanijya (that is, trade) is the inherently natural duty of the Vaishya; and in the same way, service is the inherently natural duty of the Shudra.[13]

Ambedkar concludes that *Gita* is neither a book of religion nor a book of philosophy: since the intent behind writing *Gita* was to defend certain dogmas of religion on philosophical grounds, it is "a philosophical defense of counter-revolution."[14] Against Ambedkar, Gandhi proposed a desperate reinterpretation to avoid this conclusion: he believed that *Gita* taught the principles of non-violence, self-control, and selfless action, which he used as the basis for his philosophy of Satyagraha (nonviolent resistance), so that *Gita* is far from justifying war: war is just a metaphor for the inner struggle in a soul between the Good and the Evil[15]—clearly a very problematic reading since a metaphor works both ways: inner struggle can also be an internalization into a psyche of a real warfare. (This is why today, with the world on the brink of a global war, the message of *Gita* is especially dangerous.) And this is why, today more than ever, the project of contingent universalities that I share with Simoniti provides the only serious philosophical option to enable us to think how to avoid the abyss of self-destruction.

Variation 3

Pure voice, Pure sound: Beethoven, Globokar, Act

Observation and the Act

Quantum mechanics is defined by the tension between the real of wave oscillations and what we experience as reality: reality arises when the wave function collapses. In philosophical terms, this collapse is the passage from pre-ontological real to reality as the topic of ontology, the analysis of "what is," what really exists. The mediator between the two levels is an *act* in the strongest sense of the word—what kind of act?

The discourse of ontology is sustained by what John Searle, the philosopher of speech acts, called an "indirect speech act": its assertive surface, its stating that the world "is like that," conceals a performative dimension, i.e., ontology is constituted by the misrecognition of how its enunciation brings about its propositional content. The only way to account for this "magical power" of declarations is by having recourse to the Lacanian hypotheses of the "big Other"—Searle himself has a presentiment of it when he points out that "it is only given such institutions as the church, the law, private property, the state and a special position of the speaker and hearer within these institutions"[1] that one can accomplish a declaration. In Hans Christian Andersen's "Emperor's New Clothes," all the world knows that the emperor has no clothes, and everybody knows that all the world knows it—why, then, does a simple public statement that "the emperor has no clothes" blow up the entire established network of intersubjective relations? In other words: if everybody knew it, who did not know it? The Lacanian answer is, of course: the big Other (in the sense of the field of socially recognized knowledge). Declarations imply the same logic: the meeting is closed when, by means of the utterance, "The meeting is closed," this fact comes to the big Other's knowledge.

The parallel with quantum collapse becomes clear now: in quantum mechanics, the "big Other" is the order of our everyday reality, while in quantum processes phenomena float without being rooted in a "big Other." And the "magic" of an observation/registration which affects its object is the same as that of the constative which functions as a performative. However, how can a logic which is specific to a symbolic process also structure phenomena in nature? We stumble here upon the deepest mystery of quantum physics: in it, nature is in a sense "denaturalized"; we find in it processes which we thought are specific to the symbolic universe. Collapse thus takes place neither directly in the measuring machine nor in the conscious observer but in the "big Other" which guarantees the consistency of our ordinary reality.

But there is a third problem: where precisely does consciousness enter here? Is it the space of superpositions as such or does it designate the moment of collapse, of a choice when, "in a small fraction of a second, it will become one or the other"? From a Lacano-Schellingian standpoint an immediate counter-argument imposes itself: but why the identification of (free) decision with consciousness? Are basic decisions not *unconscious*? What is missing in Penrose's mental space in which there are physical processes and consciousness is thus simply the Freudian unconscious. This is also why we should abandon the option that superpositions are unconscious, while consciousness enters at the moment of decision which causes the collapse of superpositions: decisions are unconscious, consciousness just takes note of them.

Recall the case of falling in love: it is never a conscious decision/choice—all of a sudden, I just become aware that I am deeply in love. Prior to Freud, Schelling developed the notion that the basic free decisions made by us are unconscious. So, with regard to Libet's experiment (which proved that, a split second before we made a decision to move a finger, our neurons are already sending signals to our arm), from the Freudian standpoint, the basic underlying problem is that of the status of the Unconscious: are there only conscious thoughts (my belated conscious decision to move a finger) and "blind" neuronal processes (the neuronal activity to move the finger), or is there also an unconscious "mental" process? And, what is the ontological status of this unconscious, if there indeed is one? Is it not that of a purely virtual symbolic order, of a pure logical *presupposition* (the decision *had to be made*, although it was never effectively made in real time)? At the apogee of German Idealism, Schelling deployed the notion of the primordial decision-differentiation (*Ent-Scheidung*), the unconscious atemporal deed by means of which the subject chooses his/her eternal character which, afterwards, within his/her conscious-temporal life, s/he experiences as the inexorable necessity, "the way s/he always was":

> The deed, once accomplished, sinks immediately into the unfathomable depth, thereby acquiring its lasting character. It is the same with the will which, once posited at the beginning and led into the outside, immediately has to sink into the unconscious.... Once done, the deed is eternally done. The decision that is in any way the true beginning should not appear before consciousness, it should not be recalled to mind, since this, precisely, would amount to its recall. He who, apropos of a decision, reserves for himself the right to drag it again to light, will never accomplish the beginning.[2]

Beethoven: the Reverberations of the Act

To get—not a notion but—an artistic rendering of this Schellingian act of primordial Decision, an act of pure will that precedes and grounds every dialectical process, let's deploy an analysis of Beethoven's 9th Symphony although it might seem like an eccentric exercise ... And let's begin at the beginning because in some sense everything is decided at the beginning of its first movement. A mysterious string *tremolando* breaks the silence and introduces a tension of expectation; then the stern motif 1 emerging out of the *tremolando* is gathering strength and then strikes with all brutality. What cannot but strike the eye (or, rather, the ear) of a listener used to the classical style is the precipitative character of the entrance of motif 1 in all its force: it happens all at once, it is too hasty—one would expect a slower development and ascent but we get a nervous self-overtaking.

To put it bluntly, Beethoven's music undoubtedly often verges on kitsch—suffice it to mention the over-repetitive exploitation of the "beautiful" main motif in the 1st movement of his Violin Concerto, or the rather tasteless climactic moments of the Leonora 3 overture. How vulgar are the climactic moments of Leonora 3 (and 2, its even worse utterly boring version) in comparison with Mozart's overture to *Magic Flute*, where Mozart still retains what one cannot but call a proper sense of musical *decency*, interrupting the melodic line before it reaches the full orchestra climactic repetition and, instead, jumping directly to the final staccatos! Perhaps, Beethoven himself sensed it, writing another, final, overture, the Op. 72c Fidelio—brief and concise, sharp, the very opposite of Leonora's 2 and 3. (The true pearl, however, is the undeservedly underestimated Leonora 1 Op. 138, whose very date is not sure—it is Beethoven at his best, with the beautiful rise to a climax without any embarrassing excesses.) But at the beginning of the Movement 1 of the 9th, Beethoven surpasses kitsch by way of bringing it to extreme: the climactic repetition of the motif 1 hits us preemptively with full force. The "dawn of Creation"? Maybe, but in the sense of Eric Frank Russell's short science-fiction story "The Sole Solution"[3] which begins with the confused rambling of an old lone man:

> *He brooded in darkness and there was no one else. Not a voice, not a whisper. Not the touch of a hand. Not the warmth of another heart. Darkness. Solitude. Eternal confinement where all was black and silent and nothing stirred. Imprisonment without prior condemnation. Punishment without sin. The unbearable that had to be borne unless some mode of escape could be devised. No hope of rescue from elsewhere. No sorrow or sympathy or pity in another soul, another mind.*

The old man then starts to dream about a solution:

> *The easiest escape is via the imagination. One hangs in a strait-jacket and flees the corporeal trap by adventuring in a dreamland of one's own. But dreams are not enough. They are unreal and all too brief. The freedom to be*

gained must be genuine and of long duration. That meant he must make a stern reality of dreams, a reality so contrived that it would persist for all time.

After a long hard work of planning all the details, the time comes for the act:

The time was now. The experiment must begin. Leaning forward, he gazed into the dark and said, "Let there be light." And there was light.

Here we get the ultimate *point-de-capiton* ("quilting-point"): the last lines retroactively make it clear that the ramblings are the thoughts of God himself just prior to the act of creation. The beauty of this final reversal is that it inverts the standard "twist" the reader expects, in which the thought process of God is revealed to be nothing more than the delusional rambling of a madman who thinks he is god . . . For a philosopher, however, as we have already seen, this denouement is no surprise. The beginning is not at the beginning; this is the first lesson of Schelling's *Ages of the World* fragment in which he focuses precisely on what goes on *before* the beginning.

The beginning of all the beginnings is, of course, the "In the beginning was the Word" from John; prior to it, there was nothing, that is, the void of divine eternity. According to Schelling, however, eternity is not a nondescript mass—a lot of things take place in it. Prior to the Word, there is the chaotic-psychotic universe of blind drives, their rotary motion, their undifferentiated pulsating; and the Beginning occurs when the Word is pronounced which represses, rejects into the eternal Past, this self-enclosed circuit of drives. In short, at the Beginning proper stands a Resolution, an act of Decision which, by differentiating between past and present, resolves the preceding unbearable tension of the rotary motion of drives. The true Beginning is the passage from the "closed" rotary motion to "open" progress, from drive to desire—or, in Lacanian terms, from the Real to the Symbolic.[4] It is thus the decision, *Ent-Scheidung*, primordial Difference (from Old French, from Latin *decīsiō*, literally: a cutting off).

So what is the relationship between act and anxiety? The contemporary *doxa* designates our age as the "age of anxiety" and, at the same time, as the age of postmodern reflexivity in which we are permanently bombarded with choices, with less and less certainties provided by tradition to serve as the bedrock of our choices. The *doxa* implies that anxiety is caused by the deadlock of the pressure to choose ("What should I do? Why do A instead of non-A?"). However, are these choices really so overwhelming? Are they rather not the form of appearance of their very opposite, the fundamental *lack* of (radical) choices in our "postideological/postpolitical" era. This points in the direction of Lacan who conceives anxiety as caused by the overproximity of excessive *jouissance*, and (the hysterical) acting out is, at its most basic, an attempt to evacuate the body of *jouissance*, i.e., to reassert the symbolic castration and thus open up the space for desire. In contrast to acting out, the (psychotic) *passage a l'acte* involves a direct—suicidal—identification with (or "fall into") the Real which precludes any possibility for the desire to emerge.

As is usual in the sonata form, motif 1 is followed by motif 2 which announces a "lovely pastoral world,"[5] a variation on the "Ode to Joy" melody from the last movement. The interplay of the two motifs is dazzling: 7 minutes or so into the movement, motif 1 is rendered in a lyric mode in G minor with added upper neighbour semitones, i.e., it works as the opposite of its first climactic appearance in its pure violence; no wonder that, in contrast to this lyric rendering, motif 2 appears in a more and more brutal mode. One should mention at least how, due to its eerie background provided by a "mostly chromatic meandering in the bass," the funeral march in coda "grows to terrifying proportions, as a solemn procession *for* the dead becomes more like a macabre dance *of* the dead"[6]—we get here a typical Hegelian shift of "for" to "of," of object to subject, since subject itself gets caught into the movement.[7] There is no sonata-form reconciliation at the end of Movement 1: it ends abruptly as it begins—the final bars repeat a melodic line that could easily continue. One cannot but agree that

> the first movement of the Ninth represents the interment of the great-man military heroism that the earlier symphony celebrates: the funeral march at the end of the Ninth's first movement puts the nail in the coffin of the Napoleonic dream, which had curdled so devastatingly and produced the political repressions that Beethoven was living and working under when he was writing the Ninth Symphony in the early 1820s.[8]

Movement 2 is supposed to render a lively joy, the portrait of a life of all-encompassing brotherhood, but it does it with a touch of frantic madness—Stanley Kubrick was right when he used this movement as the music for his dystopian masterpiece *A Clockwork Orange*. Similarly, Movement 3 renders peaceful pleasure, but with a touch of nostalgia and melancholy—it renders the dream of a world as it was *before* the traumatic act of decision that hits us in Movement 1. And this brings us to the notorious Movement 4 which deceptively poses as the synthetic unity and collective evolution of the preceding three movements: at its start, the main motif of each is briefly recalled by the cellos and basses in their recitative-like outbursts, the idea being that the music from the previous three movements is unfit for the grander purpose of the finale—after the motifs from the first three movements are repeated, the bass solo sings Beethoven's own words: "O Friends, not these sounds!"

Some optimist-spiritualist interpreters see in this movement nothing less that the disclosure of the "Meaning of life"—they read the notorious "Ode to Joy" (recall that its melodic line is the official anthem of the European Union!), as the first moment of a triad: the "Ode to Joy" renders the earthly brotherhood, brotherhood of men (it involves a strictly masculine standpoint: a moment of happiness includes "whoever has created an abiding friendship, or has won a true and loving wife," but nothing whatsoever is said about the happiness of wives themselves); then we pass into a "deeper" spiritual level, a call to all brothers to "be embraced, millions" in looking up to the heavenly god—"there must be a loving father" (in *Grosse Fuge* Beethoven seemed to understand that there is no such father); the complex double fugue which concludes the triad stages an intermixture of the two dimensions which should somehow render the meaning of our lives—an earthly brotherhood grounded in the awareness of a heavenly loving father that protects us.[9]

It is not only that the Movement doesn't end here—a careful listener can easily discover that something is missing in this recapitulation: "Ode to Joy" really ends a little bit after 9 minutes when a prolonged weird silence is interrupted by a vulgar "Turkish March"-style music which belies the brotherhood—some critics even designate the beginning of this "Turkish March" passage as the "fart" in the finale: "Roger Norrington's description of the intervention of the contrabassoon, two bassoons, and bass drum, in the wrong key, in a new speed, and in what you soon realize is the wrong beat of the bar, a bathetic moment that comes just after the choir have invoked a vision of God with some of the powerfully revelatory music of the symphony."[10]

So yes, all brothers are embraced, "but those who cannot must creep tearfully away from our circle"—what if *they* are referred to not so much in words as in the vulgar music which accompanies them? The words are: "Gladly, as His suns fly through the heavens' grand plan, go on, brothers, your way, joyful, like a hero to victory." But the spell is already broken, and when, after this rather creepy intermezzo the "Ode to Joy" melody is repeated, it is too late to cover up the crack. Then, as if taking cognizance of the fact that the spell of brotherhood is broken and that only a higher transcendent agency can restore order, "Be embraced millions" enters, enacting a move to god who *must be*—"Brothers, above the starry canopy there must dwell a loving Father." Here, critics have argued that Beethoven recalls the liturgical hymns of medieval sacred music:

> The religious questions are musically characterized by archaistic moments, veritable "Gregorian fossils" inserted in a "quasi-liturgical" structure based on the sequence first versicle—response—second versicle—response—hymn. Beethoven's employment of this sacred music style has the effect of attenuating the interrogative nature of the text when it mentioned the prostration to the supreme being.[11]

And then we get the double fugue as enforced reconciliation; what follows the fugue is a fake, a hysterical mess which lasts to the end of the movement. The *true* double fugue is Beethoven's quartet movement *Grosse Fuge* op. 133 which—I agree with Daniel Chua—"speaks of failure, the very opposite of the triumphant synthesis associated with Beethovenian recapitulations."[12] So, to recapitulate the advance of the entire symphony, the only moment of truth is rendered in the First Movement, and the other three enact the three modes of a fantasmatic escape: hysterically-joyful violence (which is literally the truth of joyful brotherhood); escape into romantic nostalgia; pathetic failure of the "Ode to Joy."

Beethoven's limitation is not just ideologico-political, it is strictly formal: his music still functions in the expressive mode, rendering a series of ideological and libidinal stances—it didn't yet inscribe these stances into the musical form itself. This inscription happens only with atonality—even Beethoven's *Grosse Fuge* remains within the confines of pre-modern music as an act of supplication: a call to a figure of the big Other (beloved Lady, King, God . . .) to respond, not as the symbolic big Other, but in the Real of his or her being (breaking his own rules by showing mercy; conferring her contingent love on us . . .). Music is thus an attempt to provoke the "answer of the Real": to give rise in the Other to the "miracle" of which Lacan speaks apropos of love, the miracle of the Other stretching back his or her hand to me. The historical changes in the status of "big Other" (*grosso modo*, in what Hegel referred to as "objective Spirit") thus directly concern music—perhaps, musical modernity designates the moment when music renounces the endeavour to provoke the answer of the Other: there is no one to turn to, to address, to bear witness TO, no one to receive our plea or lament. This position is extremely difficult to sustain: in modern music, Webern was the first who was able to sustain this inexistence of the Other: even Schoenberg was still composing for a future ideal listener, while Webern accepted that there is NO "proper" listener. Vinko Globokar, a Slovene composer who worked mostly in France and Germany, belongs to this line: his music is profoundly materialist—in what sense?

Globokar: From Pure Sound to Social Antagonisms

It seems that the development of all great artists proceeds in two main stages: first, the radicalization of the initial project; then the dialectical reversal into its opposite. Globokar's development is also marked by two stages: he started with the full assertion of the musical material in its autonomy—therein resides the point of Globokar's resuscitaton of the unique practice of simultaneous breathing and playing (inhaling and exhaling) the oboe, so that the sound can go on for over a minute: "When one is compelled to listen to one tone for a long time,one all of a sudden begins to hear unimagined things." What we get here is a kind of musical counterpart to anamorphosis in painting or to the extended shots in Tarkovsky. What pervades Tarkovsky's films is the heavy gravity of Earth, which seems to exert its pressure on time itself, generating an effect of temporal anamorphosis, extending the dragging of time well beyond what we perceive as justified by the requirements of narrative movement (one should confer here on the term "Earth" all the resonance it acquired in late Heidegger)—perhaps, Tarkovsky is the clearest example of what Deleuze called the time-image replacing the movement-image.

*

This protracted time is neither the symbolic time of the diegetic space nor the time of the reality of our (spectator's) viewing the film, but an intermediate domain whose visual equivalent are perhaps the protracted stains which "are" the yellow sky in late van Gogh or the water or grass in Munch: this uncanny "massiveness" pertains neither to the direct materiality of the colour stains nor to the materiality of the depicted objects—it dwells in a kind of intermediate spectral domain of what Schelling called *geistige Koerperlichkeit*, the spiritual corporeality. This dimension emerged for the first time in Romantic music which occupied itself with "a sonority that is not only unrealizable but unimaginable." Charles Rosen, who wrote this line, quotes a passage from "Abegg" variations, Schumann's opus 1, in which the impossibility arises

> because Schumann is thinking of the motto in terms of almost pure sound, in terms of release and attack as well as of pitch and rhythm . . . : a note can be attacked twice, but a double release without a second attack is nonsense on the piano.[13]

The best-known case, however, is that of Carnaval: its 21 sections intertwine in multiple ways, each of them a kind of "variation" on others, related to others through melodic or rhythmic echoes, repetitions and contrasts. In classical variations, we first get the theme "as such," followed by the multitude of its variations: as one would expect in Schumann, the "theme" is simply lacking. However, in Carnaval, these "variations" do not all possess equal weight: the eighth section ("Replique") is followed by "Sphinxes," a section which is merely written and cannot be performed. What are these mysterious "sphinxes"? The subtitle of Carnaval is "miniature scenes on four notes" [*scenes mignonnes sur quatre notes*], and "Sphinxes" provide these four notes, the musical cipher of jouissance which condenses a series of mnemonic associations: the young pianist Ernestine von Fricken, Schumann's girlfriend at the time he composed Carnaval, came from the

Bohemian town of Asch, a name whose four letters are identical with the only letters of the word "Schumann" which have note equivalents in German musical terminology (where "H" stands for B, and "B" for B flat). Furthermore, if we read "As" as A flat, we get another variant of the musical cipher, so that we obtain three brief series: SCHumAnn (E flat—C—B—A); ASCH (read as: A flat—C—B); ASCH (read as: A—E flat—C—B). In his *Psychanalyser*, Serge Leclaire reports on a psychoanalytic treatment which produced the cipher of enjoyment in his patient: the enigmatic term "poord'jeli," a condensation of a multitude of mnemonic traces (the patient's love for a girl Lili, a reference to licorne, etc.). Do we not encounter something of the same order in Schumann's "Sphinxes"?[14]

The entire piece thus turns around "Sphinxes" as its absent, impossible-real point of reference: a series of bare notes without any measure or harmony—to put it in Kantian terms, they are not musically "schematized," and therefore cannot be effectively performed. "Sphinxes" are a formula of enjoyment, not unlike Freud's formula of trimethylamin, which appears at the end of the dream of Irma's injection. As such, the absence of "Sphinxes" is structural: if "Sphinxes" were to be effectively performed, the fragile consistency of the entire piece would fall apart. (In some recordings, "Sphinxes" is effectively performed: less than half a minute of a dozen protracted tones. The effect is properly uncanny, as if we had stepped "through the looking-glass" and entered some forbidden domain, beyond (or, rather, beneath) the fantasmatic frame—or, more properly, as if we had caught sight of some entity outside of its proper element, like seeing a dead squid on a table, no longer alive and moving gracefully through the water. For this reason, the uncanny mystery of these notes can all of a sudden change into vulgarity, obscenity even—it is no wonder that the most outstanding proponent of performing "Sphinxes" was none other than Rachmaninov, one of the exemplary kitsch authors of serious music.)

Back to Globokar: then, from the mid-1970s, Globokar became aware of how this immersion into the autonomy of pure sound is a deadlock, a kind of musical hard-core pornography. Thus, he returned to the socio-ideological context of music, which affects from within the process of composing itself: "Music is for me always a consequence. Its emergence is based on an idea, a question, a care, on a problem or something taking place which at the beginning finds itself outside music. Ethics thus determines aesthetics, at the beginning at least."[15] The term "consquence" is crucial here, and has to be given the whole weight of what Alain Badiou called "fidelity" (to a truth-event): the proper domain of an artist's work is that of their fidelity to an ethical encounter or decision.

This return to the social dimension is not external to the musical material, but inscribed into its very network of formal relations. In an interview with Armin Koehler apropos "*Masse, Macht und Individuum*," Globokar pointed out how the constellation of these three terms is directly reflected in the three groups of musicians that perform the piece: a group of 21 who communicate one with another in a non-organized way (the "crowd"); the orchestra of 70 performing in a hierarchical order, under the control of a conductor ("power"); four soloists who interact and are not simply "individuals," since their interaction forms the germ of a new collective. And, as Globokar asserts, there is a fourth element present, electronic organs whose sound stands for the continuity of indestructible Life. Today, this "pure life" has a precise political equivalent in the figure of *homo sacer*, those who are excluded from the political symbolic order and reduced to bare life. In a debate about the fate of Guantanamo prisoners on NBC, one of the arguments for the ethical and legal acceptability of their status was that "they are those who were missed by the bombs": since they were the target of the US bombing and accidentally survived it, and since this bombing was part of a legitimate military operation, one cannot condemn their fate when they were taken prisoners after the combat—whatever their situation, it is better, less severe, than being dead ...

This reasoning tells us much more than it intends: it puts the prisoner almost literally into the position of the living dead, those who are in a way already dead (their right to live forfeited by being legitimate targets of murderous bombings), so that they are now cases of what Agamben calls *homo sacer*, the one who can be killed with impunity since, in the eyes of the law, his life no longer counts. (There is a vague similarity between their situation and the—legally problematic—premise of the movie *Double Jeopardy*: if you were condemned for killing A and you later, after serving your term and being released, discover that A is still alive, you can now kill him with impunity since you cannot be condemned two times for the same act. In psychoanalytic terms, this killing would clearly display the temporal structure of masochist perversion: the order of events is inverted, you are first punished and thus gain the right to commit the crime.) If the Guantanamo prisoners are located in the space "between the two deaths," occupying the position of *homo sacer*, legally dead (deprived of a determinate legal status) while biologically still alive, the US authorities which treat them in this way are also in a kind of in-between legal status which forms the counterpart to *homo sacer*: acting as a legal power, their acts are no longer covered and constrained by the law—they operate in an empty space that is still within the domain of the law.

What Globokar is proposing is thus not a new variation on the old boring opposition of individual and crowd, of the individuum "oppressed" by the crowd, etc., but the matrix of *four modalities of being-together, of sociality, which determine today's life*: the *disorganized multitude* (of, say, consumers or participants of a market-exchange); the *crowd controlled by a Leader*; the *concentration of individuals reduced to bare life*, to objects of social administration (exemplarily, in a concentration camp); and, finally, the *possibility of a new authentic collective*.

Consequently, if we are not to miss what Globokar is giving us, the first thing to do is to reject one of today's critical *topoi*, the allegedly "proto-Fascist" character of the mass choreography displaying disciplined movements of thousands of bodies (parades, mass performances on the stadiums, etc.); if one finds it also in Socialism, one immediately draws the conclusion about a "deeper solidarity" between the two "totalitarianisms." Such a procedure, the very prototype of ideological liberalism, misses the point: not only are such mass performances not inherently Fascist; they are not even "neutral," waiting to be appropriated by Left or Right—it was Nazism who stole them and appropriated them from the workers' movement, their original site of birth. None of the "proto-Fascist" elements is *per se* Fascist, what makes them "Fascist" is only their specific articulation—or, to put it in Stephen Jay Gould's terms, all these elements are "ex-apted" by Fascism. In other words, there is no "Fascism *avant la lettre*," because *it is the letter itself (the nomination) which makes, out of the bundle of constitutive elements, Fascism proper*.

Along the same lines, one should radically reject the notion that discipline (from self-control to bodily training) is a "proto-Fascist" feature—the very predicate "proto-Fascist" should be abandoned: it is the exemplary case of a pseudo-concept whose function is to block conceptual analysis. When we say that the organized spectacle of thousands of bodies (or, say, the admiration of sports which demand high effort and self-control like mountain climbing) is "proto-Fascist," we say strictly nothing, we just express a vague association which masks our ignorance. So when, decades ago, Kung Fu films were popular (Bruce Lee, etc.), was it not obvious that we were dealing with a genuine working-class ideology of youngsters whose sole outlet to success was the disciplined training of their only possession, their bodies? Spontaneity and the "let it go" attitude of indulging in excessive freedoms belong to those who have the means to afford it—those who have nothing have only their discipline. The "bad" bodily discipline, if there is one, is not the collective training, but, rather, jogging and body-building as part of the New Age myth of the realization of the Self's inner potentials—no wonder that the obsession with one's body is an almost obligatory part of the passage of ex-Leftist radicals into the "maturity" of pragmatic politics: from Jane Fonda to Joschka Fischer, the "period of latency" between the two phases was marked by the focus on one's own body.

*

Alain Badiou wrote in the fourteenth of his "Fifteen Theses on Contemporary Art": "Since it is sure of its ability to control the entire domain of the visible and the audible via the laws governing commercial circulation and democratic communication, Empire no longer censures anything. All art, and all thought, is ruined when we accept this permission to consume, to communicate and to enjoy. We should become pitiless censors of ourselves."[16] And, effectively, today, we seem to be at the opposite point of the ideology of the 1960s: the mottos of spontaneity, creative self-expression, etc., are taken over by the System, i.e., the old logic of the system reproducing itself through repressing and rigidly channeling the subject's spontaneous impetuses is left behind. Non-alienated spontaneity, self-expression, self-realization, they all directly serve the system, which is why pitiless self-censorship is a *sine qua non* of emancipatory politics. Especially in the domain of poetic art, this means that one should totally reject any attitude of self-expression, of displaying innermost emotional turmoil, desires, dreams. True art has nothing whatsoever to do with this kind of disgusting emotional exhibitionism—insofar as the standard notion of "poetic spirit" is the ability to display one's intimate turmoil, what Mayakovski said about himself with regard to his turn from personal poetry to political propaganda in verses ("I had to step on the throat of my Muse") is the constitutive gesture of a true poet. If there is a thing that provokes disgust in a true poet, it is the scene when a close friend opens up his heart, spilling out all the dirt of his inner life. Consequently, one should totally reject the standard opposition of "objective" science focused on reality and "subjective" art focused on emotional reaction to it and self-expression: if anything, true art is MORE non-subjective than science. In science, I remain a person with my pathological feature, I just assert objectivity outside it, while in true art, the artist has to undergo a radical self-objectivization, he has to die in and for himself, turn into a kind of living dead.

Furthermore, one should bear in mind that Globokar is deploying these ethico-political dimensions not as a theoretical exercise, but as a project directly embodied in the organization of musical material. How, then, are we to detect traces of the social in the musical material? Perhaps, the privileged way is through the structural absences in the vocal texture. In Schumann's "Humoresque," we have, in the written score, the famous "inner voice" [*innere Stimme*], a third line between the two piano lines, higher and lower. This absent line is to be reconstructed on the basis of the fact that the first and third levels (the right and the left hand piano lines) do not relate to each other directly, i.e., their relationship is not that of an immediate mirroring: in order to account for their interconnection, one is thus compelled to (re)construct a third, "virtual" intermediate level (melodic line) which, for structural reasons, cannot be played. Schumann brings this procedure of absent melody to an apparently absurd self-reference when, later in the same fragment of "Humoresque," he repeats the same two effectively played melodic lines, yet this time the score contains no third absent melodic line, no inner voice—what is absent here is the absent melody, i.e., absence itself. How are we to play these notes when, at the level of what is effectively to be played, they exactly repeat the previous notes? The effectively played notes are deprived only of what is not there, of their constitutive lack, or, to paraphrase the Bible, they lose even that which they never had. A true pianist should thus have the *savoir-faire* to play the existing, positive, notes in such a way that one would be able to discern the echo of the accompanying non-played "silent" virtual notes or their absence . . . and is this not how ideology works? The explicit ideological text (or practice) is sustained by the "unplayed" series of obscene superegotistic supplement.

In Really Existing Socialism, the explicit ideology of socialist democracy was sustained by a set of implicit (unspoken) obscene injunctions and prohibitions, teaching the subject how not to take some explicit norms seriously and how to implement a set of publicly unacknowledged prohibitions. One of the strategies of dissidents in the final years of Socialism was therefore precisely to take the ruling ideology more seriously than it took itself by way of ignoring its virtual unwritten shadow: "You want us to practice socialist democracy? OK, here you have it!" And when the Party apparatchiks responded with desperately trying to hint that this was not the way things worked, one simply had to ignore these hints ...

This is what *acheronta movebo* (moving the underground) as a practice of the critique of ideology means: not directly changing the explicit text of the Law, but, rather, intervening into its obscene virtual supplement. For example, the relationship towards homosexuality in a soldiers' community operates at two distinct levels: the explicit homosexuality is brutally attacked, those identified as gays are ostracized, beaten up every night, etc.; however, this explicit homophobia is accompanied by an excessive set of implicit web of homosexual innuendos, inner jokes, obscene practices, etc. The truly radical intervention into military homophobia should therefore not focus primarily on the explicit repression of homosexuality; it should rather "move the underground," disturb the implicit homosexual practices which sustain the explicit homophobia.

And, to conclude, this insight into the obscenity of the voice enables us to grasp how the two steps in Globokar's development (the assertion of the autonomy of the voice; the move towards the ethico-political dimension) are deeply co-dependent: the ultimate medium of social control and discipline is the pure voice itself. It is sufficient to cast a cursory glance at the history of music—it reads as a kind of counter-history to the usual story of Western metaphysics as the domination of voice over writing. What we encounter in it again and again is a voice that threatens the established Order and that, for that reason, has to be brought under control, subordinated to the rational articulation of spoken and written word, fixed into writing. In order to designate the danger that lurks here, Lacan coined the neologism *jouis-sense*, enjoyment-in-meaning—the moment at which the singing voice cuts loose from its anchoring in meaning and accelerates into a consuming self-enjoyment. The oldest musical text in all human history, an edict of a Chinese emperor, warns against singing which does not follow rules. In his *Republic*, Plato claims that, once non-regulated singing is allowed, the entire social structure will disintegrate and man will return to beast. In medieval times, Popes warned against free singing which is not subordinated to words as the devil's temptation. The French Revolution rejected the effeminated castrato coloraturas. Stalin prohibited Shostakovich's "Lady Macbeth" because of the wild obscene display of sounds. In the 1960s, both Soviet Communists and the US conservatives perceived Elvis Presley as a threat to our civilization . . .

The problem is thus always the same: how are we to prevent the voice from sliding into a consuming self-enjoyment that "effeminates" the reliable masculine Word? The voice functions here as a "supplement" in the Derridean sense: one endeavours to restrain it, to regulate it, to subordinate it to the articulated Word, yet one cannot dispense with it altogether, since a proper dosage is vital for the exercise of power (suffice it to recall the role of patriotic-military songs in the building-up of a totalitarian community). However, this brief description of ours can give rise to the wrong impression that we are dealing with a simple opposition between the "repressive" articulated Word and the "transgressive" consuming voice: on the one hand, the articulated Word that disciplines and regulates the voice as a means of asserting social discipline and authority, on the other hand, the self-enjoying Voice which acts as the medium of liberation, of tearing apart the disciplinary chains of law and order . . . But what about the US Marine Corps' mesmeric "marching chants"—are their debilitating rhythm and sadistically sexualized nonsensical content not an exemplary case of the consuming self-enjoyment in the service of Power? The excess of the voice is thus radically undecidable—and it is in this terrain that a composer has to fight his ethical struggle, as Globokar does.

Variation 4
Acts of reconciliation

If Hegel is the philosopher of reconciliation *par excellence*, how can we reconcile our desperate reading of Hegel with his topic of reconciliation? Let's begin with Hegel's pages on Beautiful Soul and the "hard heart" in his *Phenomenology*[1] which reverberate today as an uncanny in-advance-critique of Cancel Culture and other forms of stiff moralism—just recall his claim that the moral judgment is "envy which helps itself to the cloak of morality."(361) Reconciliation is only achieved when the judging "hard heart" itself admits its complicity in what it condemns—but how, exactly, does this happen? "The wounds of the spirit heal and leave no scars behind; it is not the deed which is imperishable, but rather the deed is repossessed by spirit into itself"(361): reconciliation "bestows recognition as good on what thought had determined acting to be, namely, evil."(362) (The question that remains here is, of course, how horrors like the Holocaust, gulags, or colonization can be "repossessed by spirit" . . .) This bestowing of recognition on the other is the obverse of fully assuming one's own evil and hypocrisy: the judging consciousness

> is hypocrisy because it pretends that such judgment is not only another manner of being evil but is rather itself the rightful consciousness of action. In his non-actuality and in the vanity he has in being such a faultfinder, it places himself far above the deeds it excoriates, and it wants to know that its speech, which is utterly devoid of any deeds, is to be taken as a superior actuality.
>
> (359)

The judging consciousness is thus a figure of clear conscience, and, as Steven Wright said: "A clear conscience is usually the sign of a bad memory." Or, as

Hegel puts it concisely, the true Evil is the gaze which sees evil everywhere around itself. Crucial to this formulation is a conception of language as the medium of truth, not just an expression of inner intention: the judging consciousness speaks the truth, it advocates universality, but (in Wittgenstein's sense) it displays the opposite attitude of non-forgiveness, of elevating its singularity above others:

> the hard heart does not recognize the contradiction it commits when it does not let the discarding that took place in speech be the true discarding, whereas it itself has the certainty of its spirit not in an actual action but in its innerness and has its existence in the speech in which its judgment is phrased. It is therefore just the hard heart itself which is putting obstacles in the way of the other's return from the deed into the spiritual existence of speech and into the equality of spirit, and through its hardness of heart, it engenders the inequality which is still present.
>
> (360)

And one has to go to the end here: the supreme figure of Evil is therefore god himself insofar as he stands above creation, judging us—this is why the true reconciliation happens only in Christianity which enacts the infinite judgment "god is a mortal man," an absolute contradiction:

> Absolute spirit comes into existence only at the point where its pure knowing of itself is the opposition and flux of itself with itself. Knowing that its pure knowing is the abstract essence, it is this duty knowingly in absolute opposition to the knowing that knows itself, as the absolute singular individuality of the self, as the essence. The former is the pure continuity of the universal which knows singular individuality knowing itself as the essence as nullity in itself, as evil.
>
> (362)

What does this imply in practical terms, as critics of philosophy like to say? Towards the end of *A River Runs Through It* (Robert Redford, 1992), Rev. Maclean gives a sermon about being unable to help loved ones who are destroying themselves and will not accept help: all that those who truly care for such a self-destructive person can do is to give unconditional love, even without understanding why.[2] This is the Christian stance at its purest: not the promise of salvation but just such unconditional love whose message is: "I know you are bent on destroying yourself, I know I cannot prevent it, but without understanding why I love you unconditionally, without any constraint." Do these lines not evoke the enigmatic scene in Gethsemane from Matthew where Jesus tells his disciples who lay tired around him: "I am deeply grieved, even to death; remain here, and stay awake with me." (Matthew 36-38)?

Liza Thompson pointed out that Jesus is here "asking for solidarity. Not followers or crowds to listen to his teachings but an act of togetherness. And it comes from a place of such radical vulnerability that it disrupts notions of Jesus as some kind of hierarchical leader."[3] Jesus himself is here on the path to his self-destruction (knowing next day he will die in terrible pain), and the only thing he asks his followers is to give him their unconditional love, even without understanding why. When we curse our fate in despair, when we courageously accept that no higher force will help us, Christ is here with us—and this is reconciliation at its most radical.

However, such a reconciliation can take different forms. Let's begin with a well-known case of operatic reconciliation. In the third act of Wagner's *Tannheuser*, the hero is on a pilgrimage in Rome where he approaches "him, through whom God speaks" (the Pope) and tells his story. However, rather than finding absolution, he is cursed and told by the pope: "As this staff in my hand, no more shall bear fresh leaves, from the hot fires of hell, salvation never shall bloom for thee." Desperate Tannhauser returns home and dies, but after his death the growing light bathes the scene as a group of younger pilgrims arrive bearing the pope's staff sprouting new leaves, and proclaiming a miracle: "Hail!, Hail! To this miracle of grace, Hail!"—Tannhauser is posthumously pardoned . . . Is this a true reconciliation?

Alain Badiou was right when, against Adorno, he pointed out that there is no true peace of reconciliation at the end of *Tannheuser*: the traumatic impact of Tannhauser's Rome narrative is far too strong to allow any peaceful resolve of its unbearable tension. (And, incidentally, the same goes for *The Twilight Of Gods* where the brutality of Siegfried's death and funeral march is not really appeased by Brunhilde's immolation.) The reconciliation that concludes the opera is purely formal, an effect of beautiful music. How could this happen?

Let's begin by recounting how Tannhauser explains to Venus what he misses in Venusberg—not spirit but peaceful nature:

> Days, moons—mean nothing to me anymore, for I no longer see the sun, nor the friendly stars of heaven; I see no more the blades of grass, which, turning freshly green, bring the new summer in; the nightingale that foretells me the spring, I hear no more. Shall I never hear it, never behold it more?

In the spirit that characterizes German Romanticism, nature and spirituality go together, so the choice facing the hero is not one between sensual reality or spirituality but both together against the excess of *jouissance*. The true opposition is thus the one between spiritualized nature and excessive *jouissance*, where Venus does not stand simply for this excess but is immanently split into two. When the pious Wolfram sings praises to the evening star ("*Oh du mein holder Abendstern*"), we should not ignore the obvious fact that he is singing praise to *Venus*: Venus is the morning star and the evening star, i.e., a figure which belongs to the same series as the Sumerian goddess Inanna:

> The discontinuous movements of Venus relate to both mythology as well as Inanna's dual nature. Unlike any other deity, Inanna is able to descend into the netherworld and return to the heavens. The planet Venus appears to make a similar descent, setting in the West and then rising again in the East.[4]

Is this not yet another argument that Venus and Elisabeth are one and the same person? That's why the same singer should sing both—even more, Venus and Elisabeth are not just the two sides of the same woman, they are the two projections of the hero himself onto the object of his love—the woman is here quite literally Tannhauser's symptom.

A hugely significant step towards the right reading of the opera was made by Romeo Castellucci in his ground-breaking 2017 staging of *Tannhauser* in the Bavarian State Opera. The first scene takes place in Venusberg, the site of carnal pleasures from which Tannhauser wants to escape; Venusberg is presented as an ugly mound full of disgusting, vaguely feminine creatures, with thick fat hanging from their bodies and intermixing into a field of flab shaking like cellulitis—an image of suffocating decay, boredom, and satiation. Tannhauser's first words in the opera, resisting the calls of Venus to stay with her, are: "*Zu viel! Zu viel!*" ("Too much! Too much!"). But this is not all: above this sleazy seething of life hangs a circular ball (a fantasy frame) in the air within which the idealized version of these same creatures (Venus and her companions) appears, this time as slim ethereal creatures floating in the air and gently dancing, deprived of their gross carnality.

One cannot but recall here the well-known scene from Terry Gilliam's *Brasil* in which, in a high-class restaurant, the waiter recommends to his customers the best offers from the daily menu ("Today, our tournedo is really special!", etc.), yet what the customers get on making their choice is a dazzling colour photo of the meal on a stand above the plate, and on the plate itself, a loathsome excremental paste-like lump: we get the split between the image of the food and the real of its formless excremental remainder, i.e., between the ghost-like substanceless appearance and the raw stuff of the realm, exactly in the same way as in Castellucci's *Tannhauser*, we get the split between the disgusting real of the flesh and the dematerialized image.

We should emphasize here that there is nothing "authentic" in the experience of this split: it doesn't render visible the disgusting reality of sex, it just bears witness to Tannhauser's psychotic split between the Real and the Imaginary which takes place when the third term, the Symbolic, is foreclosed. In other words, the shaking blob is not the Real of sex supplemented by the fantasy of ethereal girls dancing: fantasy is not only the ethereal vision of dancing slim girls but also the image of the disgusting quaking jelly whose function is to obfuscate the fact that sex is always-already "barred," thwarted by a constitutive impossibility.

So how does Elisabeth redeem Tannhauser? Does she kill herself? But this is a mortal sin ... The opera remains a mess—towards the end of his life Wagner himself remarked that he still owes his public a *Tannhauser*.[5] Jon Vickers canceled a performance of *Tannhauser* because he disagreed with its religious stance and considered it blasphemous: as a Christian he believed that Tannhauser's redemption should not come about through the love of a woman but through god himself.[6] (Incidentally, there is much more profanity in *Parsifal* in spite of its Christian aura.)

The only solution is the one offered by Istvan Szabo in his *Meeting Venus*, a wonderful movie about a staging of *Tannhauser* in Paris immediately after the fall of the Wall. The conductor (Niels Arestrup) is from Hungary, the diva (Glenn Close) is a temperamental superstar from Sweden, the baritone is a rotund East German who thinks mostly about obtaining hard currency to use in his auto-painting business, and then there are, of course, the musicians, the members of the chorus, the stagehands and electricians and painters and property masters, all members of unions that are ferociously protective of their contracts—a union man refuses to press the button to raise the curtain just before the premiere since he would thereby violate a trade union rule, and it looks like the performance will have to be canceled. But the diva proposes a simple solution: they should perform the entire opera in front of the closed curtain, directly addressing the public. The performance is a triumph, and while the camera shows the conductor during the last tones of the music, we see in reality the repeated miracle: the conductor's dry wooden stick sprouting fresh green leaves . . .

The true miracle is the spirit of community established by this performance: all their petty conflicts and sexual tensions are forgotten, we pass from *eros* to *agape*. The supreme irony is that some idiots read the film as an anti-workers manifesto: art (spirituality) wins over class struggle (trade union defense of workers' rights), but the truth is rather the opposite—the spirit of Communist solidarity wins over petty trade-unionist conflicts of interests.

Two details deserve especially to be noted about the finale. First, while everybody is in a panic at the prospect that the performance will have to be canceled, it is the diva who proposes the solution that leads to triumph, and her beatific, benevolent smile of satisfaction dominates the final moments when all others are caught in the enthusiasm of full triumph. Her gaze is directed at the conductor with whom she had a passionate love affair that ended in a fiasco during rehearsals—the way she looks at him at the end signals a profound reconciliation. Their exclusive love affair ascends to a higher level, the tumultuous *eros* (which has to end in failure since *il n'y a pas de rapport sexuel*) is transformed into the peace of *agape*. Second, the miracle (the wooden stick sprouting fresh leaves) is repeated: first just staged as a part of the story, then as an event in reality, and it is this repetition of miracle in reality that works as an authentic shock bringing us, the viewers, to the edge of tears . . .

Surprisingly (or not so surprisingly), the same reconciliation through music, through the musical form, is at work in one of Rammstein's supreme songs, "Mutter." The lyrics tell the story of a child not born from a womb but in an experiment, thus having no true father or mother; they describe his plan to kill both the mother "who never gave birth to him" and then himself. However, he fails to kill himself, instead ending up mutilated and no better off than before. The child begs and prays for strength, but his dead mother does not answer—here are the lyrics of the first strophe:

> The tears of a crowd of very old children / I string them on a white hair / I throw the wet chain into the air / and wish that I had a mother

Looking closer, one discovers that the situation of the child is ambiguous: was it an experimental birth out of the womb, an abortion so that he sings from the dead, or, at a more general level, is it a metaphor for the situation of Germans after World War II where they found their "motherland" destroyed and thus their lives ruined? One should resist here the temptation to decide what the song "really is about"—it "really is about" the formal constellation of a motherless child who survives his suicide. And a similar ambiguity is surprisingly at work in different musical versions of the song: there is the Rammstein hard rock "original," but then there are versions for solo soprano accompanied by piano or symphonic orchestra, for male chorus, even for children's chorus (with lyrics in Russian), and they all sound so "natural" in spite of the extreme brutality of the event described in the lyrics.[7] One should definitely not interpret this last version as a display of extreme irony—no, the singing children enact the only possible reconciliation of the desperate predicament of the song's hero, so they are to be taken in all naïvety.

The point is again that what Hegel calls "reconciliation" is not a reduction of the traumatic excess to a gapless totality but the acceptance of this excess in its meaningless brutality. Such a notion of reconciliation enables us to identify immediately false reconciliations or false solutions like the one that concludes *Conclave* (2024, directed by Edward Berger), a movie which clearly demonstrates the ambiguous role of the topic of trans rights in political processes. Cardinal Lawrence (superbly played by Ralph Fiennes) is tasked with coordinating the selection of a new Pope, and finds himself at the centre of the political struggles that divide the Church: there is a Black cardinal who was involved in a sexual scandal, a European conservative cardinal advocating the return to Latin masses and a tougher stance against Islam, a corrupted American liberal cardinal, etc., and their conflict threatens to shake the very foundations of the Catholic Church. The tension is resolved when a Third World cardinal nominated by the Pope just before his death appears at the conclave and instantly convinces its members with his authentic approach which focuses on global solidarity. The problem is that he is biologically an intersex person assigned male at birth who has a uterus and ovaries—Lawrence decides to ignore this and proclaims him the new Pope . . .

One should also note that the new Pope planned to submit himself to a surgery that would remove his uterus and ovaries, but cancels his plan with the argument that he wants to be the way God made him . . . In short, his argument is basically a conservative one, he wants to be in his psychic identity what he is biologically, exactly what is for the LGBT+ ideology the worst position: the gap between biological sex and symbolic sexual identity is perceived as something to be abolished. A truly subversive twist would be that the new Pope is biologically fully a man but rejects to be a man in his psychic identity since he experiences himself as trans.

Furthermore, the final solution of *Conclave* is very ambiguous: the actual problems that beset the Church are not really resolved but just magically recede into the background with the arrival of the intersex cardinal who works like a *deus ex machina*. In contrast to *Conclave*, the miniseries *Disclaimer* (2024), yet another masterpiece from Alfonzo Quaron, concludes with an outstanding case of such a Hegelian reconciliation although its narrative relies on multiple superpositions without a clear final collapse—how can this be? Here is a (simplified) resume of the narrative[8]:

Catherine Ravenscroft, a famed documentary journalist, discovers she is a prominent character in a novel *Perfect Stranger* that appeared under a pseudonym and purports to reveal a secret she has tried to keep hidden. The novel paints Catherine as a terrible mother and wife whose self-absorbed affair with 19-year-old stranger Jonathan while on vacation in Italy led to his death and the near-death of her own 4-year-old son. This story, full of juicy sexual details, disturbs the life of Catherine and all the people around her, her husband Robert, her son Nicholas, and her coworkers. We gradually learn that the book published by Jonathan's father Stephen was written by his wife Nancy, the deceased mother of Jonathan; it is a fictional account of how Nancy perceived her son's final days.

In the finale, Catherine—when she finally speaks in her own voice, after being silenced and vilified—opens up to Stephen in a harrowing monologue about the horrific night before his son's death where he brutally raped her for three-plus hours. So the following day in Italy, when Jonathan seemingly became a hero and ran out into the ocean to save a young Nicholas from drowning and Jonathan ended up drowning in the rough seas instead, Catherine didn't shout out to help her rapist. She explains to Stephen (and to viewers) that his death meant she never had to speak about that night, so she let fate take its course. She'd never had to relive her trauma out loud, until now, when she is forced to share because of Stephen's relentless and misguided pursuit of vengeance.

This brings us to the true meaning of the title: although *Perfect Stranger* begins with an inverted disclaimer ("any resemblance with actual events and persons is *not* accidental"), does the fact that the book is full of Nancy's fantasies not prove that the disclaimer is to be taken in its standard form (any such resemblance really is contingent)? The scene of Catherine flirting with and seducing Jonathan on the beach and later in her hotel room are staged in a ridiculously exaggerated non-realist way—however, such staging is justified in view of the fact that we are dealing with Nancy's imagination.

The true achievement of the series resides in the ambiguity of its ending which elicits two (almost symmetrically opposed) readings. The predominant one sees the ending as a moment of catharsis when all characters involved get rid of their illusions and are forced to assume reality as it is—to quote Cuaron himself: "Almost everyone has created a judgment of Catherine that is completely different from the ending that we reveal. It was a way for audiences to confront their own judgments."[9] To quote Hegel again, Evil is the gaze itself which perceives Evil all around itself: the Evil is not in what Catherine did with

Jonathan, the Evil is in the gaze of others who perceive her acts as evil. For this first reading, the finale thus enacts the passage from projecting onto Catherine our prejudices and desires to a sobering awakening which compels us to accept what Catherine (and Jonathan and all of us) really are.

This brutal catharsis is best exemplified in the fate of Graham: from being the instigator of the campaign against Catherine and ruthlessly pursuing his goal of revenge (killing Nicholas and Catherine), he ends up alone in the garden of his house, consigning not only the remaining copies of *Perfect Stranger* and intimate photos of Catherine but even all the personal remainders of his deceased wife Nancy to the flames. He is absolutely alone, probably considering suicide. In the last photo he throws into the fire, we see that the five-year-old Nick observed Jonathan brutally raping his mother, a fact of which Catherine herself was not aware (she thought Nick is safely asleep in his bedroom and she complied with Jonathan's orders just to keep Nick in his blessed ignorance)—so Catherine and Nick have to achieve their own awakening to the brutal reality.

However, there is another reading which captures much more adequately the final twist of the film: what if reconciliation doesn't mean a new state of peace but primarily the reconciliation with the very tensions, perversions and inconsistencies that characterize social life and especially sexuality? This sense of reconciliation is the Hegelian one: we fight a threat, an obstacle that prevents us from achieving our goal, and reconciliation doesn't mean our victory over the obstacle, the integration of the obstacle into our order as its subordinate moment, but rather the insight into how what we perceived as an obstacle is our own condition of possibility—if this obstacle disappears, our own order disintegrates. This certainly holds for Nazi anti-Semitism: the whole Nazi identity is based on fighting the Jewish plot. With regard to *Disclaimer*, this means that it is not enough to condemn the rapist and accept the truth disclosed by a woman who finally dares to say it all. What if the dark fantasies that we attribute to the enemy are part of our own identity, so that we have to learn to live with them?

It is thus all too simple to say that, at the end of the series when the evil spell cast by the book *Perfect Stranger* is broken, all the main characters are compelled to assume reality as it really was—the lesson of the end is much more ambiguous. Already earlier in the series, when Graham is forced to admit that Nancy's book doesn't fully fit facts, he justifies Nancy's small lies as part of her effort to "get rid of the ballast of truth": through her redactions, the truth (of Catherine's evil) appears in its purity, as it is, delivered of the ballast of its imperfect empirical reality. However, we should recall here the basic lesson of Hegel: when a notion is actualized imperfectly, this imperfection of reality with regard to its notion always indicates an imperfection of this notion itself. Recall Hegel's passage from state (the highest figure of objective spirit) to religion as the form of absolute spirit: really-existing states never fully fit the notion of a state—if we want to fully actualize the notion of state as a community reconciled with itself, we get a state which is no longer a state but a religious community. So if we want to represent the idea of Catherine's evil in its pure form, delivered of the ballast of empirical truth, we have to abandon this idea itself (which is false) . . .

The ending thus in no way implies that now, when the full truth is told, we can get rid of illusions and fantasies. First, at the level of facts, the character of Jonathan is morally ambiguous: yes, he brutally raped Catherine in Italy, but the next morning on the beach he immediately reacts to her desperate calls and swims into the deep sea to save Nicholas, paying the price for this heroic act when he himself drowns. Traumatized by the brutal rape, Catherine sees Jonathan drowning but doesn't do anything. She is faithful to her husband in reality but she fantasizes about flirting: while drinking wine in the bar before the rape, Catherine doesn't react to Jonathan's flirting gestures, she tells herself: "Maybe I'll fantasize about this moment later." And she left (forgets) the key in the door of her room so that Jonathan can later enter her room . . .

What this indicates is that the fantasized versions display their own libidinal truth—or, as Lacan put it, truth has the structure of a fiction. This paradox holds also (maybe even especially) for political life. There are conspiracy theories, real and fictional, which are not true but nevertheless explain everything—I have written elsewhere about Robert Harris's *The Ghost*, for example. In Lacanian terms, the clandestine meetings and secret schemes of these conspiracy theories are not part of reality, but they are real—why? Because they render visible the shared blindness of both sides. The title of Aldous Huxley's outstanding novel *Eyeless in Gaza* is taken from a phrase in

John Milton's *Samson Agonistes*: in the Old Testament, Samson was expected to deliver Israel from the Philistine yoke, but he was captured by the Philistines, his eyes were burned out and he was taken to Gaza, where he was forced to work at grinding grain in a mill: "ask for this great deliverer now, and find him / Eyeless in Gaza at the Mill with slaves." Who is today, in the war between Israel and Hamas, "eyeless in Gaza," Hamas or the Israeli racist fundamentalists? In some sense *both* are blinded by their acts: Hamas expected to deliver Palestinians from the Israeli yoke, but now it serves Israel to further enslave or expel Palestinians; Israeli fundamentalists expected to create a safe Great Israel from the river to the sea, but now they are reinforcing anti-Semitism all around the world. And although the conflict is between Hamas and Israeli hardline Zionists, we should abandon all illusions that there is a clear line to separate "extremists" from the majority of the population: today the large majority of Israeli Jews are opposed to the two-state solution.

Back to *Disclaimer* again, one should also note that, while Catherine is exculpated of her guilt at the end and recognized as a victim, the person who comes closest to being guilty (apart from Jonathan) is again a woman, his mother Nancy who wrote *Perfect Stranger*, the narrative which embellishes her son's past and fills in the gaps with her own fantasies. Emily (Graham's wife), not Graham, is the ultimate culprit for the narrative she constructs and which seduces the men (Graham, Robert, Nicholas) into surrendering to it and projecting into it their own fears and fantasies. Emily is pathologically attached to her son: after learning of his death, she moves into his room and gradually withdraws into madness. There is a strange repetition at work in the series: Nancy's pathological attachment to Jonathan after his death mirrors Catherine's self-declared full happiness on the day before the rape, alone with her son and with no husband around (a clear hint at the cracks in their marriage). Does her flirting not indicate a shadow in this happiness? And does she not reach this happiness of being alone with her son again at the very end of the series? Although her final happiness is a bitter reunion of two ruined persons, there is nonetheless a clear Christian dimension in it: "For where two or three gather in my name, there I am with them."(Matthew 18:20) Christ is neither the subject nor the object of love, he is love itself: "Whoever does not love does not know God, because God is love."(John 4:8) Christian reunion is, at its most basic, not a happy reunion which makes the couple obliterate their despair: what is shared in the reunion is the despair itself.

Am I just projecting this ambiguity into the series? No, since what points in this direction are already the formal features of the series: the story is revealed in a non-linear fashion with scenes alternating between a holiday in Italy (young Catherine's encounter with Jonathan and his subsequent death by drowning) and back home in London twenty years later (the truth emerges, the consequences). The series also uses the technique of the unreliable narrator in that the events in Italy are told twice: first from Nancy's speculative point of view and later from Catherine's first person experience. Both these features evoke the notion of quantum superpositions: reality itself, not just our (mis) perception of it, maintains itself only when it is superposed by imagined alternatives.

These imagined alternatives are not simply evil, there is also an unexpected utopian dimension in them. At the end, Catherine is not ready to pardon Robert, and her rejection is fully justified: what she cannot forgive him is that he felt relief when he learned she was brutally raped by Jonathan in the Italian hotel—so it is much easier for him to accept that she was repeatedly brutally raped than to accept that she enjoyed a passionate night of sex . . . We should go all the way in drawing the consequences of this profound insight: the passionate night of sex is not just Nancy's dirty imagination, it could have happened and it would be beautiful if it were to happen. It is a key part of reconciliation to accept *this*.

There is, however, yet another mode of reconciliation, a much more traumatic one, that we get in Mark Romanek's outstanding *Never Let Me Go* (2010, screenplay by John Garland based on the novel by Kazuo Ishiguro). *Never Let Me Go* struck me as arguably the most depressing film I've ever seen. I suspect this is because today, with all the crises that more and more affect our daily lives, from global warming to wars and the threat of digital control, we find ourselves in a position very similar to that of the heroes of Romanek's film. Its heroes are not AI creatures but humans who find themselves in a similar position of exclusion from "normal" human society.

Never Let Me Go mixes in an extraordinarily efficient way a science-fiction premise with intimate psychological drama and love story. A medical breakthrough in late 1950s has extended the human lifespan beyond 100 years, but to achieve this, the state grew clones who are destined to donate their organs to prolong the lives of mortally ill people. However, in order for this activity to become acceptable, a profound change had to occur in public morals, radically redefining what counts as socially acceptable—driven by the promise of survival, people accepted this since clones were artificially produced outside the network of kinship relations and were thus perceived as beings who didn't count as fully human.

*

The story begins in 1978 and follows three children, the young Kathy H, along with her friends Tommy D and Ruth C, who live at Hailsham, a traditional boarding school. The teachers, called *guardians*, encourage students to be health-conscious and create artwork, and they have little contact with the world beyond the school's fences. Miss Lucy, a perceptive new guardian, tells her class that they are all clones who exist to be organ donors and are destined to die, or *complete*, early in their adulthoods after a couple of donations (maximum four); she is quickly fired by the headmistress. As time passes, Kathy grows attracted to Tommy, but Ruth wins him for herself despite having engaged in teasing him. This love triangle is resolved years later when a broken Ruth reveals she only seduced Tommy because she was afraid to be alone; she is consumed with guilt and wishes to help Tommy and Kathy seek a deferral (there is a rumour circulating among the clones that if a couple proves they are really in love, their donations will be postponed). She leaves them with the address of Madame, whom she believes has the power to help them, and soon dies on the operating table during her second donation. Tommy and Kathy, now his "carer" (the one who stands by a clone during donations in order to make his/her life easier), finally enter a relationship, but after they discover that deferrals are a myth, Tommy explodes with grief and anger as he used to as a child. (One should shamelessly admit that the same scream appears at the end of a popular spy bestseller, *The Day Of the Locust* by Terry Hayes: "Tod is screaming mindlessly in imitation of the siren of the police car that has come to his rescue. This scream represents a hysterical release of the frustration and horror which he has never quite been able to put into words."[10]) Tommy dies during his fourth donation, leaving Kathy alone, and after a decade of caring, we see her contemplating the ruins of her childhood. Finally getting ready to begin her own donations, she questions in voice-over how different—or not so different—her life has been from normal people's.[11]

The book's (and the film's) big enigma remains unanswered: why the main characters never try to escape their fate of an early death (although they could easily attempt to disappear into society)? The story is pervaded by radical ambiguity with regard to this point: do the givers accept their fate because they are not fully human or do they accept it because they are in some basic sense *more* human than the rest of us, ordinary humans? Numerous comments offer a whole series of divergent answers. First, there is the obvious scientific one: the givers are "genetically engineered clones. Their genes were designed to eliminate the fright-flight response." Then, there is external control: Hailsham is surrounded by an electrified fence, all givers wear bracelets which register their movements so that they can be located at any point, etc. Finally, there is the givers' psychic stance: they have no outside perspective, they are unable to develop any kind of dream of a better outside into which to escape, plus they possess no legal documents to identify them in the external world...

However, when they reach the age to become donors, they are moved from Hailsham to Cottages, isolated countryside buildings where they see and interact with "'real' humans living their lives, growing old, having relationships, feeling and crying and laughing the same way they do. Even with the brainwashing as kids, how could they not question their rights and purpose as adults? This is how the human brain works when processing experiences, it elaborates, creates questions and motivates changes, why don't they? Why is it that every single "real" human among them has zero ethical dilemmas and doesn't rebel against the state of things, though they clearly see that those "givers" are fully humans?" They even escape to a nearby small town, visit an ordinary pub, etc.—so why do not some of them at least kill themselves?

The weirdness of this feature becomes obvious if we compare *Never Let Me Go* with *Island* (Michael Bay, 2005)—a comparison solicited by Ishiguro himself who pointed out that he wanted to do the opposite of an individual finding him/herself in a similar situation of total control and then rebelling against it. *Island* is about Lincoln Six Echo (played by Ewan McGregor), who struggles to fit into the highly structured world in which he lives, isolated in a compound on an island, and a series of strange events that unfold make him question how truthful that world is. After he learns the compound inhabitants are clones used for organ harvesting as well as surrogates for wealthy people in the outside world, he attempts to escape with Jordan Two Delta (Scarlet Johansson) and expose the illegal cloning movement... What we get here is a standard Hollywood-Leftist story of a heroic individual rebelling against the oppressing regime; he triumphs and ends up at a lone island of his own with his beloved. Nothing like this happens in *Never Let Me Go* where the lives of the three donors are meaningless—but they are meaningless precisely because the meaning of their life (in the ordinary sense of its function) is fixed in advance—they know why they are here, to serve as donors... Boris Groys wrote:

> Every generation enters history during its desiring, active phase—and then leaves it without offering anything that the next generation could embrace. On the contrary, in its second phase—after a life full of disillusionment and frustration—every generation presents itself to the next generation as historical garbage that has to be removed to make way for a new desire. It is obvious that this "tact of natality" excludes the possibility of any transgenerational project, beyond the eternal return of the desire for such a project. Thus, the return of communism is as improbable as the return of any other transgenerational project. At the same time a return of the desire for communism is not only possible but almost unavoidable.[12]

But are today, amidst the ecological crisis, transgenerational projects really impossible? And, to risk even a step further, did not some active Communist revolutionaries perceive even themselves as the last garbage to be removed (or, to use a well-known paradox, as the last cannibals to be eaten)? Or, as Brecht put it apropos of revolutionary violence in his *The Measure Taken*, one should strive to become the last piece of dirt with whose removal the room will be clean—this is Brecht's version of the justification of Stalinist purges, and the stance described by Brecht strangely echoes the stance of the donors in *Never Let Me Go*.

In a further paradoxical twist, this fixed meaning confers on their lives a depressive beauty and sustains their longing for love and vocation (painting in the movie) as a way to transcend their narrow predicament. Maybe, precisely because the fate of their lives is fixed and prevents them from dedicating themselves to love or vocation, they experience the need for love and vocation in an all the more urgent and profound way—you fully experience what really matters in your life only when you miss it. So the donors in the film are not lacking perspective on the outside reality—on the contrary, they attain a perspective which we, "normal" people fully immersed into social reality, automatically deny. It is our "normal" everyday existence which is a lie. The pessimistic conclusion to be drawn from all this is that if we fail to assume our mortality, this does not make us ethically better persons: only against the depressive background of an impenetrable deadly threat can we occasionally act in a kind and compassionate way. And is this also not the lesson for us today? Not a cheap humanist optimism but the full acceptance that we are doomed as the only ray of hope. If, maybe, an AI machine will effectively begin to think and acquire a kind of self-awareness, will its self-experience not be akin to the self-experience of the donors in Never Let Me Go?

What makes Never Let Me Go such a truly depressing masterpiece is that it provides no easy way out; part of its traumatic impact is precisely the fact that the reason why givers do not rebel (or try to escape at least) is not specified—again, in contrast to usual catastrophe movies in which the external threat (evil conspiracy, virus, aliens . . .) is sooner or later identified. We find ourselves in a situation of unspecified mortal dread which deprives individuals of their basic tendency to survive, hope, and fight, and what makes this dread all the more oppressive is its "abstract" nature, registered only as an oppressive atmosphere. Even when they still desire things (as in the love triangle of Tommy, Kathy, and Ruth where sexual passion, jealousy, and envy intermingle), the joy of love is tainted by the all-pervasive depressive background.

It is too much to say that there is a contrast between the depressive atmosphere and the intricacies of the love triangle: their love is an organic part of the atmosphere, and one should not restrain from the staggering conclusion that this depressive atmosphere make the three donors ethically much better people. The reason Ruth (superbly played by Keira Knightley) breaks down and confesses her manipulations to Tommy and Kathy is that she is well aware how close to her "completion" she is already after her first donation—one can safely presume that, without the traumatic background of being a clone raised for donations, she would remain what she was, a rather insolent seductress playing with other people's emotions and even joyfully bringing them pain. I find the crux of the film in depicting how the depressive atmosphere of knowing one's fate affects all the spheres of subjects' lives.

So let's go to the end in these risky speculations: what one should reject is the fake "wise" concluding meditation of Kathy where she arrives at the result that, in some sense, all "normal" humans resemble clones: we are all caught in destiny imposed by an anonymous other and awaiting a certain death . . . Or, to put it in a different way: *Never Let Me Go* struggles with the big enigma of our time: why do people not rebel—even when they clearly know their way of life leads to a global catastrophe? Why is indifference emerging more and more as the predominant stance of our life which is only occasionally interrupted by wild rebellions that really change nothing?

The answer suggested by the film is much more subtle than a simple critique of conformism since it introduces a key difference: we "normal" humans do not know when and how, exactly, we will die, and this uncertainly sustains our secret disavowed hope that—maybe, just maybe—we will *not* die. In other words, our "normal" everyday existence is based on a disavowal of what we all know well, but at an abstract impersonal (not-subjectivized) way. To paraphrase the well-known syllogism, all people are mortal, but maybe I am not . . . In *Never Let Me Go*, we are compelled to fully assume our mortality—the ultimate act of reconciliation.

Variation 5
Moderately conservative communism

In a recent paper,[1] Michael Millerman argues that far-right Russian philosopher Aleksandr Dugin is a legitimate heir to Heidegger. For Millerman, Heidegger is not just one of the sources or inspirations of Dugin's philosophy. A proper understanding of his thought plays a key role in determining Russia's future: to master Heidegger's thought is "the main strategic task of the Russian people and Russian society," and "the key to the Russian tomorrow."[2] This is why the question of Dugin's Heideggerianism is crucial for our understanding of what goes on now in Russia at a spiritual level. How, then, does Heidegger become "Khaydegger" (his name written in Russian)? To what subtle changes does Dugin submit Heidegger's edifice?

For Dugin, the transcendental-ontological analysis of *Dasein* that Heidegger deploys in his *Being and Time* is not universal: every civilization gives birth to its specific form rooted in a collective spirituality. The Russian *Dasein* is thus different from the German one; it focuses on "*narod*," the people in the sense of German *Volk*, not the state, not the nation (nationalism), not race (Fascism), not class (Marxism), and especially not liberal individualism. "*Narod*" is thus an ontological category, it designates a historically-specific form of the disclosure of Being, of how its members perceive what matters in their lives, what gives their lives meaning, what freedom and dignity mean in their spiritual universe. For an authentic Russian, "freedom" is something different from the liberal notion of human rights and freedoms, it is a mode of free immersion into the spiritual substance of one's people; only this can provide dignity and meaning to life .

For Dugin, philosophy is thus immanently political, inclusive of advocating war: war in Ukraine is a war between Western global modernism and the Eurasian spirituality. There is war because (as Heidegger saw) the West reached its deepest decline in global liberal hegemony, Western modernity is Evil embodied, while Russia did not yet fully articulate its Eurasian spiritual identity—this task still lies ahead, and only Russian philosophy grounded in Heidegger can do it. Here Dugin replaces Germany (for Heidegger, the unique spiritual nation) with Russia: a "new beginning"—the awakening expected by Heidegger, a new *Ereignis*—will take place in Russia, not in Germany, not even in the West. Dugin substantiates this with reference to the Russian language itself: he notes how terms that sound artificial in Heidegger's German (like "*in-der-Welt-sein*," being-in-the-world) have much more natural everyday equivalents in Russian.

Dugin is not simply a Rightist against the Left, he notices how at a certain point Bolshevism itself took a Eurasian turn.[3] One should mention here Aleksandr Blok, the great Russian poet who wrote *The Twelve*, the great ode to the October Revolution: he was quickly disappointed by the Bolshevik Revolution and his last work before his early death in 1921 was a patriotic poem "Scythians" which advocates a kind of "pan-Mongolism," a clear precursor to today's Eurasianism—Russia should mediate not only between the East and the West but also politically between the Reds and the Whites to end the self-destructive civil war. This is also why Dugin prefers Stalin to Lenin: in 1921 Lenin conceived the task of Bolshevism as bringing Russia as fast as possible to Western modernity, while this reference to the West disappears with Stalin.

Dugin is also not simply opposed to the West: his target is modernity which culminates in liberal individualism. One should note here that a similar reading of Heidegger as a tool to fend off global Western modernization is practiced not only in Russia or some other Slavic countries but also in non-Slavic countries from Romania to Iran. (In my own country, Slovenia, some Heideggerians were interpreting Dostoyevsky—whom Dugin otherwise rejects—as a case of overcoming Western nihilism.) Dugin solicits every country, every people, to get rid of the liberal-individualist yoke of global modernity and discover its own specific spirituality. The role of Russia is to defeat the global West and thus to give each country, the Western ones included, the freedom to discover its own spirituality—one may say that Dugin provides a philosophical version of the idea of a multipolar world embodied in the political notion of BRICS.

Dugin's influence should nonetheless not be overrated: he stands for an extreme tendency of creating through military victory a new Eurasian empire dominated by Russian Orthodoxy, and his partisans consider Putin way too soft. However, what Dugin writes should be taken seriously as an indicator of the dangers posed by neo-Fascism. In a short text from September 2024, Aleksandr Dugin did something that shocked even me, used to all kinds of bad surprises in theory and politics: he applied Lacan's Real/Symbolic/Imaginary triad to analyze the role of Donald Trump and Kamala Harris in the forthcoming US presidential elections. Here is how Dugin presents the triad RSI:

> The Real is the domain where every object is strictly identical to itself. This absolute identity (A=A) excludes the very possibility of becoming, i.e., of being in a state of transformation. Thus, the Real is the zone of pure death and nothingness. There are no changes, movements, or relations. The Real is true, like the truth of nothingness that has no alternatives.
>
> The Symbolic is the domain where nothing equals itself, where one thing always refers to another. It is an escape from the Real, motivated by the desire to avoid death and falling into nothingness. It is here that content, relationships, movements, and transformations are born, but always in a dreamlike state. The Symbolic is the unconscious. The essence of a symbol is that it points to something other than itself (it does not matter what specifically, as long as it is not itself).
>
> The Imaginary is the domain where the dynamic of the Symbolic stops, but without the object dying and collapsing into the Real. The Imaginary is what we mistakenly take for Being, the world, ourselves—nature, society, culture, and politics. It is everything, yet it is also a lie. Every element of the Imaginary is actually a frozen moment of the Symbolic. Wakefulness is a form of sleep that does not realize itself. Everything in the Imaginary refers to the Symbolic but presents itself as supposedly "Real."
>
> In the Real, A=A is true. In the Symbolic, A=A is false. In the Imaginary, no object is identical to itself, but unlike in the Symbolic, it doesn't want to

admit this—neither to itself nor to others. The Real is nothing. The Symbolic is ever-changing becoming. The Imaginary consists of false nodes of the frozen Symbolic.[4]

Everything is wrong in this description: what Dugin misses is precisely the interconnection of the three dimensions illustrated by the figure of the Borromean knot. The Real is not a self-identity (A=A is strictly the formula of symbolic identity) but an obstacle immanent to the Symbolic, the impossibility of A=A, of any symbolic identity to fully actualize itself. (A classic example: the Real of sexual difference means that, in a patriarchal society, a woman cannot achieve the full actualization of her potentials. Or: the Real of class antagonism means that a society is never an organic Whole.) The Symbolic itself is a system of differential identities: the identity of each element resides in its differences from other elements. In this sense, the Symbolic cannot be simply identified with the unconscious: it is primarily what Lacan calls the big Other, the socio-symbolic order which provides the basic coordinates of a society. (Along these lines, the Name-of-the-Father is a figure of the symbolic Law.) The aim of the analytic process is to bring a subject to the point at which s/he accepts that there is no big Other, that every figure of the big Other is traversed by the Real of an antagonism. The Imaginary also cannot be reduced to a frozen Symbolic: imaginary is also, at its most basic, what Lacan called the experience of a dismembered body (*le corps morcele*), the chaotic flow of bodily parts not yet united in a body . . . However, what we should focus on is how this applies to the forthcoming US elections. In Dugin's view, Kamala Harris represents the Symbolic, she

> embodies an invitation to transgression, the legalization of perversions, and liberation from all prohibitions and norms, i.e., the expansion of the Symbolic realm. The Democrats' platform is a structure of well-tempered delirium: more LGBT, more cancel culture, more illegal immigrants, more drugs and gender reassignment surgeries, more deconstruction of old orders, more BLM and critical race theory.

The Democrats' platform is thus in some sense psychoanalytic: since the Symbolic is unconscious, it repeats the old Leftist-Freudian gesture of liberating the unconscious from the constraints of oppressive order. But what Lacan knew and the Leftist Freudians ignored is the basic lesson of all revolutions: when the repressed symbolic unconscious destroys the imaginary order and is set free, such a direct assertion of the unconscious immediately gives birth to a new fixed imaginary order which is much more oppressive and totalitarian than the previous order ... It may appear that Dugin hit the right button against Lacano-Marxists—when asked "What were the political consequences of Jacques Lacan's teaching?", Jacques-Alain Miller (who really knows Lacan) replied:

> Lacan said that he was not progressive, that he did not believe in progress. For him, history was rather circular, in a way.... He was not progressive, he was not conservative and, at the same time, he did not believe in total change because he thought that if you leave a master, or destroy a master, then you will find another master. We have seen that very clearly with Soviet communism, for example. Stalin was a much fiercer master than the Tsar.[5]

But Miller is here not very original: such a warning against radical change is an old conservative-liberal commonplace first formulated by Edmund Burke in his critique of the French Revolution. (The case of Hegel is more subtle: in his *Phenomenology of Spirit* he has shown how absolute freedom necessarily turns into terror, but this passage was for him a necessary step towards the establishment of civil peace.) The gap that separates Miller and Dugin appears when we pass to the next question: how are we to counteract this radical tendency frozen in new totalitarian Imaginary? Dugin claims that the only way to really undermine Democratic delirium is to rely on right-wing symbolic delirium represented by groups like Proud Boys and pro-Trump commentators:

> Where can we find a counterattack on the frozen liberal Imaginary, which has turned into overt totalitarianism? The answer is obvious: in the opposite pole, which we can call "Trumpist Symbolic." We saw the signs of this strategy during Trump's first presidential campaign in the Alt-Right, on 4chan, in the figure of the meme Pepe the Frog, in reptilian conspiracy theories, chaos magic, and the delirious theories of QAnon. We might call this "esoteric Trumpism" or, more precisely, "psychedelic Trumpism." If the

Democrats and their transgressive practices have become the Imaginary—frozen in totalitarian prescriptive power structures—then critique from the Symbolic has naturally focused on the Republicans. Of course, not all Republicans, but the most liberated, "unhinged," and delirious factions.

And the key figure for Dugin is J.D. Vance—he even speculates Vance may be familiar with Lacan:

> In Vance, the Democrats' psychoanalytic strategy fails, as Vance himself embodies the atypical right-wing Symbolic pole. It is even possible that he understands this and is familiar with Lacan.

So here is where we finish: Vance as a Lacanian ... The underlying political vision of Dugin which sustains such madness is not just a project of European nationalists and traditional Muslims working together against global liberalism but also a project of Left and Right working together against the liberal centre:

> In the West, there are both excellent right-wing and very respectable left-wing figures. For instance, the AfD (Alternative for Germany) is a remarkable right-wing movement, and Sahra Wagenknecht is an outstanding leftist.

But the split is not only between the honest true anti-globalist Left and the globalist Left; there is a homologous split on the Right, between true anti-globalist Right and the Right which willingly participates in the globalist liberal game:

> there are European far-right individuals who join forces with Nazis from the Azov battalion to fight against us [Russia]. These far-right individuals conveniently ignore the fact that Zelensky is a Jewish liberal clown, a drug addict, and a pervert. How can these people be considered right-wing? They are merely service dogs on the liberal NATO leash.

We learn a lot from this passage with a clear anti-Semitic sting: NATO is not a right-wing organization but a liberal military union opposed by all true Right-wingers (I am tempted to agree with this claim—with some reservations). The basic implication of these lines is clear: the utter demonization of European liberalism:

> There are no good liberals. All liberals are aligned with the world government and Western hegemony. Anyone on their side is an absolute enemy of both true right-wing and true left-wing people. This is because capitalism is pure evil and must be destroyed from both the right and the left, simultaneously.[6]

These lines are not a crazy dream—in some sense they are true: the ongoing war between Russia and Ukraine is ultimately not a war for territory or economic and political influence, it is a properly metaphysical war. So what will happen when/if the joined Right and Left annihilate liberalism? Will it not be an even more brutal pure conflict? Plus how can the idea that "capitalism is pure evil and must be destroyed from both the right and the left, simultaneously" be united with Dugin's advocacy of Russia, China, etc., which are not anti-capitalist but simply authoritarian-capitalist? Dugin is anti-capitalist only insofar as capitalism is liberal, he accepts capitalism controlled and regulated by a strong nation-state grounded in national tradition—a dream of all fascists. As Lacan and Miller have been repeating for more than half a century, capitalism is global, which means that the opposition between its liberal version and its authoritarian version is immanent to it.

During the last decade of his work, Lacan was obsessed with Marx's critique of political economy. The central category of his work in this period, his notion of surplus-enjoyment (*plus-de-jouir*), is elaborated through a constant reference to Marx's notion of surplus-value. This reliance on Marx indicates that Lacan was desperately searching for a way out of capitalism, and that he

> envisioned psychoanalysis as the way out of capitalism, which in some sense, was already underway in the years after 1968. But he asks more, that psychoanalysis be the way out of capitalism for more than just some.[7]

Lacan's quest for the way out of capitalism leads him in the direction of sainthood, but he defines sainthood in a very specific way: a saint is the one who wholly adopts excremental identity, who is reduced to a piece of shit—it is not that we should all become saints in the usual sense of the term. What we should learn is to step outside the capitalist superego pressure to acquire and to be "more and more," to incessant progress, outside its economy of expanded self-reproduction which also survived in classical Marxism and really-existing

Socialism. One could speculate that what Lacan aims at with sainthood is close to *Gelassenheit*, a term used by Angelus Silesius which is generally translated as "releasement." *Gelassenheit*, a key word of Heidegger's later thought, names the fundamental attunement (*Grundstimmung*) with which human beings are to authentically relate to other beings and to being itself. It contrasts with the fundamental attunement—or rather dis-attunement—of the will.[8] Here is the key proposition from Lacan's *Television*:

> A saint's business, to put it clearly, is not caritas. Rather, he acts as trash (*déchet*); his business being trashitas (*il décharite*).[9]

And here is Francois Regnault's commentary on this proposition:

> Here begins the paradox, for in common image a saint does indeed charity. Lacan suggests that it is precisely this charity that the saint gets rid of, the saint discharges himself of the burden of charity. And in this way, "trachity" (*déchariter*) is a condensation of trash and charity and, I add, begins like *décharge*, the loaded term that it is.[10]

Lacan's stance against charity gains new force today when charitable activities have become a key component of big corporations (just recall the Bill and Melinda Gates Foundation with tens of billions of dollars' worth of donations). For Lacan, charity remains firmly within the traditional logic of the Supreme Good: it allows corporations to re-inscribe their superego incessant striving for surplus-profit into the contribution to the welfare of all. But can we effectively suspend the capitalist superego through sainthood which is ultimately an inner subjective stance?

Lacan's overall view is a pessimistic one: our future will in all probability be a new form of global capitalism supplemented by new religious nationalisms (which is effectively happening now), and psychoanalysis itself as a specific practice (in which the analyst functions as an excremental saint) will also probably disappear. Psychoanalysis is not eternal, it is possible only within specific social conditions. I remain here a Marxist: the capitalist superego is also not just an inner subjective stance, it is embedded in a complex network of social and ideological relations and in practices which materialize these relations, and the anti-capitalist struggle should go on at this level.

Miller drew the opposite conclusion about the social implications of Lacan's theory: Lacan's critique of the 1968 student protests was basically a defense of moderate and modest liberalism which compels us to avoid extremes and to maintain a fragile balance of the components of the social Borromean knot. We definitely get in Lacan a conservative aspect, a liberal aspect and a Leftist anti-capitalist aspect, but Dugin all too quickly identifies traditional liberalism and the Cancel Culture which, although it radicalizes certain liberal tendencies, is opposed by many liberals. Plus it is Dugin himself who, in his eschatological vision of the struggle to death between global liberalism and the combined "good" Left and Right, advocates a radical violent change which cannot but end in new terror.[11]

So where do I stand here? I define myself as a moderately conservative Communist. A Communist because it seems obvious to me that only a radical social change will enable us to cope with the mortal threats to our survival (the environmental changes, AI controlling our lives, new social disturbances). Conservative because, if one follows Walter Benjamin, insofar as revolutions in the linear-evolutionary sense mean big victories which leave devastation in their wake (British colonization of India pushed India towards modernity but left behind millions of dead, etc.), we should not be afraid to say that the Benjaminian revolution would be the ultimate counter-revolution: the return and revenge of all the discarded and disposable against the terrible price of progress. Moderate because we should always consider the unintended catastrophic consequences of what we are doing and learn to combine radical measures with steps back. When, in 1922, after winning the Civil War against all odds, the Bolsheviks had to retreat into NEP (the "New Economic Policy" of allowing a much wider scope of market economy and private property), Lenin wrote a wonderful short text "On Ascending a High Mountain."[12] He uses the simile of a climber who has to retreat back to the valley from his first attempt to reach a new mountain peak in order to describe what a retreat means in a revolutionary process, i.e., how does one retreat without opportunistically betraying one's fidelity to the Cause.

This triad of *moderate conservative Communism*, my own socio-political Borromean knot, perfectly fits what Lacan aims at with his recourse to this figure. Although it offers a version of politics different from Lacan's anti-progressive pessimism, it remains anti-progressive pessimist *Communism*. And it rejoins Lacan at his crucial critical insight about the May 1968 protests. Psychoanalysis is as a rule misunderstood either in a pseudo-Leftist way (we should strive for abolishing all forms of repression, for fully liberating sexuality) or in a conservative way (a level of repression is necessary to prevent social disintegration and public morality). Jacques Lacan offers here a surprise: he defines the goal of psychoanalytic treatment in our era of permissiveness as the restoration of a minimum of shame.[13] The true opposition is not the one between free sexuality and repression but the one between shamelessness and dignity. It is difficult to overestimate the political relevance of Lacan's stance: protesters attack the shamelessness of their opponents and demand to be treated with dignity.

Why shame? In his seminar "The Reverse of Psychoanalysis"(1969–1970), Lacan's reaction to the May 1968 events, he makes a much more important point than the decried provocative statement: "What you aspire to as revolutionaries is a master. You will get one."—in his critique of protesting students, he surprisingly says: "all you are lacking precisely is a bit of shame." Lacan repeatedly varies this motif, like saying that students "fear they might be carried away by buffoonery. Let us start rather from the fact that buffoonery is already there. Perhaps by mixing in a little shame, who knows, we may be able to hold it back." And he even concludes the Seminar with: "what I put forward, for the majority of you, it is just that: I manage to make you ashamed, not too much but precisely enough."[14]

Jacques-Alain Miller[15] provides the background of this statement by way of pointing out that we have to read contemporary shamelessness from the perspective of a certain mutation in capitalism, no longer a capitalism that relies on "repression of enjoyment," as in Max Weber's famous analysis of permissiveness: "the new mode—if it bears the mark of a style at all—is rather that of permissiveness, where what can sometimes be the cause of difficulty is the prohibition on prohibiting."[16]

*

Lacan doesn't advocate here a minimum of morality and/or repression that should be maintained to prevent social disintegration—on the contrary, he draws attention to what, already back in the 1940, the Frankfurt School members referred to as "repressive desublimation": what we are getting today is a kind of generalized perversion (openly doing what hysterics only dream about), and as already Freud knew, nowhere is the Unconscious more inaccessible, more repressed, than in perversion. The catch is that desire is in itself, immanently, inconsistent, self-contradictory, traversed by what Freud called "primordial repression," which is why the permissiveness of perversion ends up in a self-destructive deadlock which gives birth to the call for a new Master. And, as the ongoing wave of new populism aptly demonstrated, this new Master's shamelessness by far exceeds the shamelessness of the old Leftist protesters.

One has to be very precise here: shame is not a defense against too much of desire, it is a *defense of desire*, of the lack that constitutes it, against the excess of its over-saturation which obliterates it. At this level, desire and need can also be correlated as excess and lack: the capitalist excess of uselessness products necessarily leads to a lack of things one actually needs for survival, and this imbalance is structural: one cannot simply resolve it by way of producing things people really need.[17] And, at yet another level, is Israel now not caught in a similar paradox with regard to its territorial expansion? Israel tries to achieve security by way of occupying neighbouring territory from where an enemy may attack it, as is now the case with southern Syria—"in Netanyahu's new Middle East, Syria could become Israel's biggest strategic gain."[18] However, the more neighbouring territory it occupies (with a view to annex it or at least occupy it indefinitely), the more animosity this occupation triggers, so that Israel will then be forced to occupy even more territory—and such a situation makes one suspicious that the expansion itself is the true goal. So, again, the more Israel does to secure its safety, the more it proclaims that its very survival is in danger.

Variation 6

The painted void

The Void: Wyeth, David

Andrew Wyeth's masterpiece *Christina's World* (1948) depicting a woman (Anna Christina Olson) dragging herself through a tawny field towards a distant homestead gave birth to a whole series of more optimistic imitations, homages and versions—which could be seen as many attempts to cancel its traumatic impact.[1] The two exemplary new versions are photographer Alex Thompson's tribute to Andrew Wyeth's *Christina's World* taken in 2005 at the site of the Olsons' house in South Cushing, Maine, and the Joshua Blankinship *Modern Recreation of Christina's World by Wyeth*.[2] The main feature of these new versions are much more lively colours which obfuscate the monotone grey-brown tone of the original. One should also mention another key fact: the two buildings we see in the background are moved much closer, with almost no space between them.

Why is this last feature so important? Read properly, it belies the predominant interpretation of the painting according to which "Wyeth portrays the countryside as an escape, an arcadia. Christina leans towards her farmhouse. She longs to be home again; she wants us to come with her."[3] Really? The gap between the two buildings forms the lower part of a screen onto which we expect the crawling woman to project her fantasies—it is this frame, not the two buildings of her home, that attracts Christina, and the frame remains empty. Wyeth-the-realist working in the age of Rothko and Pollock was right to claim that he is also an abstractionist: its colours and formal dispositions are more important than the painted content.

Let us draw another analogy here—consider the uniqueness of Jean-Louis David's "*The Death of Marat*" (1793), which depicts the revolutionary journalist slumped dead in his bath, his torso twisting to face the viewer.[4] It is "the first modernist painting," according to T. J. Clark, however the oddity of the painting's overall structure is seldom noted: its upper half is almost totally black. (This is not a realistic detail: the room in which Marat actually died had lively wallpaper.) What does this black void stand for? The opaque body of the People, the impossibility of representing the People—it is as if the impenetrable dark background of the painting (the People) invades it, occupying its entire upper half.

What happens here is structurally homologous to a formal procedure often found in *film noir* and Orson Welles movies, when the discord between figure and background is mobilized: when a figure moves in a room, the effect is that the two are somehow ontologically separated, as in a clumsy rear-projection shot in which one can clearly see that the actor is not really in a room, but just moving in front of a screen onto which the image of a room is projected. In "*The Death of Marat*," it appears as if we see Marat in his bathtub in front of a dark screen onto which the fake background has not yet been projected—this is why the effect can also be described as one of anamorphosis: we see the figure, while the background remains an opaque stain; in order to see the background, we would have to blur the figure. But what is impossible is to get the figure and the background in the same focus. Is this not also the logic of the Jacobin Terror? Individuals must be annihilated in order to make the People visible; the People's Will can be made visible only through the terrorist destruction of the individual's body? Therein resides the uniqueness of *The Death of Marat*: it concedes that one cannot blur the individual in order to represent the People directly—all one can do to come as close as possible to an image of the People is to show the individual at the point of his disappearance—his tortured, mutilated dead body against the background of the blur that "is" the People.[5]

The woman in Wyeth's painting is Christina Olson, his friend, who was a disabled woman. We see her in front of her home in Maine close to the ocean, and the reason she is on the ground, almost crawling across the field towards her house, is that she was the victim of a degenerative muscular disorder.

Christina refused to use any mobility aids, so what we're seeing in the painting is her literally pulling herself across the field—back to her house—using just her arms.⁶ Therein resides the link with *Never Let Me Go*: Wyeth stated that he wanted

> to do justice to her extraordinary conquest of a life which most people would consider hopeless. If in some small way I have been able in paint to make the viewer sense that her world may be limited physically but by no means spiritually, then I have achieved what I set out do.⁷

Is this not exactly homologous with the situation of the heroes of *Never Let Me Go*? Are they also not spiritually awakened through their very physical limitation, much worse than that of Catherine's? And what all of them—the heroes of *Never Let Me Go*, David's Marat, Wyeth's Christina—share is that they don't fill in the empty frame with some ideological fantasy content (as we usual mortals do).

Courbet: The Deadlock of Male Desire

So let's risk one step more: what David was for the French Revolution, Gustave Courbet was for the Paris Commune. There is a well-known recent scandal that concerns Courbet: in Metz, an incident occurred at the exposition of art works linked to Jacques Lacan. Two feminists staged a protest in front of Gustave Courbet's *The Origin of the World* owned by Lacan; Deborah de Robertis wrote "MeToo" on the painting which depicts a headless torso of a sexually aroused naked woman's body, focused on her hairy vulva. The title of a predominant feminist reaction tells it all: "Hurrah for the Courbet vandals: defacing the vulva painting is basic feminism"—de Robertis "is right to think the painting is misogynistic: the model doesn't even have a face!"⁸ But are things really so clear and simple? While fully respecting the feminist objections as well as rejecting the traditionalist academic disdain for de Robertis's act, I think things are more complex. Yes, there is a long history of women dismembered by a (male) painter—recall *A Woman Throwing a Stone* (Picasso,

1931): the distorted fragments of a woman on a beach throwing a stone[9]—one should not forget that it was made by a male painter tearing apart a woman's body.

So let's begin with politics. Courbet was imprisoned for six months in 1871 for his involvement with the Paris Commune and lived in exile in Switzerland from 1873 until his death four years later. As for the fact that the torso is headless, we should remember that back in 2014, de Robertis already performed a feminist act in Musee d'Orsay: in front of the same painting, she sat down with her legs widely spread, fully exposing her vulva to the spectators.[10] This confrontation of the real displayed vagina with her fantasmatic double in a painting produces the effect of "This is not a vagina," like that of "This is not a pipe" in the famous Magritte painting—the scene in which a real person is shown side by side with the ultimate image of what she is in the fantasy for the male Other. But is a woman really more "objectivized" when painted as a headless torso?

To grasp what is happening here, one should recall the paradigmatic hardcore sexual position (and shot) which is easy to identify: the woman is lying on her back with her legs spread wide backwards and with her knees above her shoulder; the camera is in front, showing the man's penis penetrating her vagina (his face is as a rule invisible, he is reduced to an instrument), but what we see in the background between her thighs is her face in the thrall of orgasmic enjoyment. This minimal "reflexivity" is crucial: if we were just to see the close-up of penetration, the scene would soon turn boring, disgusting even, more of a medical showcase—one has to add the woman's enthralled gaze, the subjective reaction to what is going on. Furthermore, this gaze is as a rule not addressed at her partner who is producing the supposed pleasure but directly at us—we, the spectators, clearly play the role of the big Other who has to register her enjoyment. The pivot of the scene is thus not male (her sexual partner's or the spectator's) enjoyment: the spectator is reduced to a pure gaze, the pivot is woman's enjoyment (staged for the male gaze, of course). The sad irony here is that the very fact that the woman is not "objectivized" but rendered as a subject makes her humiliation worse: she has to fake her enjoyment. Being compelled to enact fake subjective engagement is much worse than being reduced to an object.

So, back to the photo of the painting and the "real" de Robertis displaying her vulva: the paradox is that, no matter what her intentions were, the real de Robertis displaying her vulva is much closer to pornography than Courbet's painting precisely because her vulva is accompanied by her gaze (her head looking at us), while the effect of Courbet's painting is much more disturbing— why, precisely? While it is not, of course, a feminist painting in any sense (it clearly addresses a male gaze), it clearly renders the deadlock (or dead end) of the traditional realist painting, whose ultimate object—never fully and directly shown, but always hinted at, present as a kind of underlying point of reference— was the naked and thoroughly sexualized feminine body as the ultimate object of male desire and look. The exposed feminine body functioned here in a way similar to the underlying reference to the sexual act in classic Hollywood, best described in the famous instruction of the movie tycoon Monroe Stahr to his scriptwriters from Scott Fitzgerald's *The Last Tycoon*:

> At all times, at all moments when she is on the screen in our sight, she wants to sleep with Ken Willard. . . . Whatever she does, it is in place of sleeping with Ken Willard. If she walks down the street she is walking to sleep with Ken Willard, if she eats her food it is to give her enough strength to sleep with Ken Willard. But at no time do you give the impression that she would even consider sleeping with Ken Willard unless they were properly sanctified.

The exposed feminine body is thus the impossible object, it functions as the ultimate horizon of representation whose disclosure is forever postponed—in short, it functions as the Lacanian incestuous Thing. Its absence, the Void of the Thing, is then filled in by "sublimated" images of beautiful, but not totally exposed, feminine bodies, i.e., by bodies which always maintain a minimum of distance towards That. But the crucial point (or, rather, the underlying illusion) of the traditional painting is that the "true" incestuous naked body nonetheless waits there to be discovered—in short, the illusion of traditional realism does not reside in the faithful rendering of the depicted objects; it rather resides in the belief that, *behind* the directly rendered objects, there effectively IS the absolute Thing which could be possessed if we were only able to discard the obstacles or prohibitions that prevent access to it.

We can read many pre-modern paintings as pointing towards the Thing which remains off frame—suffice it to recall the (wrongly) so-called mystery of Mona Lisa's smile. I think it is a fake mystery—there is no secret behind her smile. Its best explanation is provided by Slovene (my own) language—every (honest) Slovene knows what the smile of Mona Lisa is about. Slovenes do not have their own dirty words, they have to borrow them, mostly from Serbo and Croat, but also from Italian. We know that "Mona" is a popular Italian name for vagina, and "lisa" (pronounced "leeza") is the root of the Slovene verb "to lick"—Mona Lisa's smile is the satisfied smile of getting a gentle cunnilingus. There is a modern parodic painting *The real Mona Lisa* which, I think, renders her quite appropriately in her stupid satisfaction after the cunnilingus.

What Courbet accomplished in his *Origin* is the gesture of radical desublimation: he made the risky move and simply went all the way, directly depicting what the previous realistic art was just hinting at as its withdrawn point of reference—the outcome of this operation, of course, was the reversal of the sublime object into abject, into an abhorring, nauseating excremental piece of slime. This disgusting slime is not the "truth" of the sublime appearance: true love is able to assert the identity of the two—here is a nice case of it. A classic (not always) comic film scene is that of the (persecuted) hero finding himself in front of a large audience, mistaken for another; he has to improvise a talk about a topic of which he is wholly ignorant (Robert Donat in Hitchcock's *39 steps*, mistaken for a local politician, improvises an electoral speech; Joseph Cotten in *The Third Man*, mistaken for a serious writer, answers questions about James Joyce, etc.). The latest version occurs in *Bean* (directed by Mel Smith, with Rowan Atkinson), in which Bean, a disastrously stupid low-level employee of the English National Gallery, is sent to Los Angeles to present Whistler's portrait of his mother, bought by a rich local gallery from Musee d'Orsay for 50 million dollars. Here is Bean's short speech:

> Well, hello, I'm Dr Bean, apparently, and my job is to sit and look at paintings. (Applause) So what have I learnt that I can say about this painting? Well . . . Well, firstly, it's quite big, which is excellent, because if it was really small, you know, microscopic, then hardly anybody would be able to see it, which

would be a tremendous shame. And secondly, and I'm getting quite near the end now of this analysis of this painting, secondly, why was it worth this man here spending 50 million of your American dollars on this portrait? And the answer is, well, this picture is worth such a lot of money because it's a picture of Whistler's mother, and as I've learnt by staying with my best friend, David Langley, and his family, families are very important, and even though Mr Whistler was perfectly aware that his mother was a hideous old bat who looked like she had a cactus lodged up her backside, he stuck with her and even took the time to paint this amazing picture of her. It's not just a painting. It's a picture of a mad old cow who he thought the world of, and that's marvelous. Well, that's what I think, anyway.

This speech is far from nonsense: it plays with the gap between the sublime and the ridiculous, relying on the notion of true love as the ability to find the sublime IN the ridiculous. This, however, is not Courbet's line: Courbet masterfully continued to dwell at the very blurred border that separates the sublime from the excremental: the woman's body in *Origin* retains its full erotic attraction, yet it becomes repulsive precisely on account of this excessive attraction. (Courbet painted also the head that belongs to the naked body in *Origin*—a proof that he knew very well that the head should not be included in the painting.) Courbet's gesture is thus a dead end: the dead end of traditional realist painting—but precisely as such, it is a necessary "mediator" between traditional and modernist art, i.e., it stands for a gesture that had to be accomplished if we are to "clear the ground" for the emergence of the modernist "abstract" art. How?

With Courbet, we learn that there is no Thing behind its sublime appearance, that if we force our way through the sublime appearance to the Thing itself, all we get is a suffocating nausea of the abject—so the only way to reestablish the minimal structure of sublimation is to directly stage *the void itself*, the Thing as the Void-Place-Frame, without the illusion that this Void is sustained by some hidden incestuous Object. One can now understand in what precise way, and paradoxical as it may sound, Malevitch's *Black Square* as the seminal painting of modernism is the true counterpoint to (or reversal of) *Origin*: in Courbet, we get the incestuous Thing itself which threatens to implode the

Clearing, the Void in which (sublime) objects (can) appear, while in Malevitch, we get its exact opposite, the matrix of sublimation at its most elementary, reduced to the bare marking of the distance between foreground and background, between a wholly "abstract" object (square) and the Place that contains it. The "abstraction" of the modernist painting is thus to be conceived as a reaction to the over-presence of the ultimate "concrete" object, the incestuous Thing, that turns it into a disgusting abject, i.e., that turns the sublime into an excremental excess.

Far from being a simple male-chauvinist depiction of the object of desire, Courbet's *Origin* thus confronts the male desire with its deadlock: what you really desire is a headless monster, and it is your gaze (sustained by desire) which decapitates the woman. The title of Courbet's painting could have been a version of Magritte's "*ita Ceci n'est pas une pipe*": "*Ceci n'est pas une vagine!*" In French vagina is masculine ("*le vagin*"), so why feminize it? Vagina in feminine ("*la vagine*") is a part of the entire feminine body (head, legs and arms included), while "*le vagin*" is not feminine but part of a headless monstrosity constructed by masculine fantasy. "*Ceci n'est pas une vagine*" is thus quite literally true: what we see on the painting is *le vagin*, so it should be "*ceci est un vagin.*"

Tristan's Chord and his Death

One should not be surprised to see this same void of desire staged in what is perhaps the first work that breaks the chains of classic tonality, Richard Wagner's *Tristan*. As we have already seen,[11] the axiom of the analytic interpretation holds that whenever a new Master-Signifier emerges and structures a symbolic field, we must look for the absent centre excluded from this field. Insofar as, in classical tonal music, the dominant plays a role similar to the Master-Signifier, it is the Prelude to *Tristan* which brings out for the first time the tension between multiple dominants (which are all absent, just implied) in a way which uncannily resembles quantum superpositions. Matthew Cord described perspicuously how, at its beginning,

> Wagner has made the key very clear from the outset, and you'll wonder why. The first reason why is because we're in a minor, but a minor is never stated

explicitly. What we're given is the Tristan chord turning to the dominant seven of a minor, so that could go to a minor—it never does but it implies that the tonality is a minor. We don't hear a minor, what we hear is the second phrase which takes us to C major. Well, we don't hear that either but it is implied, and then finally the third phrase takes us to the dominant of e minor.[12]

So not only is the resolution of the tension in the dominant forever postponed, not only does the dominant never directly appear, even this absent centre constantly changes. From a purely musical standpoint, we could argue that we get the resolution at *Tristan*'s very end, with the peace established by the *Liebestod*. But do we really get it? Recall what is for me the definitive staging of *Tristan*, Jean-Pierre Ponnelle's Bayreuth version (conducted by Daniel Barenboim in 1981, filmed in 1983): in Act III, Tristan dies alone (Isolde stayed with her husband, King Marke, her appearance at the opera's end is merely the dying Tristan's hallucination). The gap that prevents any resolution is here staged as the tension between the resolution in music and the reality of what we see on stage. Johanna Meier (the soprano who sang Isolde) reported about this ending:

> Ponnelle imagined Isolde would never appear, but sing from the pit, which idea was not favoured by me, nor by Barenboim, nor by Wolfgang Wagner, so in the final week of rehearsal Ponnelle began experimenting with various possibilities. Isolde here, Isolde there, Isolde arrives early, Isolde arrives late, etc. .... The final staging was decided on Opening Night, when I was informed in my dressing room between the 2nd and 3rd Act which version we would do. This version was used in all three years of the production, although it has been erroneously reported both in reviews and books that Ponnelle's first concept of Isolde singing from the pit was used.[13]

I think that while Ponnelle was playing with multiple superposed versions, his solution was the correct one—it clearly demonstrates that in *Tristan*, the very opera which elevates the lovers' shared death into its explicit ideological goal, this, precisely, is NOT what effectively happens. They approach this moment in the duet at the end of Act II ("*so stürben wir, um ungetrennt*"—"so we are dying, undivided"), but their orgasmic self-annihilation is cut short first by the warning of Brangaene and then by the brutal intrusion of King Marke. At the opera's end, they die one AFTER the other, each immersed in his/her own solipsistic dream. Along these lines, one should read Isolde's ecstatic death at the end of Tristan as the ultimate operatic prosopopea: Tristan can only die if his death is transposed onto Isolde. When Tristan repeats his claim that death could not destroy their love, Isolde provides the concise formula of their death: "But this little word 'and'—if it were to be destroyed, how but through the loss of Isolde's own life could Tristan be taken by death?"—in short, it is only in and through her death that he will be able to die.

Does Wagner's *Tristan* not then offer an example of the interpassivity of death itself, of the "subject supposed to die"? Tristan can only die insofar as Isolde experiences the full bliss of the lethal self-obliteration for him, in his place. In other words, what "really happens" in Act III of Tristan is *only Tristan's* long "voyage to the bottom of the night" with regard to which Isolde's death is Tristan's own fantasmatic supplement, the delirious construction that enables him to die in peace. Isolde's final appearance and ecstatic death in *Tristan* is the hallucination of the dying Tristan, so that the entire Act III, inclusive of the ending, is Tristan's monologue. Thomas May wrote about the long monologue of the dying Tristan:

> As the music heats up to the fever pitch in his staggered states of delirium, its excitement evokes nothing of the erotic character heard earlier in the drama. Its depiction of an emptiness at the core of desire is nothing short of terrifying, and this very realization fuels Tristan's suffering. This is what the word *passion* after all signifies in its root meaning.[14]

Ponnelle brings out this "emptiness at the core of desire" in a painfully-palpable way: when Isolde stops singing her *Liebestod*, the entire stage is enveloped in darkness for a couple of seconds, and then (a much weaker and greyish) light returns, showing the dead Tristan alone under the gigantic dead tree. Moreover, Isolde did not appear to the dying Tristan: she appears as an extra-bright hallucination *behind his back*. Tristan looks at us, the spectators, as if he sees Isolde in our gaze.[15] As in hardcore porn, we—the spectators—are reduced to a pure gaze, and the pivot is woman's enjoyment (here Isolde's ecstatic death) staged for the male gaze, but in a more complex way: a man (Tristan) sees the gaze seeing her dying. After Isolde disappears we see the dead Tristan deprived of all fantasmatic support, alone as he always was in the emptiness of his desire. Note that Isolde appears to the dying Tristan in the void that separates the two stems of the gigantic tree—the void which corresponds to the void that separates the two houses in Wyeth's painting, making the parallel between Christina and the dying Tristan perfect.

Variation 7

The many monsters of the cinema

Not only is appearance inherent to reality; what we get beyond reality is a weird split in appearance itself, an unheard-of mode designating "the way things really appear to us" as opposed to both their reality and their (direct) appearance to us. This shift from the split between appearance and reality to the split, inherent to appearance itself, between "true" and "false" appearance, is to be linked to its obverse, to a split inherent to reality itself. If, then, there is appearance (as distinct from reality) because there is a (logically) prior split inherent to reality itself, is it also that "reality" itself is ultimately nothing but a (self-)split of the appearance? However, how does this *topos* differ from the old boring Rashomon-motif of an irreducible multiplicity of the subjective perspectives on reality, with no way (no exempted position from which) to establish the one truth represented in a distorted way by these multiple perspectives?

The East: Rashomon

What better way to clarify this point than to refer to the very film (and the short story on which the film is based) whose title was elevated into a trope, Akira Kurosava's *Rashomon*? As the legend goes, it was through *Rashomon* that the Western public in the early 1950s discovered the "Oriental spirit" in cinema;

the lesser-known obverse of this legend is that *Rashomon* was a failure in Japan itself where it was perceived as all too "Western"—and one can well see why. When the same tragic event (in a lone forest, a well-known bandit rapes the samurai's beautiful wife and kills the samurai) is retold by four witnesses-participants, the effect (pertaining to the very Western realism of the cinematic image) is simply that we are told four different subjective perspectives. However, what effectively distinguishes the so-called "Oriental spirit" from the Western attitude is that, precisely, ambiguity and indecidability are not "subjectivized": they should not be reduced to different "subjective perspectives" on some reality beyond reach—they rather pertain to this "reality" itself, and it is this ontological ambiguity-fragility of the "thing itself" that it is difficult to render through the realism of the cinematic medium. What this means is that the authentic "rashomon" has nothing to do with the pseudo-Nietzschean perspectivism, with the notion that there is no objective truth, just an irreducible multitude of subjectively distorted-biased narratives.

*

The first thing to do apropos *Rashomon* is to avoid the formalist trap: what one is tempted to call the film's formal-ontological thesis (the impossibility to arrive at truth from multiple narratives of the same event) should NOT be abstracted from the particular nature of this event—the feminine challenge to the male authority, the explosion of feminine desire. The four witness-reports are to be conceived as four versions of the same myth (in the Levi-Straussian sense of the term), as a complete matrix of variations: in the first (bandit's) version, he raped the wife and then, in an honest duel, killed her husband; in the second (surviving's wife's) version, in the course of the rape, she got caught up in the passion of the bandit's forceful love-making and, at the end, tells him that she cannot live in shame with both the men knowing about her disgrace—one of them should die, and it is then that the duel ensues; in the third version (told by the ghost of the dead husband himself), after the husband is set free by the bandit, he stabs and kills himself out of shame; in the last version, told by the woodcutter who observed the events hidden in a nearby bush, when, after the rape, the bandit cuts the rope tying the husband, and the husband furiously rejects his wife calling her a dishonored whore, the ecstatically furious wife explodes against both men, reproaching them with weakness and challenging them to fight for her. The succession of the four versions is thus not neutral, they do not all move at the same level: in the course of their progression, the male authority is step by step weakened and the feminine desire asserted. So when we privilege the last (woodcutter's) report, the point is not that it tells what "truly happened," but that, within the immanent structure that links the four versions, it functions as the traumatic point with regard to which the other three versions are to be conceived as defenses, defense-formations.

The "official" message of the film is clear enough: at the very beginning, in the conversation that provides the frame for the flashbacks, the monk points out that the lesson of the events recounted is more terrifying than the hunger, war, and chaos that pervaded society at that time—in what does this horror reside? In the disintegration of the social link: there was no "big Other" on which people could rely, no basic symbolic pact guaranteeing trust and sustaining obligations. The film is thus not engaged in ontological games about how there is no ultimate unambiguous reality behind the multitude of narratives; it is rather concerned with the socio-ethical consequences of the disintegration of the basic symbolic pact that holds the social fabric together. However, the story—the incident retold from different perspectives—tells more: it locates the threat to the big Other, the ultimate cause that destabilizes the male pact and blurs the clarity of the male vision of a woman, of *feminine desire*. As already Nietzsche put it: in its very inconsistency and lack of any ultimate point of reference beneath multiple veils, truth is feminine.

The East: Monsters, Handmaiden

There are clear indications that the so-called Oriental spirituality, especially that of Japan and South Korea, provides a privileged site of superpositions in cinema. The definitive movie about superpositions is without doubt *Monsters* (Hirokazu Kore-Eda, Japan, 2023)—here is the outline of the story. Saori Mugino, a single mother, is raising her fifth-grade son Minato who begins exhibiting strange behaviour (cutting his own hair, coming home with only one shoe). One night, Minato does not come home at all and after calling around, Saori finds him in an abandoned train tunnel. Saori begins to suspect her son's teacher, Hori, is abusing him and confronts the school about it. She is treated coldly by the faculty, culminating in Hori making a disingenuous apology. When she confronts Hori directly, he asserts that Minato is actually bullying another student named Yori. Saori visits Yori's house and discovers that Yori, despite his strange behaviour, is fond of and concerned for Minato. Hori is eventually fired from the school, but returns there days later; Minato falls down a flight of stairs trying to escape from him. Hori later comes to Saori and Minato's house during a rain storm, but Minato has gone missing. At this point, a flashback returns to the beginning of the film from Hori's point of view. He notices Minato exhibiting disruptive behaviour, such as throwing other students' belongings around the classroom and seemingly locking Yori in a bathroom stall. Hori too visits Yori's house, where he discovers that his father, Kiyotaka, is an abusive alcoholic. When Saori begins inquiring about her son, the faculty requires Hori to resign. Hori returns to the school to confront Minato, and contemplates jumping from the roof. Back at home, Hori notices a pattern in Yori's old homework that seems to spell out Minato's name. Realizing the two boys were actually in love, Hori rushes to the Mugino household to apologize. When Saori tells him Minato is missing, they go to the train tunnel to find him. They find an abandoned railcar nearly buried in mud, but only see Minato's poncho inside. The final flashback begins from Minato's point of view. Yori plays with Minato's hair, which the latter then impulsively cuts off. The two boys grow close and Minato begins defending him from other bullies, which Hori confuses for bullying. As the two become closer, Minato is distressed that his feelings are becoming romantic and that he is not a worthy son to his father. One night when he goes to Yori's house, Yori and Kiyotaka declare that Yori has been "cured," though Yori quickly recants, which incites his father's wrath. During the rainstorm, Minato finds Yori fully clothed in his bathtub, covered in bruises, and the two escape to the abandoned railcar, which has become their hideout. After the rain subsides, they emerge from the bottom of the railcar and question whether they have been reborn, and run through a field together.[1]

Monsters is a movie about neighbours in the strict Judeo-Christian meaning of the term. One should clearly distinguish "neighbour" from merely a fellow man: fellow men are those who are like us, we immediately recognize in them the common ground that we share. Fellow men are friends, members of my family, co-workers, those whom I think I know intimately. A fellow man transforms himself into a neighbour when I detect in him a feature or a gesture which makes him a total strangers to me: "How could he do THAT? I never expected this from him. Is he one of us at all or an alien monster?" It is on account of this monstrosity of the neighbour that Lacan applies to the neighbour the term Thing (*das Ding*), used by Freud to designate the ultimate object of our desires in its unbearable intensity and impenetrability. One should hear in this term all the connotations of horror fiction: the neighbour is the (Evil) Thing which potentially lurks beneath every homely human face. Just think about Stephen King's *The Shining*, in which the father, a modest failed writer, gradually turns into a killing beast who, with an evil grin, goes on to slaughter his entire family. But a neighbour can also imply an unexpected positive surprise: a fellow man whom we considered just an ordinary person with all its weaknesses becomes a neighbour when he displays an unexpected courage or honesty.

In *Monsters*, we see how, first, Minato becomes a monster for his mother due to his weird acts, and to account for his weird acts and simultaneously de-monstrify Minato, she projects monstrosity onto his teacher Hori. In the first flashback, Hori is de-monstrified: we see him from his own standpoint as a modest and compassionate teacher who perceives a monstrosity in Minato, but is then compelled to see the inner tension of Minato who is not able to come to terms with his affection towards Yori. The interest of the film resides in the fact that it repeatedly performs the operation that is the exact opposite of a fellow man becoming a monstrous neighbour: when we shift the perspective to the inner experience of the monster him/herself, we see s/he is really a fellow man like us . . .

The obvious lesson of the film is that the ultimate monster is the patriarchal order itself, and for that reason, the only person who remains a monster is Kiyotaka, Yori's abusive and alcoholic father who wants to brutally "renormalize" his son and make him act as befits a boy—we never see the other side of his character that would made him more sympathetic since he is reduced to a ridiculous embodiment of the patriarchal stance. This fact indicates the limit of the film's ideological coordinates: the opposition of patriarchal culture and gay love is unconditional, there is no process of de-monstrification of patriarchy and of monstrification of gay love in this universe. (One should add here that the couple is not yet sexualized, so that the love of the two boys is asexual—a further compromise, because the asexual character of their love makes this love pure and innocent. Sexualization always implicates duplicity, deceit and a kind of monstrosity.)

The multiple standpoints of the film's narrative—flashbacks make us see the same events in a different light—are a strategy to de-monstrify someone who is perceived/constructed in the eyes of the others as a monster. What I find problematic here is the underlying premise which comes close to the utter fatuity masquerading as a deep wisdom: "An enemy is someone whose story you have not heard."[2] Are we also ready to affirm that Hitler was our enemy only because his story was not heard? Is it not that the more I know about and "understand" Hitler, the more Hitler is my enemy? Not to mention the fact that stories we are telling to ourselves are as a rule a lie manufactured to justify the horrors I am doing to others—the truth is out there, in what we are doing in reality. Every aggressor presents itself as a victim reacting to an aggression. That's why my motto is "no ethnic cleansing without poetry," that's why wars are sustained not only by an industrial-military complex but also by what one should call the *poetic-military complex*. We saw this complex at work in the post-Yugoslav war in the early 1990s, but to avoid the illusion that the poetic-military complex is a Balkan specialty, one should mention at least Hassan Ngeze who, in his journal *Kangura*, was systematically spreading anti-Tutsi hatred and calling for their genocide.

The predominance of religiously (or ethnically) justified violence can be accounted for by the very fact that we live in an era that perceives itself as post-ideological. The large majority of people are spontaneously "moral": killing another human being is deeply traumatic for them. So, in order to make them do it, a larger "sacred" Cause is needed, which makes petty individual concerns about killing seem trivial. Religion or ethnic belonging fit this role perfectly. Of course there are cases of pathological atheists who are able to commit mass murder just for pleasure, just for the sake of it, but they are rare exceptions. The majority needs to be "anaesthetized" against their elementary sensitivity to the other's suffering. For this, a sacred Cause is needed. More than a century ago, in his *Brothers Karamazov*, Dostoyevsky warned against the dangers of godless moral nihilism: "*If God doesn't exist, then everything is permitted.*" The lesson of today's terrorism is, on the contrary, that if there *is* a God, then everything, even blowing up hundreds of innocent bystanders, is permitted to those who claim to act directly on behalf of God, as the instruments of His will, since, clearly, a direct link to God justifies our violation of any "merely human" constraints and considerations. The "godless" Stalinist Communists are the ultimate proof of it: everything was permitted to them since they perceived themselves as direct instruments of their divinity, the Historical Necessity of Progress towards Communism. Religious ideologists usually claim that, true or not, religion makes some otherwise bad people do some good things; from today's experience, one should rather stick to Steven Weinberg's claim that, while, without religion, good people would have been doing good things and bad people bad things, only religion can make good people do bad things.

This is why the shifting perspectives in *Monsters* tell only half of the story. In the film, all characters (except Kiyotaka) are ethically rehabilitated when we hear their side of the story; even the headmistress of the school who treats Saori in a polite but brutally-dismissive way, ignoring her pain, is rehabilitated when we learn about the tragic accident that ruined her life. But one should still insist that this inner experience of trauma in no way justifies her brutal treatment of Saori: whatever her inner experience, the truth is that she acted in an ethically unacceptable way—or, in quantum mechanics terms, a superposition of two stances irreducibly marks her life.

There are some unexpected parallels between *Monsters* and *The Handmaiden*, Park Chan-wook's 2016 South Korean movie based on Sarah Waters' *Fingersmith*, a 2002 novel with a similar plot set in Victorian time which, prior to Chan-wook's movie, was already twice adapted: a BBC TV adaptation in 2005 and a stage adaptation in 2015. *The Handmaiden* also uses shifting perspectives (the same event, depicted from a different perspective, appears in a wholly new light), plus it praises homosexual (here lesbian) sexuality as resistance against violent patriarchy; the difference is here that same-sex love is here fully sexualized (some critics accused the film of getting too close to pornography), not just a pre-sexual gentle feeling of affection (as is the case in *Monsters*). What makes the movie interesting is that its shifts of perspective work in the opposite direction with regard to *Monsters*: the two women who first appear as naïvely-innocent are revealed to be involved in almost diabolically-evil plots (their naïvety was a fake), while the two main masculine persons are from the beginning presented as almost ridiculously evil, and in the course of the film their evil gradually gets even more diabolical. (There is no radical shift of perspective here, no other view that would at least partially justify their acts—to make a more general point, it is as if there are not enough flashbacks here, not enough shifts of standpoint.) It goes without saying that toxic masculinity is exploding all around the world, not only in new Right's male chauvinism in the "developed" West but also in Africa: in Kenya, the manosphere—a brutal polemics against the kind of behaviour deemed to devalue a man's worth, thereby making him a "simp"—is exploding in the last years. "Simp" means being overly submissive or attentive to women or begging or nagging for a woman's attention after rejection, and any men seeking validation from women through excessive or demeaning actions, such as apologizing or proposing marriage; such a stance should be opposed by proud assertion: "I'm an alpha male, you can't speak to me like this. I need to be treated like a king." Amerix, the main proponent of the manosphere, is also well known for his advocacy of fertility and men's health, often emphasizing diet, virility and the belief that men, especially Africans, should have many children.[3] However, one should add that, in all such cases, the manosphere is not a true display of strength but a clear sign of weakness and panic.

What redeems the two women is that, although each of the two is involved in a deadly plot against the other, they fall passionately in love with each other, and this love allows them to exit the vicious cycle of evil, while the two men both end up dead. One has to add here that the way the two women exit the circle of male domination is no less criminal—they both act in a brutal manipulative way against others. The world we end up in *The Handmaiden* is thus a world of global violence, manipulation and exploitation: there is no way out of it, the escape of the two women is limited to their sexual intimacy, while in their relations to others they fully remain within the world of corrupted manipulation. What if they—the two woman—are the paradigmatic subjects of our time (with "authentic" intimate experience somehow justifying their social behaviour), while one of the men at least (the fake "Count") is much more honest in his open admission of total corruption not justified by any inner authenticity?

Surprisingly (or not so), this brings us back to our first case, *Rashomon*. As we have already seen, the succession of the four versions is not neutral: in the course of their progression, the male authority is step by step weakened and the feminine desire asserted. This brings us to Lacan and his theory of feminine sexuality (and subjectivity): the multiplicity of superpositions is not a formal scheme indifferent with regard to sexual difference. The (irreducible) multiplicity of superpositions is as such, in itself, feminine, and its collapse into a single point is masculine. This in no way implies that femininity is reduced to a confusing ground which is magically turned into a single consistent order through the intervention of a masculine Master-Signifier (Sl)—quite on the contrary, the imposition of a single Master-Signifier obfuscates the multiplicity of Master-Signifiers themselves.

The East in the West: Romance Sentimentale

The very first episode of the first season of *The Twilight Zone* begins with a man who finds himself walking down a country road, not knowing who, nor where he is. He comes across a diner with a jukebox blaring and hot coffee on the stove—only no one's there. A little further down the road, he comes to the picturesque town of Oakwood, and finds it, too, seems deserted. The only sounds he hears are a clock tower and a pay phone ringing. At the local movie theater, an ad for *Battle Hymn* leads him to believe he's in the Air Force. In spite of there being no people to be found, he can't shake off the feeling that he's being watched. Finally he realizes that his experience in Oakwood was his hallucination—he is actually in an isolation booth being observed by a group of uniformed servicemen. He has been undergoing tests to determine his fitness as an astronaut and whether he can handle a prolonged trip to the Moon alone; the town was an hallucination caused by sensory deprivation.[4] While watching this episode (and not knowing the final twist), I was expecting a different final turn (remember that the episode was shot in 1958, in the midst of the Cold War): a nuclear bomb explodes above the empty Oakwood and totally destroys it—the man finds himself in a fake empty city which was constructed by the US Army to test how much and what kind of destruction is caused by a nuclear explosion ... The fact that he is a military pilot explains how he found himself at this spot: USA Army effectively made such experiments in the 1950s. My point is that we have here a genuine superposition: for a typical TV spectator at that time the testing of the effects of a nuclear explosion was a much more credible event. It is thus a safe presupposition that this version was the first that popped up in the minds of the TV spectators, and the creators of the episode were fully aware of this and were counting on it: the final twist only works because it avoids the superposed different twist.

This brings us to the second axiom of the analytic interpretation: the excluded dimension inscribes itself into the form of a work of art in its excess over its content, which is why for a Marxist the truth of an event or work resides in its form itself. Take George Orwell's *Animal Farm*: the story is obviously an account of how the October Revolution regressed into Stalinism. However, let's imagine that we would re-translate the story about animals rebelling against humans into a direct realist story about exploited humans rebelling against their masters, the result of their rebellion being an even worse tyranny—what we would get is a totally boring and predictable story without any artistic or political interest. All the libidinal charm comes from replacing humans with animals (the new nomenklatura are pigs, etc.). Animals are not just a metaphor: they confer on the story about a human rebellion a specific flavour.

Let's complicate this dialectic between form and content even further by another unexpected example. Sergei Eisenstein's and Grigori Aleksandrov's *Romance Sentimentale* (1930)[5], a 20-minute movie accompanied by music, is arguably the point of exception (and as such the symptomal point) in Eisenstein's entire work. In 1930, when Eisenstein and Aleksandrov found themselves on a tour of Western Europe before moving to the US and Mexico, a rich French businessman invited them to do a short film dedicated to his mistress who was also to star in it; Eisenstein and Aleksandrov accepted the task and quickly made a 20-minutes long *"romance sentimentale"* whose title perfectly fits the content. No wonder Eisenstein later not only disavowed the film but even denied having anything to do with it (Louis Bunuel, who at that time worked in the same Paris studio in which Eisenstein and Aleksandrov did their romance, confirmed it was their work).

One can easily understand the reason for Eisenstein's shame: the film demonstrates how his "revolutionary" procedure of montage of attractions can be used without any problem to film a "sentimental romance," the very epitome of bourgeois ideology. It is as if, in *Romance Sentimentale*, Eisenstein traversed the path from Grail to cream separator in the opposite direction. That is to say, in his remarks on the Jesuit techniques of meditation, he elaborated how the procedure which, according to Loyola, enables us to attend ecstatic contact with god can also be mobilized to attend ecstatic revolutionary engagement. The most famous example is the cream separator scene from *The Old and the New* in which the protagonist Marfa experiences a moment of pure bliss while, kneeling before the cream separator, she observes how the flow of cream begins to flow out of it. Eisenstein strives here to infuse the idea of collectivization and technological progress with the fervour of the "ecstasy of economics," i.e., to discern in the impact of elementary agricultural technology a properly religious ecstasy. In *Romance Sentimentale*, on the contrary, the procedure of generating ecstatic revolutionary fervour is used to give rise to moribund romantic sentimentality. In the first case, ideological ecstasy is reduced to its material base (production process), while in the second case, revolutionary material practice is used as a tool of ideological mystification.

Upon a closer look, however, we can see how things get more complex. *Romance Sentimentale* is composed of four parts. The first part (*ca.* 5 minutes) is a pure exercise in montage of fragments destined to render what Deleuze would have called pure impersonal intensity: turbulent nature, waves crushing, trees falling, hectic forward movement, etc., accompanied by fragmentary modern music (even some siren sounds), gradually slowing down and passing into the melody of the elegiac love song. The turbulent passion is pacified, burns out, in the second (longest) part; we find ourselves in an opulent dark room where a lady—the heroine—stands at a window and then sits behind a black piano and sings the song, the "sentimental romance." So the first part is the objective correlate which renders—what? Not the heroine's inner state at the time when we see her (in the second part) but her state of excitement when her passionate affair was still going on. It is, we can surmise, done in an impersonal way because it is something too strong and intense to be subjectivized by her. In the third part passionate confusion returns as a renewed erotic explosion, but structured in a different way—subjectivized, a mixture of dynamic fragments, clock, a dog, stills of Rodin's statue of lovers combined in montage cuts that generate the impression of movements (as with the Czar's statue falling down in October), with an almost ridiculous drawn star exploding . . . all this against the same background of the heroine sitting behind a piano in darkness. The part ends with return to sadness, with the lady behind the piano in a dark night. Fade out—fade in to the last shortest part, morning sun, brightness, bursting flowers, interchanged with the heroine now in white behind a white piano, singing (the same song) in happiness, in an almost kitschy way . . .

If, then, the impersonal libidinal intensity of part 1 passes into the melancholic calm song of part 2, why does the subjectivized libidinal intensity of part 3 pass into a short vision of happiness where the same song is performed in the opposite mood? Is it simply that non-subjectivized intensity leaves the subject at a distance, unable to assume it, and therefore in a melancholic mood of loss, while subjectivized libidinal intensity brings happiness? I think the opposite is true: we can enjoy ourselves only when the fundamental crazy dance of fantasies is kept at a distance, which is why melancholy, melancholic loss, is the only way to sustain the core of enjoyment. When this core engulfs us, our subjectivity dissolves, we turn into living dead. Here one should note a crucial detail: in Eisenstein's film the passage from part 3 to part 4 is a clear cut indicated by the fade out and fade in. After this cut we enter another dimension—her white dress and the white piano signal that she is dead.

The lesson of this very basic interpretation is nonetheless an important one: although we are dealing with a kind of Greimasian semiotic square of four stances, all four are not at the same level, they do not operate within the same space. The fourth position is an impossible one, it stands for nothing, for obliteration of the subject, and the white-coloured part just fills in the gap of this void. This is why one should not dismiss this short film just as a commercial compromise: it brings out something that remains repressed in the "revolutionary" political use of Eisenstein's procedure: the impossibility to sustain the full subjective assumption of libidinal madness—the moment I do it, I obliterate myself. In other words, while the first three parts are focused on the heroine, part four is our own (viewer's) dream, totally disconnected from the heroine, our own kitschy projection of a happy ending onto her disappearance.

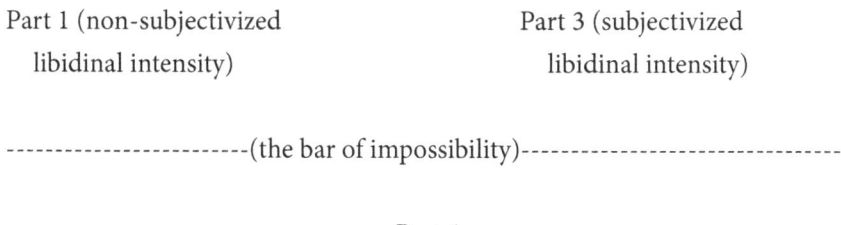

What we get here is not a linear progress from 1 to 4 but a 3 + 1: a pseudo-Hegelian triad supplemented by a radically heterogeneous fourth term. We begin with non-subjectivized libidinal intensity which is then negated by a melancholic subject unable to appropriate/subjectivize it, and what follows is a "synthesis," an attempt of the subject to subjectivize/assume libidinal intensity. However, this "synthesis" fails, the subject pays the price for its risky assumption of libidinal intensity by its self-obliteration. However, the subject beneath the bar of impossibility is not simply dead, it survives what Lacan calls subjective destitution and emerges as a living dead, the pure void of subject deprived of its subjectivity, a subject who is no longer a person.

Variation 8
Sexual superpositions

According to the popular (mis)conception of psychoanalysis, sex (the sexual relationship) serves as the ultimate reference of all our activities: everything we do and feel has a sexual connotation. Along these lines, one is tempted to rewrite the entire history of modern philosophy:

- Descartes: "I fuck, therefore I am," i.e., only in the intense sexual activity do I experience the fullness of my being (Lacan's "decentering" answer to it would have been: "I fuck where I am not, and I am not where I fuck," i.e., it is not me who is fucking, but "it fucks" in me);
- Spinoza: within the Absolute as Fuck (*coitus sive natura*), one should distinguish, along the lines of the distinction between *natura naturans* and *natura naturata*, between the active fucking penetration and the object being fucked—there are those who fuck and those who get fucked;
- Hume introduces here the empiricist doubt: how do we know that fuck as a relationship exists at all? There are just objects whose movements appear coordinated;
- Kant responds to this crisis: "the conditions of possibility of fucking are at the same time the conditions of possibility of the objects of fucking";
- Fichte then radicalizes this Kantian revolution: fucking is a self-positing unconditional activity which divides itself into fucker and the fucked object, i.e., it is fucking itself which posits its object, the fuckee;

- Hegel: "it is crucial to conceive Fucking not only as Substance (the substantial drive overwhelming us), but also as Subject (as a reflective activity embedded in the context of spiritual meaning)";
- Marx: one should return to real fucking against the idealist masturbatory philosophising, i.e., as he literally put it in *German Ideology*, real, actual life is to philosophy as real sex is to masturbation;
- Nietzsche: the Will is, at its most radical, the Will to Fuck, which culminates in the Eternal Return of "I want more," of a fuck going on forever;
- Heidegger: in the same way as the essence of technology is nothing "technological," the essence of fucking has nothing to do with fuck as a simple ontic activity; rather, "the essence of fucking is the fucking of the Essence itself," i.e., it is not only we, humans, that fuck up our understanding of Essence, it is the Essence which is already in itself fucked up (inconsistent, withdrawing itself, erring);
- and, finally, this insight into how the Essence itself is fucked up, brings us to Lacan's "there is no such thing as a sexual relationship."

Heidegger's and Lacan's "pessimist" reversal of Nietzsche's Eternal Return of a fuck going on forever is actually a happy one. Recall the key turn in Hamlet's "To be or not to be" soliloquy: "To die, to sleep, To sleep, perchance to Dream; aye, there's the rub, For in that sleep of death, what dreams may come, When we have shuffled off this mortal coil, Must give us pause." So let's go to the end and imagine the most terrifying eternal dream: to fuck endlessly, without interruption, without any chance of escape. At the end of this soliloquy, when Hamlet says to Ophelia whom he sees reading a religious book: "Nymph, in thy orisons [prayers] be all my sins remembered," he is basically asking her to pray for him and for the forgiveness of his sins. What Lacan means by "there is no big Other" is precisely that there is no place where all Hamlet's sins are remembered, nor mine, which means that they cannot be obliterated—they will haunt me forever.

Furthermore, if there is no big Other, we also have to abandon the idea of sexuality as the ultimate reference of all that we say and do. We have to do this if we want to be true dialectical materialists: the notion of "pan-sexism" is clearly non-dialectical, it is a mechanic-materialist thesis. In quantum terms, sexuality is immanently crossed by detours and displacements, and these detours and displacements evoke the topic of superpositions—so what can the quantum approach tell us about sexuality? The first obvious implication is that we should replace the rather boring topic of sexual *positions* (how to do the sexual act, what positions bodies should assume) with the topic of sexual *superpositions*. How is a sexual identity formed? It (mostly) "collapses" into a particular form (gay, hetero, lesbian ...), but to understand how this form emerged we have to accept that the subject in their fantasies played with many possible forms, and that these multiple and inconsistent "superposed" forms continue to echo in the final form.[1]

The main source of these superposed fantasies is so-called infantile sexuality, and the basic insight of psychoanalysis is that, even if a subject finally adopts a single "mature" sexual identity, infantile sexual fantasies do not disappear but continue to serve as a fantasy support of the "actual" sexual activity. This conclusion clearly follows Freudian orthodoxy: the basic premise of his *Three Essays on Sexuality* (1905) is that perversions exist in normal people also, in multiple deviations of sexual aims, as well as in the tendency to linger over preparatory sexual aspects such as looking and touching. Then there are situations in which someone acts as if they are sincerely attracted to another person, but in reality they act like this in order to be in contact with someone close to this person—say, I regularly visit an older professor and engage in passionate debates with him, but in reality I do this just to be close to his daughter who lives with him and with whom I am passionately in love ... But what about the opposite situation: I say to myself that I tolerate talking to her father while in reality I enjoy talking to her father more than being close to her? In this case, pretending (to enjoy talking to her father) is not a lie covering my real intention—the lie is the very act of pretending to like what I really like. Pretending is thus redoubled, reflected into itself: I don't just pretend, I *pretend to pretend*. From here it is just a short step towards perversion: in perversion I don't just pretend to pretend, I openly focus on what is supposed to be just a detour, a foreplay to the main event—say, in sexuality, I endlessly postpone the act proper and remain at the level of caressing other parts of the body ... Freud formalized the distinction between the "fore-pleasures" of infantile sexuality and the "end-pleasure" of sexual intercourse; children have sexual urges, from which adult sexuality only gradually emerges via psychosexual development. So

> a disposition to perversions is an original and universal disposition of the human sexual instinct and . . . this postulated constitution, containing the germs of all the perversions, will only be demonstrable in *children*.[2]

This can be taken a step further: we (some of us) arrive at the heterosexual norm only through deviations, and this path through deviations is not an organic "natural" process but a process of brutal symbolic cuts, prohibitions and impositions. This is the basic paradox of human sexuality: what appears as a "natural" sexual orientation, the way in which reproduction (the biological function of copulation) happens, is the final outcome of a complex socio-symbolic process. The "progress" from infantile sexuality to the heterosexual norm is not the process which follows a pattern of natural development. What, then, is so scandalous about infantile sexuality? It is not the sole fact that even children, presumed innocent, are already sexualized. The scandal resides in two features (which are, of course, two sides of the same coin). First, infantile sexuality is a weird entity which is neither biological(ly grounded) nor part of symbolic/cultural norms. Jean Laplanche elaborated this weirdness when he shows how the Freudian topic of seduction effectively reproduces the precise structure of a Kantian antinomy. On the one hand, there is the brutal empirical realism of *parental sexual abuse*: the ultimate cause of many later traumas and pathologies is that children effectively have been groomed and abused by adults; on the other hand, there is the (in)famous reduction of the abuse scene to the patient's fantasy. As Laplanche points out, the ultimate irony is that dismissing sexual abuse as fantasy often passes for the "realistic" stance, while those who insist on its reality sometimes end up identifying all kinds of abuse, up to and including satanic rites and extra-terrestrial harassments . . . Laplanche's solution is precisely the transcendental one: while what he refers to as "seduction" cannot be reduced to the subject's fantasy, while it does refer to a traumatic encounter of the other's "enigmatic message," bearing witness to the other's unconscious, it also cannot be reduced to an event in the reality of the actual interaction between a child and adults. "Seduction" is rather a kind of transcendental structure, the minimal a priori formal constellation of the child confronted with the impenetrable acts of the Other which bear witness to the Other's unconscious—and we are never dealing here with simple "facts," but always with facts located into the space of indeterminacy between "too soon" and "too late": the child is originally helpless, thrown into the world when unable to take care of itself, i.e., their survival skills develop too late; at the same time, the encounter of the sexualized Other always, by a structural necessity, comes "too soon," as an unexpected shock which cannot ever be properly symbolized, translated into the universe of meaning.[3] The fact of "seduction" is thus again that of the Kantian transcendental X, a structurally-necessary transcendental illusion ... However, this excess, this weirdness, is not sublated by adult "normal" sexuality—this latter also is always distorted, displaced:

> when it comes to sexuality, man is subject to the greatest of paradoxes: what is acquired through the drives precedes what is innate and instinctual, in such a way that, at the time it emerges, instinctual sexuality, which is adaptive, finds the seat already taken, as it were, by infantile drives, already and always present in the unconscious.[4]

The "natural" form is the outcome of a complex symbolic process: the starting point (infantile sexuality) is not yet fully "cultural," but it is also not "natural," so that perversions (whose model is infantile sexuality) do not simply disappear, they are not simply left behind in normal adult heterosexuality. They remain in the form of kissing, touching, and the eroticization of non-sexual parts of the body: "normal" sexuality erotically works only through the shadows and remainders of these elements, otherwise it is just raw coupling, like the insemination in *Handmaid's Tale*. Perverse "deviations" are thus necessary, we arrive at the norm only through them, so that (to put it in Hegelian terms) what appears as "the norm" is the ultimate self-sublated perversion. We encounter here what Hegel called "absolute recoil": as deviations from the Norm, perversions presuppose the norm, the pleasure they generate resides in the transgression of the Norm; however, this Norm itself arises through deviations, as the ultimate deviation. In other words, the very process of deviation retroactively constructs what it deviates from, or, as Hegel would have put it, perversion is an act which posits its own presupposition, it is an effect which retroactively posits its cause.

This circularity is rendered at its purest in *M Butterfly* (directed by David Cronenberg, script by David Henry Hwang from his own play), a movie whose narrative is utter improbability: without the advertisement, in the credits, that the story is based on true events, nobody would take it seriously. During the Great Cultural Revolution, a minor French diplomat in Beijing (Jeremy Irons) falls in love with a Chinese opera singer named Song Liling who sings some Puccini arias at a reception for foreigners (John Lone). His courting leads to a lasting love relationship; Song, who is to him the fatal love object (with reference to Puccini's opera, he affectionately calls her "my butterfly"), gets pregnant and bears him a child. While their affair goes on, she induces him to spy for China, claiming that this is the only way the Chinese authorities will tolerate their association. After a professional failure, the diplomat is transferred to Paris where he is assigned to the minor post of diplomatic courier. Soon afterwards, his love joins him there and tells him that if he will carry on with spying for China, the Chinese authorities will allow their child to join them. When, finally, French security discovers his spying activities and they are both arrested, it turns out that Song is not a woman at all but a man—in his Eurocentric ignorance, the hero did not know that in Chinese opera feminine roles are sung by men.

It is here that the story stretches the limits of our credulity: how was it that the hero, in the long years of consumed love, did not see that he was dealing with a man? The singer incessantly evoked the Chinese sense of shame, s/he never undressed, they had (unbeknownst to him, anal) sex discreetly, s/he sitting on his lap . . .—in short, what he mistook for the shyness of the "Oriental" woman was a deft manipulation destined to conceal the fact that "she" was not biologically a woman at all. The choice of the music that obsesses the hero is crucial: the famous aria "*Un bel di, vedremo*" from *Madama Butterfly*, perhaps the most expressive example of Puccini's gesture that is the very opposite of bashful self-concealment—the obscenely candid self-exposure of the (feminine) subject that always borders upon kitsch. The subject pathetically professes what she is and what she wants, she lays bare her most intimate and frail dreams—a confession that, of course, reaches its apogee in the desire to die (in "*Un bel di, vedremo*", Madama Butterfly imagines the scene of Pinkerton's return: at first, she will not answer his call, "in part for fun and in part not to die at the first encounter [*per non morir al primo incontro*]").

From what we have just said, it may seem that the hero's tragic blunder consists in projecting his fantasy-image onto an inadequate object, i.e., in mistaking a real person for his fantasy-image of the love object, the "Oriental" woman of the Madame Butterfly type. However, things are definitely more complex. The key scene of the film occurs after the trial, when the hero and Song, now wearing an ordinary man's suit, find themselves alone in the closed compartment of a police car on their way to prison. Song takes off his clothes and offers himself naked to the hero, desperately proclaiming his availability: "Here I am, your butterfly!" He proposes himself as what he is outside the hero's fantasy frame of a mysterious Chinese woman. At this crucial moment, the hero retreats: he avoids looking at his lover and rejects the offer. It is here that he compromises his desire and thus contracts an indelible guilt—he betrays the true love that aims at the real kernel of the object beneath the fantasmatic envelopes.

The painful final scene of the film conveys the hero's full recognition of his guilt (in clear contrast to Ponelle's staging of Wagner's *Tristan* in which Tristan is not ready to abandon the fantasy of Isolde: he can only die imagining her presence). In the prison, he stages a performance for his vulgar and noisy fellow-prisoners: dressed as Madama Butterfly (the Japanese kimono, heavily made-up face) and accompanied by excerpts from Puccini's opera, he retells his story; at the very climax of "*Un bel di, vedremo*", he cuts his throat with a razor and collapses dead. This act of a man dressed as a woman who performs a public suicide is of a strictly ethical nature: the hero stages a psychotic identification with his love object, with his *sinthome* (synthetic formation of the nonexistent woman, "Butterfly"), i.e., he "regresses" from the object-choice to an immediate identification with the object; the only way out of the insoluble deadlock of this identification is suicide qua the ultimate *passage a l'acte*. By way of his suicidal act, the hero makes up for his guilt, for his rejection of the object when the object was offered to him outside the fantasy-frame.

In other words, the hero experiences the separation, the gap between the idealized image of his love object and the reality of the Chinese man who assumed this image, and is thus confronted with the fact that his love object was his own fantasmatic construct, a mere semblance. At this point, his desperate stratagem is to supplement this semblance, to provide for its "flesh," by directly offering his own body as its "stuff." In this way, he becomes his own object-cause, i.e., he assumes the object-cause of his desire as his own—such a direct identification, of course, is lethal, impossible to sustain. The identification with the lost object is here brought to its logical (suicidal) conclusion: if I *am* the lost object, then I can fully and authentically "be" only insofar as I lose (obliterate) myself ... *This* is the authentic melancholic ethics, in contrast to the "postmodern" compromise solution, where the uprooted subject retains the melancholic fidelity to his lost ethnic roots, while fully participating in the global capitalist economy.

The film thus also implicitly echoes Freud's infamous statement concerning the status of sexual difference: "Anatomy is destiny." This statement should be read as a Hegelian "speculative judgement" in which the predicate "passes over" into the subject. That is to say, its true meaning is not the obvious one, the standard target of feminist critique ("the anatomical difference between the sexes directly founds, is directly responsible for, the different socio-symbolic roles of men and women"), but rather the opposite one: the "truth" of the anatomy is "destiny," i.e., a symbolic formation. In the case of sexual identity, an anatomic difference is "sublated," turned into the medium of appearance/expression—more precisely, into the material support—of a certain symbolic formation.

Does this mean that the space of sexuality is irredeemably chaotic, resisting any systematization? No—and here we can bring in Hegel once more. Since the topic of the diversity of sexual practices is much more openly and widely discussed today than in Hegel's time, one cannot avoid the task of introducing into the messy space of sexuality some conceptual order, of deploying not the empirical history of sexuality but the immanent dynamic of the concept of sexuality. The task is thus not just classifying sexual practices but also displaying how the sequence of different stances forms a properly dialectical process in which each particular form resolves the antagonism of the previous form and gives birth to a new antagonism of its own since *il n'y a pas de rapport sexuel*. The task is thus nothing less than a Hegelian *system of sexuality* in the standard form of successive triads.

Where to begin then? Human sexuality emerges through a clear cut with animal copulation which aims at procreation, so at its zero-level it implies that every bodily contact with another is excluded: sexual pleasure should be explicitly posited as an end-in-itself, serving no biological function. The only form of sexuality that fully meets this condition is masturbation—but not masturbation alone (which is also practiced by some animals). Since a human being is a spiritual being, a being whose mind is plagued by products of its creative (and destructive) imagination, the zero-level of human sexuality is masturbation accompanied and sustained even by imagination, by sexual fantasies—to put it in a somewhat vulgar way, while I do it to myself, I dream about doing it with others. Kant was quite right to claim that masturbation with imagination is the lowest degeneration of sexuality, the most radical abandonment of its natural goal:

> Lust [the "impetus" to sexual "pleasure"] is called unnatural if one is aroused to it not by a real object but by his imagining it, so that he himself creates one, contrary to [natural] purpose; for in this way imagination brings forth a desire contrary to nature's end.[5]

But those who today celebrate masturbation as the most basic and democratic form of sexual activity are, in their own way, also right: "masturbathon" (a large group of people masturbating openly at the same place) builds a collective out of individuals who are ready to share the solipsism of their own stupid enjoyment, and is as such the form of sexuality which fits these cyberspace coordinates perfectly. Here is how Dr. Carol Queen justifies masturbation:

> Masturbation is our first sexual activity, a natural source of pleasure that's available to us throughout our lives, and a unique form of creative self-expression. Each time you masturbate, you're celebrating your sexuality and your innate capacity for pleasure, so give yourself a hand! . . . Masturbation can be a radical act, and the culture that suppresses masturbation may suppress many other personal freedoms as well.[6]

This is why Lacan suggests that, whereas the basic form of sexuality for animals is copulation, the basic form of sexuality for humans is masturbation. The structure of masturbation sustained by (and simultaneously split from) fantasizing is a universal feature of human sexuality, it is operative in all of its forms. "The act of sex for humans is so much caught up in our fantasies (our idealized images of both ourselves and our sexual partners) that it is ultimately narcissistic."[7] This is what Lacan had in mind with his *il n'y a pas de rapport sexuel*: not only is masturbation sex with an imagined partner (one does it to oneself, arousing oneself with imagined activity with partners); in a strictly symmetrical way, "real sex" has the structure of *masturbation with a real partner*: I effectively use the flesh-and-blood partner as a masturbatory prop for enacting my fantasies. In other words, what makes this notion of sexuality so traumatic for those attached to "real communication with real people" is not that the link to a flesh-and-blood person is cut, but that we are forced to realize how sex always-already was "virtual," with flesh-and-blood persons used as masturbatory props for dwelling in our fantasies.

The next step is the return to the bodily form of animal copulation—*coitus a tergo*—but with a new function: since the two partners don't face each other, each of them is free to pursue its own fantasies during the sexual act, and these fantasies are not linked to the fantasies that sustain the other partner. When the division between fantasy and bodily reality becomes too strong, the only way out is the desperate attempt to unite the bodily and the spiritual dimension—we are, of course, talking about the so-called missionary position (advocated by the Catholic Church precisely for this reason: the face-to-face conjunction is meant to establish a spiritual proximity). But it is obvious that the gap returns in an even stronger form because the face-to-face encounter renders palpable the discord of the underlying fantasies. The worst solution occurs when the lovers decide to accompany their bodily activity with talking, trying to stimulate each other with tender or dirty details—the gap is exposed in all its ridicule.

*

Now the real mess begins with an almost endless series of desperate attempts to close the gap between fantasy and the miserable reality of sex by way of improvising different bodily positions, under the implicit motto "if the words fail let's try to achieve it with our bodies." The obvious first variation is to change the partner: a man instead of a woman or vice versa. (One could, of course, replace the human partner with an animal. From my youth in the 1960s and 1970s, I remember short illustrated handbooks teaching men how to penetrate a goat or a cow and women how to arouse a dog or a horse to penetrate them.)

The next step is to experiment with all possible variations of group sex: two couples doing it together, a group of men in a circle penetrating each other, etc. One popular variation involves one woman with three man penetrating her simultaneously: vaginally, anally and orally; however, the paradigmatic case is what one might call "the Swiss army wife" position, a woman who is able to use all her holes and limbs to simultaneously satisfy a group of men.

This important dialectical-materialist concept of "Swiss army wife" points towards the next variation: all possible combinations between the three main holes (vaginal, anal, mouth) and the three main penetrating instruments (penis, tongue, hand). This brings us to the next step: the gradual disappearance of the distinction between foreplay and the sexual act proper (penetration): mostly what was traditionally considered from a heteronormative point of view a form of foreplay (kissing, fingering, and other forms of caressing) becomes an end-in-itself, so that the big penetrative act is simply no longer needed. There are, of course, many other attempts to reconcile the contradictions we have identified, including extreme forms of masochism like coprophagia (compulsive eating of feces) or brutal masochism (like self-castration), but all this obviously ends up in a deadlock—so how can we get out of it?

We must conceptualize the self-sublation of sexuality in a truly dialectical-materialist way, as an act of immanent self-overcoming, not just external negation from some "higher" spiritual position. Perhaps we should take inspiration from the corporate world and overcome sexual activity by outsourcing it. Recently, the so-called "Stamina Training Unit" appeared on the market, a masturbatory device that resembles a battery powered light (so we're not embarrassed when carrying it around). You put the erect penis into the opening at the top, push the button, and the object vibrates till satisfaction . . . So let's say I am flirting with a lady and we decide to do it: we meet at her place or mine, she brings her vibrator and I my Stamina Training Unit, we plug both toys into a source of electricity, then we push the vibrator into the Stamina Training Unit, turn them both on and leave all the fun to this ideal couple. Accompanied by the pleasant background buzzing, we—the two real human partners—then sit down at a nearby table, drink tea and eat cake, both of us calmly enjoying the fact that, without great effort, we have fulfilled our duty to enjoy through the machines. In this way, we are free to engage in a nice talk, with no pressure that this talk must lead to sexual activity: we can just enjoy it and become asexual friends.

The Scriptures defined this passage from sexual coupling to asexual friendship in terms of *eros* (sexual love) and *philia* (asexual affection/ friendship), and added two further types of love to this taxonomy: *storge* (parental familial love) and *agape* (the unconditional love that unites individuals who dedicate their lives to a Cause). At the level of *agape*, feelings (sexual or not) no longer matter, what remains is just Holy Spirit, an egalitarian community of comrades dedicated to a Cause.[8] As a comrade, I can involve myself sexually with another comrade, I can become his/her friend, but this doesn't really matter: if the situation of a struggle demands it, I should be ready to betray him/her because only the Cause matters. And if my comrade is a true comrade s/he will fully understand me and even despise me if I allow any weakness for him/her to overcome my fidelity to the shared cause and am not ready to betray him/her. There is nothing spontaneous about such an egalitarian community of comrades—it requires hard work and full commitment, so it is the very opposite of "egalitarian" morality as it was nicely summed up by Rúben Gallo: "human beings, regardless of gender, race, social class, or nationality, are invariably selfish, cruel, and corrupt."[9]

At the other end of the spectrum, there is the deliberate ignoring of the link between sexuality and (sexual) *love* as another form of the self-sublation of sexuality. As Lacan put it, love supplements the impossibility/failure of sexual relationship: it is not an imaginary illusion destined to obfuscate the ultimate failure of any sexual relationship, but, on the contrary, the only link to another human being which is open to another human being in its radical alterity, accepting it without any idealization. It is only love that makes a sexual act non-masturbatory. But here another deadlock emerges, that of the excess of love itself perspicuously encapsulated by Neil Gaiman:

> You build up all these defenses, you build up a whole suit of armor, so that nothing can hurt you, then one stupid person, no different from any other

stupid person, wanders into your stupid life . . . You give them a piece of you. They didn't ask for it. They did something dumb one day, like kiss you or smile at you, and then your life isn't your own anymore. Love takes hostages. It gets inside you. It eats you out and leaves you crying in the darkness . . . It hurts. Not just in the imagination. Not just in the mind. It's a soul-hurt, a real gets-inside-you-and-rips-you-apart pain. I hate love.[10]

This is why one should fearlessly endorse the result of the study from the University of Valencia: "Just five minutes alone with an attractive female raise the levels of cortisol, the body's stress hormone."[11] However, as Hegel hinted in some passages, there is a cure for the horror of intense love—it's called marriage. A (not too) vulgar joke provides an insight into a truly happy marriage. Late in the evening, a wife and a husband lie in bed; the wife is trying to fall asleep, while the husband is reading a book. Every couple of minutes, he reaches with his hand over to the wife and gently rubs her vaginal lips with his finger. After this goes on for half an hour, the wife explodes: "I am trying to fall asleep! If you want to have sex, do it fast, don't play with me like that!" The husband replies: "Sorry, it is not about sex. I am just reading a book and every couple of minutes I need to wet my finger to turn a new page . . ." This brings us to Pascal: the true Pascalean formula of marriage is not "You don't love your partner? Then marry him or her, go through the ritual of shared life, and love will emerge by itself!"; it is, on the contrary: "Are you too much in love with somebody? Then get married, ritualize your love relationship, in order to cure yourself of the excessive passionate attachment, to replace it with the boring daily custom . . ." Marriage is thus a means of re-normalization which cures us of the violence of falling in love. (And, incidentally, are many "radical" Leftist intellectuals not doing something similar to the unfortunate husband? Afraid to approach the real of actual political struggle they just touch it fleetingly to wet their finger and go on reading and writing academic books which criticize actual fighters.) Today, unfortunately, marriage is less and less needed because in our time of permissiveness a passionate sexual love for a single person is quite often dismissed as too fixating—you can play (consensual) sexual games with many people, just don't get too stuck on one of them.

To conclude, let's raise the final question: what can psychoanalysis do when confronted with a trans patient caught in the mess of multiple identities and modes of enjoyment, unable to decide what he/she/it "really is"? In an interview published a couple of years ago ("The Trans Solution,"[12] in which he also passingly dismisses Lacan's use of mathematical formulas as "just parodies"), Jacques-Alain Miller clarifies his (and, by extension, what he considers the Lacanian) stance towards the transactivists who are

> full-fledged political activists, and with that, very sensitive. They promote a "gender identity" that is intimate, innate and definitive. The subject would be the only one to know in its heart of hearts who it is, as it were, gendered. In short, "I am what I say I am," all trans people are transparent to themselves. So they demand an immediate transition, and at all ages, as soon as a subject, even a child, says it is uncomfortable with its body. This is the famous "gender self-determination" on which, in Western countries, the public authorities are gradually aligning themselves. *Victoire*! Will it be sustainable? The bets are open. Still, it is the exact opposite of psychoanalysis whose act is based on interpretation, that is to say on the fact that the subject does not really know what it is saying.

While I agree with Miller's basic line of argumentation, I find many of its details incorrect and deceiving. For many trans subjects, their gender identity is NOT "innate and definitive" but an everlasting process of performative transformation since all trans people are NOT "transparent to themselves." For them, psychoanalysis is not problematic because it presumes that the subject "does not really know what it is saying" but because the analytic process of interpretation is not neutral: it is sustained by an implicit normative dimension. Someone gave me a badge with an (apocryphal, of course) quote from Stalin: "I trust no one, not even myself." The real Stalin was precisely not able to include himself into the list of people he didn't trust. And the same should be said about trans subjects: not only are they not what they appear to others ("people around me take me for a man, but I am a woman"), they are also not what they themselves think they are.

I would only add to this that today this dimension is not predominantly patriarchal/heterosexual but tends precisely towards a notion of infinite plasticity of sexual identities. The implication of this fact is that (today, at least) we cannot simply say that the analytic process really reaches its conclusion when "the subject has completed its speaking journey (*son parcours de parole*), that it has clarified its desire or its conviction"? And can we really simply say that after this point "the choice is theirs"? Does a subject ever reach this point at which its libidinal economy becomes transparent to him so that he can from some neutral position make a choice? When Miller concludes that "we see suffering subjects who finally find relief in the transition, and their particular definition as sexual beings," how can we be sure that this "relief" is not a fake, i.e., that the newly-found "particular definition" of a subject as a sexual being is not just a new symptom-formation destined to obfuscate the trauma of sexuality? Does this not bring us to late Lacan's modest determination of the psychoanalytic treatment whose goal is just to enable the patient to construct a symptom which would enable him/her/it to lead a relatively tolerable life?

At a more formal level, the question of how to measure the truth of sexual intercourse gets even more complex. Let's turn to two different versions of the same joke which will hopefully enable us to clarify a key conceptual difference. I knew for years a classic vulgar joke about an American who seduces a Japanese lady during a business trip to Tokyo; they end up in bed, and during their passionate love-making, the woman is repeatedly shouting two words in Japanese that the American doesn't understand but presumes they express her full pleasure. The next day he goes to play golf with his business partners and after he hits the ball, his partners shout the same words as the lady the previous night. Perplexed, he asks them what these words mean, and they explain it to him: "Wrong hole!" Recently I was told another version: after he hits the ball on the golf course, all his partners applaud passionately because he put the ball into a hole with the first strike. He wants to join their celebration and repeats loudly the two words he heard during the love-making, presuming they express pleasure and satisfaction, but his partners' faces reveal surprise and consternation. He asks one of them what was wrong, and gets the answer: "Are you making fun of us? Why are you shouting 'Wrong hole!' when you put the ball into the right hole?" The vulgarity of the joke notwithstanding, the difference between its two versions is worth a closer look. In both cases, the first act is a double failure: not only with regard to what went on (he penetrates the "wrong hole") but also a misunderstanding (the American misreads the woman's cries as praise); the misunderstanding is clarified in the second act, but in the opposite direction. In the first version, the American's golf partners repeat the same words because, as with the Japanese lady, he missed the proper hole; in the second version, he himself repeats the two words he doesn't understand because this time he did hit the right hole, and he thinks he is joining the celebration of his success. You do the wrong thing (miss the proper hole), and the words are used (by the partners) in its right meaning; you do the right thing (ball in the hole), and you use the words in the wrong meaning. As in hardcore movies, the penetrated woman is presumed to enjoy it ecstatically even if the male partner put it into a wrong hole—and in some sense, since "there is no sexual relationship," the sexual encounter is always a failed one, the hole is always a wrong one, the man misreads his act as a triumph. If the man repeats the act of filling a hole in a non-sexual context (like playing golf), there are two options. If you miss the hole again, the big Other (embodied here in your partners on the golf course) will repeat the women's words, and you will finally get the message that your "triumph" was a painful fiasco. If you hit the right hole, you appear an even greater idiot because, unknowingly, you declare it a failure, and the big Other is offended . . .

The key feature here is that this joke works only when the first act is sexual and the second is asexual (playing golf). Let's try to reimagine it in the opposite order: I play golf with my partners, I miss the hole and I hear them shouting two words that I don't understand; the same evening, I make love with a Japanese woman and hear her shouting the same two words which I don't understand, so I ask her what they mean . . . but wouldn't it be more logical to ask already my partners on the golf course than to raise the question in the middle of (what was for me at least) a passionate intercourse? So the joke works because (due to a vulgar association of the two holes to be filled in) in sex the hole is always in some way missed and the communication misunderstood, while in asexual life (overdetermined by sexual innuendos) I may hit the right hole or not, but the misunderstanding persists. We can speculate that this is the general structure of our lives as sexed beings: sex remains a mess, and the only way to introduce a little bit of order into this mess is through engaging in non-sexual activities which, although they remain overshadowed by sex, allow us to escape the vortex of sex. My reading is thus that the second version of the joke is the right one: I hit the right hole, but my mistake (shouting "Wrong hole!") is also right at the level of sexuality because there is no sexual relationship—I am right without knowing it, of course, and the big Other which corrects my misunderstanding is wrong.

Aaron Schuster notes how Josephine the singing mouse from Kafka's last story "simulates her self-loss in order to truly lose herself without psychotically falling apart, without this loss turning to anxiety, panic, or revulsion. She thus creates a true illusion."[13] Every word counts here—"true illusion" is not simply an illusion (product of our mind) which happens to represent correctly external reality; the content of the illusion is true, but the only way for me to accept it, not to be crushed by it into a psychotic breakdown, is to treat is as a mere illusion. The same holds also for a fundamentalist political passion: you have to maintain a minimal distance towards it if you are to avoid psychotic breakdown. And the same holds for love: when we are passionately in love, we struggle to retain a minimal distance towards it, we tell ourselves "I am just playing at being fully in love" because we are afraid that fully assuming the sexual passion will drive us crazy.

Variation 9
Make the kitchen maid king

As is well known, Hegel advocated constitutional monarchy as the only appropriate form of political order that fits modern society. His numerous critics see this weird advocacy either as a clear sign of Hegel's immanent philosophical limitation or as a sign of his political conformism, with some more benevolently disposed critics interpreting it as a cunning trick to delude state censorship (first among these sarcastic critics is none other than Marx).[1] Klaus Vieweg's critique of Hegel's deduction of monarchy is by far the most thoughtful in this vein: what he tries to prove is that Hegel's deduction is wrong in Hegel's own terms. Hegel justifies the necessary role of the monarch with reference to the syllogism, to the syllogistic structure of the state power, but Vieweg claims that the very form of syllogism to which he refers (disjunctive syllogism) would impose a democratic solution with people as the ultimate source of legitimate power.[2] So can Hegel be fully defended today? Let's begin with Mark Tunick's concise summary of Hegel's position:

> Hegel is not a democrat. He is a monarchist. But he wants monarchy because he does not want strong government. He wants to deemphasize power. He develops an idealist conception of sovereignty that allows for a monarch less powerful than a president . . .[3]

That is to say, less powerful than a *democratically elected* president. How would this work in practice?

Hegel supposes that the monarch's counsel, whose members are chosen by objective criteria, can resolve an issue at least to the point where only an arbitrary will can choose among the options. The counsel rules out all the bad alternatives (which democracy doesn't do), until the remaining options are equally meritorious. Even if the monarch decided every political issue, the issues he'd be deciding would be different than the issues as they first appear, and which a democratic vote would have resolved. The monarch makes a "groundless" decision that still has grounds.

Tunick uses the example of prison overcrowding: some of the potential solutions to the problem (such as letting convicted criminals go free or killing all the prisoners) will be eliminated by the counsel. "The remaining alternatives are grounded (i.e., in the principle that we must not kill, or that we must punish wrongdoers), but suppose it's arbitrary which of them we choose. The monarch decides this."[4]

It should be clear from this example what Hegel fears (as well as why his fear is even more urgent today): the direct rule of experts which justify their decisions with (pseudo-scientific) reasons incomprehensible to the majority of ordinary citizens. Just recall how today economic decisions are legitimized by experts as simple neutral scientific insight, and in this way the political bias of these decisions disappears from view, dismissed as "ideological" ... Hegel is aware that a Master who is elevated above the system of knowledge (in Lacanian terms, of the "discourse of university") is needed, so he wants to keep the power that decides outside expert knowledge. However, he is at the same time aware that a return to the premodern master who reigns directly is unacceptable in modern times; his solution is therefore a monarch whose function is ultimately just to dot the s's and cross the t's, to sign his name on decisions prepared and proposed by qualified experts.

Vieweg is right in claiming that the key for the proper understanding of Hegel's notion of monarch is provided by his notion of disjunctive syllogism (as a further development of the syllogism of necessity); but he accuses Hegel of misreading the political implications of this syllogism. Its structure is that of PUI: the universal dimension (people represented in legislative assembly) mediates between the particular dimension (executive power) and the individual (monarch as the decision-maker). In short, in contrast to the premodern monarchy where the king directly rules over its subjects, in a modern state the people in their universal dimension regulate and control both extreme, executive and deciding power:

> The application of the disjunctive syllogism to the structure of the state's internal constitution leads to a most surprising result in contrast to what the Outlines (of the Philosophy of Right) claims: it affects the theoretical legitimization of a republican, democratic constitution and reveals the fundamental importance of the legislative assembly as an expression of a representative-democratic structure.[5]

But does Hegel really violate the logic of disjunctive syllogism? It is Vieweg himself who ignores what its name indicates, the dimension of *disjunction* located by Hegel into the mediating universality itself—here is a passage from Hegel's small logic (*Encyclopaedia*, par 191) which already points towards the role of the monarch:

> the mediating Universal is explicitly put as a totality of its particular members, and as a single particular, or exclusive individuality—which happens in the *Disjunctive* syllogism. It is one and the same universal which is in these terms of the Disjunctive syllogism; they are only different forms for expressing it.[6]

Disjunction thus divides Universality itself into the totality of its particular members and the exclusive individuality which directly gives body to the universality—as we say in everyday jargon, the monarch does not represent the people, the monarch IS the people, only through the monarch is the universality of the people actualized. In his precise essay "The Jurisdiction of the Hegelian Monarch,"[7] Jean-Luc Nancy emphasizes this performative dimension of the monarch (to use today's parlance) which comes close to what Lacan called the pure signifier (the Master-Signifier, a signifier which falls into the signified and is as such a signifier without signified). This is how one should read the tautology "Socialism is socialism"—recall the old Polish anti-Communist joke: "Socialism is the synthesis of the highest achievements of all previous historical epochs: from tribal society, it took barbarism, from antiquity, it took slavery, from feudalism, it took relations of domination, from capitalism, it took exploitation, and from socialism, it took the name." Does the same not hold for the anti-Semitic image of the Jew? From the rich bankers, it took financial speculation, from capitalists, it took exploitation, from lawyers, it took legal trickery, from corrupt journalists, it took media manipulation, from the poor, it took indifference towards washing one's body, from sexual libertines it took promiscuity, and from the Jews it took the name ... And this is also why a king is a king: he just adds his/her name. But, again, why is a monarch needed? Why is it that representative democracy (or, even better, some form of direct self-organization of the people) cannot do the job?

To fully grasp this, one should take note of the gap that separates two syllogistic triads: that of the entire society (individual family life, market and production in civil society, state) and that of the state as institution (legislative power, executive power, decider-monarch: UPI). When Vieweg elevates the political form of universality ("legislative assembly as an expression of a representative-democratic structure") into the central mediating role, he ignores another disjunction: however it is formed (even in the most open democratic elections with universal right to vote), legislative power is always by definition at a gap from "actual people."

In past decades, a whole series of events made this gap palpable. Remember the protests of yellow vests (*gilets jaunes*) in France that went on for over twenty weekends from late 2018 to early 2019. They began as a grassroots movement that grew out of widespread discontent with a new eco-tax on petrol and diesel, seen as hitting those living and working outside metropolitan areas where there is no public transport. The movement has grown to include a panoply of demands, including "frexit" (the exit of France from EU), lower taxes, higher pensions, and an improvement in ordinary French people's spending power. They offer an exemplary case of the Leftist populism, of the explosion of people's wrath in all its inconsistency: lower taxes and more money for education and health care, cheaper petrol and ecological struggle ... Although the new petrol tax was obviously an excuse or, rather, pretext, not what the protests are "really about," it is significant to note that what triggered the protests was a measure intended to act against global warming. No wonder Trump enthusiastically supported yellow vests (even hallucinating shouts "We want Trump!" from some of the protesters), noting that one of the demands was for France to step out of the Paris agreement. The thing to note here is that when representative of yellow vests met with government representatives, the talks were a total failure—they simply didn't speak the same language.

Or recall the UK elections of 2005: in spite of the growing unpopularity of Tony Blair (he was regularly voted the most unpopular person in the UK), he won the general elections—there was no way for this discontent with Blair to find a politically effective expression. Something is obviously very wrong here—it is not that people "do not know what they want," but, rather, that cynical resignation prevents them from acting upon it, so that the result is the weird gap between what people think and how they act (vote); such a frustration can foment dangerous extra-parliamentary explosions, especially in the form of rage in today's populism.

Years ago, the Spanish Podemos undoubtedly stood for the populist protests against the state mechanisms at its best: against the arrogant Politically Correct intellectual elites which despise the "narrowness" of the ordinary people who are considered "stupid" for "voting against their interests," its organizing principle was to listen to and organize those "from below" against those "from above," beyond all traditional Left and Right models. The idea was that the starting point of emancipatory politics should be the concrete experience of the suffering and injustices of ordinary people in their local life-world (home quarter, workplace, etc.), not abstract visions of a future Communist or whatsoever society. (Although the new digital media seem to open up the space for new communities, the difference between these new communities and the old life-world communities is crucial: these old communities are not chosen, I am born into them, they form the very space of my socialization, while the new (digital) communities include me into a specific domain defined by my interests and thus depending on my choice.)

Far from making the old "spontaneous" communities deficient, the fact that they do not rely on my free choice makes them superior with regard to the new digital communities since they compel me to find my way into a pre-existing not-chosen life-world in which I encounter (and have to learn to deal with) real differences, while the new digital communities depending on my choice sustain the ideological myth of the individual who somehow pre-exists a communal life and is free to choose it.) While this approach undoubtedly contains a (very big) grain of truth, its problem is that, to put it bluntly, not only, as Laclau liked to emphasize, society doesn't exist, but *"people" also doesn't exist* ... However, problems arose when Podemos decided to change into a political party and entered a government: its politics there was indistinguishable from a moderate social-democratic party.

*

Can this gap be filled by deliberative democracy, composed of popular assemblies composed of civil experts and individuals chosen by lot to debate a certain topic? Deliberative democracy can help, but it must be sustained by a clear structure of decision—the key point is that the deliberative assemblies *don't decide*. This is why, today even, *something like* monarchy is needed. As the top-decider, he is not qualified by any characteristics, he stands for the people as such, in its universality, which are excluded not only from the state institutions but also encompass all inner divisions and factional struggles. This disjunctive unity is best rendered by the fact that media report on the personal habits and preferences of the monarch and his family (music, books, gardening, sports . . .), things that are totally uninteresting in an ordinary person—who cares what food my neighbour likes! The king is a common man elevated into the top-decider—more radically, we can even say that he is a member of the rabble, of those with no determinate place in social hierarchy. We must take into account here the difference between sublation (*Aufhebung*) and sublimation: when an object is sublated into a higher form, it is not sublimated. Sublimation occurs when what resists sublation, its indivisible/non-sublatable remainder, is elevated from the status of trash to a sacred object, to a stand-I for the void, for what is excluded from the symbolic order. In Hegel's theory of monarchy, the monarch is a non-sublated rest of the social edifice, his position is not mediated through its social achievements, it is just determined by the biological contingency of his birth, he is with regard to his properties like any other ordinary citizen, and he is as such elevated to a sacred status, to the sublime embodiment of society as a whole. One thing is sure: the way to reinvent something-like-a-king today should definitely include a lottery aspect, it should be left to chance. What is expected from a monarch is just some common sense since, to quote Bill Murray: "Common sense is like deodorant. The people who need it most never use it." Was Lenin himself not on the path towards this solution when, in his *State and Revolution*, he proposed the famous slogan: "Every Kitchen Maid Should Learn to Rule the State"? It is worth taking a closer look at the precise context of Lenin's justification of this slogan which, at a first sight, may appear extremely utopian, especially since he emphasizes that the slogan designates something that "can and must be made at once, overnight," not in some later Communist future: "the mechanism of social management is here already to hand"[8] in modern capitalism—the mechanism of the automatic functioning of a large production process where the bosses (representing the owner) just give formal orders. This mechanism runs so smoothly that, without disturbing it, the role of the boss is reduced to simple decisions and can be played by an ordinary person. So all the Socialist revolution has to do is to replace the capitalist or state-appointed boss with an (randomly selected) ordinary person.

*

But it didn't work in this way, and it is interesting to see *how* it didn't work: there is one title which condenses what went wrong, that of the "General Secretary" of the Party. After the Bolshevik victory in the Civil War, the Office of General Secretary was created by Lenin in 1922 with the intention that it serve a purely administrative and disciplinary purpose. Prior to Stalin's accession, the position was not viewed as an important role in Lenin's government: previous occupants had been responsible for technical rather than political decisions. Its primary task was to determine the composition of party membership and to assign positions within the party. The General Secretary also oversaw the recording of party events, and was entrusted with keeping party leaders and members informed about party activities.[9] So how did we arrive from this non-political "technical" role to the position of the absolute Master not only of the Party but also of the state and its entire population? The problem was not that the General Secretary was a new form of monarchic dictatorship, but the exact opposite: the General Secretary, imagined as a modest non-political post, filled in the gap opened up by the absence of a monarchic (purely symbolic) power.

*

In some countries (the US, Israel) in which the executive branch is perceived as getting too strong, the role of the monarch can be partially taken over by the Supreme (or Constitutional) Court—is this not why, in the months before the Hamas attack of October 7, 2024, the political struggle that triggered mass demonstrations in Israel was the opposition's attempts to prevent the government from abolishing the autonomy of the Supreme Court? Although the function of the Supreme Court is just to protect the rule of law, it often has to decide in ambiguous or open situations. Another social institution which can (rarely, but nonetheless) play this role is

> the army, as none other than Fredric Jameson argued in his magisterial *An American Utopia: Dual Power and the Universal Army*[10]—his point is that the army could play this role precisely because it is organized in a non-democratic way (top generals are not elected, etc.).

That's why Hegel fanatically opposes all reasoning about the justification of a king's authority: this authority is not a topic of debate, it is *unconditional and, as such, empty*. The best argument against the monarch's actual power is the tautology: "The king is a king." In his brief outline of social ontology, Kafka distinguishes three levels that he designates with A, B, and C.[11] To put it in a very simplified way, A is the One, the core of our being out of our direct reach, or (politically) the summit of power. As such, A is always minimally transcendent, its signs cannot be read in an unambiguous way, so they have to be interpreted, transformed into fixed regulations, by some form of B: ideological institutions, interpreters of the obscure Sacred Word which bombard individual subjects (C) with messages that remain ambiguous since their A remains blurred. Is there a solution to this predicament? The worst option by far is B without A, i.e., a reign of experts with no higher authority—this is the most concise definition of totalitarianism where inconsistent institutions reign. An A is thus needed, but how to avoid a traditional authority like monarchy? I am more and more inclined to claim that a monarchy with a stupid monarch who is selected by a lot and is just like one of us, with no expert knowledge (like Lenin's kitchen maid) is the only realistic solution even if it appears the most utopian.

To venture further still, the structure should be triple: not just democracy plus a stupid monarch elected by a lot, but a collective body standing for social wisdom, not just experts (disgusting as this word is). Take ecology: the necessary tough measures needed to cope with ecological threats cannot be left to democratic vote. Today, in an age when the fateful limitation of the Western model of multiparty liberal democracy is becoming more and more obvious, the need to supplement liberal democracy with another mechanism of power is also growing. Attempts in this direction are already taking place, although they largely pass unnoticed. Recall Switzerland, a definitely successful and stable country. Very few people know who are the ministers there or which parties have majority—government is considered a kind of neutral mechanism that one can safely ignore. Plus in Switzerland they often have referendums, but with a nice totalitarian touch: when a citizen goes to vote, he gets two pieces of paper—his ballot, and a leaflet where the state gives him/her the advice on how to vote. (It is through a referendum held in February 1971 that women got the right to vote, and women's suffrage didn't affect in any serious way the relationship between the political parties.) A couple of decades ago, a Communist served as the mayor of Geneva, a city which embodies modern capitalism, and life just went on, with no disturbances (the same thing in 2024 is going on in Graz, Austria). The secret is that, elevated above the state administration, there is a kind of state council composed of less than 10 (financially, economically . . .) important members who, although they mostly stay in the shadows, effectively control and regulate social processes.

With all the inevitable critiques of Iran, one must admit that, when Khomeiny took power, he took great pains to formalize a quite similar structure: a democracy, but with an external body controlling it, deciding, vetoing, etc. This body is the Guardian Council composed of the top representatives of the Muslim Clergy and led by the Supreme Leader (first Khomeiny himself, now Khamenei). Iran has a democratically-elected parliament, prime minister and president, but all candidates have to be confirmed (and are often vetoed) by the Supreme Leader to safeguard the Islamic purity of Iran. Iranian constitution has thus been called a "hybrid" of "theocratic and democratic elements." While Articles 1 and 2 vest sovereignty in God, Article 6 "mandates popular elections for the presidency and the Majlis, or parliament."[12]

But what about China today (and Vietnam and . . .)? Do we not have there the Communist Party as the non-elected guardian which controls and directs the state apparatus inclusive of all elected bodies? There are obvious problems with this model: elected bodies are a rubber stamp for the decisions of the party (which, interesting to note, is excluded from the legal system: it doesn't exist from the standpoint of the law, it is nowhere registered as a legal entity) plus what is obviously missing is a stupid monarch elected by lot. China is thus further away from this goal than Iran, where there is a minimum of public political struggles (between "moderates" and "hardliners").

But the main problem here is, of course: how will this controlling body be nominated? Who will do it? Of course it should NOT be democratically elected, and it is also not "apolitical"—in some sense, it is the most political body of them all, the outcome of an informal class struggle. Ideally, its basic orientation should be that of a moderately-conservative Communism (aware of the urgency of radical changes, but cautious in their realization—my own stance, curiously enough!). In contrast to the democratic state administration, it clearly stands for a dictatorial element.

I am far from suggesting that we need the same (Iranian) model in Europe (after all, Iran is an Islamic republic based on a sacred book); however, we in Europe (and all around the world) are facing the same problem: how to combine a secular democracy with a non-elected advisory body plus a non-sacred quilting point, a top agent or agency of formal decision which performs a political collapse, deciding among democratic superpositions.

Conclusion: The hunger to be something

Hegelian dialectics, Lacanian psychoanalysis, and quantum mechanics may seem like an oddly-assorted trio, a motley crew. But what they have in common (apart from my interest in all three) is that they all operate in the mode of *paraconsistent* logic, which challenges the predominant model of logic. According to that traditional logic, from contradictory premises, anything follows. A logical consequence relation is *explosive* if according to it any arbitrary conclusion is entailed by any arbitrary contradiction. Inconsistency, according to received wisdom, cannot be coherently reasoned about. Paraconsistent logic challenges this standard view: a logical consequence relation is said to be paraconsistent if it is not explosive. Thus, if a consequence relation is paraconsistent, then even in circumstances where the available information is inconsistent, the consequence relation does not explode into *triviality*. Thus, paraconsistent logic accommodates inconsistency in a controlled way that treats inconsistent information as potentially informative.[1] This certainly holds for Hegel in whose thought inconsistency obeys an iron logic; for Lacan, where inconsistency indicates an intervention of the unconscious dimension; and for quantum mechanics in which inconsistency is what defines superpositions (a particle is simultaneously here and there and . . .)?

We experience this dimension of paraconsistency at its purest when we stumble upon the reversal of mediation into a new shape of immediacy. Today,

Marxists as a rule reject any form of immediacy as a fetish that obfuscates social mediation. However, in his masterpiece on Adorno,[2] Jameson has shown how dialectical analysis includes its own point of suspension: in the midst of a complex analysis of mediations, Adorno suddenly makes a vulgar gesture of "reductionism," interrupting the flow of dialectical finesse with a simple point like "ultimately it is about class struggle." This is how class struggle functions within a social totality: it is not its "deeper ground" or its profound structuring principle that mediates all its moments, but something much more superficial—the point of failure of endless complex analysis. It is a gesture of jumping ahead to a conclusion, when, in an act of despair, we raise our hands and say: "But after all, this is all about class struggle!" What we must bear in mind here is that this failure of analysis is immanent to reality itself; it is how society totalizes itself through its constitutive antagonism. In other words, class struggle is a quick and easy pseudo-totalization when proper totalization fails; it is a desperate attempt to use antagonism itself as the principle of totalization.

Recall that during Joe Biden's inauguration, there was a lone figure who stole the show by just sitting there, sticking out as an element of discord disturbing the spectacle: Bernie Sanders. The effect was not that of a person left out at a party but rather of a person who has no interest in joining. Every philosopher knows how impressed Hegel was when he saw Napoleon riding through Jena—it was for him like seeing the world spirit (the predominant historical tendency) riding a horse ... The fact that Bernie stole the show and that the image of him just sitting there instantly became an icon means that the true world spirit of our time was there, in his lone figure embodying scepticism about the fake normalization staged in the ceremony—there is still hope for our cause, people are aware that a more radical change is needed. Lines of separation thus seemed clearly drawn: liberal establishment embodied in Biden versus democratic socialists whose most popular representative is Bernie Sanders.

But my point here is not a political one, it concerns the inherent necessity for a general spiritual tendency to "collapse" in a particular person. This is why one cannot reduce this "collapse" to a form of fetishism in which a complex web of mediations appears as an immediate presence: only through such a "collapse" does this complex web (in our case, all the tendencies and hopes that Bernie personifies) acquire a form of actuality, a positive force that sustains political engagement. If we take away this collapse we don't get the general spirit of a world in its clean form, without any contingent empirical elements—what we get is a mess with no mobilizing force. And it is important to note the difference between this image of Bernie and the photo of a defiant Trump with blood on his ear and cheek, being rushed off stage by Secret Service agents, fist raised with an American flag in the background. Although this photo also became instantly iconic, it did not acquire the same mobilizing force as the much more modest, less spectacular, photo of Bernie sitting alone.[3]

Perhaps, we can also say that paraconsistency belongs to the field some call "metamodernism." Metamodernism presents itself as a dialectical "negation of negation" of modernism: postmodernism negates modernism (traditional rationalist progressism) with ironic deconstruction or historicist relativization of modernist universal rationalism, while metamodernism brings postmodernism to its immanent self-negation, maintaining its critical stance but combining it with a reassertion of hope and positive values which survive relativist deconstruction—it is not enough to demonstrate how every ideology is rooted in a particular socio-symbolic context, one also has to translate this demonstration into a positive ethico-political stance. Metamodernism mostly locates this stance in a reference to authentic subjectivity, as well as in ecological concerns or social solidarity . . .

*

There are two problems with this notion of metamodernism. First, according to the definition given above, were Marx, Nietzsche, and Freud not already metamodernists, even though they preceded postmodernism? Moreover, was Hegel himself not the first major metamodernist, since his dialectical procedure endeavours precisely to undermine every fixed universal notion? Second, modernism is not the beginning of the story but a reaction to the vast field usually referred to as "traditional societies"—and is our time not characterized precisely by a weird co-existence of postmodern cynicism and a resuscitated *pre*modern fundamentalism? If—as Fred Jameson pointed out—postmodernism introduced a false permissiveness (everything is permitted on condition that it does not disturb the free circulation of the capital, all "subversive" acts are even solicited insofar as they can be integrated into the self-reproductive movement of the capital), an exemplary feature of metamodernist ideology is the so-called Cancel Culture in which exclusion, brutal censorship, is reintroduced on behalf of inclusion and diversity themselves: you are excluded if you do not fit our definition of inclusion and diversity. To put it in another way, while postmodernism stands for the (appearance of the) end of history when all epochs coexist in an eternal Now, metamodernism designates a return of history with its radical breaks, tensions and antagonisms, something nicely captured by the term "bend of History":

> A bending of History may simultaneously imply forcing History into a different direction or shape as well as causing History to deflect from the more or less straight line of teleological narrative. It also captures the increasing awareness across culture that there is something at stake, yet we are still very much unsure what this something—hidden around the bend, as it were—might be (and we will only really know in hindsight).[4]

In quantum mechanics, paraconsistency resides in the parallax gap between our common reality and the quantum proto-reality means that each domain is contained in its opposite. As Bohr liked to repeat, the only reality that exists for us is our common reality, and all we know about quantum proto-reality are the measurement data we see in our common reality—they appear within a frame, i.e., on a screen of our measuring devices. At the same time the implicit ontological premise of quantum mechanics is that what we perceive (and interact with) as reality is the outcome of the collapse of wave functions, so that—as, among others, Rovelli claims—the ultimate reality is that of the complex network of wave oscillations, and our common reality is something that appears (and exists) only within the frame generated by wave oscillations. This duality is strictly homologous to the duality of nature and culture: human culture is part of nature since nature is "all there is," but at the same time, to paraphrase Lukacs, nature is a cultural category, i.e., what we perceive as "natural" is always overdetermined by a social-cultural historical context.

Consequently, paraphrasing Lacan's well known "*Kant avec Sade*", we should say "Gettier with Rumsfeld." A brief reminder: back in 1963, Edmund Gettier imagined counterexamples which challenge the predominant justified-true-belief (JTB) account of knowledge. The JTB account holds that knowledge is equivalent to justified true belief; if all three conditions (justification, truth, and belief) are met of a given claim, then we have knowledge of that claim. Gettier attempts to illustrate by means of two counterexamples that there are cases where individuals can have a justified, true belief regarding a claim but still fail to know it because the reasons for the belief, while justified, turn out to be false—the JTB account is thus inadequate because it does not account for all of the necessary and sufficient conditions for knowledge.[5]

*

Here is one counterexample: I am interviewed for a job and I am told by the interviewer that my answers were excellent so that the job is mine for sure; on my way out, I put my hand into my pocket and discover that I have there two coins, so I conclude that the person who will get the job has two coins in his pocket. What then happens is that there was another guy interviewed after me and he was even better than me, so that he got the job; on the top of it, by a strange coincidence this guy also has two coins in his pocket. All three conditions of true knowledge are thus met: I know the guy who got the job has two coins in his pocket, the guy really has two coins in his pocket, and my claim that he has two coins in his pocket is justified (I reached this conclusion with clear reasoning)—however, intuition tells me that we are dealing here with a rare coincidence so that we cannot really say that I *knew* the guy who got the job has two coins in his pocket.

Among the dozens of attempts to resolve the problem by way of redefining knowledge, the predominant one adds a fourth condition which concerns causal power: my justification of a fact must designate the true cause of that fact. This condition is clearly not met in our counterexample: my justification (I checked my pocket and there were two coins in it) has nothing to do with the fact that the winner (not me) had two coins in his pocket... Instead of proposing the right solution, I'll limit myself here to the obvious fact that at least two further distinctions are needed here: between belief and opinion (which are both unjustified in the usual sense of the term), and between knowledge in the strict sense of the world (the French *savoir*) and a more vague sense of knowing something or someone (the French *connaissance*). An authentic religious belief is not only not justified in the usual sense of the term, true theologians even despise so-called rational proofs of god's existence as an obscene abomination: belief is not a matter of objectively knowing that something is true, it implies full subjective engagement (which is why the statement "I know god exists but I don't believe in him" is one of the most brutal expressions of radical atheism). The same holds for political engagement: if I say "I believe people are equal," I am not asking for a further justification in order to make this belief true knowledge—"I believe people are equal" is a political stance, a norm to which I am fully committed, not a statement of objective knowledge.

Belief is also to be distinguished from opinion (a not fully justified presumption)—say, I think Trump really lost the 2020 presidential elections, but this opinion is not grounded in my detailed knowledge, I've just decided to trust the media reports. Another distinction is here the already-mentioned one between *savoir* (strict knowledge) and *connaissance* (*connaitre* in the sense of knowing someone, being acquainted with him): there is no contradiction in saying "Yes, I know that guy, but I don't *really* know him." Say, I know my neighbour, I met him regularly on the stairs, we nod to each other, but I know practically nothing about him.

Then there are rumours[6] which function in a strange way with regard to truth: the fact itself, the factual truth of a rumour, is suspended (or, rather, treated as indifferent—"I don't know if it is true, but this is what I heard..."), while the content of a rumour retains its full symbolic efficiency—we enjoy them, retelling them with passion. So it's not the same as the fetishist disavowal ("I know very well it's not ture, nonetheless... I believe in it"), but, again, its inversion, something like "I cannot say that I believe this is true, this really happened, but nonetheless... here is what I know." With regard to the exercise of power, the space of rumours is ambiguous. "Dirty" rumours can sustain power and its authority (from Ataturk to Tito), but rumours also play an often decisive role in unrests and revolutionary upheavals, inclusive of anti-immigrant revolts (Europe is now full of rumours of immigrants raping our women, and of how authorities censor news about these rapes). There are also what one may be tempted to call "good rumours" which are needed to trigger a revolutionary explosion. Exemplary here is the Great Fear (*la Grande Peur*), the general panic that took place between July 17 and August 3, 1789, at the start of the French Revolution:

> Rural unrest had been present in France since the worsening grain shortage of the spring, and, fueled by rumors of an aristocrats' "famine plot" to starve or burn out the population, both peasants and townspeople mobilized in many regions. In response to these rumors, fearful peasants armed themselves in self-defense and, in some areas, attacked manor houses. The content of the rumors differed from region to region—in some areas it was believed that a foreign force was burning the crops in the fields, while in other areas it was believed that robbers were burning buildings.[7]

From what we know, there was no "famine plot," and the very fact that the content of rumours varied demonstrates their factual non-truth: however, even if false ("fake news"), they played an indispensable role in mobilizing the people. Every revolutionary upheaval, from the October Revolution to the Khomeini movement overthrowing the regime of the Shah in Iran, was also a conflict of rumours. During the October Revolution, rumours were circulating that Bolshevik units were commanded by German officers, etc., together with rumours that drunken Bolsheviks were serially raping women ...

What complicates things further is the precise reflexive status of my knowledge: is being aware of some knowledge necessary for it to qualify as knowledge? This brings us again to "Gettier with Rumsfeld"—back in March 2003, Rumsfeld engaged in a little bit of amateur philosophizing about the relationship between the known and the unknown: "There are known knowns. These are things we know that we know. There are known unknowns. That is to say, there are things that we know we don't know. But there are also unknown unknowns. There are things we don't know we don't know."[8] What he forgot to add was the crucial fourth term: the "unknown knowns," things we don't know that we know—which is precisely the Freudian unconscious, the "knowledge which doesn't know itself," as Lacan used to say. If Rumsfeld thought that the main dangers in the confrontation with Iraq were the "unknown unknowns," the threats from Saddam we were not even aware of, our reply should be that the main dangers were, on the contrary, the "unknown knowns," the disavowed beliefs and suppositions we are not even aware of adhering to ourselves. This distinction between unknown unknowns and unknown knowns is today more pertinent than ever. In the case of ecology, disavowed beliefs and suppositions are the ones which prevent us from taking seriously the prospect of a catastrophe. So let me propose here my own thought experiment on "Gettier with Rumsfeld" which involves racism or sexism and works in both ways. Let's imagine a black single mother applied for a job, was fully qualified for it (surpassing all competitors), and got it: a sexist racist may claim that she didn't really get the job because she was qualified for it but because she was a black woman. Or the opposite case: she wasn't the most qualified for the job and she didn't get it, but a feminist anti-racist will claim that the real reason she didn't get the job is, again, that she was a black woman.

Things get here very complicated—first, how does affirmative action work? Is it just that between equally qualified persons we should choose the (racially, sexually ...) underprivileged one, or is it that the underprivileged status can to some extent prevail over qualifications? There are some arguments for this more radical stance: the features we rely on in measuring qualification are often not socially neutral—which is also why some versions of John Rawls's famous principle of the "veil of ignorance" (not knowing some things like colourblindness) cannot and should not always be applied. Unknown knowns are not just a negative feature (unconscious prejudices, etc.); they can also play a different role. What if deep in my psyche I know that I did something horrible and inexcusable, and while I rationalized this betrayal by a series of arguments which make it acceptable, the pressure of guilt secretly permeates my entire life.

The status of true knowledge is in itself ambiguous, not only in the obvious sense that, while all the data I enumerate are true, the selection of some data and ignorance of other data betray a hidden (or even not so hidden) bias. Knowledge doesn't concern just individuals: it is a social fact embedded in the predominant notion of the big Other. Let's take the obvious example: yes, the Earth circulates around the Sun, but only if we accept in advance the coordinates of classical modern physics—the moment relativity theory and quantum mechanics enter the game, such statements should be qualified. However, in our common universe, it is accepted as a fact that the Earth circulates around the Sun.

Does this imply epistemic or moral relativism? Does it mean that what is at one level a terrible crime is at another level a neutral fact? The best-known example: if brain science demonstrates that there is no free will, was then Hitler really responsible for Shoah? Is it not all too easy to reply that we have to distinguish levels here (in our human universe, Hitler was evil, while as a living organism his freedom was just a "user's illusion"): brain science pretends to explain how the experience of freedom as a "user's illusion" emerges out of and is a moment of natural mechanisms. This is why even those who reject free will resort to evoking complex inscrutability of our brain processes to leave some space open for freedom—here is an exemplary case of this strategy:

> So there is no "ghost" inside the cerebral machine. But as researchers, we argue that this machinery is so complex, inscrutable, and mysterious that popular concepts of "free will" or the "self" remain incredibly useful. They help us think through and imagine—albeit imperfectly—the workings of the mind and brain. As such, they can guide and inspire our investigations in profound ways—provided we continue to question and test these assumptions along the way.[9]

While here is not the place to confront these deadlocks,[10] what we must insist on is that complexity and inscrutability are not just an effect of the limitation of our knowledge—they reside in the thing itself. True knowledge and freedom are proofs that reality itself is antinomic and "contradictory" in the Hegelian sense—in short, that it is paraconsistent. With the wonderful irreverence that is so rare among today's Leftists due to our Cancel Culture, Alain Badiou asserts that philosophy emerged in Ancient Greece:

> I, for one, can say that in pre-colonial Africa, or even in ancient China, there was no philosophy at all, without feeling guilty of cultural colonialism, and actually without feeling guilty of anything.[11]

Why? Because philosophy can only emerge when two conditions are met: democracy and mathematics. Badiou immediately notices the tension between these two conditions: freedom implies indeterminacy and chaos, while mathematics implies following rules and the procedures of demonstration. (More precisely, "freedom" stands here for a gap between truth and power: truth is not dependent on some higher authority—god, state power and its institutions—but should be demonstrated with rational reasoning. This is why Badiou also claims that mathematics itself begins in Ancient Greece: only there mathematical axioms become something to be demonstrated—this is not what we get in much praised ancient Indian or Arab mathematics. Even the great Srinivasa Ramanujan (1887–1920), praised as "the man who knew infinity"—reshaped twentieth-century mathematics with his various contributions in several mathematical domains, including mathematical analysis, infinite series, continued fractions, number theory, and game theory—is regularly reproached for just formulating his intuitions without any formal procedures of demonstration.)

This "Eurocentrism" is already detectable in the triadic structure of the present book. Let me attempt the impossible and provide a brief description of the basic ontological premise of all my work, the premise best rendered by Mladen Dolar's thesis that *being is a failed nothing*.[12] One could also add here Emil Cioran's notion of the "inconvenience of existence," and, of course, Peter Wessel Zapffe, a Norwegian thinker for whom humanity is "an evolutionary error"—its excessive self-awareness may appear to heighten its chances of survival, but it effectively limits its ability to act.[13] Let me emphasize that there is absolutely no contradiction between such a "pessimist" view and a dedication to Communism: today's Communist has to accept the immanent despair of the human condition and propose Communism as a strategy to cope with it.

In other words, one should drop the implicit humanist optimism of the standard Left: a human being has the potential for a happy life, for solidarity and cooperation, suffering and despair predominate just in alienated societies ... Without asserting the tendency towards evil as constitutive of being human (the figure of a utilitarian-egotist human nature is clearly a product of capitalist modernity), one should unconditionally abandon the idea of some essential creative potential of human beings which is thwarted in capitalism. This idea was superbly deployed in Ray Brassier's outstanding *Fatelessness: Freedom and Fatality After Marx*, where he systematically and in a true philosophical spirit demonstrates how the Marxist concept of deactualization "challenges Hegel's yoking of possibility to actuality":

> capital is not just a loosely coordinated aggregate of social phenomena but a self-reproducing social totality that, although of historically recent provenance, is compelled to subordinate the present and future of human history to ensure its own perpetuity. Thus capital is not just one of a succession of shapes of spirit but its fatal estrangement; a specific mode of production that coopts generic human productivity (human genus being or *Gattungwesen*) for its own limitless yet pointless expansion. ... Thus humanity's actualization in and through capital (working to live) is coupled to capital's actualization in and through humanity (the exploitation of labour). But there is an asymmetry in this coupling because while labour's actualization actualizes capital, the actualization of capital simultaneously actualizes *and* deactualizes labour.[14]

From my standpoint, Brassier here re-Aristotelianizes Marx, mobilizing the tension between the essential possibility of being-human and its contingent actualization. For Hegel actualization is a truth of a possibility, i.e., it brings out what a possibility effectively amounted to—say, from Hegel's standpoint, Stalinism was the truth of the Leninist (or even Marxist) project, not just its secondary deviation. For Marx, there is a split in every actualization, and this split becomes palpable in capitalism: the creative potential that defines being-human and tends towards its actualization effectively is actualized in capitalism (workers collectively produce immense material and spiritual wealth), but this actualization is simultaneously the workers's de-actualiztion, their reduction to poor, suffering, dominated and exploited instruments of capital's self-reproduction. This de-actualization is not necessary, it is necessary just for the reproduction of capital, while from the creative human essence immanently contains the possibility of eradicating contingent suffering and domination—a revolutionary effort is sustained precisely by the awareness that the capitalist actualization is something historically contingent that could be abolished.

I think this critique of Hegel should be rejected from the very Marxist standpoint: in *Grundrisse* Marx makes it clear that only in and through capitalism the working class emerges as a substance-less subjectivity which can then (through the revolutionary act as a collective subject) re-appropriate its alienated substance as its own product. Exploitation and domination are thus necessary for human actuality: they give rise to the subject of potential liberation, and this is why Marx even says that capitalism is already liberation in itself (and will become for itself through a revolution). Pre-capitalist societies are less "alienated" than capitalism because in them workers are not excluded from objective social totality, they are just still reduced to moments of the organic social process of production, i.e., they still appear to have their proper place within a social totality and are not reduced to a "place of no-place."

One should be careful not to confuse this movement with the standard misunderstanding of the Hegelian triad: it is not that the (collective) subject objectivizes itself in its product in which he no longer recognizes itself and thus (mis)perceives it as an alien entity, finally recognizing itself in it and appropriating it as its own product. There is no subject prior to alienation: it is the process of alienation itself which creates the subject in its distinction to objective order.

To follow this through as far as it goes, what happens in the third moment of a dialectical movement is neither that the subject recognizes itself in its other, appropriates it as its own product, nor does the subject recognize itself in its other in the sense of acquitting a fixed proper place in it. The solution is a properly Hegelian one: the subject recognizes itself in the lack/inconsistency/impossibility that traverses the Other, it experiences itself as correlative to the lack in/of the Other. This solution implies that the only appropriate ontological stance of revolutionary Marxism is a radical ontological pessimism, which is why another key name must be added to the list of ontological pessimists: Philipp Mainländer, a more or less forgotten German "philosopher of pessimism" from the mid-nineteenth century who split from Schopenhauer. While Mainländer follows Schopenhauer in his basic claim that the only redemption is death, a return to void, for him Will is not not a will to live (which we should fight to extinguish it) but the will to die, to vanish.

So how did our world of suffering arise in the first place? In a crazy cosmic extrapolation, Mainländer interprets creation as a kind of Big Bang in which the singularity of god (a name for the primordial Void) exploded, i.e., in which he killed himself, dispersed himself into a chaotic multitude: "The world is nothing but the decaying corpse of God." And since "non-being is better than being," all of creation strives to return to the primordial Void.[15] Here we should disagree with Mainländer: the explosion does not follow the divine Void, it is itself the primordial fact—this is the only way to reply to the obvious counter-argument: why did god not remain a peaceful Void? Yes, the primordial fact is death drive, but death drive is not (as Freud himself sometimes misunderstands his own discovery) a tendency towards nirvana, it is uncannily close to an obscene immortality, a drive which persists beyond the circle of life and death.

Mainländer's philosophy was for him not just a theory, it involved a full engagement (like Otto Weininger's thought): the day he received copies of his *Philosophy of Redemption*, he accepted that he had done what he could for the benefit of humanity and decided to kill himself—he hanged himself on April 1, 1876 (the fool's day!). But here comes a big surprise: he considered another way that he could remain useful to humanity and go on living, a radical Leftist political engagement. (He did not take this path because his sister to whom he was very close opposed Leftist politics.) The contrast between Mainländer and Schopenhauer's political conservativism and anti-feminism strikes the eye: for Mainländer, the fact that for a large majority of people life is one long suffering and misery pushed him to social engagement to lessen suffering—a convincing case of how ontological pessimism goes hand in hand with compassionate radical politics. Mainländer goes very far in this direction, he argues not only against Schopenhauer but also against Buddhism:

while these systems provide pathways for individual alleviation of suffering, they fall short of addressing the broader societal implications of existential suffering. He contends that such quietisms can perpetuate injustice by failing to empower those who lack the means to achieve personal moral development. For Mainländer, the ethical pursuit of personal goodness must be accompanied by a commitment to social justice, ensuring that all individuals have access to the education and resources necessary to develop an awareness of the lack of value of life.

The central premise of Mainländer's activism is thus that a truly pessimistic ethics *must* advocate for the dismantling of social and political structures that perpetuate inequality and suffering: the pursuit of social and political equality is a natural extension of the compassion that arises from recognizing existence as fundamentally evil. This perspective leads him to champion not only Communism but also the free love movement (*freie Liebe*), including feminism and gay rights, as essential components of a just society: "Communism serves as a vehicle for achieving social and economic equality, allowing individuals to transcend the selfish impulses inherent in the will to survive. By eliminating class distinctions and ensuring equal access to education and resources, Mainländer believes that society can cultivate a collective commitment to alleviating suffering."[16] Should we be surprised that two great figures of the German Social Democracy in the late nineteenth century, August Bebel and Eduard Bernstein, sympathized with Mainländer? Today, in a society in which the striving for pleasure and happiness fully display their self-destructive potential, only figures like Mainländer can save us.

*

To return to the main thrust of my argument, the only candidate for being as a non-failed nothing that I know would be viruses like Covid: they are beings in which nothing (force of destruction) succeeded[17]; plus one may add abortion. In Sophocles' *Oedipus at Colonus*, the Chorus says: "Not to be born at all / Is best, far best that can befall"—could these famous chorus lines not be actualized today as the best argument for abortion? "Do you worry about the kind of world your child will live in? We can secure its greatest luck by aborting it . . ." All positively-existing entities are quite literally *less than nothing*, they emerge because of the immanent antagonism/contradiction that cuts across the primordial void, the tension between the void in the sense of the Buddhist *sunyata* (the primordial void as the background of all ephemeral appearances that exist only in their interrelations) and the void in the sense of self-relating negativity, a singularity that excludes and threatens to destroy all positive content. This tension between the all-encompassing Void of eternal pace and void of negativity, a point of pure singularity, is the ultimate identity of the opposites, a new version of the first couple of Hegel's logic, Being and Nothingness, a pre-dialectical tension which sustains all dialectical process:

> *Pure Being* and *pure nothing* are, therefore, the same. What is the truth is neither being nor nothing, but that being—does not pass over but has passed over—into nothing, and nothing into being. But it is equally true that they are not undistinguished from each other, that, on the contrary, they are not the same, that they are absolutely distinct, and yet that they are unseparated and inseparable and that each immediately *vanishes in its opposite*.[18]

The key claim in this quote is that being "does not pass over but has passed over" into nothing: it is a pre-dialectical passage which always-already took place. This dimension is missing in Rovelli's *Helgoland* where, in order to explain his notion of interrelatedness of all entities, i.e., of how every entity is what it is only in its relations with all others (in itself it is a void), he enthusiastically refers to Nagarjuna, the great Mahayana Buddhist.[19] It is because of this tension in the void itself that we should reject all stories of the Origin, of a Fall from some primordial peace, or, more appropriate to our times, the idea that wave oscillations are the ultimate true reality, the productive origin of everything, and object of our ordinary reality just the (ontologically) secondary "objectification" (reification) of the primary productive flow, the result of its collapse, a kind of ontological Fall of the primordial productivity. The fluid domain of wave oscillation is in itself an index of instability and tension, wave oscillations in their multiplicity of superpositions are the reaction to a fundamental impossibility. Collapses of wave functions are local and ultimately failed attempts to stabilize the situation, to resolve the (pre)ontological tension that permeates the quantum domain. So we have, roughly said, three domains or levels: the absolute contradiction of the primordial void, quantum oscillations, our ordinary reality.

As we have already seen, Rovelli seems to come dangerously close to the typical modern view which turns around the traditional view of material things which all the time change as originating from an eternal immovable Absolute: what we get in modernity is the idea that fixed self-identical objects, material things, are a "reified" result of a fluid non-substantial productive process—movement comes before fixed identity. My Lacanian counterpoint is that one should introduce here the distinction between objects in reality and what Lacan, following Freud, called the Thing (*das Ding*), the impossible Real Thing which coincides with its own opposite, the Thing which has no substantial content but stands for pure difference. It is because the quantum processes are always-already haunted by this gap of the Thing that they immanently tend to collapse in order to resolve their constitutive tension—or, as Schelling put it two centuries back, because of this gap or tension there is a "hunger to be something" in every Nothing.

The next key point is that we should not see these three levels as three steps in the self-deployment of the Absolute: the circular logic of retroactivity is at work here also. The primordial Void is also a retroactive product of the failure of quantum wave to actualize their potentials, the point of impossibility around which they circulate, and these waves themselves can also be conceived as a cloud of virtualities which float around a real object or process. And this brings us also to history and politics proper. Read against the background of such quantum ontology, history is a process whose necessity and direction are always determined retroactively: once the multiplicity of options collapses in a contingent way, the past is structured as a necessary process that had to lead to the present state of things. And, last but not least, this collapse is not a neutral "objective" process but a contingent political act.[20]

This is how we are to understand more closely the triadic structure of this book: quantum inspired ontology as the new form of dialectical materialism; historical materialism reconstructed so that it excludes the progressive-evolutionist aspects of traditional Marxism; chances of radical emancipatory acts today. This structure of UPS is not that of a linear progress: it is not that we (in the logical order) first formulate a general ontological vision, then we apply this vision to social development, and finally we draw from it political implications. (If a reader will take the book in this way, s/he deserves a lifelong place in gulag.) The notion of hologram, retroactivity, and the collapse of superpositions, the central motif of the book, also underlies its tripartite structure: a radical political act is the singular point which retroactively grounds its historical and philosophical superpositions. The true starting point is thus not a panoramic view of the entire cosmos but the unbearable tension of a political moment, of what Walter Benjamin called *Jetztzeit*:—let me shamelessly quote the Oxford Reference description:

> a notion of time that is ripe with revolutionary possibility, time that has been detached from the continuum of history. It is time at a standstill, poised, filled with energy, and ready to take what Benjamin called the "tiger's leap" into the future. It isn't naturally occurring, however, and takes the intervention of the artist or revolutionary to produce it by "blasting" it free from the ceaseless flow in which it would otherwise be trapped. Benjamin contrasts *Jetztzeit* with the "homogeneous empty time" of the ruling class, which is history written from the perspective of the victors.[21]

So it is not only quantum physics which describes the level where the linear flow of time is suspended—at the opposite end of quantum speculations, in a moment of extreme political engagement, we find a homologous paradox. This in no way implies historicist relativization—our historical moment *is* unique, a moment at which god (the big Other) is effectively dead, at which the death of god became a moment of our social life itself, not just a brief traumatic experience covered up by new illusions. In some sense which is far from merely metaphorical, god is dead and we are dead with it. If we still live, we are living dead. Being undead is our only space of freedom—or, to quote James Baldwin:

> Any real change implies the breakup of the world as one has always known it, the loss of all that gave one an identity, the end of safety. And at such a moment, unable to see and not daring to imagine what the future will now bring forth, one clings to what one knew, or dreamed that one possessed. Yet, it is only when a man is able, without bitterness or self-pity, to surrender a dream he has long possessed that he is set free, he has set himself free for higher dreams.[22]

Is my ultimate stance then a pessimist one? Yes and no. Yes, since I am ready to renounce the standard Leftist idea that, at some point in the future, the majority of the people will awaken, throw off the shackles of the ruling ideology and engage in radical emancipatory action. What we are witnessing now is a step in the opposite direction: a gradual *normalization* of Rightist and Leftist "excesses" (like Fascism and Stalinism). Although Alternative for Germany from time to time slips into open racism, it mostly speaks a "civilized" moderate language. Even the radical Left is recently trying to normalize itself: there is a new tendency on the fringes of our political spectrum, something we cannot but call a "moderate far Left"; its main proponents are Domenico Losurdo (who recently died) and Gabriel Rockhill (who analyzed the link between Adorno and Horkheimer and the CIA, and also dismissed me as "capitalist's court jester").

This tendency is far Left because it breaks the firewall that defined the post-World War II Western Left: it rehabilitates "really existing Socialism," inclusive of Stalin and Mao. But it does this not in exalted Stalinist language: its language is that of moderation and non-dogmatic realist pragmatism, so that it's not so much a rehabilitation but rather the normalization of Stalinism and Maoism. Stalinism should be viewed as one of the stages in the complex development of Socialism; yes, it had its excesses, but also its great achievements, and it emerged as an understandable reaction to the boycott and pressure on Socialist countries. This is how the followers of this line explain the repressive features of the Socialist regimes (strong secret police, etc.): they construct a narrative which I find thoroughly ridiculous: when revolutionaries took power, they thought they were now in a free society, but they were soon compelled to realize that they were under siege, encircled by internal and external enemies bent on their destruction through direct military intervention, economic boycott, corruption, etc.

The sad conclusion was that, in order to survive and protect their revolution, they also needed secret police and other means of social control and oppression ... [23] In a similar vein, the deadly excesses of the Chinese revolutions (like the tens of millions of dead in the "great leap forward" in late 1950s) are dismissed as part of the contradictory gradual development of Socialism, with the oscillation between two extremes (revolutionary terror and a partial return to capitalist economy) ... it is easy to recognize in this normalization an exact mirror-image of the far Right attempts to "normalize" Fascism by situating it into its historical context.

What I find problematic is the suggestion that the revolutionaries enjoyed an intermediary state of naïve belief that they and their society were now free. There was no utopian moment of freedom; even before their victory, the revolutionaries were well aware of the necessary terror and well prepared to apply it. The first thing to do to clarify this mess is to problematize democracy itself (at least the way this term functions today)—one has to gather the courage to reject the simple explanation that what is missing is the mobilization of the people, a true democracy sustained by the popular engagement. If there is a lesson to be learned from the latest Right-populist protests, it is that the time has come to turn around what Abraham Lincoln once said: "You can fool all people some of the time and some people all of the time. But you can never fool all people all of the time." Today's version is: most people can avoid being fooled some of the time and some people can avoid being fooled all the time. But most people can never avoid being fooled all the time.

The classic wisdom-of-the-crowds finding involves point estimation of a continuous quantity. At a 1906 country fair in Plymouth, 800 people participated in a contest to estimate the weight of a slaughtered and dressed ox; the median guess, 1,207 pounds, was accurate within 1% of the true weight of 1,198 pounds. However, one should note that in this case each person made its estimation alone, without consulting others: when individuals were allowed to consult with each other prior to making their guess, the accuracy of the median guess decreased considerably—a convincing argument against the free debate prior to making a choice.[24] It's difficult not to draw the obvious link to the low quality of democratic choices in our era of Facebook, X, Instagram, and other "free" digital links.

*

A genuine emancipatory engagement of the people is a rare event which quickly disintegrates. And we are not talking only about Western democracy here: recall how, in the time of the Cultural Revolutions, Mao Ze-dong was sending thousands of intellectuals to the agricultural communes to learn from ordinary farmers whom he elevated into "subjects supposed to know"—one can argue that it was good for intellectuals to get acquainted with the actual life on the countryside, but what they definitely did not get is some deeper wisdom about social life. Today, there is no privileged group which harbors an authentic understanding of society.

To be more precise, it's not so much that the majority is fooled, it is that they basically don't care—their main concern is that the relatively stable daily life goes on unperturbed. The majority doesn't want actual democracy in which they would really decide: they want the appearance of democracy where they freely vote, but some higher authority which they trust presents them with a choice and indicates how they should vote. When the majority doesn't get such clear hints, people get perplexed and the situation in which they are supposed to really decide is paradoxically experienced as a crisis of democracy, as a threat to the stability of the system. However, when the so-called silent majority begins to care, when they feel like victims and explode in real anger, things as a rule get much worse. As the ongoing wave of Rightist populism vastly demonstrates, they expose themselves even more to manipulation, falling prey to conspiracy theories. If we read Hamlet's well-known line (from act 1, scene 4) about the custom being "more honored in the breach than in the observance" as "it is a custom *that would be better honored* by breaking rather than adhering to," might we then not say that today democracy itself is more honored in the breach (when its rules are not respected) than in the strict observance of its rules? We should not be afraid to go to the end in this line and assume the lesson rendered long ago by Athena towards the end of Aeschylos' *Eumenides*:

> As for terror, / don't banish it completely from the city. / What mortal man is truly righteous / without being afraid? Those who sense the fear / revere what's right. With citizens like these / your country and your city will be safe, / stronger than anything possessed by men.[25]

We should understand here fear not as being afraid of singular powerful persons, but as being afraid of a strong social organization which is today needed more than ever—Kurt Vonnegut was right when he wrote: "There is no reason why good cannot triumph as often as evil. The triumph of anything is a matter of organization. If there are such things as angels, I hope that they are organized along the lines of the Mafia." Only in this way we'll be able to cope with the catastrophes that are awaiting us. What is missing in today's mess is not some larger unity but its very opposite. Alain Badiou was right to say that true ideas are those which enable us to draw the true line of division, a division that really matters, that defines what a political struggle is really about—and today's hegemonic Master-Signifiers (freedom, democracy, solidarity, justice . . .) are no longer able to do this (if they were ever able to do it is another question). "Democracy" is regularly used to justify neocolonialism, plus some hardline Socialist countries (East Germany, North Korea . . .) called themselves democratic. "Freedom" is often used as an argument against public healthcare ("it limits our freedom of choice") or universal public education, "justice" can also mean "everyone should act according to his/her/their proper place in social hierarchy," etc. To confront the great challenges today, it is crucial to learn to draw the proper lines of division—the old motto "United we stand, divided we fall" should be turned around: *divided we stand, united we fall.*

And I am not a pessimist precisely because my pessimism is much deeper that the usual one: I see the existing global system gradually moving towards its own self-destruction. The main threat to it are not external enemies but its own self-undermining dynamic. The more and more obvious global dangers (environmental destruction, global war, the role of Artificial Intelligence, etc.) will lead to a growth of fear and horror, to some kind of permanent emergency state, and this fear is deeply ambiguous. It may give rise to a new authoritarianism or chaotic world order, or it may sober up people and compel them to engage themselves for a simple survival. So how should we (by "we", I mean those who perceive these dangers as a serious threat) react to this situation? The commonsense answer—keep a cool head, carefully analyze the situation and see what can realistically be done—is obviously too flat: everybody would in principle agree with it, which makes it toothless. A much better approach is to see what options are at our disposal—as far as I can see, there are three:

- Outright denial: it's all overblown, let's just carry on with our lives as usual. This strategy is mostly used by the new Right and its conspiracy theories (climate change denialism, vaccinations are the cause of autism, etc), although recently Leftist versions have also begun to emerge (variations on the theme that the ecological panic, Covid pandemic, and the war in Ukraine are all inventions by big capital to keep workers under control).

- A fascination with the apocalyptic threat that accepts it as inevitable and something, perversely, which we are to enjoy. This stance is, of course, rarely formulated in an explicit way, but it often pervades our thinking as its obscure foundation.
- The third and most interesting option: disavowal. As Alenka Zupančič[26] demonstrated, disavowal best renders the structure underlying our contemporary social response to traumatic and disturbing events, from climate change to unsettling tectonic shifts in our social tissue. Unlike denialism and negation, disavowal functions by fully acknowledging what we disavow—its logic is that of the well-known French phrase *je sais bien, mais quand meme . . .*, "I know very well (it's true), but all the same (I don't really believe in it)." Such a stance is fast becoming the predominant mode in which we live our social and political lives. We see it lived out among the vast swathes of people who fully accept climate change and impending environmental collapse as scientific realities, but nevertheless continue to reproduce, drive cars, eat meat, rely on technologies and so on, just as if the planet's resources are limitless rather than exhausted: "I know very well we are in serious trouble with our environment, but nonetheless . . . (life must go on, our individual desires are still worth pursuing, fundamentally it's business as usual)."

How are we to counteract this disavowal? Not just by simply taking our knowledge seriously, without disavowal, but by enacting the opposite disavowal: we knew well that the situation is desperate, that what awaits us is a catastrophe, but nonetheless we should act with full engagement to prevent it. How can this apparently irrational strategy work? Because the knowledge contained in "of course, we know very well" *is not neutral*: its objectivity is already biased. What we "know very well," what is "obvious," what is accepted as a matter of course, is not written in stone, but in shifting sand; it is a socially-constructed shared hegemonic opinion which obfuscates its owns cracks and inconsistencies in order to seem immutable, and our task is to change it. The point is not to provide "alternate facts," but to undermine the framing that makes us select some facts and ignore others. This is why we are not dealing here with the usual disavowal but with a courageous act of taking a risk and ignoring our apparent limitations. Our stance should be: we know we appear weak and divided, but we should nevertheless do what has to be done. We know (or feel with the force of seeming knowledge) that we cannot avert environmental collapse, but we should still take the actions that would give us the best chance of doing so. In such a situation where apocalypse is on the horizon, one should bear in mind that the standard logic of probability no longer applies—we need a different logic described by Jean-Pierre Dupuy:

> The catastrophic event is inscribed into the future as a destiny, for sure, but also as a contingent accident ... if an outstanding event takes place, a catastrophe, for example, it could not not have taken place; nonetheless, insofar as it did not take place, it is not inevitable. It is thus the event's actualization—the fact that it takes place—which retroactively creates its necessity.[27]

This, according to Dupuy, is also how we should approach the prospect of an ecological or social catastrophe: not to "realistically" appraise the likelihood of the catastrophe, but to accept it as our fate, as unavoidable, and then, on the basis of this acceptance, mobilize ourselves to perform the act which will change destiny itself and thereby open up new possibilities within the situation. Instead of saying "the future is still fluid, we still have time, time to act and prevent the worst," one should accept the catastrophe as inevitable and then act to undo the destiny which is already "written in the stars". G.K. Chesterton saw clearly how such sober acting has to combine opposite emotions and desires:

> A soldier surrounded by enemies, if he is to cut his way out, needs to combine a strong desire for living with a strange carelessness about dying. He must not merely cling to life, for then he will be a coward, and will escape. He must not merely wait for death, for then he will be a suicide, and will not escape. He must seek his life in a spirit of furious indifference to it; he must desire life like water and yet drink death like wine.[28]

An outstanding recent movie renders perfectly such a combination of the opposites: Oleh Sentsov's *Real* which consists of 90 minutes of frontline action captured when he didn't realize his camera was on. Sentsov, who spent several years a political prisoner in Russia and is now fighting in the Ukrainian army, found the 90 minutes of shaky footage six months after the battle while he was on a short leave at home (he is now back on the front). He was going through old files on his GoPro camera and realized it had been switched on that day. Presented unedited, it manages to capture the terror and boredom of life on the frontline: "I was about to delete everything when I found this and I realized I had a very interesting imprint of that battle and of war how it truly is—ugly, incomprehensible, twisted, and stupid." "Real" of the title does not refer to any kind of "real"—it is named after the position where the wounded men are stuck (all the positions in the battle are named after football teams: "Real" refers to Real Madrid). Sentsov's position is Marseille and a nearby position is Chelsea. The movie's title is accurately ambiguous: the name of a big sports club and war in its ugly, incomprehensible, twisted, and stupid nature—in short, in its Real in the Lacanian sense.

The same duality traverses the entire film: the meaningless and boring brutality of the real is intercepted by magical moments of what one cannot but designate as meaningless meaning. Sentsov recalled a moment from the same day, which took place about an hour before the footage in *Real* begins. "There was a soldier with the call sign Johnny, a veteran of the Afghan war. He was going there to evacuate the wounded but he was hit, and he managed to make one last radio transmission, in which he said: 'This is Johnny. I'm dead.'"[29] A moment of an authentic metaphysical absurdity.

Reviewers of the film often comment that *Real* shows "the war as it really is," but this claim is one-sided and deeply deceiving. If this were to be the message of the film, it would be yet another pacifist depiction of the meaningless absurdity of war, yet another variation on the motif "when you experience the brutality of warfare, when you see bodies dismembered, when you hear cries of the dying soldiers, you become aware that all the appeals to sacrifice yourself for your country, to fulfil your highest duty, etc., are just empty phrases serving those in power" . . . Sentsov is unique in that, while bringing out all the horror and boredom of fighting, he doesn't draw from this the expected cynical-pacifist conclusion—while accepting its brutal meaninglessness, *fighting for a just cause has to go on*. Deprived of all pathetic-emotional romanticization of the heroic fighting, *Real* displays what true courage means: to heroically accept the misery of a military struggle and not to obfuscate its Real with pathetic fantasies.

This Real is hard to swallow without being fascinated by it. Centuries ago the Dutch colonizers in the far East (probably Indonesia) submitted a prisoner to a terrible water torture: they tied him to a tree and then put a narrow tube out of which water continuously flowed into his mouth so that if he wanted to breathe he had to swallow water. After two hours the prisoner's belly was overblown, but he wasn't yet dead, and the people observing the torture took this as a proof that he is evil, possessed by the devil who gave him the unnatural strength to survive his ordeal—in short, instead of some compassion with the tortured prisoner, his unexpectedly prolonged survival in terrifying pain triggered hatred and rage . . . Is this really something alien to our enlightened times? Is something similar not going on now, at the beginning of 2025, in Gaza? The more the Palestinians survive the genocidal violence of the IDF in Gaza, the more their unexpected survival is taken as a proof that they are all Hamas supporters, while their torturers led by the war criminal Benjamin Netanyahu fortify their status as warriors against terror. What "Israel as the only democracy in the Middle East" actually amounts to is made clear in a weird incident that occurred in mid-January 2025: some starving Gazans caught a dolphin in the sea and ate it—and were immediately attacked by some Israelis for non-ecological behaviour, as barbarians eating endangered species.[30] The horror of this attack is double: not only is it obscene to reproach starving people for eating whatever they can get their hands on, it is even more obscene that IDF itself changed Gaza into an area of ecological catastrophe. The well-known joke from Ernst Lubitsch's *To Be Or Not to Be* (told in the movie by a Nazi called "concentration camp Erhardt" who terrorizes the Poles) thus applies perfectly to "concentration-camp-Bibi": "We do the concentrating, Palestinians do the camping."

The genocidal activity of IDF in Gaza confronts us with heart of what Markus Gabriel, a young philosopher who emerged as a superstar of German philosophy, characterized as our "dark times"—although, Gabriel sees the greatest manifestation of this setback in the Hamas October 7, 2023, attack, not in what goes on in Gaza:

We are in the midst of a crisis of humanity on a global scale. The greatest manifestation of this setback is the barbaric massacre in Israel committed by the terrorist organization Hamas in Gaza.[31]

Does this passage not demonstrate that Gabriel himself is part of the ongoing "dark times": his judgment bears witness to a conspicuous lack of moral universalism, of measuring different events with the same standard.

We should assert moral universalism, but as a notion which is at the same time *necessary* and *impossible*, penetrated by immanent tensions and antagonism. The first step in this direction is not to conceive the perversion of (what presents itself as) a universal value as its secondary deformation but as something immanent to this value itself—in short, to be always attentive to the ambiguities of any notion of progress.[32] What one should avoid at any price is a vague common sense universal progressism: a large majority of people know what is bad and what is good, and we should just push forward in this direction, gradually expanding solidarity and compassion . . .

Moral universalism is not necessarily idealist, it can also be formulated outside the space of Kantian transcendental apriorism, as moral realism grounded in facts. Markus Gabriel, who adopts this position, assumes that universal moral arguments are not dependent on specific historical circumstances—if slavery is wrong now, it has always been wrong (I am tempted to add: slavery has always been wrong *measured by today's predominant standards*). Moral categories exist independently of human beings, and they should be obvious to everyone, even in the most oppressive circumstances. Gabriel asserts the objectivity of moral facts, their universality, and their essential knowability by human beings—although he concedes that in "dark times" (like ours) they can be obscured by ideology, propaganda, psychology and manipulation. In this way, Gabriel seems to join the ranks of Habermasian normative progressism which can be vaguely defined by the premise that,

> through large-scale cooperation between the humanities, the social sciences, and even other fields of expertise if necessary, we are able to discover normative facts that are guiding for nonacademic sectors.[33]

Philosophy is thus no longer like the owl of Minerva, as it was for Hegel, but future-oriented ... how, exactly? First, how did the dark times arrive? Gabriel provides no realist analysis, he simply claims that universal values "can be obscured by ideology, propaganda, psychology, and manipulation"—a claim that I consider ultra-naïve since it disregards how ideology, manipulation, etc., are an aspect of complex social processes which need them for their reproduction. And the same holds for getting out of the "dark times": what one should change is the entire social edifice, not just the ideology that sustains it. Can such a change really be set in motion by philosophers and social theorists? Gabriel mentions (approvingly) Germany where politicians often seek advice from philosophers—obviously, their advice didn't prevent Germany from entering a deep crisis ... The main argument Gabriel offers for his moral realism rests on a thought experiment called the "Day of Judgment".: he

> asks us to consider what our reaction would be if we were facing God's judgment and God commended us for all the bad things we have done and condemned us for the good. We would find this judgment incomprehensible. A god whose judgments had no continuity with our own would not be God, but a "terrible demon."[34]

Gabriel's notion of a Judgment Day is not as eccentric as it may appear: many scientists refer to something similar when they talk about a (virtual, not really existing) Book in which all the laws of nature that we are gradually discovering are already written in their perfect form. For example, the great Hungarian mathematician Paul Erdős,

> although an agnostic atheist, spoke of "The Book," a visualization of a book in which God had written down the best and most elegant proofs for mathematical theorems. Lecturing in 1985 he said, "You don't have to believe in God, but you should believe in *The Book.*" He himself doubted the existence of God whom he playfully nicknamed the SF (for "Supreme Fascist").[35]

I immensely admire Erdős, as a person as well as a thinker; his lifestyle had something of the practicing Communist—most of his belongings would fit in a suitcase; he donated what he earned to people in need; and he lived an itinerant lifestyle, traveling between scientific conferences, universities and the homes of friends and colleagues: "He would typically show up at a colleague's doorstep and announce 'my brain is open,' staying long enough to collaborate on a few papers before moving on a few days later. In many cases, he would ask the current collaborator about whom to visit next."[36] However, his idea of a Book was a mistake—a necessary one, but nonetheless a mistake. What a truly materialist science compels us to accept is that *there is no Book*, not only in reality but also as an inaccessible ideal (therein resides the basic lesson of quantum mechanics).

Back to Gabriel, I reject his thought experiment with the Day of Judgment for two reasons. If taken literally, it ignores the lesson of the Book of Job, arguably the first text that practices critique of ideology, which is that the discontinuity between our judgments and the putative divine judgment is irreducible—every authentic Protestant dismisses as an obscenity the idea that we have direct access to god's judgment. If taken metaphorically, it relies on a non-historical notion of big Other which is obviously ideological: every idea of a Judgment Day (which would enable us to measure our historical moment with standards that are in some sense absolute) is clearly marked by its own historical moment—history and eternity are not simply exclusive, every historical epoch creates its own notion of what is trans-historical. A clear proof of the historical roots of Gabriel's moral universalism, of his premise that "moral categories exist independently of human beings, and they should be obvious to everyone, even in the most oppressive circumstances," is that he ends up with a vision of ethical capitalism[37]—here is its brief characterization:

> Ethical Capitalism has at least two essential ingredients: a focus on creating long-term economic and social value, and a commitment by business to act as stewards of the full spectrum of its constituencies—customers, employees, suppliers, investors, and society. Ethical Capitalism seeks to build deep, trust-based relationships in the service of society as well as the bottom line. In other words, it is a business model with a higher purpose.[38]

This stance relies on a rather flat commonsense logic: capitalism is the only thing that functions economically, but today's capitalism privileges profit; so we need a different capitalism which will privilege solidarity and the environment

. . . I think the basic lesson of Marx remains fully valid here: capitalism obeys its own immanent logic (what Adrian Johnston called the "capitalist drive" independent of capitalists' personal virtues or vices, a drive to expanded self-reproduction which inherently ignores social and natural consequences[39]). Mandeville's idea of the "invisible hand of the market" implies that, pursuing their egotist desires, individual capitalists work for the common good—but does this still hold (or did it ever hold)? Gabriel's notion of ethical capitalists as the "stewards" of community (the role today played in public by Elon Musk, Bill Gates, and other new feudal lords) pretends to turn around the logic of the "invisible hand of the market": acting as ethical subjects, pursuing common good and charity, these new lords just enable the capitalist drive to function more smoothly—no wonder they are getting richer and richer. The axiom to be followed is here: never trust a project which relies on moral values of individuals.

If I remain a Marxist, then I would define myself as an anthropologically pessimist one, and this puts me in good company: the Brechtian extraneation is not just a procedure of acquiring intellectual distance, it is itself an emotion, an atmospheric stance, the "feeling" that things are weird, out of joint. Therein resides the importance of Hanns Eisler's music to Brecht's poems: it renders the emotional atmosphere which fits the critical stance of extraneation. And although Eisler was a dedicated Communist, this emotion is as far as possible from cheap socialist optimism and trust in a bright future. For Eisler, as for any authentic Communist, revolutionary engagement always occurs against the background of sadness, despair even—despair at all the meaningless suffering that abounds in the long series of catastrophes called "human history." This inescapable atmosphere of sadness is grounded in our finitude: there is no way for us to extract ourselves from the texture of history and assume the external position of an agent and observer to whom history is a transparent process. Eisler's two songs with words based on Pascal (nos. 17 and 18 from the *Hollywood Songbook*) display a similar dark vision:

> Despite these miseries, man wishes to be happy, / and only wishes to be happy, and cannot wish not to be so. / But how will he set about it? To be happy he would have to / make himself immortal. But, not being

able to do so, / it has occurred to him to prevent himself from thinking of death

(no. 17).

The only thing which consoles us for our miseries is diversion, / and yet this is the greatest of our miseries. / For it is this which principally hinders us from reflecting upon ourselves, / and which makes us insensibly ruin ourselves. Without this / we should be in a state of weariness, and this weariness would spur us / to seek a more solid means of escaping from it. / But diversions amuse us and lead us unconsciously to death

(no. 18).

Again, such a dark vision of humanity is the necessary background of authentic Communism—without it, we end up in the Stalinist optimism which is the front side of terror. Nowhere is this ontological sadness more clearly expressed than in Eisler's *Serious Songs* for baritone and chamber orchestra which accompanies the voice in a Mahlerian mode. The cycle culminates in the outrightly pessimistic "Despair" (words based on Hamerling and Leopardi):

There is nothing worthy of your efforts / And the earth doesn't deserve a sigh. / Pain and boredom are our lot / And the world is dirt, nothing more. / Be calm.

Yes, there are small rays of hope that may shine through clouds in the periods of retreat and defeat of the radical emancipatory movement—*every* emancipation has to emerge against the background of despair. So why not read Brecht and Eisler together with Peter Wessel Zapffe, who wrote in 1939 about the Book of Job and how God answers when Job asks him why misfortunes have been heaped upon him:

God does not attempt to answer Job on the questions of morality or justice that he raises, rather it is a demonstration of might. Human beings are firmly put in their place and the most important creature is revealed as none other than the hippopotamus! Although Job is overwhelmed by God's appearance he comes to the realization that God is no more than "a universal ruler of grotesque primitivity, a cosmic caveman, a show-off." Job realizes that there is no further point in arguing, in bringing up "theoretical topics" because God is not simply unwilling to engage, he is "unable to understand." As a result Job in his replies pretends to agree with God "as one does with irresponsible people." He becomes acutely aware of God's shortcomings.[40]

One should also note another feature that confirms God's primitivity: his vulgar-materialist notion of restoration—as if getting back his material wealth will somehow erase Job's meaningless suffering . . . At the end of the Book of Job, Job is thus compelled to assume the despair of human existence, and what remains open to him are the four strategies devised by humanity to cope with its basic predicament: isolation (ignore the disturbing thoughts and feelings), anchoring (the "fixation of points within, or construction of walls around, the liquid fray of consciousness": "God, the Church, the State, morality, fate, the laws of life, the people, the future"—in short, different forms of what Lacan calls the "big Other"), distraction ("one limits attention to the critical bounds by constantly enthralling it with impressions" to prevent the mind from turning in on itself—a trend which reaches its apogee with our chaotic digital culture of surfing), sublimation (the refocusing of energy away from negative outlets: writers, poets, painters—but I would add here vocation and events in Badiou's sense of the term).[41]

This is why, with all my admiration of Sally Rooney, a self-designated feminist Marxist who advocates a feminist demystification of love, she also falls short: yes, love is always grounded in (and part of) concrete material and social circumstances of exploitation and domination, but it cannot be reduced to them: love is an event, a miraculous excess. To avoid a fatal misunderstanding: love is not a happy interruption of our miserly life, it is in itself experienced as a traumatic intrusion which derails the established rhythm of our lives.

We confront here yet again the elementary question: why this detour through the stupid fantasy of evil-indifferent god, a Supreme Fascist, why should we not just directly assert that there is "no god"? Because this terrifying notion of an evil-indifferent god *is the immanent truth of the notion of god*, its unconscious support, its Real. That is why, if we want to assume atheism as a subjective stance, not just as an objective fact, we have to undermine the notion of god from within, to bring it to its truth.

*

After finishing this book, I gave it to a deeply religious friend to read, and his reaction surprised me. He told me that he absolutely disagrees with my position, but that nonetheless the book gave him such nightmares that the world would be a better place if my book disappeared from it leaving no trace. I tend to agree with this reader. If, for some putative reader, this clarification renders things even more abstruse, he/she/they/it (or whoever does not recognize itself in this list) should simply read this book again from the beginning.

Notes

Introduction: Materialism and quantum criticism

1 Flatland - Wikipedia (https://en.wikipedia.org/wiki/Flatland, last accessed 10 July 2025). I owe this reference to *Flatlands* to Tim Salecl.

2 See Thomas Hertog, *On the Origin of Time*, London: Penguin 2023, p. 225.

3 J. Barbour (1982), "Relational concepts of space and time", *Brit. J. Phil. Sci.* 33, p. 265.

4 Available online at marxists.org (https://www.marxists.org/archive/lenin/works/1908/mec/, last accessed 10 July 2025).

5 See, among numerous podcasts, Physicists Proved the Universe Isn't Real (https://www.youtube.com/watch?v=YSAhtl7BVtE, last accessed 10 July 2025); Quantum Theory PROVES You Never Die | Unveiled (https://www.youtube.com/watch?v=78onGajtyZw, last accessed 10 July 2025); Quantum Realities: How Your Mind Alters the Universe (https://www.youtube.com/watch?v=q0HRZW-ZzWs, last accessed 10 July 2025); God is Spirit: Quantum Physics and God (https://www.youtube.com/watch?v=W6WV9JXHWrA, last accessed 10 July 2025); Quantum Physics Debunks Materialism (https://www.youtube.com/watch?v=4C5pq7W5yRM, last accessed 10 July 2025). Plus, of course, Jung is never far from such speculations—see The Hidden Message in Synchronicities | 5 Different Types of Synchronicity—(https://www.youtube.com/watch?v=KvKTyQNaRvw, last accessed 10 July 2025).

6 See Carlo Rovelli, *Helgoland*, London: Penguin 2022, pp. 103–15. Needless to add that I am generally very sympathetic to Rovelli's political stances—to add a joke (an obvious misreading), here is a sentence from Rovelli's *The Order of Time* about how "a duration can be associated only with the movement of something, with a given trajectory": "'Proper time' depends not only on where you are and your degree of proximity to masses; it depends also on the speed at which you move." I am tempted to read this sentence as a Leninist advice on political intervention: the proper time to intervene politically depends not only on where you are socially, on your proximity on the masses (working classes); it depends also on the "speed" of your political organization, on how it is able to move faster than the inert social body.

396   Notes

7 Some philosophical readings of quantum mechanics fall into a similar trap, equating the role of observation with the Kantian transcendental constitution.

8 The obvious alternative to it is: I take an atheist to the main concentration camps and torture houses, and then ask him: "Do you believe there is a divine monster who created these places?"

9 Harmeet Kaur, "Atheist chaplains are forging a new path in a changing world", CNN. com (https://www.cnn.com/2024/11/07/us/atheist-chaplains-humanist-cec, last accessed 10 July 2025).

10 Louis Althusser, "Philosophy as a Revolutionary Weapon", first published 1968, accessed via marxists.org (https://www.marxists.org/reference/archive/althusser/1968/philosophy-as-weapon.htm, last accessed 10 July 2025).

11 Edmund Husserl, *Logical Investigations*, Vol. II, London: Routledge 2001, p. 76.

12 Aaron Schuster, *How to Research Like a Dog*, Cambridge: MIT Press 2014, p. 112.

13 Agon Hamza, "Untruth and Directness" (unpublished manuscript).

14 Quoted in Ian H. Birchall, *Sartre Against Stalinism*, New York: Berghahn Books 2004, p. 166.

15 Slavoj Žižek, *Pandemic*, New York: OR Books 2020.

1 Why a Hegelian needs quantum mechanics

1 iHeart, "Here's how David Copperfield made the Statue of Liberty disappear" (https://www.iheart.com/content/2017-09-26-we-finally-know-how-david-copperfield-made-the-statue-of-liberty-disappear/, last accessed 10 July 2025).

2 Along the same lines, a very critical review of my *Christian Atheism*—see Rupert Shortt, "What does Christian atheism mean?", *The Spectator*, 27 April 2024 (https://www.spectator.co.uk/article/what-does-christian-atheism-mean/, last accessed 10 July 2025)—totally misses the central enigma of my atheism: why a true atheism cannot be asserted directly, why does it have to pass through (not any religion but specifically) Christian religion? I take Lacan's (and already Hegel's) axiom *la verite surgit de la meprise* (the truth arises out of misrecognition) quite literally—it concerns truth in itself, not just our approach to truth; it concerns truth immanent to mistake itself, not truth arrived at through our learning from mistakes.

3 Alenka Zupančič, *The Odd One In: On Comedy*, Cambridge: MIT Press 2008, p. 171.

4 Philip Ball, "Physics experiments spell doom for quantum 'collapse' theory", *Quanta*, 20 October 2022 (https://www.quantamagazine.org/physics-experiments-spell-doom-for-quantum-collapse-theory-20221020/, last accessed 10 July 2025).

5 Op. cit.

6 The theories of David Bohm (especially the deterministic de Broglie-Bohm interpretation of quantum mechanics) and the "Many-Worlds Interpretation," which removes randomness and action at a distance from quantum theory by postulating the existence of many worlds which exist in parallel to our own, are significant examples.

7 Quoted from Gali Weinstein, "Time Travel in Feynman Diagrams", Quora post, 2019 (https://qr.ae/pA3QgK, last accessed 10 July 2025).

8 Joanne Baker, *50 Quantum Physics Ideas You really Need to Know*, London: Greenfinch 2013, p. 171.

9 Quantum eraser experiment—Wikipedia (https://en.wikipedia.org/wiki/Quantum_eraser_experiment, last accessed 10 July 2025).

10 Joanne Baker, *50 Quantum Physics Ideas You really Need to Know*, London: Greenfinch 2013, p. 171.

11 See Thomas Hertog, *On the Origin of Time*, London: Penguin 2023. Numbers in brackets that follow indicate the pages of this book.

12 Avery Thompson and Jessica Coulon, "The logic-defying double slit experiment is even weirder than you thought", *Popular Mechanics*, 5 April 2023 (https://www.popularmechanics.com/science/a22280/double-slit-experiment-even-weirder/, last accessed 10 July 2025).

13 Quoted from Thomas Hertog, *On the Origin of Time*, London: Penguin Books 2023, p. 197.

14 Claude Levi-Strauss, "Do Dual Organizations Exist?", in *Structural Anthropology*, New York: Basic Books 1963, pp. 131–63; the drawings are on pages 133–4.

15 I am, of course, not able to pass a qualified judgment on the cosmological constant which "fills spacetime with energy and pressure," the idea being that with it, "everything happens as though the energy in vacuum would be different from zero."(57–8) In other words, although the cosmological constant adds energy to a vacuum, a vacuum remains a vacuum. Only against this background of a vacuum which is not a zero can the symmetry-breaking transition of the Higgs field to a nonzero that endows particles with a mass occur, a vital step on the long road towards complexity."(139)

16 John Horgan, "Do our questions create the world?", *Scientific American*, 6 June 2018 (https://www.scientificamerican.com/blog/cross-check/do-our-questions-create-the-world/, last accessed 10 July 2025).

17 Charlie Wood, "How our reality may be a sum of all possible realities", *Quanta*, 6 February 2023 (https://www.quantamagazine.org/how-our-reality-may-be-a-sum-of-all-possible-realities-20230206/, last accessed 10 July 2025).

18 Entropy - Hmolpedia 2020 (https://eoht.info/page/Entropy, last accessed 10 July 2025).

19 Lee Smolin, "Democracy and science need each other to thrive", *Maclean's*, 15 September 2017 (https://macleans.ca/society/science/democracy-and-science-need-each-other-to-thrive/, last accessed 10 July 2025).

20 Carlo Rovelli, *The Order of Time*, London: Penguin 2019, p. 30. Numbers in brackets that follow indicate the pages of this book.

21 "Lee Smolin on time, philosophy and the nature of reality", *Sean Carroll's Mindscape*, 31 May 2021 (https://www.preposterousuniverse.com/podcast/2021/05/31/149-lee-smolin-on-time-philosophy-and-the-nature-of-reality/, last accessed 10 July 2025).

2 Why quantum mechanics needs Hegel

1 Thomas Hertog, *On the Origin of Time*, London: Penguin 2023.

2 Jason Fernando, "Trillion dollar coin: Meaning, examples, and use cases", *Investopedia*, 24 March 2024 (https://www.investopedia.com/terms/t/trillion-dollar-coin.asp, last accessed 10 July 2025).

3 Conor Costick, "Quantum holography and the origin of time", *Independent Left*, 2 June 2023 (https://independentleft.ie/quantum-holography/, last accessed 10 July 2025).

4 Andrew Jaffe, "The illusion of time", *Nature*, 16 April 2018 (https://www.nature.com/articles/d41586-018-04558-7, last accessed 10 July 2025).

5 See Carlo Rovelli, *Reality Is Not What It Seems* (all non-accredited numbers in brackets refer to the pages of this book).

6 User question, "What does 'God is subtle, but He is not malicious' mean?", *English Language & Usage* (https://english.stackexchange.com/questions/35517/what-does-god-is-subtle-but-he-is-not-malicious-mean, last accessed 10 July 2025).

7 Op. cit.

8 Hertog, op. cit., p. 246.

9 Op. cit., p. 247.

10 Op. cit., p. 249.

11 Op. cit., p. 248.

12 Op. cit., p. 225.

13 See Alenka Zupančič presents: "Is the Logic of Fantasy the Lacanian Transcendental?" (https://www.youtube.com/watch?v=Ktg2oawcHaY, last accessed 10 July 2025).

14 *The Seminar of Jacques Lacan, Book XI*, New York: Norton 1991, pp. 105–6.

15 Joanne Baker, *50 Quantum Physics Ideas You really Need to Know*, London: Greenfinch 2013, p. 169.

16 Steve Paulson, "Roger Penrose on why consciousness does not compute", *Nautilus*, 27 April 2017 (https://nautil.us/roger-penrose-on-why-consciousness-does-not-compute-236591/, last accessed 10 July 2025).

17 Gödel's incompleteness theorems—Wikipedia (https://en.wikipedia.org/wiki/G%C3%B6del%27s_incompleteness_theorems, last accessed 10 July 2025).

18 Quoted from Paulson, "Roger Penrose on why consciousness does not compute".

19 Although one must add that some of the new experiments appear to confirm Penrose's and Hameroff's hypothesis—see Sabine Hossenfelder, "Brain really uses quantum effects, new study finds", 12 May 2024 (https://www.youtube.com/watch?v=R6G1D2UQ3gg, last accessed 10 July 2025).

20 Quoted from Penrose, op. cit.

21 Quoted from op. cit.

22 Quoted from op. cit.

23 Hans Busstra and Federico Faggin, "Quantum fields are consciousness: A groundbreaking new theory by the inventor of the microprocessor", *Essentia Foundation*, 16 June 2016 (https://www.essentiafoundation.org/quantum-fields-are-consciousness-a-groundbreaking-new-theory-by-the-inventor-of-the-microprocessor/seeing/, last accessed 10 July 2025).

24 Richard Gould and Jane Clarke, "Consciousness as the ground of being", *Beshara*, 20:2022 (https://besharamagazine.org/science-technology/consciousness-as-the-ground-of-being/, last accessed 10 July 2025).

25 Michael Marder & André Geremia Parise, "Extending cognition: a vegetal rejoinder to extensionless thought and to extended cognition", *Plant Signaling & Behavior*, 19(1) (https://www.tandfonline.com/doi/full/10.1080/15592324.2024.2345984#, last accessed 10 July 2025).

26 See Matteo Smerlak and Carlo Rovelli, "Relational EPR" (arXiv:quant-ph/0604064, last accessed 10 July 2025). Non-assigned quotes that follow are from this source.

27 The Einstein–Podolsky–Rosen (EPR) paradox is a *thought experiment* proposed by *Albert Einstein, Boris Podolsky* and *Nathan Rosen*, which argues that the description of physical reality provided by *quantum mechanics* is incomplete. They argued for the existence of "elements of reality" that were not part of quantum theory, and speculated that it should be possible to construct a theory containing these *hidden variables*. I've dealt with this paradox in detail in many of my books, first in *The Indivisible Remainder,* London: Verso Books 2007.

28 "Lee Smolin on time, philosophy and the nature of reality", *Sean Carroll's Mindscape*.

29 Lee Smolin author page, *Scientific American* (https://www.scientificamerican.com/author/lee-smolin/, last accessed 10 July 2025).

30 See Chapter 1 of this book.

31 Again, see Chapter 1 of this book.

32 Brian Greene, *The Elegant Universe,* New York: Norton, 1999, 116–19.

33 Hegel, G.W.F., *Philosophy of Mind*, Oxford: Clarendon Press 1971, p. 315.

34 Bruce Rosenblum and Fred Kuttner, *Quantum Enigma: Physics Encounters Consciousness*, Oxford: Oxford University Press, 2006, 171.

35 I condense here a line of thought with which I've dealt in many of my books, especially in Chapter 1 of *Disparities*, London: Bloomsbury Press 2016.

36 Aage Petersen, "The Philosophy of Niels Bohr", *Bulletin of the Atomic* Scientists, 1963, 19(7) (https://www.tandfonline.com/doi/abs/10.1080/00963402.1963.11454520, last accessed 10 July 2025).

37 Nikki Westeijn, "Wigner's friend and Relational Quantum Mechanics: A Reply to Laudisa", *Foundations of Physics* 51(4):1–13 (https://philarchive.org/rec/WESWFA, last accessed 10 July 2025).

38 Westeijn, op. cit. One should thus not confuse the pre-ontological Real-in-itself implied by the quantum theory (a Real composed of quantum processes) with the pre-ontological Real that we find in Lynch's or Tarkovsky's films (an impenetrable density which ultimately remains fantasmatic/imaginary).

39 Harmut Neven, "Meet WIllow, our state-of-the-art quantum chip", 9 December 2024 (https://blog.google/technology/research/google-willow-quantum-chip/, last accessed 10 July 2025).

40 J. Barbour (1982), "Relational concepts of space and time", *Brit. J. Phil. Sci.* 33, p. 265.

41 Jacques Lacan, *The Four Fundamental Concepts of Psycho-Analysis*, New York: Norton 1978, p. 96 (translation corrected).

42 Mauro Dorato, Rovelli's relational quantum mechanics, anti-monism and quantum becoming", accessed via PhilPapers.org (https://philpapers.org/rec/DORRRQ, last accessed 10 July 2025).

43 Ricardo Muciño, Elias Okon and Daniel Sudarsky, "Assessing relational quantum mechanics", *Synthese* 200.5 (2022): 399 (https://arxiv.org/abs/2105.13338, last accessed 10 July 2025).

3 Noncommutativity in the symbolic and in the (quantum) real

1 Carlo Rovelli, *Helgoland*, London: Penguin Books 2021, p. 52. Numbers in brackets in the text that follows refer to the pages of this book.

2 See Slavoj Žižek, *Less Than Nothing*, London: Verso Books 2012.

3 As for the double cone from an event into its past and future, do these cones include quantum wave oscillations or just the speed-of-light links to other events?

4 Carlo Rovelli, *Helgoland*, London: Penguin Books 2021. Numbers in brackets in this text refer to the pages of this book.

5 *The Seminar of Jacques Lacan, Book XI*, New York: Norton 1991, p. 40.

6 Quoted in Ian H. Birchall, *Sartre Against Stalinism*, New York: Berghahn Books 2004, p. 166.

7 See Jean-Pierre Dupuy, *Economy and the Future*, East Lansing: Michigan State University Press 2014, p. 24.

8 Op. cit., p. 110.

9 Gilles Deleuze, *Difference and Repetition*, New York: Columbia University Press 1994, p. 119.

10 Deleuze, op. cit., pp. 119–20.

11 Ian Buchanan, *Deleuzism*, Durham: Duke University Press 2000, p. 5.

12 The Symptom 10 " The Seminar of Jacques Lacan Bruce Fink."

13 Jacques Lacan, La troisième [The third]. *Lettres de l'Ecole freudienne 16 (1975)*, p. 186.

14 Another case of such asymmetry: in an apparently "irrational" way, economic and financial agents, when confronted with the possibility of a catastrophic outcome, choose to ignore it: "They eliminate it from their calculations, on the ground that it is too horrible to bear close scrutiny. But it is precisely in removing it that they give it a place; in fact, a quite considerable place" (op. cit., p. 86). If the 50/50 alternative is either that our stocks will further grow or that a total collapse of the market will render them worthless, it may appear "rational" to diminish their value for half—but the truly rational strategy is to retain their full price, since, in this way, we win if things turn out OK, and if they turn out bad it doesn't matter what we did.

15 G.W.F. Hegel, *Vorlesungen ueber die Philosophie der Religion II*, Frankfurt: Suhrkamp Verlag 1969, p. 206.

16 Op. cit., p. 207.

17 Op. cit., p. 205.

18 Op. cit., ibid.

19 Jean-Pierre Dupuy, *La Catastrophe ou la vie—Pensées par temps de pandémie*, Paris: Editions du Seuil 2021, p. 16.

1 Names for finitude: Hegel, Heidegger, Pippin

1 Robert Pippin, *The Culmination*, Chicago: The University of Chicago Press 2024.

2 *The Journals of Kierkegaard*, New York: Harper and Brothers 1959, p. 98.

3 I developed a detailed analysis of Schelling's pre-ontology in my *The Indivisible Remainder*, London: Verso Books 1996.

4 I resume here the line of argumentation from the subchapter "Absolute Knowing" of the Chapter 6 of my *Less Than Nothing*, London: Verso Books 2012.

5 G. W. F. Hegel, *Philosophy of Right*, accessed via marxists.org (https://www.marxists.org/reference/archive/hegel/works/pr/*philosophy-of-right*.pdf, last accessed 10 July 2025).

6 Robert C. Solomon, *In the Spirit of Hegel*, Oxford: Oxford University Press 1983, p. 639.

7 I resume this line of thought from Chapter 9 of my *Disparities*, London: Bloomsbury 2016.

8 Michael Wigglesworth, "The Day of Doom", accessed via allpoetry.com (https://allpoetry.com/The-Day-Of-Doom, last accessed 10 July 2025).

9 Jacques Lacan, *Le séminaire, livre XIX: . . . ou pire* (Paris: Seuil 2011, 43.

10 Stephen Hawking and Leonard Mlodinow, *The Grand Design*, New York: Bantam 2010, p. 5.

11 G.W.F. Hegel, *Phenomenology of Spirit*, Oxford: Oxford University Press 1977, p. 21.

12 Jacques Lacan, *The Four Fundamental Concepts of Psychoanalysis*, New York: Routledge 2004, p. 34.

13 Sigmund Freud, *The Standard Edition*, London: Hogarth Press 1953–1974, Vol 1, p. 356.

14 Op. cit, p. 349.

15 See Franz Kafka, "Investigations of a Dog", accessed via gwern.net (https://gwern.net/doc/fiction/humor/1922-kafka-investigationsofadog.pdf, last accessed 10 July 2025).

16 Aaron Schuster, *How to Research Like a Dog*, Cambridge: MIT Press 2014, p. 35.

17 Aaron Schuster, "Kafka swims: The champion of the impossible", *Cabinet*, 20 May 2020 (https://www.cabinetmagazine.org/kiosk/schuster_aaron_28_may_2020.php, last accessed 10 July 2025).

18 Op. cit., ibid.

19 See Darian Leader, *Is It Ever Just Sex?*, London: Hamish Hamilton 2023.

2 The night of the world

1 See Anil Seth, *Being You: A New Science of Consciousness*, London: Dutton 2021.

2 See John A. Johnson, "Consciousness as controlled and controlling hallucination: My review of Anil Seith's *Being You*", *Psychology Today*, 24 November 2021 (https://www.psychologytoday.com/gb/blog/cui-bono/202111/consciousness-as-controlled-and-controlling-hallucination#:~:text=Key%20points,supports%20our%20survival%20and%20flourishing., last accessed 10 July 2025).

3 See Alain Badiou, *In Praise of Philosophy*, Cambridge: Polity Press 2025 (quoted from the manuscript).

4 The Seminar of Jacques Lacan, Book 1, *Freud's Papers on Technique*, New York: Norton 1991, pp. 232–3.

5 The Seminar of Jacques Lacan, Book 20, *On Feminine Sexuality*, New York: Norton 1999, p. 76.

6 Jacques Lacan, *Seminar XVI, D'un Autre à l'autre,* session of June 25, 1969, Staferla edition, http://staferla.free.fr/S16/S16.htm; quoted from the unpublished Cormac Gallagher's translation.

7 See S14 LOGIQUE.docx (live.com)

8 See Martin Heidegger, *The Question Concerning the Thing: On Kant's Doctrine Of the Transcendental Principles*, Blue Ridge Summit: Rowman and Littlefield 2018.

9 Michael L. Thompson, *Imagination in Kant's Critical Philosophy*, Berlin, Boston: De Gruyter 2013.

10 G.W.H. Hegel, *Phenomenology of Spirit*, Oxford: Oxford University Press 1977, pp. 18–19.

11 G.W.F. Hegel, "Jenaer Realphilosophie," in *Fruehe politische Systeme*, Frankfurt: Ullstein 1974, p. 204; translation quoted from Donald Phillip Verene, *Hegel's Recollection*, Albany: Suny Press 1985, pp. 7–8.

12 Hegel, *Encyclopaedia,* Par. 408, Addition. Accessed via marxists.org (https://www.marxists.org/reference/archive/hegel/works/sp/ssintrod.htm, last accessed 10 July 2025).

13 Ibid.

14 Quoted from Untitled Document (luc.edu).

15 I resume here my argumentation from "On David Lynch" (https://zizek.uk/2012/03/01/on-david-lynch/, last accessed 10 July 2025).

16 Martin Heidegger, *Beitraege zur Philosophie*, in *Gesamtausgabe,* Frankfurt: Vittorio Klostermann 1975 ff., Vol. 65, p. 338.

17 Martin Heidegger, "'Hoelderlin's Hymne, Der Ister,'" *Gesamtausgabe 53*, Frankfurt: Vittorio Klostermann 1984, p. 94.

18 Martin Heidegger, *Heraclitus Seminar* (with Eugen Fink), Tuscaloosa: University of Alabama Press 1979, p. 146.

19 Martin Heidegger, *Zollikoner Seminare*, Frankfurt: Vittorio Klostermann 2017, p. 260.

20 See John Sallis, "Deformatives: Essentially Other Than Truth," in John Sallis, ed., *Reading Heidegger*, Bloomington: Indiana UP 1993. For a more detailed analysis of this key point, see my *Fragile Absolute*, London: Verso Books 2000.

21 When Hegel mocks Schelling's thesis on identity of subject-object as a night in which all cows are black, one should nonetheless remember that in his account of this identity Schelling provides a beautiful description of the basic mystical experience of the unity of activity of passivity, of identifying with the neutral (subject-object) flow of the Absolute.

22 David Barnett, "Liu Cixin: 'I'm often asked - there's science fiction in China?'", *The Guardian*, 28 March 2024 (https://www.theguardian.com/books/2024/mar/28/liu-cixin-author-three-body-problem-netflix-science-fiction, last accessed 10 July 2025).

23 TIKHistory, "Hegel's ideobabble is the basis of Marxism and Fascism" (https://www.youtube.com/watch?v=6kzZoK5CtJ8, last accessed 10 July 2025).

24 Alain Badiou, *In Praise of Philosophy*, Cambridge: Polity Press 2025 (quoted from the manuscript).

25 Nikolai Berdyaev, "Jakob Bohme: The tragedy of freedom and the curse of the law", accessed via criticallegalthinking.com (https://criticallegalthinking.com/2012/08/16/jakob-bohme-the-tragedy-of-freedom-and-the-curse-of-the-law/, last accessed 10 July 2025).

26 Private conversation.

27 I owe this idea to Udi Aloni.

28 See DOMJAT, "Patrick Stewart as Lenin (All Scenes)" (https://www.youtube.com/watch?v=dsiU0P-swYE, last accessed 10 July 2025).

29 For a report sympathetic to these protests, see Eliav Breuer, "Ministers, MKs enraged by arrests of soldiers suspected of terrorist prisoner abuse", *The Jerusalem Post*, 29 July 2024 (https://www.jpost.com/israel-news/article-812376, last accessed 10 July 2025).

30 Sophie Wahnich, "*Faire entendre la voix de la verite, un droit revolutionaire eternel*" (manuscript, June 2010). All further non-attributed quotes are from this outstanding text.

31 V.I. Lenin, *Collected Works*, Vol. 33, 4th edition, Moscow: Progress Publishers 1966, p. 422.

3 Heidegger's politics of finitude

1 Schema - Wikipedia (https://en.wikipedia.org/wiki/Schema, last accessed 10 July 2025).

2 Quoted from ibid.

3 Martin Heidegger, *The Basic Problems of Phenomenology*, Bloomington: Indiana University Press 1988, p. 132.

4 See Kafka, "Investigations of a Dog".

5 Aaron Schuster, *How to Research Like a Dog*, Cambridge: MIT Press 2014, p. 91.

6 I rely here on ideas developed by Alenka Zupančič (private conversation).

7 Martin Heidegger, *Überlegungen* XII, GW 96, Frankfurt: Vittorio Klostermann 2014, p. 56.

8 See Something Worth Writing, "The Usual Suspects: The Devil's Reveal" (https://www.youtube.com/watch?v=6LNBmX4guCs, last accessed 10 July 2025).

9 Martin Heidegger, *Anmerkungen I-V*. GW 97, Frankfurt: Vittorio Klostermann 2015, p. 82.

10 Not to mention the obvious fact that there is a rich tradition of Jewish spirituality which absolutely cannot be reduced to Heidegger's rather caricatural notion of *Judentum*.

11 Martin Heidegger, *Gesamtausgabe* Vol. 8, p. 71.

12 Martin Heidegger, "Anmerkungen I," in *Anmerkungen I–V, Gesamtausgabe* Vol. 25, Frankfurt: Vittorio Klostermann 1997, p. 151.

13 Peter Trawny, "Heidegger and the Shoah," in *Reading Heidegger's Black Notebooks 1931–1941*, Cambridge: MIT Press 2016, p. 175.

14 I got this information from Wolfgang Schirmacher in Saas-Fee.

15 OMERTA, "Patrick Buisson, La fin d'un monde" (https://www.youtube.com/watch?v=2gPYGIAOgcE, last accessed 10 July 2025).

16 Peter Trawny, *Hitler, die Philosophie und der Hass: Anmerkungen zum identitätspolitischen Diskurs*, Berlin: Matthes&Seitz 2022.

17 See the listing on the publisher's website for Peter Trawny, *Hitler, Philosophy and Hatred: Notes on the Discourse on Identity Politics* (https://www.matthes-seitz-berlin.de/book/hitler-die-philosophie-und-der-hass.html, last accessed 10 July 2025).

18 To avoid embarrassment, I will of course not name him.

19 Franco "Bifo" Berardi, "Sabotage and Self-Organization", interview with Chandler Dandridge, *Ill Will*, 7 May 2024 (https://illwill.com/sabotage-and-self-organization, last accessed 10 July 2025).

20 Quoted from Steven Müller-Doohm, *Adorno: A Biography*, Cambridge: Polity Press 2005, p. 438.

21 Franz Kafka, "Before the Law", accessed via *Franz Kafka Online* (https://www.kafka-online.info/before-the-law.html, last accessed 10 July 2025).

22 This is the topic Liu Cixin deals with in his novels.

23 This saying was first reported by Max Brod, in "Der Dichter Franz Kafka," *Die Neue Rundschau* 32 (November 1921), p. 1213.

24 Jacques Lacan, *Seminar XVI, D'un Autre à l'autre,* session of June 25, 1969, Staferla edition, http://staferla.free.fr/S16/S16.htm; quoted from the unpublished Cormac Gallagher's translation.

25 Franz Kafka, *The Blue Octavo Notebooks*, ed. by Max Brod, Cambridge, MA: Exact Change 1991, p. 41.

26 Schuster, op. cit., p. 193.

27 Antonio Gramsci, *Quaderni del Carcere*, vol. 1, Quaderni 1–5, Turin: Giulio Einaudi editore 1977), p. 311. English translation quoted from *Selections from the Prison Notebooks of Antonio Gramsci*, London: Lawrence & Wishart 1971, p. 276.

28 Joseph Brodsky, *Less Than One. Selected Essays*, New York: Farrar Strauss Giroux 1986, p. 118.

29 Personal communication.

1 The hologram of conflicting universalities

1 Alain Finkielkraut, "It's back to 50", *Le Monde*, 21 September 2015 (https://www.lemonde.fr/idees/article/2015/09/22/c-est-reparti-comme-en-50_4767144_3232.html, last accessed 10 July 2025).

2 Quoted from http://th-rough.eu/writers/bifo-eng/journey-seoul-1.

3 I follow here the suggestion of my Korean friend Alex Taek-Gwang Lee.

4 Xinhua staff, "Xi's article on cultural heritage, fine traditional Chinese culture to be published", *Xinhua*, 15 April 2024 (https://english.news.cn/20240415/2a5ad40d1f054413a49500bf668b613a/c.html, last accessed 10 July 2025).

5 Available online at https://dokumen.pub/america-against-america.html.

6 See Yanis Varoufakis, *Technofeudalism: What Killed Capitalism*, London: Vintage 2024

7 Private exchange.

8 Private exchange.

9 The Poetry of Predicament, "The end of organized humanity: Noam Chomsky" (https://www.youtube.com/watch?v=VY9PZvK6CZs, last accessed 10 July 2025).

10 Jonathan Watts, "Climate engineering off US Coast could increase heatwaves in Europe, study finds", *The Guardian*, 21 June 2014 (https://www.theguardian.com/environment/article/2024/jun/21/climate-engineering-off-us-coast-could-increase-heatwaves-in-europe-study-finds, last accessed 10 July 2025).

11 See Liu Cixin, *The Three-Body Problem*, London: Head of Zeus 2015.

12 Paul Sutter, "Physicists predict Earth will become a chaotic world, with dire consequences", *Live Science*, 25 May 2022 (https://www.livescience.com/humanity-turns-earth-chaotic-climate-system, last accessed 10 July 2025).

13 Op. cit.

14 Lili Bayer, "Europe must get ready for looming war, Donald Tusk warns", *The Guardian*, 29 March 2024 (https://www.theguardian.com/world/2024/mar/29/europe-must-get-ready-for-looming-war-donald-tusk-warns, last accessed 10 July 2025).

15 Thomas Hertog, *On the Origin of Time*, London: Penguin Books 2023, p. 255. Numbers in brackets in the text that follows refer to the pages of this book.

16 See Alex Taek-Gwang Lee, "Capitalism in Asia," in *Made in Nowhere*, Sublation Press 2024.

17 See David Graeber and David Wengrow, *The Dawn of Everything*, New York: Farrar, Straus and Giroux 2021.

18 John Millbank and Slavoj Žižek, *The Monstrosity of Christ*, Cambridge: MIT Press 2011.

19 The are other similar differences at work in our languages—for example, a different reference to age: when a mature woman is considered sexually attractive, we use the term "milf," while for an elder man the term is "gilf" (grandfather I would like to f . . .): a father (middle-age man) is not "filf," he is automatically presumed fuckable, but not a mother—not to mention the fact that a fuckable grandmother is not called "gilf" because fuckable grandmothers are supposed to be very rare, in contrast to men who are supposed to maintain or even strengthen their charm with age.

20 See especially Lacan_SemXVIII_710120 (psychaanalyse.com).

21 See Walter Benjamin, "On the Concept of History", accessed via marxists.org (https://www.marxists.org/reference/archive/benjamin/1940/history.htm, last accessed 10 July 2025).

22 Letter from October 11, 1931, *Martin Heidegger—Elisabeth Blochmann. Briefwechsel 1918–1969*, Marbach: Deutsches Literatur-Archiv 1990, p. 44.

23 Martin Heidegger, *The Fundamental Concepts of Metaphysics*, Bloomington: Indiana University Press 1995, p. 271.

24 Quoted from Karl Marx, "Introduction", *Grundrisse*, accessed via marxists.org (https://www.marxists.org/archive/marx/works/1857/grundrisse/ch01.htm#3, last accessed 10 July 2025).

25 See Pierre Bayard, *Le plagiat par anticipation*, Paris: Editions de Minuit 2009.

26 Benjamin, "On the Concept of History".

27 See Old Believers - Wikipedia (https://en.wikipedia.org/wiki/Old_Believers, last accessed 10 July 2025).

28 "The Patriarch of Putin, on the nuclear danger: Christians should not fear the end of the world (Video)", *spotmedia*.ro, 28 November 2024 (https://spotmedia.ro/en/news/news/the-patriarch-of-putin-on-the-nuclear-danger-christians-should-not-fear-the-end-of-the-world-video, last accessed 10 July 2025).

29 www.exclusion.net/images/. . ./772_nudaq_RBbrazil_suplicy_en.pdf.

---

30 William McGovern, quoted Orville Schell, *Virtual Tibet*, New York: Henry Holt and Company 2000, p. 230.

2 Can artificial intelligence really think?

1 See LittleSis, "BlackRock vies for the 2022 corporate hall of shame", *Corporate Accountability*, 27 June 2022 (https://corporateaccountability.org/blog/blackrock-for-2022-corporate-hall-of-shame/, last accessed 10 July 2025).

2 See Aladdin (BlackRock)—Wikipedia.

3 To quote Zorana Baković, an outstanding Slovene journalist specialized in China, "for quite some time the Chinese leader was not as relaxed and loquacious as he was during the meeting with the presidents on the greatest American companies": "The only serious interlocutor of the Communist Party of China is for a long time the capital. And the only argument the Chinese party and state leader Xi Jinping is ready to comply with and then maybe even to change a little bit some of the segments of his politics is something that relates to the question if the Western investments with continue to participate in the market idyll on the Chinese ground or will they find a better domain for their profitable enrichment." Zorana Baković, "Edini sogovornik Xi Jinpinga je zahodni kapital", *Delo*, 30 March 2024 (https://www.delo.si/novice/svet/edini-sogovornik-xi-jinpinga-je-zahodni-kapital, last accessed 10 July 2025). When, on June 16, 2023, Xi Jinping met Bill Gates in Beijing, he called Gates "an old friend" and said he hoped they could cooperate in a way that would benefit both China and the United States. (Op. cit.)

4 See CNN staff, "July 19, 2024, global tech outage news", *CNN*, 19 July 2024 (https://edition.cnn.com/business/live-news/global-outage-intl-hnk, last accessed 10 July 2025).

5 Yuval Abraham, "'Lavender': The AI machine directing Israel's bombing spree in Gaza", *972mag.com*, 3 April 2024 (https://www.972mag.com/lavender-ai-israeli-army-gaza/, last accessed 10 July 2025).

6 Mia Jankowicz, "Ukrainian soldier credits video-game obsession for his ability to strike Russian targets with drones", *Yahoo*, 14 August 2023 (https://www.yahoo.com/news/ukrainian-soldier-credits-video-game-154351722.html?guccounter=1&guce_referrer=aH

R0cHM6Ly93d3cuZ29vZ2xlLmNvbS8&guce_referrer_sig=AQAAAAaHpiG-027ysVq7dc v8qSkbMFf2YPMWuI7FHreFX6chdKjVAsrwppmIsJ__kWfPUlb-ZhbmMBnaL5VUOJW fg8yU1SS75swea2k0QtmEO-__WF6rTHoNwj6MmY1E8iOGMJ20GnA12Ygd2Y 7mtXY61vQteVitOO8lDUNZ1KEs64ES, last accessed 10 July 2025).

7 For a popularly written report on what AI can now do in the field of mathematics, see Oxford Mathematics, "The potential for AI in science and mathematics - Terence Tao", 7 August 2024 (https://www.youtube.com/watch?v=_sTDSO74D8Q, last accessed 10 July 2025), and also Terence Tao, "What's new", terrytao.wordpress.com (https://terrytao.wordpress.com/, last accessed 10 July 2025).

8 Sana Noor Haq, "Global water crisis could 'spiral out of control' due to overconsumption and climate change, UN report warns", *CNN*, 22 March 2023 (https://edition.cnn.com/2023/03/22/world/global-water-crisis-un-report-climate-intl, last accessed 10 July 2025).

9 Patrick Greenfield, "What happens to the world if forests stop absorbing carbon? Ask Finland", *The Guardian*, 15 October 2024 (https://www.theguardian.com/environment/2024/oct/15/finland-emissions-target-forests-peatlands-sinks-absorbing-carbon-aoe, last accessed 10 July 2025).

10 I owe this parallel to Gregor Golobič, Ljubljana.

11 See Harriet Marsden, "Have we reached 'peak cognition'?", *The Week*, 19 March 2025 (https://theweek.com/science/have-we-reached-peak-cognition, last accessed 10 July 2025).

12 George Fitzmaurice, "'We're not going to hit the climate goals anyway': Eric Schmidt has a plan to drive sustainable data center and AI development—and it involves more AI", *IT Pro*, 7 October 2024 (https://www.itpro.com/technology/artificial-intelligence/were-not-going-to-hit-the-climate-goals-anyway-eric-schmidt-has-a-plan-to-drive-sustainable-data-center-and-ai-development-and-it-involves-more-ai, last accessed 10 July 2025). I owe this reference to Eric Schmidt to Tim salcl, Ljubljana.

13 Ian Sample, "'Unprecedented risk' to life on Earth: Scientists call for halt on 'mirror life' microbe research", *The Guardian*, 12 December 2024 (https://www.theguardian.com/science/2024/dec/12/unprecedented-risk-to-life-on-earth-scientists-call-for-halt-on-mirror-life-microbe-research, last accessed 10 July 2025).

14 Condensed from Paul Batters, "City Lights (1931): Charlie Chaplin's most poignant masterpiece", *Silver Screen Classics*, 17 April 2018 (https://silverscreenclassicsblog.wordpress.com/2018/04/17/city-lights-1931-charlie-chaplins-most-poignant-masterpiece/, last accessed 10 July 2025).

15 Condensed from Ahmed Banafa, "Bridging the gap between symbolic and subsymbolic AI", *LinkedIn*, 7 April 2024 (https://www.linkedin.com/pulse/bridging-gap-between-symbolic-subsymbolic-ai-prof-ahmed-banafa-ujkjc, last accessed 10 July 2025).

16 See Neural network (machine learning)—Wikipedia (https://en.wikipedia.org/wiki/Neural_network_(machine_learning), last accessed 10 July 2025).

17 I rely here on the insights of Primož Krašovec—for a resume of his ideas, see "Inteligenca, ki opušča intelektualnost" (in Slovene) in *Cukr*, Ljubljana 2024, p. 94-100.

18 Krašovec, op. cit., p. 100.

19 Schuster, op. cit., p. 183.

20 David Chalmers, *Reality+*, London: Penguin Books 2023.

21 Chalmers, op. cit.

22 Op. cit., p. 413.

23 John Searle, *Intentionality*, Cambridge: Cambridge University Press 1984, p. 252.

24 Slavoj Žižek, *The Sublime Object of Ideology*, London: Verso Books 1989, pp. 103–4.

25 Christopher Hitchens, "Visit To a Small Planet," *Vanity Fair*, January 2001, p. 24.

26 Michael Norton, *The Ritual Effect*, London: Penguin Life 2024.

27 Étienne Balibar, "Citizen Subject," in *Who Comes After the Subject?*, ed. Eduardo Cadava, Peter Connor, and Jean-Luc Nancy, New York: Routledge, 1991.

28 Aaron Schuster, *How to Research Like a Dog*, Cambridge: MIT Press 2014, p. 139.

29 See Chapter 8 in Slavoj Žižek, *The Year of Dreaming Dangerously*, London: Verso Books 2012.

30 Schuster, op. cit., p. 151.

31 Quoted from the bilingual edition of Ludwig Wittgenstein, *Tractatus-Logico-Philosphicus*, accessed via umass.edu (https://people.umass.edu/klement/tlp/, last accessed 10 July 2025).

32 Wigglesworth, "The Day of Doom".

33 Jon Elster, "States that are Essentially by-products," in *Social Science Information*, vol. 20, no. 3 (1981).

34 Op. cit.

35 Op. cit.

36 David Chalmers, *Reality+*, London: Penguin Books 2023, p. 144.

37 In Bertrand Russell's "Foreword" to the original English edition of *Tractatus*, accessed via umass.edu (https://people.umass.edu/klement/tlp/, last accessed 10 July 2025).

38 Henrik R., "Lavrov: Russia open to talks, but only if Ukraine meets these two conditions", *Dagens*, 29 September 2023 (https://www.dagens.com/news/lavrov-russia-open-to-talks-but-only-if-ukraine-meets-these-two-conditions, last accessed 10 July 2025).

39 Quoted from Suzanne Moore, "Banning free speech in the name of inclusivity and diversity is the Fringe's sickest joke", *The Telegraph*, 18 August 2023 (https://www.

telegraph.co.uk/comedy/comedians/graham-linehan-edinburgh-fringe-banning-free-speech/, last accessed 10 July 2025).

40 Jon Elster, "Some Notes on 'Populism,'" *Philosophy and Social Criticism* vol. 46, no. 4 (2020).

3 The politics of vocation

1 Best Documentary, "Bhutan: the dictatorship of happiness", 14 June 2023 (https://www.youtube.com/watch?v=yaobUyL77RA, last accessed 10 July 2025).

2 Milan Thomas and Yangchen C. Rinzin, "Your Questions Answered: What is Bhutan's Gross National Happiness Index?", *Asian Development Blog*, 20 March 2023 (https://blogs.adb.org/blog/your-questions-answered-what-bhutan-s-gross-national-happiness-index, last accessed 10 July 2025).

3 Hanif Kureishi, *Shattered*, London: Penguin 2024, pp. 154–5.

4 Op. cit., p. 156.

5 Sigmund Freud, "The Ego and the Id," quoted from https://www.sigmundfreud.net/the-ego-and-the-id-pdf-ebook.jsp.

6 This line of thought was suggested to me by Aaron Schuster (personal communication).

7 John le Carré, *The Little Drummer Girl*, London: Penguin Books 2018, p. 295.

8 Private communication.

9 Rowan Williams, *Dostoyevsky*, London: Continuum 2008, p. 8.

10 Jacques Lacan, *Ecrits*, New York: Norton 2007, p. 691.

11 Personal communication.

12 Vatican News staff, "Pope Francis grants approval for Medjugorje devotion", *Vatican News*.

13 G.W.F. Hegel, *Vorlesungen ueber die Philosophie der Religion II*, Frankfurt: Suhrkamp Verlag 1969, p. 206.

14 Op. cit., p. 205.

15 Harriet Sherwood, "Led not into temptation: pope approves change to Lord's Prayer", *The Guardian*, 6 June 2019 (https://www.theguardian.com/world/2019/jun/06/led-not-into-temptation-pope-approves-change-to-lords-prayer, last accessed 10 July 2025).

16 See List of common misconceptions—Wikipedia (https://en.wikipedia.org/wiki/List_of_common_misconceptions, last accessed 10 July 2025).

17 Op. cit.

18 George Grimbilas, "Lead us not into mistranslation", *The New Criterion*, 19 December 2017 (https://newcriterion.com/dispatch/lead-us-not-into-mistranslation/, last accessed 10 July 2025).

19 Soren Kierkegaard, *Fear and Trembling*, Princeton: Princeton University Press 1983, p. 115.

20 Elise Ann Allen, "Pope in multi-faith Singapore says 'all religions are a path to God'", *Crux*, 13 September 2024 (https://cruxnow.com/2024-pope-in-timor-leste/2024/09/pope-in-multi-faith-singapore-says-all-religions-are-a-path-to-god, last accessed 10 July 2025).

21 Filosofikalanen, "Louis Althusser: The crisis of Marxism (interview)", 12 July 2017 (https://www.youtube.com/watch?v=feepQg_Dx7U, last, accessed 10 July 2025).

22 Steven Wedgeworth, "What is Calvinism? A simple explanation of its terms, history & tenets", *Logos*, 26 June 2023 (https://www.logos.com/grow/nook-what-is-calvinism/, last accessed 10 July 2025).

23 Gilbert Keith Chesterton, *Quotes*, Mineola: Dover Publications 2015, p. 1.

24 G.W.F. Hegel, *Lectures on the Philosophy of Religion*, vol. 3, Berkeley: University of California Press 1987, p. 84.

25 See his outstanding *The Sexual Economy of Capitalism*, Redwood City: Stanford University Press 2024.

26 Karl Marx and Friedrich Engels, *Selected Works*, Volume 1, Moscow: Progress Publishers 1969, p. 83.

27 See Jacques Lacan, *The Ethics of Psychoanalysis*, New York: Routledge 2015.

28 Romans 7 NIV, quoted from *Bible Gateway*.

29 See Russell Sbriglia, "Minus One, or the Mismeasure of Man" (unpublished manuscript).

30 Joan Copjec, *Read My Desire: Lacan Against the Historicists*, Cambridge: MIT Press, 1994, p. 87. Numbers in parentheses refer to the pages of this book.

31 Aaron Schuster, *The Trouble with Pleasure: Deleuze and Psychoanalysis*. All unattributed quotations in the present chapter are from this work.

32 Quoted from Friedrich Nietzsche, *Ecce Homo*, accessed via Classicly (https://www.classicly.com/bibi/pre.html?book=1501.epub, last accessed 10 July 2025).

33 See Alain Badiou, *The Century*, Cambridge: Polity Press 2007.

34 Quoted from Friedrich Nietzche, *The Will to Power*, accessed via Project Gutenberg (https://www.gutenberg.org/files/52914/52914-h/52914-h.htm, last accessed 10 July 2025).

35 For a more detailed elaboration of this line of thought, see miy *Zero Point*, London: Bloomsbury 2025.

Variation 1   Frozen beauty: Rovelli, Deleuze and the Stoics

1 Gilles Deleuze, *The Logic of Sense*, New York: Columbia University Press 1990, p. 80.

2 Gilles Deleuze and Felix Guattari, *What is Philosophy?*, New York: Columbia University Press 1994, p. 59.

3 Gilles Deleuze, *The Logic of Sense*, New York: Columbia University Press 1990, p. 5.

4 Op. cit., p. 7.

5 See Gabriel Nuchelmans, *Theories of Proposition. Ancient and Medieval Conceptions of the Bearers of Truth and Falsity*, Amsterdam: North-Holland 1973.

6 For this line of thought, I am indebted to Alenka Zupančič.

Variation 2   No substitute for true universals

1 See Jure Simoniti, *The Contingent Universal*, manuscript (to appear at Bloomsbury).

2 J. Barbour (1982), "Relational concepts of space and time", *Brit. J. Phil. Sci.* 33, p. 265.

3 See Chapter 1 on Plato in my *Less Than Nothing*, London: Verso Books 2013.

4 *Analects* 13:3, available via classics.mit.edu (https://classics.mit.edu/Confucius/analects.html, last accessed 10 July 2025).

5 Jonathan Clements, *The First Emperor of China*, Chalford: Suton Publishing 2006, p. 34.

6 Aguslord31, "I think Zizek doesn't get Eastern philosophy", Reddit post (https://www.reddit.com/r/zizek/comments/1bt8wyu/i_think_zizek_doesnt_get_eastern_philosophy/?utm_source=share&utm_medium=web3x&utm_name=web3xcss&utm_term=1&utm_content=share_button, last accessed 10 July 2025).

7 *Bhagavad Gita*, translated by W. Johnson, Oxford: Oxford University Press 1994, pp. 44–5.

8 See Piers Morgan Uncensored, "Piers Morgan vs Slavoj Zizek on Israel, Hamas, Putin and more", 15 March 2024 (https://www.youtube.com/watch?v=Otsv5sHHzs8, last accessed 10 July 2025).

9 See ET Online, "'Remove it across the world': Bhagavad Gita reference in 'Oppenheimer' sex scene sparks outrage", *The Economic Times*, 23 July 2023 (https://economictimes.indiatimes.com/industry/media/entertainment/remove-it-across-the-world-bhagavad-gita-reference-in-oppenheimer-sex-scene-sparks-outrage/articleshow/102051810.cms?from=mdr, last accessed 10 July 2025).

10 Swami Revatikaanta, "Refuting Slavoj Žižek's Misinformed Take On The Bhagavad Gita", 19 July 2024 (https://www.youtube.com/watch?v=OSQ_jkGZjTs, last accessed 10 July 2025).

11 Clarice Lispector, quoted from lit.snaps post on Threads, 12 January 2024 (https://www.threads.com/@lit.snaps/post/DDDOFQmTcNw, last accessed 10 July 2025).

12 Kate Buck, "Putin would prefer nuclear strike to defeat in Ukraine, says Russian state TV chief", Yahoo, 28 April 2022 (https://uk.news.yahoo.com/putin-rather-press-nuclear-button-lose-ukraine-war-rt-broadcaster-151707840.html, last accessed 10 July 2025).

13 Nalini Pandit, "Ambedkar and the 'Bhagwat Gita'", *Economic and Political Weekly*, vol. 27, no. 20/21, 1992, pp. 1063–65 (http://www.jstor.org/stable/4397889, last accessed 10 July 2025).

14 Op. cit.

15 See Mahadev Desai, *The Gospel of Selfless Action or the Gita According to Gandhi*, August 1946 (https://www.mkgandhi.org/ebks/gita-according-to-gandhi.pdf, last accessed 10 July 2025).

Variation 3 Pure voice, Pure sound: Beethoven, Globokar, Act

1 John Searle, *Expression and Meaning*, Cambridge: Cambridge University Press 1979, p. 18.

2 F.W.J. von Schelling, *Ages of the World*, Ann Arbor: The University of Michigan Press 1997, pp. 181–2. See also Chapter 1 of Slavoj Zizek, *The Indivisible Remainder*, London: Verso Books 1997.

3 Eric Frank Russell, "Sole Solution", accessed via avalonlibrary.net (https://avalonlibrary.net/ebooks/Eric%20Frank%20Russell%20-%20Sole%20Solution.pdf, last accessed 10 July 2025).

4 For a more detailed account of this topic, see the first part of Slavoj Zizek, *The Indivisible Remainder*, London: Verso Books 2007.

5 The Music Professor, "Beethoven's 9th: the dawn of Creation!", 15 June 2024 (https://www.youtube.com/watch?v=ZkkQKqMmxl4, last accessed 10 July 2025).

6 Chairat Chongvattanakij, "Lecture on Beethoven's Ninth Symphony (Part 1)", 23 August 2020 (https://www.youtube.com/watch?v=S-WrQzw1RLc, last accessed 10 July 2025).

7 Something similar happens at the beginning of the act III of Wagner's *Flying Dutchman*: the chorus of Norwegian sailors provoking the ghosts on the Dutchman's ship is overtaken and eclipsed by the phantom dance and eerie singing of the living dead, Dutchman's crew.

8 Tom Service, "Symphony guide: Beethoven's Ninth ('Choral')", *The Guardian*, 9 September 2014 (https://www.theguardian.com/music/tomserviceblog/2014/sep/09/symphony-guide-beethoven-ninth-choral-tom-service, last accessed 10 July 2025).

9 See Enjoy Classical Music, "Beethoven's Meaning of Life - The double fugue in the ninth symphony", 15 April 2023 (https://www.youtube.com/watch?v=8TMDW18mPKc, last accessed 10 July 2025).—this podcast induced the following comment: "Beethoven's 9th is the highest mountain of all music history, and the double fugue is its top peek."

10 Service, "Symphony guide".

11 Symphony No. 9 (Beethoven)—Wikipedia (https://en.wikipedia.org/wiki/Symphony_No._9_(Beethoven), last accessed 10 July 2025).

12 Daniel K.L. Chua, *The "Galitzin" Quartets of Beethoven*, Princeton: Princeton University Press 1965, p. 240.

13 Charles Rosen, *The Romantic Generation*, London: Harper Collins 1996, p. 175.

14 See Serge Leclaire, *Psychanalyser*, Paris: Editions du Seuil 1968.

15 Jakob Jež, "Interview with Vinko Globokar and Lojze Lebič on the occasion of their 60th anniversary," *Naši zbori* 3-4/1994.

16 "Alain Badiou // Fifteen theses on contemporary art", chtodelat.org (https://chtodelat.org/b8-newspapers/12-69/fifteen-theses-on-contemporary-art/, last accessed 10 July 2025).

Variation 4 Acts of reconciliation

1 G. W. F. Hegel, *The Phenomenology of Spirit*, trans. Terry Pinkard, accessed via libcom.org (https://files.libcom.org/files/Georg%20Wilhelm%20Friedrich%20Hegel%20-%20The%20Phenomenology%20of%20Spirit%20(Terry%20Pinkard%20Translation).pdf, last accessed 10 July 2025). Numbers in brackets in the text that follows refer to the pages of this book.

2 A River Runs Through It (film) - Wikipedia (https://en.wikipedia.org/wiki/A_River_Runs_Through_It_(film), last accessed 10 July 2025).

3 Liza Thompson, personal communication.

4 Venus - Wikipedia (https://en.wikipedia.org/wiki/Venus, last accessed 10 July 2025).

5 See "The Problem with Tannhauser", monsalvat.no (https://www.monsalvat.no/tannhauser.htm, last accessed 10 July 2025).

6 Jon Vickers - Wikipedia (https://en.wikipedia.org/wiki/Jon_Vickers, last accessed 10 July 2025).

7 See Schitorama, "Mutter - Rammstein (children's choir cover)", 18 June 2016 (https://www.youtube.com/watch?v=BzF-JEZ1RMo, last accessed 10 July 2025).

8 See the basic info at Disclaimer (TV Series) - Wikipedia (https://en.wikipedia.org/wiki/Disclaimer_(TV_series), last accessed 10 July 2025).

9 Jackie Strause, "What does the 'Disclaimer' ending say about us? Alfonso Cuarón explains his intention", *Hollywood Reporter*, 11 November 2024 (https://www.hollywoodreporter.com/tv/tv-features/disclaimer-ending-alfonso-cuaron-explains-finale-twist-1236058412/, last accessed 10 July 2025).

10 Nathanael West, *The Day of the Locust*, "Chapter 27", cliffnotes.com (https://www.cliffsnotes.com/literature/d/the-day-of-the-locust/summary-and-analysis/chapter-27, last accessed 10 July 2025).

11 One should mention here also Liane Moriarty's novel *Here One Moment*, London: Penguin Books 2024, which begins on an ordinary short domestic flight where something extraordinary happens: all people on board learn how and when they are going to die. For some, their death is far in the future, but for six passengers, their predicted deaths are not far away at all . . . Moriarty's story doesn't involve any clairvoyance: the apparent fate is rationally accounted for.

12 Boris Groys, "History as the 'Tact of Natality'", *e-Flux*, September 2024 (https://www.e-flux.com/notes/625463/history-as-the-tact-of-natality), last accessed 10 July 2025).

Variation 5 Moderately conservative communism

1 Michael Millerman, "Alexander Dugin's Heideggerianism", *International Journal of Political Theory* 3:1(2018), accessed via philpapers.org (https://philarchive.org/archive/MILADH-2, last accessed 10 July 2025).

2 Dugin quoted from op. cit.

3 See Aleksandr Dugin, *Templars of the Proletariat*, London: Arktos 2023, a close analysis of the metaphysics of national Bolshevism.

4 Quoted from Alexander Dugin, "Lacan and Psychedelic Trumpism", *Arktos*, 19 September 2024 (https://arktos.com/2024/09/19/lacan-and-psychedelic-trumpism/, last accessed 10 July 2025).

5 Oscar Ranzani, "Jacques Alain Miller: 'Lacan foresaw the global domination of capitalism'", New Lacanian School, 8 August 2022 (https://www.amp-nls.org/nls-messager/jacques-alain-miller-lacan-foresaw-the-global-domination-of-capitalism/, last accessed 10 July 2025).

6 Alexander Dugin, "A Right-Left union against liberals", *Arktos*, 7 September 2024 (https://arktos.com/2024/09/07/a-right-left-union-against-liberals/, last accessed 10 July 2025).

7 Jacques-Alain Miller, "A reading of some details in television in dialogue with the audience", *Newsletter of the Freudian Field* 4:1 & 2, accessed via missouri.edu (https://return.jls.missouri.edu/NFFvol4no12/NFF412_Jacques_Alain_Miller.pdf, last accessed 10 July 2025).

8   See Bret W. Davis, "Will and *Gelassenheit*" in *Martin Heidegger: Key Concepts*, ed. Bret W. Davis, Acumen Publishing 2009 (https://www.cambridge.org/core/books/abs/martin-heidegger/will-and-gelassenheit/52C3B6B12EA46AEEA9B3432FD2735051, last accessed 10 July 2025).

9   Jacques Lacan, *Television*, accessed via monoskop.org (https://monoskop.org/images/f/f2/Lacan_Jacques_Television_A_Challenge_to_the_Psychoanalytic_Establishment.pdf, last accessed 10 July 2025).

10 Francois Regnault, "Saintliness and the Sainthood (excerpt)", *Lacanian Ink* (https://www.lacan.com/lacinkXXXIII6.html, last accessed 10 July 2025).

11 Incidentally, in a podcast debate between Dugin and Haz, a self-declared Stalinist Communist, Dugin directly replies to my critique of his use of Lacan. I consider his reply so ridiculous that it doesn't deserve my reaction. See Infrared, " HAZ x DUGIN: Fascism, Žižek and Lacan", 7 January 2025 (https://www.youtube.com/watch?v=xjeozrLaIkM, last accessed 10 July 2025).

12 *Quoted from V. I. Lenin,* "On Ascending a High Mountain", *Notes of a Publicist*, accessed via marxists.org (https://www.marxists.org/archive/lenin/works/1922/feb/x01.htm, last accessed 10 July 2025).

13 Thanks to Mladen Dolar for his analysis on the link between shame and '68 events. (Private communication.) I elaborated this motif more extensively in my *Zero Point*, London: Bloomsbury 2025.

14 Jacques Lacan, *The Seminars of Jacques Lacan: Book XVII, Psychoanalysis upside down/ The reverse side of psychoanalysis*, accessed via lacaninireland.org (http://www.lacaninireland.com/web/wp-content/uploads/2010/06/Book-17-Psychoanalysis-upside-down-the-reverse-side-of-psychoanalysis.pdf, last accessed 10 July 2025).

15 Miller, J.-A. "On Shame," in *Jacques Lacan and the Other Side of Psychoanalysis*, ed. Justin Clemens and Russel Grigg (Durham: Duke University Press, 2006.

16 Soren Larson, "For Shame", *The Lacanian Review*, 7 December 2022 (https://www.thelacanianreviews.com/for-shame/, last accessed 10 July 2025).

17 See Todd MacGowan, *Pure Excess*, New York: Columbia University Press 2025.

18 Mostafa Salem, "In Netanyahu's new Middle East, Syria could become Israel's biggest strategic gain", *CNN*, 14 March 2025 (https://edition.cnn.com/2025/03/14/middleeast/syria-netanyahu-new-middle-east-gain-mime-intl, last accessed 10 July 2025).

Variation 6 The painted void

1   MoMA, "Andrew Wyeth: *Christina's World*, 1948", *MoMA.com* (https://www.moma.org/collection/works/78455, last accessed 10 July 2025).

2 See listing for "'Modern Recreation of Christina's World by Wyeth 30″ × 40″ Acrylics", paintingsbyjoshua.com (https://www.paintingsbyjoshua.com/store/p45/%22Modern_Recreation_of_Christina%27s_World_by_Wyeth_30%22_x_40%22_Acrylics.html#/, last accessed 10 July 2025).

3 Zachary Small, "The controversial story behind Andrew Wyeth's most famous painting", *Artsy*, 31 August 2017 (https://www.artsy.net/article/artsy-editorial-controversial-story-andrew-wyeths-famous-painting, last accessed 10 July 2025).

4 MuseumTV, "'The Death of Marat' by Jacques-Louis David", 23 April 2021 (https://www.museumtv.art/artnews/oeuvres/la-mort-de-marat-de-jacques-louis-david/, last accessed 10 July 2025).

5 For a more detailed analysis of David's painting, see the chapter on "Objects, Objects Everywhere" in my *Less Than Nothing*, (London: Verso Books 2013.

6 Davis Dunavin, "Christina's World: The woman behind the painting", WSHU, 3 August 2023 (https://www.wshu.org/off-the-path/2023-08-03/christinas-world-the-woman-behind-the-painting, last accessed 10 July 2025).

7 Quoted from Small, "The controversial story behind Andrew Wyeth's most famous painting".

8 [TO COME]

9 For a more detailed analysis of Picasso's painting, see "The Lesson on Superpositions in Art" I Part II of this book.

10 See Etienne Dumont, "Deborah de Robertis adds another layer to Metz", *Bilan*, 7 May 2024 (https://www.bilan.ch/story/ed-deborahderobertis-788035082610, last accessed 10 July 2025).

11 See Variation 4.

12 The Music Professor, "The Tristan Chord Revealed", 14 September 2024 (https://www.youtube.com/watch?v=Aya6rG0PgRs, last accessed 10 July 2025).

13 Porgy Amor, "I saw three ships", *Parterre Box*, 20 September 2016 (https://parterre.com/2016/09/20/i-saw-three-ships/, last accessed 10 July 2025).

14 Thomas May, *Decoding Wagner*, Milwaukee: Amadeus Press 2004, p.77.

15 The production can be watched at Stage+ (https://www.stage-plus.com/video/vod_concert_APNM8GRFDPHMASJKBSOJIE8, last accessed 10 July 2025).

Variation 7 The many monsters of the cinema

1 Monsters (2023 film)—Wikipedia (https://en.wikipedia.org/wiki/Monster_(2023_Japanese_film), last accessed 10 July 2025).

2 Epigraph of "Living Room Dialogues on the Middle East," quoted from Wendy Brown, *Regulating Aversion*, Princeton: Princeton University Press 2006.

3 CNN, "'The hostility was something I'd never experienced before': The cost to women of the overlooked rise of Kenya's manosphere" (https://edition.cnn.com/interactive/asequals/kenya-manosphere-toxic-masculinity-as-equals/, last accessed 10 July 2025).

4 See Where is Everybody - Wikipedia (https://en.wikipedia.org/wiki/Where_Is_Everybody%3F, last accessed 10 July 2025).

5 You can watch *Romance Sentimentale* online via YouTube (https://www.youtube.com/watch?v=5PAgAdXN0wQ, last accessed 10 July 2025).

Variation 8 Sexual superpositions

1 I owe this thought to Jacqueline Rose.

2 Sigmund Freud, *Three Essays on the Theory of Sexuality*, New York: Basic Books 1962, p. 155.

3 See Jean Laplanche, *New Foundations for Psychoanalysis*, Oxford: Basil Blackwell 1989.

4 Jean Laplanche, "Sexuality and Attachment in Metapsychology," in *Infantile Sexuality and Attachment*, edited by D. Widlöcher, New York: Other Press 2002, p. 49.

5 Immanuel Kant, *The Metaphysics of Morals*, Cambridge: Cambridge University Press 1996, p. 178. For a detailed study of Kant's propositions of sexuality, see Alain Soble, "Kant and Sexual Perversion", *The Monist* 86:1, January 2003, accessed via philpapers.org (https://philpapers.org/archive/SOBKAS.pdf, last accessed 10 July 2025).

6 Quoted from http://www.masturbate-a-thon.com.

7 Dino Felluga, "Modules on Lacan: On Desire", *Introductory Guide to Critical Theory*, Purdue U (http://www.purdue.edu/guidetotheory/psychoanalysis/lacandesire.html, last accessed 10 July 2025).

8 Jodi Dean developed this notion in her wonderful "Comrade: A Body for Politics" (unpublished manuscript).

9 Rúben Gallo, *Freud's Mexico: Into the Wilds of Psychoanalysis*, Cambridge, MA: MIT Press 2010, pp. 169–70,

10 Available online at http://w.thinkexist.com/quotation/have-you-ever-been-in-love-horrible-isn-t-it-it/347156.html (last accessed 10 July 2025).

11 Bill Mouland, "How a beautiful stranger will send a man's stress hormones soaring… especially if he's not in the same league", *Daily Mail*, 5 May 2010 (https://www.dailymail.co.uk/sciencetech/article-1270271/Beautiful-women-bad-health-raise-stress-hormones.html, last accessed 10 July 2025).

12 See "The Trans Solution", interview with Jacques-Alain Miller, Lacan.com (https://www.lacan.com/symptom/the-trans-solution/, last accessed 10 July 2025).

13 Aaron Schuster, *How to Research Like a Dog*, Cambridge: MIT Press 2014, p. 82.

Variation 9 Make the kitchen maid king

1 See Karl Marx, "Critique of Hegel's Philosophy of Right", accessed via marxists.org (https://www.marxists.org/archive/marx/works/1843/critique-hpr/, last accessed 10 July 2025).

2 For a very balanced critique of Vieweg, see Sebastian Stein, "Review Article: Hegel's Monarch, the Concept and the Limits of Syllogistic Reasoning", *Hegel Bulletin*, Cambridge University Press (CUP), 2016, accessed via academia.edu (https://www.academia.edu/88394992/Review_Article_Hegel_s_Monarch_the_Concept_and_the_Limits_of_Syllogistic_Reasoning_Hegel_Bulletin_, last accessed 10 July 2025).

3 Philip J. Kain, "Hegel on Sovereignty and Monarchy", 2015, accessed via Santa Clara University Scholar Commons (https://scholarcommons.scu.edu/cgi/viewcontent.cgi?article=1059&context=phi, last accessed 10 July 2025).

4 Mark Tunick, "Hegel's justification of hereditary monarchy", *History of Political Thought* 12(3), 1991, accessed via core.ac.uk (https://core.ac.uk/download/pdf/492522394.pdf, last accessed 10 July 2025).

5 Klaus Vieweg, *Das Denken der Freiheit*, Paderborn: Wilhelm Fink Verlag 2012, p. 429.

6 See *Part One of the Encyclopedia of Physical Sciences: The Logic*, "(c) The Syllogism", accessed via marxists.org (https://www.marxists.org/reference/archive/hegel/works/sl/slsyllog.htm, last accessed 10 July 2025).

7 See Jean-Luc Nancy et al., "The jurisdiction of the Hegelian monarch", *Social Research* 49:2, 1982 (http://www.jstor.org/stable/40970873., last accessed 10 July 2025).

8 Quoted from V. I. Lenin, *The State and Revolution*, accessed via marxists.org (https://www.marxists.org/archive/lenin/works/1917/staterev/, last accessed 10 July 2025).

9 See General Secretary of the Communist Party of the Soviet Union—Wikipedia (https://en.wikipedia.org/wiki/General_Secretary_of_the_Communist_Party_of_the_Soviet_Union, last accessed 10 July 2025).

10 See Fredric Jameson, *An American Utopia: Dual Power and the Universal Army*, London: Verso Books 2016.

11 See Aaron Schuster, *How to Research Like a Dog*, Cambridge: MIT Press 2014.

12 See S. Sayyid, "Khomeini and the Decolonization of the Political", *A Critical Introduction to Khomeini*, ed. Arshin Adib-Moghaddam, Cambridge: Cambridge

University Press 2014 (https://www.cambridge.org/core/books/abs/critical-introduction-to-khomeini/khomeini-and-the-decolonization-of-the-political/1E96B4D224EABE3516EEFC3CBC32C427, last accessed 10 July 2025).

Conclusion: The hunger to be something

1 "Paraconsistent Logic", *Stanford Encyclopedia of Philosophy*, 21 February 2022 (https://plato.stanford.edu/entries/logic-paraconsistent/, last accessed 10 July 2025).

2 See Chapter 1 in Fredric Jameson, *Late Marxism: Adorno, Or, The Persistence of the Dialectic*, London: Verso Books 1990.

3 Did not something similar happen after Luigi Mangione was arrested on December 9, 2024, and charged with murder in the fatal shooting of UnitedHealthcare CEO Brian Thompson? (See UnitedHealthcare CEO shooting latest: Luigi Mangione has been charged with murder—ABC News.) Although people generally condemned his act, something unexpected happened. UnitedHealthcare was well-known for refusing to pay its clients the insurance money they deserved, so Brian Thompson was perceived as a symbol of big companies which ruthlessly profit from small people, and this triggered a large wave of sympathy for Mangione, a wave which went across the usual party divisions. As in the case of Bernie, Mangione became a symbol of the oppressed in the class struggle—a proof that class struggle is lurking beneath the official political lines of division, unable to express itself adequately within the existing political coordinates and waiting to explode when opportunity arises.

4 *Metamodernism*, Robin van den Akker, Alison Gibbons and Timotheus Vermeulen, New York: Rowman and Littlefield 2017, p. 2.

5 See Gettier problem - Wikipedia (https://en.wikipedia.org/wiki/Gettier_problem, last accessed 10 July 2025).

6 I rely here on Mladen Dolar, *Rumours*, Cambridge: Polity Press 2024.

7 See Great Fear - Wikipedia (https://en.wikipedia.org/wiki/Great_Fear, last accessed 10 July 2025).

8 I have used this example many times in my work, most extensively in Chapter 9 of my *Defense of Lost Causes*, London: Verso Books, 2017.

9 Alessandra Bucella and Tomas Dominik, "Free will is only an illusion if you are too", *Scientific American*, 16 January 2023 (https://www.scientificamerican.com/article/free-will-is-only-an-illusion-if-you-are-too/, last accessed 10 July 2025).

10 I did it in chapters 1 and 2 of my *Freedom: A Disease Without Cure*, London: Bloomsbury Press 2023.

11 Alain Badiou, *In Praise of Philosophy*, Cambridge: Polity Press 2025 (quoted from the manuscript).

12 See Mladen Dolar, "Sophist's choice", *Crisis Critique* 6:1 (https://www.crisiscritique.org/storage/app/media/2019-04-02/dolar.pdf, last accessed 10 July 2025). Incidentally, Dolar's thesis also has interesting implications for the so-called ontological proof of god's existence (god is a perfect being, and since existence is one of the features of perfection, god has to exist, i.e., existence follows from its notion). If being (existence) is a failed nothingness, it means it is an imperfection, so it follows from the very notion of god that it doesn't exist.

13 See Wise Daily Reflections, "The Ultimate Solution to Human Suffering According to Peter Wessel Zapffe | The Last Messiah", 3 January 2025 (https://www.youtube.com/watch?v=aChGPS0lqnM, last accessed 10 July 2025).

14 To appear in 2025 at MIT Press.

15 See Philipp Mainländer, *Philosophy of Redemption*, Brisbane: Irukandji Press 2025.

16 Condensed from Philipp Mainländer—Wikipedia (https://en.wikipedia.org/wiki/Philipp_Mainl%C3%A4nder, last accessed 10 July 2025).

17 I owe this idea to Jela Krečič, Ljubljana.

18 Quoted from *Hegel's Science of Logic*, vol. 1, book 1, § 134, accessed via marxists.org (https://www.marxists.org/reference/archive/hegel/works/hl/hlbeing.htm, last accessed 10 July 2025).

19 See Carlo Rovelli, *Helgoland*, London: Penguin 2022, pp. 121–31.

20 A careful reader must have noticed the parallel between this triad and the political triad proposed in Variation 6: universal (the domain of free elections), particular (a non-elected controlling body), singular (a monarch chosen by a lot).

21 "Jetztzeit", Oxford Reference (https://www.oxfordreference.com/display/10.1093/oi/authority.20110803100020224, last accessed 10 July 2025).

22 James Baldwin, *Nobody Knows My Name: More Notes of a Native Son*, accessed via Internet Archive (https://archive.org/details/nobodyknowsmynam0000jame_r2m5, last accessed 10 July 2025).

23 *Actually Existing Socialism*, "Understanding siege socialism with Gabriel Rockhill", 7 September 2024 (https://directory.libsyn.com/episode/index/id/32038762#:~:text=Unlike%20most%20episodes%20of%20this,of%20the%20Critical%20Theory%20Workshop%2C, last accessed 10 July 2025).

24 See Wisdom of the crowd—Wikipedia (https://en.wikipedia.org/wiki/Wisdom_of_the_crowd, last accessed 10 July 2025).

25 Aeschylos, *Eumenides*, Ian Johnston's translation (2003), available online at www.mala.bc.ca/~Johnstoi/aeschylus/aeschylus_eumenides.htm.

26 See Alenka Zupančič, *Disavowal*, Cambridge: Polity Books 2024.

27 Jean-Pierre Dupuy, *Petite metaphysique des tsunami*, Paris: Seuil 2005, p. 19.

28 Gilbert Keith Chesterton, *Orthodoxy*, San Francisco: Ignatius Press 1995, p. 9.

29 Shaun Walker, "'War how it truly is': Ukrainian director turns accidental footage into a film", *The Guardian*, 22 June 2024 (https://www.theguardian.com/world/article/2024/jun/22/oleh-sentsov-ukrainian-director-turns-accidental-footage-film, last accessed 10 July 2025).

30 See תושדחה—N12—דיגייס עוזית םיתפ דוליפו ואכלו אותו. קנויה . . . | Facebook.

31 Naoki Yamamoto, "Western philosophers are too low-level", X post, 21 February 2024 (https://x.com/NaokiQYamamoto/status/1760234807672312147, last accessed 10 July 2025).

32 See Slavoj Žižek, *Against Progress*, London: Bloomsbury Press 2024.

33 See Markus Gabriel, *Moral Progress in Dark Times: Universal Values for the 21st Century*, Cambridge: Polity Press 2022.

34 Denise Gamble, "Do universal values exist? A philosopher says yes, and takes aim at identity politics—but not all of his arguments are convincing", *The Conversation*, 23 August 2023 (https://theconversation.com/do-universal-values-exist-a-philosopher-says-yes-and-takes-aim-at-identity-politics-but-not-all-of-his-arguments-are-convincing-208014, last accessed 10 July 2025).

35 See Paul Erdős—Wikipedia (https://en.wikipedia.org/wiki/Paul_Erd%C5%91s, last accessed 10 July 2025).

36 Op. cit.

37 See Markus Gabriel, *Gutes tun: Wie der ethische Kapitalismus die Demokratie retten kann*, Berlin: Ullstein Verlag 2024.

38 Stanley M. Bergman, "Ethical Capitalism? It's worth a try", *HuffPost*, 27 March 2014 (https://www.huffpost.com/entry/ethical-capitalism-its-wo_b_4666325#:~:text=This%20year's%20World%20Economic%20Forum,to%20give%20it%20a%20try., last accessed 10 July 2025).

39 See Adrian Johnston, *Infinite Greed*, New York: Columbia University Press 2024.

40 Katharine J. Dell & Arnoldus Schytte Blix, "The Norwegian philosopher Peter Wessel Zapffe (1899-1990) and the Book of Job", *The Royal Norwegian Society of Sciences and Letters*, 1, 2022 (https://www.dknvs.no/wp-content/uploads/2022/09/DKNVS_Skrifter1_2022_Scr.pdf, last accessed 10 July 2025).

41 See Peter Wessel Zapffe - Wikipedia (https://en.wikipedia.org/wiki/Peter_Wessel_Zapffe, last accessed 10 July 2025).

Index

abortion 29, 376
Abraham 218
Absolute
    and Hegel 50, 83, 86, 257
    idealism 90–1
    knowledge 85–6, 90
    and love 211
    not reality-in-itself 52
    and Rovelli 378
    and the Void 58
'absolute recoil' 339
acheronta movebo 276
actualism 243
Adam and Eve 73–6, 216
Adorno, Theodor 87, 140, 200, 364
Against Progress 169
Agamben, Giorgio 272
agape 284, 346
Ages of the World (Schelling) 84, 265
Aladdin system 175–6
Aleksandrov, Grigori 330
Allais, Alphonse 76
Alternative for Germany (AfD) 302, 380
Althusser, Louis Pierre 4–5, 221
Ambedkar, B. R. 260
America against America (Wang Huning) 152
An American Utopia: Dual Power and the Universal Army (Jameson) 360
Amerix 328
Amish 172–3
ANC 163
Andersen, Hans Christian 261
Angelou, Maya 195

Angelus Silesius 102
Animal Farm (Orwell) 330
Anthropocene Age 158
anti-de-Sutter universe 2
anti-Semitism 131, 148, 150, 192–3, 288
anti-Vietnam-war protests (1968) 139
antidescriptivism 191
anxiety 125–7, 265–6, 351
apes 168
The Archaeology of Knowledge (Foucault) 237–8
Arendt, Hannah 159–60
Arestrup, Niels 284
Aristotle 5, 13, 37
Armand, Inessa 211
Arse, Lucho 221–2
articulated Word 277
Artificial Intelligence (AI) 142, 175, 177–86, 194–5, 205
Artificial Neural Networks (ANN) 184
artificial neurons 184
'Assessing Relational Quantum Mechanics' (Muciño/Okon/Sudarsky) 55
asymmetry 72, 373, 400n.14
atheism
    and Christianity 214, 222, 224
    crack in texture of reality 12–13, 396n.2
    introduction 3–4, 395n.8
    not free decision 115–16
    as a subjective stance 393
Augustine, St. 74–6, 217
Auschwitz 200
authenticity 201–3, 328

Badiou, Alain
  'censors of ourselves' 274
  and creation of God 115
  drawing truc line of division 382–3
  and fidelity 272
  metaphor for XXth century 232
  multiplicity of multiplicities 240
  opposes mysticism/philosophy 101
  philosophy in Ancient Greece 372
  Seoul term 150
  and 'symptomal torsion' 249
  and *Tannheuser* 281
Bahia, Brazil 171
Baldwin, James 379
Balibar, Etienne 196
Bataille, Georges 225
Baudelaire, Charles 131–2
Bayard, Pierre 168
Bean (film) 314
Bebel, August 376
Beckett, Samuel 140
Beckett, Thomas 216
becoming-it-itself 237–8
Beethoven, Ludwig van 263–4, 266–8
Being
  and Alain Badiou 101
  anxiety faced with mortality 126
  disclosure of meaning 89–91
  and Hannah Arendt 160
  and Hegel 81
  and Imaginary 299
  and Kant's *Critique* 123
  and language 109
  and man 111
  meaning of 109, 134–5, 137
  place of disclosure of 110
  predominant temporality of 237–8
  question of 96
being is a failed nothing (Dolar) 372
Being and Time (Heidegger) 197
Being You: A New Science of Consciousness (Seth) 99
being-in-the-world 107, 203
Bell's theorem 46
Ben Gvir, Itamar 149

'bend of History' 366
Benjamin, Walter 61, 144, 157, 167–9, 305, 379
Bentham, Jeremy 226
Berardi, Franco 139–40, 150
Berger, Edward 285
Berkeley, George 3
Bernstein, Eduard 376
Bhagavad Gita 179, 256–60
Bhutan 207
Bible, the 13
Biden, Joe 364
Big Bang 27, 33–4, 36, 108
'big Other'
  absence in *Rashomon* 323
  and Beethoven 269
  and Einstein 36
  and God's judgement 390
  and knowledge 371
  and Lacan 12, 261–2, 393
  and proto-reality 49, 51
  and Rovelli 40
  and sex 336
  see also God
Bill and Melinda Gates Foundation 304
biofriendliness 159
Black Notebooks (Heidegger) 135, 148
'Black Square' (Malevitch) 315–16
BlackRock 175–6
Blade Runner (film) 186
Blair, Tony 224, 357
Blankinship, Joshua 309
'block universe' 29–30
Blok, Aleksandr 298
Blue Velvet (Lynch) 107–8
Bogdanov, Aleksandr 2–3
Böhme, Jacob 113–15, 250
Bohr, Niels 23, 25, 52, 208, 367
Boko Haram 172
Bolivia 221–2
Bolshevism 170, 211, 298, 305, 359
Bonhoffer, Dietrich 213
Borromean knot 300, 305
borrowing 49–50
Brandom, Robert 92, 98

Brasil (Gilliam) 283
Brassier, Ray 373
Brecht, Bertolt 294, 391–2
BRICS 299
Brod, Max 94, 142
Brodsky, Joseph 143–4
Brooks, Mel 198
Brothers Karamazov (Dostoyevsky) 326–7
Buchanan, Ian 70
Buddhism
    attaining inner peace 226
    and capitalism 151
    and Enlightenment 111–12
    and Mainländer 375–6
    and the self 99–100, 260
    and *sunyata* 377
    Tibetan 172
    understanding 255–7
    and the Void 58
Buisson, Patrick 138
Bukharin, Nikolai 160
Bunuel, Louis 330
Burke, Edmund 301

Calvinism 221–2
Cancel Culture 156, 203–4, 279, 305, 366, 372
Cantor, George 86
Canudos 171–2
capitalism
    and commodification 209
    and creative potential of humans 373–4
    crisis of 143–4
    de-totalization of meaning 150–1
    and Heidegger 137–8
    and history 162–3, 165, 173–4
    and Miller 306
    and Protestantism 222–3
    'pure evil' 303
    reaching its notion 154
    and socialism/communism 165, 223
    trans-cultural global 147
    vision of ethical 390

Carlsen, Magnus 205
Carnaval (Schumann) 270–1
Carroll, Sean 62
Castellucci, Romeo 282
The Castle (Kafka) 83
castrato coloraturas 277
causal theory 188
'Ceci n'est pas une pipe' (Magritte) 316
Censor Librorum 215
The Century (Badiou) 232
Chalmers, David 186–90
Chaplin, Charles 181
ChatGPT 181
chemistry 149–50
Cherubinic Wanderer (Angelus Silesius) 102
Chesterton, G. K. 85, 107, 222, 385
China
    and Confucius 246–7
    Dugin's view of 303
    ongoing campaign in 152–3
    state control 362–3, 380–1
    war plans 178
    and Western investments 176, 406n.3
Chinese Communist Party 152
Chinese Cultural Revolution 144
Chomsky, Noam 156
Christ! 198–9
Christianity
    anti-Christian logic in Russia 259
    and atheism 224
    Calvinism as ex-timate point of 222
    and capitalism 151
    cultural 214–16, 219, 220–1
    and the Devil 223
    and existence of God 113, 213
    fundamentalism 149
    and 'God is Christ' 12, 16
    Good and Evil 74
    and immaculate conception 217
    and Martin Luther 194
    modernity 164
    the only universal religion 224
    theological revolution of 92

and true reconciliation 280-1
and unconditional love 21
and universality 244
Christie, Agatha 195
Christina's World (Wyeth) 309
Chua, Daniel 268
Cioran, Emil 372
City Lights (Chaplin) 182
Cixin Liu 113-14, 157-8
Clark, T. J. 310
Claudel, Paul 218
climate change 156-8, 180
clitoridectomy 136
A Clockwork Orange (Kubrick) 267
Close, Glenn 284
coitus a tergo 344
colonization 163, 172-3, 305
commodification 209, 223
Communism
　and Althusser 221
　authentic 392
　author's position 305, 362
　and capitalism 222-4
　egalitarian emancipatory Idea 249
　and the human condition 373
　and Mainländer 376
　return of desire for 294
　and truth 161
　undermining cultural values 214
'complementarity' (Bohr) 23
Conclave (film) 285-6
Confucius 246-7
Connes, Alain 30
consciousness 43-5, 106, 262
Conselheiro, Antônio 171
The Contingent Universal (Simoniti) 244
controlled hallucination 99
Copenhagen interpretation 2, 25
Copenhagen QM 48
Copjec, Joan 226
Copperfield, David 12
coprophagia 345
Cord, Matthew 316-17
cosmology 19, 23-6, 33, 38, 88, 108, 159
cosmos 20, 24-6, 55, 245, 379

Costick, Conor 34
Cotten, Joseph 314
counterfactual situations 68, 73, 77
Courbet, Gustave 311-16
Covid pandemic 7, 77, 376
Critique of Pure Reason (Kant) 103, 123, 127
Cuarón, Alfonso 286-7
The Culmination (Pippin) 81, 91, 96-7
Cultural Revolution 144, 153, 381
cunnilingus 314

Dark Night (St John of the Cross) 102
dark precursors 70
Darwin, Charles 24, 33, 163
das Man 126
Dasein 84, 88-90, 110, 125, 297
David, Jean-Louis 310
Dawkins, Richard 215
The Dawn of Everything (Graeber/Wengrow) 163
The Day of Doom (Wigglesworth) 87, 199-200
The Day of the Locust (Hayes) 292
de Gaulle, general 120
de Robertis, Debcourorah 311-13
de Sade, Marquis 87, 227-30
death 87, 230, 233, 318
death drive 229, 252-3, 375
'The Death of Marat' (David) 310-11
Death Valley, California 157-8
Deleuze, Gilles
　abandoning god 116
　and becoming 237-8, 241
　choosing/chosen 208
　and dark precursor 70
　and impersonal intensity 331
　perspectival distortion 86
　productive-immanent 'One' 240
　time/movement image 270
democracy 29, 118, 203-4, 301, 358, 383
Democrats 300-2
derangement 109-10
Derrida, Jacques 277
Descartes, René 62, 71, 133, 166, 186, 335

description 188, 191–2
Destiny 125, 135, 137, 296, 342, 385
determinism 36, 68–9, 93, 160, 248
Detour (Ulmer) 82
Deutsch, David 54
Devil, the 131–3, 223, 277, 387
Dharma 258
dialectics 5, 8, 12–15, 103, 116, 253, 364, 378
Dickens, Charles 195
Die Frage nach dem Ding (Heidegger) 103
Difference and Repetition (Deleuze) 70
differentiality 52, 78, 109, 255
Diósi, Lajos 14
disavowal 296, 369, 384–5
Disclaimer (Quaron) 286–90
disjunctive syllogism 354–5
diversity 204, 366
The Doctrine of Fascism (Gentile/Mussolini) 243
Dolar, Mladen 372
Donat, Robert 314
Donnellan, Keith 190
Dostoyevsky, Fyodor 213, 298, 326–7
Double Jeopardy (film) 272
double-slit experiment 19, 25
drugs 149–50
dualism 16, 164, 238, 246
Dugin, Aleksandr 297–303, 305, 413n.11
Dupuy, Jean-Pierre 68, 72–3, 94, 385

Ecce Homo (Nietzsche) 232
Eckhart, Meister 113–14
Eddington, Arthur 28
Ego 32, 209
Egypt 173
Einstein, Albert 27, 36, 47–8, 208
Einstein–Podolsky–Rosen paradox (EPR) 46–8, 398n.27
Eisenstein, Sergei 330–2
Eisler, Hanns 391–2
electrons 18, 20, 25, 43, 45, 51
Elephant Man 108
Eliot, T. S. 216
Elster, Jon 202–3

'Emperor's New Clothes' (Andersen) 261–2
end of philosophy 87–8
Enlightenment 116, 226
entropy 27–32, 35
Erdős, Paul 389–90
eros 346
eukaryotic cells 43
Eumenides (Aeschylos) 382
'Eurocentrism' 372
European liberalism 302–3
Evil
    description of 129–30
    and the Devil 132
    and existence 376
    the gaze itself 286–8
    and good 216–17, 259–60, 382
    human tendency towards 373
    indestructible 87
    meaning of 73–7
    origin of 109, 114
    supreme figure of 280
    and Thing 325
    and Ukraine war 298
Eyeless in Gaza (Huxley) 289–90

Faggin, Federico 44–5
Fall, the 74–7
fascism 144, 156, 231, 243, 273–4, 297, 381
Fatelessness: Freedom and Fatality After Marx (Brassier) 373
feminism 148, 311, 375–6
feudalism 162, 173, 190, 356
Feynman, Richard 15–16, 25–6
Fichte, Johann 88, 335
Fiennes, Ralph 286
Fingersmith (Waters) 327
finitude 86, 125, 162
Fink, Bruce 70
Fink, Larry 175
Finkielkraut, Alain 148
Finland 180
Flatland: A Romance of Many Dimensions (Abbott) 1
Foreword to Phenomenology 103
Foucault, Michel 127–8, 185, 237–8

Four Weddings and a Funeral (film) 201
fourth dimension 1
France 118–21
Francis, Pope 214, 217–20
Frankfurt School 306
free love movement 376
free will 44–5, 100, 221, 371
freedom
    another name for ignorance 159–61
    and evil 217
    a Fascist nation-state 243
    gift of 74–5
    and Kant 226–7
    and knowledge 372
    repressed 130
    space of 93–4
    in Ukraine 230
    and the Ungrund 115
French Revolution 230, 301, 369
Freud, Sigmund
    and the death drive 229, 252–3, 375
    Ego and Id 209
    importance of appearance 201
    and metamodernism 366
    and oppression 127
    pansexualism of 198
    and primordial repression 14, 307
    and the Real 122
    and reconstruction 70–1
    and screen-memory 90
    and sex 337, 342
    status of the Unconscious 262–3
    and the 'thing' 103, 325
    trimethylamin formula 271
    and 'trivialities' 6
    the unconscious 92–3, 97, 110–11, 300–1, 370
    and workings of non-commutativity 66–7
fuck 197–9, 335
'The Fundamental Concepts of Metaphysics' (Heidegger lectures) 167
fundamentalism 21, 121, 149, 156, 172–3, 214

Gabriel, Markus 387–90
Gaiman, Neil 346–7
Gallo, Rúben 346
Gandhi, Mahatma 117, 229–30, 260
Garland, John 291
Gaza 129, 134, 142, 178, 290, 387–8
Gegenwart 250
geistige Koerperlichkeit 270
Gelassenheit 304
Gentile, Giovanni 243
Germany 120, 133–6, 259, 282, 297
Gettier, Edmund 367
'Gettier with Rumsfeld' 367, 370
The Ghost (Harris) 289
gilets jaunes 356–7
Gilliam, Terry 283
Gipfel 82
Girondins 119
global capitalism 134, 147, 149, 151, 153
global warming *see* climate change
Globokar, Vinko 269–77
God
    abandoning of 115–16
    and Adam and Eve 73–6, 216–17
    and atheism 13
    and Calvinism 221
    and Christ 92, 124–5
    and creation of the world 115
    death of 222, 379
    decaying corpse of 375
    divided from himself 113
    and Eric Liddell 208
    existence of 213–14, 327
    fate of 168
    and human ethics 218
    is love 290
    and Job 392–3
    judgement of 389
    and Judgment Day 199–200
    as majestic creator of everything 83
    need of humans 114
    omnipotent not omniscient 51
    rational proof of existence 368
    reading the mind of 90

religions as paths to reach 220
sensed by Boehme 114–15
supreme figure of Evil 280
taking refuge in 3–4
and teleology 20
thought processes of 265
the ultimate/absolute observer 37
vision of 59
see also 'big Other'
Gödel, Kurt 43
Good 74–7, 129, 216–18, 259–60
Google 54
Gould, Stephen Jay 273
Gracq, Julien 230
Graeber, David 163, 173
Gramsci, Antonio 143
The Grand Design (Hawking) 88
The Great Dictator (Chaplin) 183
Great Fear (1789) 369
Greece 173, 245, 372
Greek Orthodox Church 170
Gregoire, abbe 120
Grosse Fuge (Beethoven) 268–9
Groys, Boris 294
Grundrisse (Marx) 168, 374
Guantanamo Bay 272–3
Guardian Council (Iran) 361
Guattari, Félix 238
Guevara, Che 136

Habermas, Jürgen 126, 196, 388–9
Haiti 149
hallucination 99–100
Hamas 134, 139, 142, 179, 290, 360, 387–8
Hameroff, Stuart 43–4
Hamlet (Shakespeare) 68, 190, 336
Hamza, Agon 6–7, 40
Han Fei 247
Handmaiden (film) 327, 328
Handmaid's Tale 339
Harris, Kamala 299–300
Harris, Robert 289
Hawking, Stephen 20, 24, 26, 33, 37–8, 88
Hayes, Terry 292

Hegel, Georg
and the Absolute 50, 85–6, 90–1, 110, 257
and 'absolute recoil' 190
actualization, truth of possibility 373–5
and Adam and Eve 216
closed circle system 144
and constitutional monarchy 353–5, 358, 360
dialectical process of 73–4, 113, 204, 363
disparity of substance 92
end of philosophy 87–8
and Evil 287–8
'for-us' distinction 100
formula of phrenology 220
formula of reconciliation 3
and Foucault 127–8
and freedom 301
and French revolution 230
and Giovanni Gentile 243
and Gödel 43
and Habermas 196
and Heidegger 81–2, 96–7, 134, 137
and the Holy Spirit 222
idealism of 123
and imagination 103–5
and infinite judgment 25
and insanity 106
and Jacob Böhme 114
and knowledge 75
and Kojeve 151
and *Logic* 246
logic of 101, 363, 377
and metamodernism 366
and Napoleon 364
need for appearance 201
'night of the world' 32
notion of historicity 8
and 'objective Spirit' 269
and the 'One' 240
paradox of existing 49
and Pippin 84, 97–8, 203–4
and quantum mechanics 12–17
and reconciliation 279–80, 285, 289
resistance between object/subject 67

and schematism 124–5
second death 228
self-relating negativity 252–3
and sex 336, 339, 342, 347
space and time 31
and true thinking 109
and the Void 58
Heidegger, Martin
  and Being 106, 174, 203
  end of philosophy 87–91
  and freedom 161
  and Freud 110–11
  and *Gelassenheit* 304
  and Hannah Arendt 160
  and Hegel 81–4, 96, 113
  and imagination 103
  and Jews 148
  man as *Dasein* 110–11
  and Millerman/Dugin 297–8
  notion of historicity 8
  and onto-theological structure of metaphysics 37
  pain in nature 112, 167–8
  and Pippin 97–9
  and poetry 95–6
  politics of finitude 123–39, 404n.10
  and pre-human nature 167
  and the Real 113
  relating to mortality 76
  sexual angle 336
  and 'thing' 103
  and truth 108–9
Helgoland (Rovelli) 2, 254, 377
Heraclitus 36
Hertog, Thomas 18, 26–7, 32–3, 37–8, 159–60
Himmler, Heinrich 255–6, 258–9
Hinduism 112, 151, 255, 260
history 162–4, 167–74, 238
History of the World: Part I (Brooks) 198
Hitchens, Christopher 192
Hitler, Adolf 120, 138, 193, 214, 326, 371
Hitler, Philosophy and Hatred (Trawny) 138

Holocaust, the 133–6, 176–7, 200, 259
holographic cosmology 23
holography 1, 21, 24, 27, 162, 173
Holy Ghost 244
Holy Spirit 222–3, 346
homelessness 126
homo sacer 272–3
homosexuality 276
honesty 201
Hossenfelder, Sabine 39, 100
'Hugh-Grant-paradox' 201
human beings 166, 184–6, 212, 405–6n.19
human rights 130
Hume, David 335
'Humoresque' (Schumann) 275
hur 217
Husserl, Edmund 5
Huxley, Aldous 289–90
hypocrisy 279

Id 209
Idea 50, 101
idealism 24, 243, 250
Ideas 246
IDF 118, 129, 142, 179, 387
IG Farben 176
'il n'y a pas de grand Autre' (Lacan) 54
The Iliad (Homer) 184
Imaginary, the 299–302
imagination 103–4
immanentism 243
immortality 86–7
Incas 163, 173
incest 199
inclusion 204
'inconvenience of existence' (Cioran) 372
India 155, 305
indicative propositions 68
'indirect speech act' 261
inert in-itself 42
infantile sexuality 338–9
infinite judgment (Hegel) 25
insanity 105–6
intellectuality 185
Interpretation of Dreams (Freud) 122

'Investigations Of a Dog' (Kafka) 93–4, 128
Iran 215, 361–2
Iraq 370
Irgolič, Rafko 95
Is It Ever Just Sex? (Leader) 94–5
Isaac 218
Ishiguro, Kazuo 291, 293
ISIS 172
Islam 149, 155, 172, 217
Island (Bay) 293–4
Israel
    actions in Gaza 133–4, 142, 179, 290, 387
    caught in a paradox 307
    a failed state 149
    mass demonstrations in 360
    raid on Sde Teiman base 118

Jacobin Terror 118, 310
Jameson, F. 112–13, 154, 164, 360, 364, 366
Japan 151, 322–3
Jaurès, Jean 221
Jenaer Realphilosophie (Hegel) 103, 105
Jesus Christ
    dying on the cross 244
    experiencing unity with god 113
    fake paintings of 34
    and fall of man from god 83
    and God 125
    liberation of 212–13
    and love 115, 290
    practice of judgment 72
    and solidarity 281
    the 'vanishing mediator' 223
Jetztzeit (Benjamin) 379
Johnston, Adrian 391
jouissance 87
Judaism
    and anti-Semitism 192
    and gas chambers 257
    and Heidegger 131–4, 139, 148–9
    and Himmler 256, 259
    and Hitler 214
    and the Nazis 176–7

Judgment Day 199–200, 389–90
Julius Caesar 69
'The Jurisdiction of the Hegelian Monarch' (Nancy) 355
justified-true-belief (JTB) 367

Kafka, Franz 83, 93–4, 140–4, 185, 351, 360
kangaroos 192
Kant, Immanuel
    and Christianity 92
    and de Sade 229
    ethics of 224–5
    and evil 129
    finitude 125
    and freedom 226
    and Heidegger 88, 103
    and imagination 104
    moral struggles 168
    'musical schematizing' 271
    noumenal domain 199
    a priori 'feelings' of 127
    and reality 103, 112
    schematism 124
    and sex 335, 338
    things-in-themselves 193
    and transcendental schematism 123
Karamazov Brothers (Dostoyevsky) 213
Karma Yoga 258
Kautsky, Karl 22, 160
Kenya 328
Khomeini, Ayatollah 155
Khovanshchina (Khovansky affair) 170
Khovanshchina (Mussorgsky) 170
Khovansky, Prince Ivan 170
Khrushchev, Nikita 7
Kierkegaard, Søren 75, 83, 86, 199, 216, 218
Kill Bill (Tarantino) 7
Kim Yong Il 192–3
King, Martin Luther 163
King, Stephen 325
Kirill, patriarch 171
Knightley, Keira 295
knowledge 367, 370–2
'knowledge in the real' (Lacan) 48
Koehler, Armin 272

Kohei Saito 151, 181
Kojeve, Alexandre 151
Koji Yakusho 151
Kotkin, Stephen 69
Kubrick, Stanley 267
Kung Fu films 274
Kureishi, Hanif 207–8
Kurosava, Akira 321
Kurukshetra war 258

'la Femme n'existe pas' (Lacan) 54
Lacan, Jacques
   anti-progressive pessimism 305–6
   and anxiety 266, 269
   and the big Other 12, 36, 40, 261–2, 300–1
   and capitalism 303–5
   and de Sade 228
   and death 233
   and desire 124, 213
   disparity between subject and substance 91–2
   and enunciation 63, 204
   ethics of 257
   and failure 140
   and Freud 70–2
   and immortality 86–7
   inconsistency of 363
   and J. D. Vance 302
   and *jouis-sense* 276–7
   and *jouissance* 87
   and Kafka 143
   and Kant 225–7, 230, 367
   'knowledge in the real' 48
   and lies 133
   logic of non-all 53–5
   and mysticism 102–3
   no clear view 183
   and non-commutativity 66, 77
   and *Origin of the World* 311
   and Pippin 98
   and 'primordial' speech acts 195
   and progressive evolution 167
   and Real 220, 222, 255, 265, 299, 386
   remembrance 67
   revolutions 119
   and Richardson 111
   Sartrean duality 42–3
   and sex 124, 329, 336, 343–4, 346, 348–9
   and signifier 5, 355
   status of the unconscious 93
   and structure 190–1
   and 'subjective destitution' 100
   and subjective destitution 333
   superegos of dogs 198
   and surplus-enjoyment 127–8
   and teleology 167
   and the Thing 378
   and truth 90, 121, 289
Laclau, Ernesto 358
language 40, 109, 196–9, 239
Laplanche, Jean 338
The Last Tycoon (Scott Fitzgerald) 313
Lavender (programme) 178–9
Lavrov, Sergey 203
le Carré, John 211, 218–19
Le horla (Maupassant) 103
Leader, Darian 94–5
Leclaire, Serge 271
Leibniz, Gottfried 45, 55
lekta 239–41
Lenin, Vladimir
   and Bolshevism 298, 305
   famous slogan of 359–60
   and Hamza 40
   and Inessa Armand 211
   and Jacobin legacy 118–19
   and *Materialism/Empiriocriticism* 2–6
   rethinking a Communist revolution 244
   and Stalinism 373
   and Stolypin 117
'less than nothing' 58
Levi-Strauss, Claude 21
LGBT movement 155–6
liberalism 305, 361
Libet, Benjamin 262
Liddell, Eric 208
light, speed of 26, 50, 53, 59, 61

Lincoln, Abraham 381
Lispector, Clarice 259
The Little Drummer Girl (le Carré) 211–12
Loch Ness monster 3–4
logic 239, 363
Logic (Hegel) 50
Logical Investigations (Husserl) 5
logos 91, 109
Losurdo, Domenico 380
love 210–11, 213, 223, 262
Love, Actually (film) 205–6
Lubitsch, Ernst 387
Luther, Martin 194
Lutheran Protestantism 222
Lynch, David 42, 107–8

M Butterfly (film) 340–2
McGowan, Todd 144
MAD (Mutually Assured Destruction) 178
Madama Butterfly (Puccini) 340–1
Magic Flute (Mozart) 264
Mahayana Buddhist ontology 58
Mainländer, Philipp 375–6
Malevich, Kazimir 316
Mallarmé, Stéphane 229
man 109–11, 165–8
Mandelstam, Osip 232
Mankell, Henning 154
manosphere 328
Many Worlds Interpretation 57, 62
Mao Zedong 244, 380–2
Marder, Michael 46
marriage 25–6, 223, 347
Marx, Chico 192
Marx, Groucho 181, 192
Marx, Karl
    anatomy of the ape 168
    and Aristotle 373
    and capitalism 374, 391
    and Christian atheism 224
    and commodity fetishism 147, 177
    critique of political economy 303–4
    and history 162, 173, 190
    importance of appearance 201
    and Lenin 118
    and metamodernism 366
    and ontological pessimism 375
    opposed to philosophy 88
    and Pippin 97
    and radical conservatives 138
    and religion 149
    sexual angle 336
    value of a commodity 129
    and the working class 249
Marxism
    and capitalism 165
    cultural 214
    and the Jacobin legacy 118
    and predestination 112–13
    primacy of interaction over observation 40
    rejection of immediacy 364
    traditional 378
    truth resides in form itself 330
    Western 215
Mary 215
Master-Signifiers 316, 329, 355, 383
materialism 2, 4, 107
Materialism and Empiriocriticism (Lenin) 2–3
The Matrix (film) 186
Matthew 281
Maupassant, Guy de 103
May, Thomas 318
Mayakovsky, Vladimir 274–5
Meaningfulness 138
meaninglessness 106
The Measure Taken (Brecht) 294
Medjugorje 214–15, 219
Meeting Venus (Szabo) 284
Meier, Johanna 317
Mein Kampf (Hitler) 138
Mer-Khamis, Juliano 212
metamodernism 365–6
metaphysics 90–1
microtubules 43–4
Mikado (Gilbert and Sullivan) 5
Millbank, John 101, 164
Miller, Jacques-Alain 301, 305–6, 348–9
Millerman, Michael 297

Milton, John 290
mirror bacteria 182
missionary position 344
Modern Recreation of Christina's World by Wyeth (Blankinship) 309
modernism 164, 365
Moliere 76
Mona Lisa 314
'monad of the monads' (Leibniz) 55
monadology (Leibniz) 45
monism 55
Monsters 323–8
Moral Majority 173
moral universalism 388
Morales, Evo 221–2
Moralista movement 221
Morgan, Piers 257
Muciño, R. 55
multiverse 27, 54
Munch, Edvard 270
Murder in the Cathedral (Eliot) 216
Murphy, Mark 213
Murray, Bill 359
Musk, Elon 154
Muslims *see* Islam
Mussorgsky, Modest 170
'Mutter' (Rammstein) 285
mystic materialism 101–2
mysticism 101–2

Nagarjuna 58, 377
Name-of-the-Father 300
Nancy, Jean-Luc 355
Napoleon 68, 364
'narod' 297
National Socialism 135–6, 138
NATO 176, 302
Nature 157, 228–9, 367
nausea 106
Nausea (Sartre) 106
Nazism
    and anti-Semitism 288
    disclosure of reality 150
    and Heidegger 138–9
    and Himmler 258–9
    and Hitler 120, 193
    and the Holocaust 176–7
    and Judaism 134–6
    and workers' movement 273
neo-Fascism 299
Netanyahu, Benjamin 307, 387
neufeudalism 153–4
neurons 43, 220
neurotheology 220
Never Let Me Go (Romanek) 291–6, 311
New World Order 155
Newton, Isaac 60
Newtonian physics 37
Ngeze, Hassan 326
Nietzsche, Friedrich 232, 336, 366
'night of the world' 83, 100–1, 105, 125
nihilism 130–1, 134–5
9th symphony (Beethoven) 263–4, 266–8
Nogaro, Padre Raffaele 212–13
non-commutativity 65–7
Norma (Bellini) 241
normativity 196
Norrington, Roger 267–8
North Korea 140–1, 151–2, 192–3
nothing 58, 114–15
NWO 155

'objective reality' 100–1, 113
objet petit a (Lacan) 124, 127
observer/observation 40–1
October Revolution 69, 143–4, 170, 330, 369
'Ode to Joy' (Beethoven) 266–8
Oedipus 135
Oedipus at Colonus (Sophocles) 376
Okon, E. 55
Old Believers 170–1
The Old and the New 331
Olson, Christina 310–11
On the Origin of Time (Hertog) 32
'One' (energy) 44–5
One, the 45, 101, 240–1, 248
ontology 261, 375

The Opposing Shore (Gracq) 230–1
Orban, Viktor 231
Oriental spirituality 323
The Origin of the World (Courbet) 311, 314–16
original baptism 191–2
Orwell, George 330
Other, the
  becoming a real object 142
  and child sexuality 339
  and de Sade 228
  and Ego 32
  and Freud 111
  and God 116
  and Hegel 3, 374–5
  and Heidegger 126
  and language 196, 198
  and Lenin 119
  North Korea 141
  and populist fundamentalism 172
over-excitement 150

Palestine 118, 133–4, 139, 149, 178, 387
'Pan-Asianism' 163
Pandemic (Žižek) 7
paraconsistency 363–7
Paradise 217–18
Paris Commune 311–12
Park Chan-wook 327
Parmenides (Plato) 36, 246
Parsifal (Wagner) 27, 216
Pascal, Blaise 212, 347
past, the 169
Patriarch Nikon of Moscow 170
Paul, St. 225
Penrose, Roger 11, 14, 43–4, 194, 262, 398n.19
People 310
Perfect Days (film) 151
The Perfect Number (Zanussi) 209–10
pessimism 375–6, 383
Peter the Great 169–70
Phenomenology of Spirit (Hegel) 83, 91, 104, 279
philia 346

philosophy 87–8, 188, 245, 249–50, 253, 298, 372
Philosophy of Redemption (Mainländer) 375
photons 17, 19–20, 26, 42, 65–6
phrenology 220
'physical collapse' 14
Pinker, Steven 162
Pippin, Robert
  and Hegel 81, 84, 90–2, 203
  and Heidegger 95–8, 126, 134, 136–8
  present-at-hand 128
Pius VI, Pope 227–8
plants 46
Plato 3, 21, 115, 238, 240, 246, 277
Platonism 239
pleasure 127, 226
Plekhanov, Georgi 68–9, 160
Podemos 357
poetic-military complex 326
poetry 95–6, 200
Pokemon Go (AR game) 187, 193
Politburo Standing Committee (CCP) 152
polytheism 220
Ponnelle, Jean-Pierre 317–18, 341
positrons 15–16
postmetaphysical idealism 107
postmodernism 365–6
Presley, Elvis 277
primordial collapse 14
primordial decision-differentiation notion 263
primordial repression 14, 307
Prison Notebooks (Gramsci) 143
prison overcrowding 354
prisoner's dilemma 205
Protestantism 222–4
proto-consciousness 44
Proud Boys 301
Puccini, Giacomo 340–1
Pugh, Florence 212
PUI 354–5
pure 237
Putin, Vladimir 155, 169, 171, 173, 259, 299

Qin government 247
QU 194
quantum computing 43
quantum eraser experiment 17–18
Quantum events 47
quantum holography 34, 36
quantum information 44
quantum mechanics
    and AI 186–7
    appearances 100
    borrowing energy 49
    cannot describe observers 63–4
    and Carlo Rovelli 35–6
    and Hegel 50
    holography 162
    and Kafka 141
    and microtubule symmetry 44
    most successfully tested theory 52–3
    not a complete theory 194
    and objective reality 33, 40, 42
    and paraconsistency 366–7
    and Real 98
    relational (RQM) 46, 64
    and Rovelli 54
    status of waves 57, 122, 251–4
    superpositions *see* superpositions
    and supreme Observer 37–8
    and Thomas Hertog 159
    wave oscillations/reality 261–2, 378
quantum phenomena 45
quantum physics 25, 37, 43, 45, 51, 193–4, 379
quasars 38
qubits 24, 43, 45
Queen, Carol 343

racism 370
racist phallogocentrism 218
Ranciere, Jacques 249
Rashomon (Kurosava) 321–2, 329
Rawls, John 370
Reagan, Ronald 3
Real
    and Beethoven 266–7
    core of social antagonism 22–3
    and global market mechanism 151
    independent of us 113
    of madness 106
    neurological 220–1
    pre-ontological 42, 98, 103, 107–8, 122, 255
    reaching through observer 13, 15
    and reality 91, 193
    and 'subjective destitution' 100–2
    and the Symbolic 299–300
    and *Tannhauser* 283
Real (Sentsov) 385–7
real-in-itself 41–2, 52, 86, 102
Reality+ (Chalmers) 187–8, 193
reality
    and Absolute 52
    and AI 182
    and appearance 321
    and ideality 250
    infinitely divisible 107
    and Real 193
    and the Void 58
reality-as-it-is 99
Reason 104, 125
reconciliation 279, 285
reductionism 364
Regnault, Francois 304
relational quantum mechanics (RQM) 46–8, 52–3, 55, 63, 241, 254
relationality 46–55
religion 149, 368
religious fundamentalism 212, 218
'Remembering, Repeating and Working Through' (Freud) 66–7
repressive desublimation 306–7
Republic (Plato) 277
republicanism 224
Republicans 302
Revatikaanta, Swami 257–9
'The Reverse of Psychoanalysis' (Lacan) 306
revolution 117, 211
Rhapsody (Vidor) 210–11
Rhine mystics 114
Richardson, William 111
River Runs Through It (film) 280–1

Robespierre, Maximilien 118–20
Rockhill, Gabriel 380
Roman Catholicism 164, 215, 217, 221–3, 344
Romance Sentimentale (Eisenstein/Aleksandrov 330–3
Romanek, Mark 291
Romans 7 (Paul) 225
romanticism 282
Rooney, Sally 393
Rosen, Charles 270
Rovelli, Carlo
   and becoming 241
   epistemic approach 57
   exposure of entity to multiple interactions 39
   and *Helgoland* 2, 395n.6
   interactions between particles 40–1
   interrelatedness of all entities 377–8
   looking outward at the universe 244
   and objective reality 141–2
   observation/consciousness 45
   and quantum events 255
   and quantum mechanics 54, 254
   and reality 36, 63–5, 237
   reduction of wave function 58–63
   and relationality 46–7
   and RQM 52
   and time 30, 35
   and 'traces' of the past 32
   and wave oscillations 367
   and Zeilinger's experiment 77
royalism 224
rumours 369
Rumsfeld, Donald 370
Russell, Bertrand 202
Russell, Eric Frank 264
Russell's paradox 63
Russia
   and Alexandre Kojeve 151
   anti-Christian logic in 259
   conflict with the West 155, 169–70
   and freedom 297–9
   metaphysical war in Ukraine 303
   and Putin's regime 173, 178
   and Ukraine war 129, 169, 176–7, 179, 203, 231, 233
Russia House (le Carré) 218–19
Russia today! 259
Russian Orthodox Church 170–1

Sacred Word 360
Saint Helena 207
Saint Theresa of Avila 218
Sallis, John 112
Samson Agonistes (Milton) 290
Sanders, Bernie 364–5
'sartorial superego' (Copjec) 226
Sartre, Jean-Paul 7, 106, 197
Satan *see* Devil, the
Satie, Eric 221
Satyagraha (non-violent resistance) 260
Saussure, Ferdinand de 78
Sbriglia, Russell 226
Schelling, Friedrich von
   and *Ages of the World* fragment 265
   and consciousness 262
   geistige Koerperlichkeit 270
   and Hegel 97, 403n.21
   and Heidegger 82, 84, 109
   'hunger to be something' 378
   meta-transcendental approach 113
   and primordial decision-differentiation 263
   and Simoniti 250
schematism 123
Schmidt, Eric 180–1
Schopenhauer, Arthur 375
Schroedinger's cat experiment 57, 59, 61
Schumann, Robert 270–1, 275
Schuster, Aaron 5, 128, 142–3, 197, 228, 351
Scott Fitzgerald, F. 313
Scott, Ridley 103
Scott, Walter 28
screen-memory 90
Sde Teiman base 118
Searle, John 261
Second World War 134, 136, 176–7
seduction 72–3

Self 99–102, 104
self-consciousness 96
self-relating negativity 252–3
Seminar 18 (Lacan) 121
Seminar I (Lacan) 70
Seminar XI (Lacan) 67
Seminar XIV (Lacan) 102
Seminar XVIII (Lacan) 166
*seminar XX (*Encore*)* (Lacan) 102
Sense 238–9, 241
Sentsov, Oleh 385–6
Serious Songs (Eisler) 392
Seth, Anil 99–100
sex
    with animals 95, 345
    difference 329
    disgusting reality of 283
    homosexual 327
    implications of sexualization 326
    and language description 199
    masturbation 343–6
    pan-sexism 336–7
    passion and social-revolutionary activity 208
    practices 342
    private formula for 124
    the right hole 349–51
    sexism 370
    sexual identity 286
    trans subjects 348
    and vocation 208
Shattered (Kureishi) 207–8
Shining (King) 325
Shoah 371
Shostakovich, Dmitri 277
signifiers 5–6, 67, 77, 190–1
Simoniti, Jure 244, 247–55, 260
Simonyan, Margarita 259
'simp' 328
Sin 76–7
Singer, Bryan 131
singing 277
singularities 27, 62, 247–8, 254
sinthome 341
'six-crises problem' 158

slavery 388
Sloterdijk, Peter 115
Slovenia 298
Smerlak, Matteo 46–7
Smolin, Lee 32, 48
socialism 119, 165, 273, 276, 355–6
Socrates 245–6
Sofia Alekseyevna, regent 170
'The Sole Solution' (Russell) 264–5
somata 239–40
songs 162
Sophocles 135, 376
South Korea 140–1, 150–1, 323
Soviet Union 137
space
    Hegel's notion of 50
    holding the universe 37
    location of thoughts in 36
    pre-existence of 108
    sense illusory 62
    space-time 244
    universal form of 29–32
Spartacus 169
Spinoza, Baruch 36, 335
Spirit 97
'Spirit is a bone' (Hegel) 12
spiritualism 2, 3–5, 102, 107
Srinivasa Ramanujan 372
Stahr, Monroe 313
Stalin, Joseph
    admirer of Peter the Great 169–70
    and Bolshevism 298
    Brecht and the purges 294
    finding another master 301
    and General Secretary post 359
    and godless communists 327
    Great Purges of 144
    and inevitability of Stalinism 68–9
    prohibition of 'Lady Macbeth' 277
    and trust 348
Stalinism
    and *Animal Farm* 330
    normalization of 380
    rise of 68–9, 143
    truth of the Leninist project 373

Stamina Training Unit 345
State and Revolution (Lenin) 359
Statue of Liberty 12
Stewart, Patrick 117
Stoicism 239
Stolypin, Pyotr 117
storge 346
Structural Anthropology (Levi-Strauss) 21
structuralism 52, 189–90
Subject 58, 257
'subjective destitution' 100
subjectivity 122–4, 245
sublimation 358
Substance 58, 83, 91, 229, 257
subsymbolic AI systems 183–4
Sudan 154
Sudarsky, D. 55
superego 198, 227
superpositions
    collapse of 53
    'democratic' Inca society 173
    and *Monsters* 323
    and the One 45
    and quantum mechanics 162, 363
    sexual 329, 335–51
    unconscious 262
    and wave functions 68, 377, 379
surplus-enjoyment 127–8
surplus-value (Marx) 303
Sutlić, Vanja 136
'Swiss army wife' position 345
Swissair flight 111 73
Switzerland 361
Symbolic, the 299–302
Symphony No. 1 (Schumann) 270
Syria 307
Szabo, Istvan 284

Taek-Gwang Lee, Alex 162
Talmud 115
Talmudic texts 139
Tannheuser (Wagner) 281–5
Tarantino, Quentin 7
Tarkovsky, Andrei 42, 106–7, 269–70
techno-feudalism 154, 176

teleology 167–8, 251
Television (Lacan) 304
thermodynamics, second law of 27–8
Theses on History (Benjamin) 167
Thing, the 103, 125, 313–16, 325, 378
things-in-themselves 22, 91
The Third Man (film) 314
Third Way Social Democracy 224
Thompson, Alex 309
Thompson, Liza 281
Three Essays on Sexuality (Freud) 337
The Three-Body Problem (Cixin Liu) 113, 157
time
    and Deleuze 238
    and holography 34–5
    nature of 26–32
    ontological origin of 23
    sense illusory 62
    and thoughts 36
Tito je vaš (Tito Is Yours) (Riblja Corba) 116
Tito, Josip 116
To Be or Not to Be (Lubitsch) 387
Tom and Jerry 87
'top-down view' (Hertog) 32
topoi 273
Tractatus (Wittgenstein) 199–201
Tramp 182–3
transcendental schematism 123–4
'transference' 50
transhumanism 248
Trawny, Peter 135–6, 138–9
Treatise on Human Freedom (Schelling) 109
tree of knowledge 73–6
Trial, The (Kafka) 140
'trillion-dollar coin' strategy 33–4
Tristan da Cunha 207–8
Tristan und Isolde (Wagner) 316–19, 341
Trotsky, Leon 69
Trump, Donald 22, 152–3, 183, 299, 301, 356–7, 365
truth
    and appearance 90
    contingent events 253

and correctness 109
deeper spiritual 201
and democratic elections 120
in the empirical sense 6–7
and fundamentalism 172
and hallucination 100
importance of factual 68
and man 111–12
as a minority position 121–2
monstrosity of 112
of a (symbolic) fiction 196
violence of 116–22
Tunick, Mark 353
Tusk, Donald 159
Twain, Mark 71
The Twelve (Blok) 298
The Twilight of Gods (Wagner) 281
The Twilight Zone (series) 329–30

Ukraine war
'clash of cultures' interpretation of 169
metaphysical 303
necessary risk 231
'reflecting' interests of West 176–7
Russian view 129, 203, 230–1
and video game help 179, 407n.6
and Western global modernism 298
Ulmer, Edgar G. 82
'Un bel di, vedremo' (song) 340–1
uncertainty principle (Heisenberg) 49, 65
unconscious 71, 93, 262–3, 299, 301
Understanding 103–5, 125, 196
Ungrund 114–15
United States 137, 149, 175, 178
universality 147–9, 244, 246, 248–9, 355
universe, the
abandoning notion of whole 63–4
anti-de-Sutter 2
the block 29–30, 35–6
divine global gaze 254
echoes of Big Bang 108
the holographic 34–5
and laws of physics 33
and man 112
quantum 38, 251

and space-time 55, 244
true origin of 24, 33
unknown unknowns/knowns 370–1
unnamable 202
UPS 378
user's illusion 100, 371
The Usual Suspects (Singer) 131–2
utilitarianism 226
Utopia 171

Vaccari, Ulisses Razzante 103
van Gogh, Vincent 270
Vance, J. D. 302
Varoufakis, Yanis 153–4
'veil of ignorance' (Rawls) 370
Vertigo (Hitchcock) 69
Vichy regime 120
Vickers, Jon 283
Vidor, King 210
Vietcong 139
Vieweg, Klaus 353–4, 356
violence 117
Virgil 122
Virgin Mary 215, 219
vocation 207–9, 211
Void
and Badiou 101
Buddhist opposite 257
of eternal pace/negativity 377
and matter 107
notion of 58
Oriental thought 255
primordial 375, 378
as principle of motion 91
and Space 108
of the Thing 313, 315–16
Vollendung 82
Voltaire 215
von Fricken, Ernestine 270–1
Vonnegut, Kurt 382
Vorhandenes 107

Wagenknecht, Sahra 302
Wagner Group 179
Wagner, Richard 216, 316–18, 341

Wakefulness 299
Wallace, David Foster 6
Wang Huning 152
water 189, 191
Waters, Sarah 327
wave functions
  and AI 187
  collapse of 11, 13–15, 44, 194, 367
  collapsed by God 51
  and Copenhagen orthodoxy 25
  domain of quantum 57, 122, 251–4
  indexes of instability/tension 377
  and particles 62
  reduction of 58–9
  space for 41
  superpositions 53–5, 68, 163
  weird logic of 92–3
Waverly (Scott) 28
Weber, Max 222, 306
Weinberg, Steven 327
Weininger, Otto 375
Welles, Orson 310
Wengrow, David 163
Weststeijn, Nikki 53, 399n.38
Wheeler, John 17–18, 20, 23–4, 38–9
Whole 62
Wigglesworth, Michael 87, 199
Wigner, Eugene 41, 44
Wigner's Friend problem 41, 44
Will 375
The Will to Power (Nietzsche) 232

Williams, Serena 195
Willow 54
Winnebago tribe 21
Wire I/4 197–8
Wittgenstein, Ludwig 199–205, 239, 280
Wolfman 93
'A Woman Throwing a Stone' (Picasso) 312
women 166
working class 249
World 107
Worstward Ho (Beckett) 140
Wright, Steven 279
Wyeth, Andrew 309–10, 319

Xi Jinping 152
Xunzi 247

Yuran, Noam 154, 223

Zanussi, Krzysztof 209–10
Zapffe, Peter Wessel 372, 392
Zeilinger, Anton 59–60, 64–6, 77
Zelenskyy, Volodymyr 302
Zen 179
Zero Point 169
zero-point 251, 257
zhengming 246–7
Zionism *see* Judaism
Žižek, Slavoj 248, 252, 255
Zollikoner Seminare (Heidegger) 110–11
Zupančič, Alenka 13, 40, 42, 51, 154, 384